📞 01603 773114
email: tis@ccn.ac.uk 🐦 @CCN_Library Ⓦ ccnlibraryblog.wordpress.com

21 DAY LOAN ITEM

Please return <u>on or before</u> the last date stamped above

A fine will be charged for overdue items

CITY
COLLEGE
NORWICH

The Whole House Book

The Whole House Book

Ecological building design & materials
Cindy Harris and Pat Borer

Illustrations by Graham Preston, Pat Borer and Benedicte Foo

Centre for
Alternative
Technology
Publications

Photographic credits: those not by the authors, or from the libraries of the
Centre for Alternative Technology have been generously lent by those credited.
Cover image of Great Bow Yard, Langport, courtesy of Ecos Homes Ltd., Architect – Stride Treglown plc.
The Whole House Book by Cindy Harris and Pat Borer
© July 1998, 2005 Centre for Alternative Technology.
All rights reserved.
Centre for Alternative Technology
Machynlleth, Powys SY20 9AZ.
Tel. 01654 705950   Fax. 01654 702782.
email: info@cat.org.uk
Website: www.cat.org.uk
Charity No. 265239.
With assistance from Rick Dance, John Willoughby and Peter Harper.
Illustrations by Graham Preston, Pat Borer and Benedicte Foo.
Designed by Graham Preston.
Edited by Caroline Oakley, Julie Stauffer and Stokely Webster.

2nd Edition April 2005.   ISBN 978-1-902175-54-6.

Printed in Great Britain by Cambrian Printers, Aberystwyth (01970 627111).
Originally published with support, gratefully acknowledged, from the Department of the
Environment, Environment Wales and the Ecology Building Society.

Printed on Era Silk paper and board. FSC certified under Mixed Sources label
50% post-consumer waste

ACKNOWLEDGEMENTS

We would like to acknowledge our debt – both intellectual and practical – to the late Walter Segal, whose original timber frame construction method helped us both to understand how buildings are really put together. It was in the context of this method and its later adaptations that we began to develop our ideas about ecological design and construction.

The Centre for Alternative Technology has generously provided us with the space and opportunity to put some of these ideas into practice. Building projects at CAT have always been a unique experience in that, within one organisation, people act as designer, contractor and client. This has meant that an essentially co-operative approach prevails, as opposed to the sadly more usual adversarial one. In addition, there has always been a willingness to experiment with unconventional design solutions. We trust that CAT as a whole has benefitted from this as much as we have. We would like to thank Maureen Richardson for thinking of the title for this book, a task which we failed miserably to do.

Cindy would like to thank her son, Jude Harris, and her partner, Rob Gwillim, for practical help and suggestions and unfailing support.

Contents

Foreword by Richard Rogers

Cities are at the centre of the environmental debate because they consume the largest share of our resources and produce the largest proportion of waste and pollution.

The Whole House Book tackles this issue head on by bringing together the many diverse standards of sustainable design. The authors promote the central theme of a holistic approach to design that combines social, economic and environmental objectives and that evaluates buildings against their local and global impact.

This excellent book challenges architects and designers to incorporate sustainable thinking as well as sustainable technologies into their work.

Introduction

We have tried to present an approach to ecological design and building that will enable those who are interested to access the relevant information, and that will inspire all those involved in eco-construction to take responsibility for the environmental impact of their decisions.

The route to sustainability is what this book tries to describe: small and large lifestyle changes, dramatic and subtle technical fixes, radical solutions as well as practical compromises. The first priority of a green householder is to reduce the energy consumption of the home by energy conservation techniques and building with low-energy materials. Figure 1.1 shows that once we start to reduce the house energy use, then transport energy and the production and transportation of food soon dominate our personal energy usage. So, as well as trying to construct a low-energy house, we should be aiming to eat low-energy food such as locally grown, organic wholefoods and use low-energy transport, walking or cycling wherever viable.

DESIGN CHOICES

This book is about design choices. This doesn't just mean planning a new home. We are designing all the time: where to put furniture, what to paint a shelf with, what to clean the floor with, how to draughtstrip, where and how to build a conservatory or an extension. Decisions are often interrelated. Design is a circular or iterative process where, after investigating a subject, you keep returning to your original question with new, enlightening information. Just as every action we take in life has an effect on other people and other environments, so it is difficult to look at one subject area without reference to others.

Certain areas of energy efficiency, environmental pollution or human health impacts are covered by legislation. These areas will inevitably increase, but will only ever be a bedrock of minimum standards. Over and above these, we will have to arrive at our own conclusion of what is ideal, or acceptable, or even intolerable, for any given situation. The solution we end up with will have been influenced by cost, availability and convenience, as well as by environmental impact.

HOLISTIC DESIGN

What is certain, is that any useful and meaningful approach must be holistic. That is to say, it must take as wide a perspective as possible and foster an understanding of the complex interrelationships between different kinds of impact.

'For a building to be "green", it is essential for the environmental impact of all its constituent parts and design decisions to be evaluated. This is a much more thorough exercise than simply adding a few green elements, such as a grass roof or a solar panel.'[1]

But even a building with the best green credentials can fail to delight and inspire. It is very important that in the search for the perfect eco-friendly house, we do not lose sight of people's desire for beauty, richness and variety. A soulless building will win few friends and no converts.

An environmentally-friendly building has to be people-friendly too. This usually means being designed and built in such a way that it can respond to changing demands on its function, layout and technical performance. Buildings designed to be flexible and adaptable, with an obvious and accessible structure and built-in

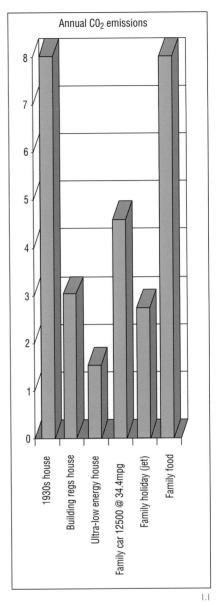

1.1

Fig. 1.1 Average annual household CO_2 emissions in tonnes/year.
Source: John Willoughby and Pat Borer.

ease of maintenance, are the most loved and cared for and therefore the most long-lasting.

According to John Ruskin: 'When we build, let us think that we build forever. Let it not be for present delight nor for present use alone; let it be such work as our descendants will thank us for[2].'

[1] Tom Woolley, *Green Building Handbook: vol 1*, E&FN Spon, 1997
[2] John Ruskin, *The Seven Lamps of Architecture*, New York: Dover, 1849

Users and builders

'Our houses are such unwieldy property that we are often imprisoned rather than housed in them.'

Alex Ely[01]

SUSTAINABLE HOUSING

All exemplars of sustainable development need to address social and economic, as well as environmental, considerations. This is the so-called 'triple bottom line' so beloved of public policy makers. They are right to make the links between housing and community; people and jobs; comfort and deprivation. The complex interface between the physical fabric of a building, its impact on the people who live or work within it, and its further impact on an ever-widening circle of locality, country, and planet, constitutes the main subject area of this book.

Housing or shelter is one of our basic needs. The quality of our built environment, like the quality of our natural environment, affects our lives in many ways. It should benefit our health, well-being, and ability to function in the outside world. Ideally, we should be able to influence our immediate physical surroundings, the four walls within which we spend the bulk of our time, and not just by choosing a colour scheme, but through a critical appreciation of the building's structure, function and general arrangement. This would allow us to interact effectively with our homes and for them to become expressions of individuality and objects of pride.

All too often, in practice, the situation is very different. Although 70% of us now own our own homes and the DIY trade is booming, the variety of houses on offer is not great. On the whole we have to fit our lives and our families into what is already there, with the small number of new houses being constructed to a few standard design types and layouts. According to Richard Rogers, the main criterion governing these development decisions is maximum profit: 'The search for profit determines (a building's) form, quality and performance. This strategy is the antithesis of sustainable thinking and provides no incentive to... use good materials, to landscape a building or even plant a tree.'[1]

In terms of the existing housing stock, latest official figures show that 1.5 million homes are officially classified as unfit[2]. This represents 7.5% of homes in the UK and is the same proportion as was unfit in 1991. (However, the Government's third annual report on sustainable development found an improvement in housing conditions between 1996 and 2001, with the percentage of 'non-decent' homes falling from 46% to 33%.) Dampness, disrepair and unsatisfactory facilities for food preparation were major causes of unfitness. Another report, commissioned by the Joseph Rowntree Foundation and published in 1996 by the National Housing Forum, came to a sobering conclusion, sensationalised in newspaper headlines: 'Thousands Die of "Home Sickness" – Bad Housing Kills'[3]. Poor housing conditions were found to contribute to 'chronic chest disease, hypothermia, digestive problems, schizophrenia, even cancer'.

A combination of poor quality housing, low disposable income, and under-occupation leads to a situation known as 'fuel poverty', where more than 10% of net disposable income is spent on heating costs. This affects nearly eight million homes across the UK and occurs because energy-inefficient houses take more energy to achieve a desirable temperature. Thermal comfort therefore becomes a relatively more expensive item for those who most need it and can least afford it. As a consequence, poorer families and the elderly in particular will go without heat, and the knock-on effect of this deprivation, in personal, social and economic terms, can be catastrophic.

The state of our current housing stock makes dismal reading from an energy efficiency perspective. The average SAP rating of UK Houses (a measure of energy use, where a higher score is better) is about 42 out of 100. New houses built in the UK typically use 3.5 times as much energy as their counterparts in Denmark and Germany. Overall, the UK has probably the worst insulated housing stock in Northern Europe.

In addition, much of our housing stock is inappropriate for modern households in terms of its size, layout, and location. Issues of accessibility and flexibility, which could enable a building to respond to the changing need of its occupants, need to be addressed, as in the Lifetime Homes Standard developed by the Joseph Rowntree Trust. Directed mainly at policy makers, this project sets out a number of standards to be met if the physical arrangement of homes is to be made more convenient for those with young children, frail older people or those with temporary or permanent disabilities.

As a nation, the UK still needs more homes and major housing expansion is planned for certain areas of the country, such as the Thames Gateway, over the next few years. (The current official estimate is that we will need 3.8 million new homes by 2021.) Recent demographic changes have shown a shift away from the conventional two-parent family towards an increasing number of single parents and single people wanting independent accommodation. The number of households in England and Wales rose by 31% in the period 1971-2001[5].

Improvement is needed in housing quality as well as quantity. Bad housing and poverty tend to be mutually reinforcing, creating a depressing cycle of poor health, low self-esteem, educational failure, unemployment and crime. The effects of this cycle are not just personal and local, but global as well. When people are faced with difficulties in securing the basics of life, it is hardly surprising that more remote and longer term problems of environmental degradation are seen as relatively unimportant. As the Brundtland report put it in 1987, 'Poverty reduces people's capacity to use resources in a sustainable manner: it intensifies pressure on the environment'.

THE POLITICAL CONTEXT

The present Government promotes energy efficiency in the home as this feeds into two of its major policy objectives – reductions in CO_2 emissions and the elimination of 'fuel poverty'. Improving the thermal performance of new and existing houses, through changes to the Building Regulations, is part of the Government's commitment to achieve a 20% reduction in CO_2 emissions, on 1990 levels, by 2020.

Legislation is planned to make information on energy performance available to potential house buyers in a 'seller's pack', so that high efficiency and low bills could become an extra marketing asset. European requirements for a minimum standard of energy performance in buildings have been adopted in the UK and will become legally binding from 2006. We can expect more measures in the future to reduce buildings-related carbon emissions, as long as these can be made economically feasible.

The Sustainable Buildings Task Force, a Government-commissioned group of experts, has called for an enforceable Code for Sustainable Buildings (CSB) based on the Building Research Establishment Energy Assessment Method (BREEAM). The campaign launched by the WWF at the Rio summit in 2002 for 'One Million Sustainable Homes in the UK' has led to the introduction of the Sustainable and Secure Buildings Act, 2004.

These various political measures directed at improving domestic energy efficiency are likely to have social and economic benefits, as well as environmental ones. The expected benefits include reduced fuel costs, reduced pressure on the NHS and more jobs in the construction industry – an estimated saving to the taxpayer of £2.5bn over 15 years[6].

SUSTAINABLE CITIES

Around 75% of the European population live in urban or suburban areas. With the growth in the size and number of cities, and the globalisation of trade, the traditional link between town and country has been broken. Imported food swamps local production, the environmental footprint of the city bears no relation to the carrying capacity of the surrounding countryside, and the image and culture of the city refers more to international standards than to local ones. The ecological footprint of London, for example, is 293 times its geographical area[7].

According to UK Government estimates, 3.8 million more homes will be needed in the next 15 years. It is important that the design of new residential developments does not stop at the building envelope, but extends to creating secure, sheltered and landscaped open spaces. Mixed residential tenure, and mixed use developments seem to be the best recipe for ensuring lively neighbourhoods and sustainable communities.

In inner city areas, however, residential populations are declining and there is a serious lack of accommodation for single people and young families, particularly 'key workers', on moderate incomes. We need to reverse this situation if we are to avoid city centres populated exclusively by the very poor and the very rich. In one attempt at addressing this issue, the Joseph Rowntree Foundation (JRF) has commissioned and invested in two high-density CASPAR developments in Birmingham and Leeds. CASPAR stands for City Centre Apartments for Single People at Affordable Rents and development costs compare reasonably favourably with social housing in the same area. In both schemes, JRF claims a return of over 6% per year on their investment, while keeping basic rents at around £100/week.

2.1a

2.1b

Fig. 2.1a CASPAR in Leeds.
Architect: Levitt Bernstein.
Fig. 2.1b CASPAR in Birmingham's jewellery quarter.
Architects: Allford, Hall Monaghan Morris.

Mix of apartments, maisonettes and townhouses

Photovoltaic panels

Workspace and community facilities

Rainwater store

Green roof and roof gardens

Mews type access roads

2.2

There seems to be a prevailing consensus, backed by Government policy and public opinion, that as much new development as possible should be on 'brownfield' sites. (In February 1998, the Government announced a national target for England that at least 60% of new homes are to be built on previously developed (brownfield) land by 2008.) There is, however, a strong argument for a more flexible approach, treating each proposal on its merits. Some environmentally sensitive developments in untouched rural locations could add to an area's diversity and prosperity, while some derelict sites in cities should be left as pockets of greenery and wildlife.

With the development of sustainable cities, comes the question of appropriate density. Increasing density beyond a certain threshold can trigger the viability of providing a public transport system, and other facilities such as schools, shops and open spaces, all within the locality. Compact developments offer the potential for greater resource efficiency and CO_2 reductions, for example by achieving viability for district heating schemes. Care should be taken, however, that higher densities do not compromise access to daylight and sunlight.

High densities – of, say, 100-150 dwellings per hectare – can create communities similar to the traditional street rather than the suburban estate. The Council for the Protection of Rural England (CPRE) is lobbying to prevent 'sprawl' in new developments and recent revision to planning policy (PPG3) recommends minimum densities of 30-50 dwellings/hectare. According to one author, 'High density, mixed use neighbourhoods give back the sense of place that 20th century planning policies have undermined.'[8]

Current standards for the space needed for new houses, are determined more than anything by the perceived need for high levels of car parking. Any sustainable development must examine and implement ways of minimising reliance on motor vehicles. One of the best ways of doing this is to provide a reliable public transport system, which will require a certain density of habitation to be viable. Alternatively, some eco-developments have undertaken to reduce reliance on cars as part of their initial brief.

The BedZED project (figure 2.2) in South London has a density of over 100 units per hectare, while maintaining good solar access. Their green transport plan aims to reduce the level of car use, by providing facilities for working at home, prioritising pedestrians and cyclists on the site, and making available cleaner, cheaper, community-based alternatives.

Fig. 2.2 BedZED, a sustainable suburban community.

A SUSTAINABLE COUNTRYSIDE

Recent housing development in the countryside has taken the form of suburban sprawl on greenfield sites around towns and villages, or dormitory suburbs serving cities. There has been a drift of population away from cities – 20% now live in rural areas, compared with 10% in the 1980s. This sort of development has a high impact: it generates lots of traffic, covers more countryside in more roads, is not built of local materials, has been built to the minimum standards of energy conservation, and is obtrusive.

2.3

The countryside itself is now thought of by many as a cross between a food factory and a heritage museum, dedicated to preserving misguided agricultural policies and practices. There seems little room for people to live and work in a way that develops the land sustainably. Britain has had a glorious history of building progressive housing developments: Robert Owen's New Lanark; the philanthropic industrialists' Port Sunlight, New Earswick, and Bournville; and the Garden City movement. The Chartist smallholders' settlements, the utopian Whiteway colony, and the present-day co-housing scheme, in Stroud, are examples of deliberate community design. We have a surfeit of examples of better ways to build. Even the Prince of Wales' village of Poundbury, often seen as 'pastiche', is based on good planning principles and uses local references and materials.

Simon Fairlie, in his book *Low Impact Development*, argues that 'by giving people the opportunity to live in the countryside in return for ecological improvements and a commitment towards sustainability, the planning system could reinvigorate the land-based economy, create a more diverse rural environment and facilitate the provision of affordable housing.'[9]. There are efforts presently being made to have low-impact or sustainable developments incorporated as a distinct category of development within Local Planning policies in the countryside*.

The distinction has already been made by West Lothian District Council, near Edinburgh, in their 'Lowland Crofting' or 'Very Low Density Housing and Woodland Development' scheme.

Fig. 2.3 Homes for soap factory workers, Port Sunlight, Wirral.

*Planning Policy Statement [PPS] 7 was published in September 2003 and includes the notorious 'Country House', exemption, which allows development of isolated new houses which can demonstrate 'truly outstanding and groundbreaking, design'. A group called Chapter 7 is campaigning to have this exemption changed to include 'groundbreakingly sustainable, and low-impact rural developments', (chapter7@tlio.demon.co.uk). At the moment, large prestigious country houses are allowed by PPS7 while low-impact homes and sustainable developments are not [10].

2.4

The 'Lowland Crofting' concept pioneered by West Lothian Council harnesses the demand for rural living to secure an improved landscape and other natural heritage benefits as a contribution to the development of the Central Scotland Forest. Development involves the subdivision of marginal farms in areas of poor environmental quality to create serviced plots within a restructured landscape incorporating substantial areas of new woodland.
Lowland Crofting development, West Harwood.

Since its adoption in 1994, the Lowland Crofting policy has resulted in the establishment of substantial areas of new broadleaved woodland, secured the future of sensitive natural heritage features, facilitated the creation of new wildlife habitats, and improved public access to the countryside by providing new footpath networks. It is also offering new opportunities for people to live and develop businesses in the area. The environmental objectives of the policy are likely to be applicable in other parts of Scotland.
Planning for Natural Heritage: Planning Advice Note 60
http://www.scotland.gov.uk/library/pan/pn60-11.asp

THE ECOLOGY OF SELF-BUILD

Until recent times, and in many parts of the world today, building one's own home was and is the normal thing to do. For most people it was the only way to get a roof over their heads. In Wales, landless peasants would work round the clock to complete the shell of a 'tai unnos', or one-night house, as a right of tenure would be gained if smoke was seen rising from the chimney before sunrise on the following day. The shell could then be finished off and added to as time and resources allowed. The first building societies were in fact mutual savings clubs that were dissolved after all the members had built their own homes.

Sustainable building means, among other things, thermal comfort, healthy living, lower heating costs, and a high degree of user satisfaction. As such it is almost certain to appeal to those fortunate enough to have an input into the design and construction of their own homes. Indeed a desire to live in a more eco-friendly home than can usually be found on the market, is often the motive behind self-building in the first place.

For the television series *Grand Designs*, presenter Kevin McCloud has worked closely with many self-build projects, following their progress over months and even years. He found that environmental issues were taken on board by nearly all the participants and that 'suit-wearing fathers of 2.4 children become overnight disciples of solar power, power-dressing mothers leave their chargecards on the hall table and step out into a brave new world of composting toilets, and retired couples experience Damascene conversions to ecological living.'[11]

Fig. 2.4 Lowland Crofting.

Recent examples of low-energy self-build houses are among the best national examples of environmentally sound building, with high NHER (National Home Energy Rating) scores of 9 or 10 (out of 10)[12]. In other countries too, self-builders are sidestepping the mainstream construction industry and leading the way in low-energy building. For example, financial incentives, for all eco-building measures made available by the German Government to raise the standard for eco-materials. The building industry has now had to accept these standards – in the beginning the incentives were mainly claimed and used by self-builders[13].

Very often in conventional construction projects, designer, contractor and client will have separate and different interests in terms of costs, timing, and build quality and this can generate conflict, or at least a lack of combined effort. One partner in the project will often blame one of the others for a failure to deliver the best environmental option. In situations where these different roles are united in one person or interest group, there is scope for effective decision making about the longer term benefits of certain eco-measures, and a commitment from the beginning to integrate them into the design and planning process.

For many people of course, self-build is a daunting prospect and the mystique surrounding buildings and how they work can deter even the most enthusiastic amateur. Construction professionals, like professionals everywhere, guard the secrets of their skills. Dire warnings are often issued on the dangers of amateurs getting involved. As a result, decisions about building design and construction are removed from the people most affected by those decisions. Buildings are seen as pre-determined structures, which we have to fit our lives around, rather than flexible objects which can adapt to changing family or employment conditions.

Of course, there are skills involved in building a house but many of these can be learned quite easily on the job, given proper site supervision. Some methods of building, however, are inherently more user-friendly than others.

THE SEGAL METHOD

The post-and-beam, timber frame building method, developed in the 70s and 80s by architect Walter Segal, has proved to be particularly appropriate for self-builders with no previous experience of construction. For many years CAT has run self-build courses based on the Segal Method, and these have always been popular and usually oversubscribed.

The original Segal Method was essentially eco-friendly, relying as it did on timber as the main structural material; minimum use of concrete and land disturbance; and the built-in option of reusing all materials. Above all, the Segal approach put the self-builder at the heart of the process. Segal trusted his self-builders to make sensible decisions about the design of their houses, and he trusted their practical competence, fuelled by a desire to improve their housing conditions. And he was proved right.

Designers and builders working in the Segal tradition, are developing the method to incorporate energy efficiency and low environmental impact. They have been able to do this because of the system's inherent simplicity and flexibility, and a basic low-tech, low-waste approach[13a].

Self-build is about more than just acquiring a new building or home. It is often a process of self-discovery, development and empowerment. Kevin McCloud ranks it with the birth of a new child, or writing a novel, or crossing the Sahara, and describes

2.5a

Fig. 2.5a Hedgehog self-build project in Brighton, completed summer 2000, consisting of ten detached bungalows.

it as 'one of the last great adventures open to us'[14]. The return on the effort invested is immense, not just in the financial and physical sense, but also in the enormous satisfaction and self confidence that comes from having created one's own home and the continuing enjoyment that brings.

Self-build can also be used to skip a few rungs on the way up the housing ladder, given a certain amount of capital to begin with. It is an entirely honourable way of 'bucking the system' – individuals, couples and families can self-build in order to enjoy a bigger and better house than they could otherwise afford.

For those on middle to high incomes, there is a burgeoning market in 'designer self-build', based on the appeal of a totally unique and individual home. The ultimate in DIY, self-build in this situation can include an input into design or managing the process, as well as doing some or all of the construction work. Sometimes it is no more than a minimal input, but the sense of having overall control makes it feel very different from buying an 'off-the-peg' house. Glossy magazines aimed at this market offer many examples of couples or families building their 'dream home', and are full of adverts for financial packages, insurance and building plots.

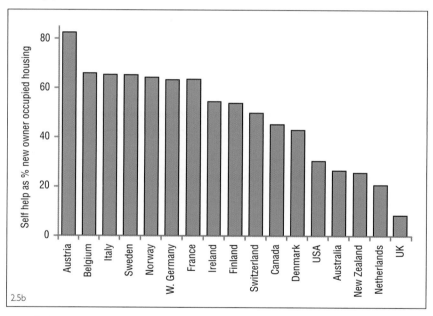

2.5b

Unfortunately, those on lower incomes who succeed in self-building usually have done so in spite of our current system of housing provision, rather than because of it. As Jon Broome points out 'Britain has a disabling framework for self-help housing...compared with other countries.'[15]. The number of self-build completions, as a percentage of all new housing, is lower for the UK than for any other European country.

This is due to several factors: the relatively high cost of land; the lack of suitable financial packages allowing for the release of capital before the house is completed; and restrictive planning regulations. Still, groups of people in housing need may attract funding through the Housing Corporation or, with appropriate support from a local authority or Registered Social Landlord (RSL), private finance through banks or building societies. It is possible to include a training element such as NVQs into these self-build schemes, so that young unemployed people end up with their own home, and the prospect of employment.

Fig. 2.5b Reproduced from Duncan & Rowe (1992).

Bournemouth Churches Housing Association has developed a 'Build and Train' model, designed to deliver a fast-track training package, of a minimum NVQ level 2 qualification, to young long-term unemployed and homeless people. In collaboration with Purbeck District Council, who provided the land free of charge on a long-term lease, Bournemouth & Poole College, which provided the training, and Oregon Partnerships, who provided the timber frame structure and specialist training, six low-energy flats were constructed that in the first year showed a 35% saving on heating bills. Construction costs were estimated to be 5-8% lower than for conventional masonry construction. [Sourced from Sustainable Homes]

For many self-build groups, it can take years of battling with various bureaucracies before they can start to build. Individual self-builders, especially those who are not professional builders, are often regarded as high-risk by mortgage lenders. Yet in a scheme run by Stockholm City Council, where self-builders were given the help and facilities they needed such as access to land and finance, only 1 in 1000, once started, failed to complete their houses, and only 1 in 100 were more than 2 months late[17].

What is more, with most of the labour donated free by the self-builders, these houses can be built within Housing Corporation cost guidelines. The recently completed Hedgehog self-build scheme in Brighton was made possible by treating the self-builders' labour as match funding to complement a Social Housing Grant. Their rents are set at a discounted rate and heating bills are expected to be around £80/yr. In an earlier Brighton scheme (Diggers), also funded by South London Family Housing Association, the self-builders paid rents that were only two thirds of the NFHA (National Federation of Housing Associations) rent indicator levels for 1993[18].

2.6

Fig. 2.6 Segal Method in Scotland, Benarty Self Build.
Architect: Duncan Roberts.

The future for self-build

People building their own homes or property will tend to take more care, and spend more time getting details just right, than those building for profit. Because self-builders have an intimate knowledge of the way their houses are built, any necessary maintenance tasks are usually obvious, and they are carried out conscientiously, as a means of protecting the initial investment of time and effort. Thus, these houses tend to have a longer life. They are also much more likely to be altered and renovated, as family circumstances change, both because self-builders see such work as within their sphere of competence, and because they are understandably reluctant to move.

Self-build also provides the option of 'building in stages': adding rooms as a family grows or more money becomes available; converting former living space to work or hobby space. Indeed, there is a lot to be said for not attempting to complete a house in one go. Vernacular houses were often deliberately built unfinished, and evolved over time as circumstances changed and finances permitted. After all, 'if a building is perceived to have been completed and not capable of change, (it) ceases to provide us with the enriching experience of imagining alternatives[19]'. Many self-builders have learned the wisdom of Stewart Brand's warning: 'A building is not something you finish. A building is something you start.'[20]

Groups of people working together for a common aim will often build up a sense of community and mutual help, thereby laying the basis for a well integrated, sustainable neighbourhood in the future. In the Diggers scheme in Brighton, and more recently at Hockerton in Nottinghamshire, this is reflected in the decision to create communal leisure and play spaces, community enterprises and growing areas on surrounding land and collectively-owned renewable energy systems.

Durable, flexible houses, which suit the particular needs of their inhabitants, whose construction has enhanced self esteem and community relationships, and which have low embodied energy and energy efficiency built in, seem as close to a definition of sustainable housing as one can reasonably get. Not everyone would choose to build for themselves, but for those who do it should be a viable option. Access to land and finance could be further improved and planning conditions be made more sympathetic to individual designs. Deprived of its mystique, the process of building could become much more open, enlarging and enriching the pattern of housing provision in this country.

References

[01] Alex Ely, *The Home Buyer's Guide*, Black Dog Publishing Ltd/ CABE 2004

[02] Curwell et al, *Hazardous Building Materials*, chapter 7

[1] Richard Rogers, *Cities for a Small Planet*, Faber & Faber 1997

[2] The English House Conditions Survey, Energy Report DETR, 1996

[3] *Observer*, 2/6/96

[4] The English House Conditions Survey, Energy Report DETR, 1996

[5] National Statistics, DEFRA 2002

[6] Warm Homes website: www.nea.org.uk

[7] www.citylimitslondon.com

[8] Brian Edwards, *Rough Guide to Sustainability*, RIBA Publications 2001

[9] Simon Fairlie, *Low Impact Development*, Jon Carpenter, 1997

[10] Sustainable Homes and Livelihoods in the Countryside, Chapter 7 and the PPG7 Reform Group, Jan 2003

[11] Kevin McCloud, *Grand Designs*, Channel 4 Books, 1999

[12] Review of Ultra Low Energy Homes, Ten UK Profiles, David Olivier and John Willoughby, Building Research Establishment, 1996

[13] Report on PassivHaus conference in *Building for a Future* magazine, vol 11, no 1

[13a] Pat Borer and Cindy Harris, *Out of the Woods*, CAT Publications, 1997

[14] Kevin McCloud, as [10]

[15] Jon Broome, *Housing and the Environment: A New Agenda*, Mark Bhatti et al (eds), Chartered Institute of Housing, 1994, p 169.

[16] S. Duncan and A. Rowe, 'Self-Help Housing', Working Paper 85, Centre for Urban and Regional Research, University of Sussex, 1992

[17] Jon Broome and Brian Richardson, *The Self Build Book*, Green Books, Devon, 1991, p. 226

[18] Jon Broome as [14] p 186

[19] Richard Burnham, 'Ecology in Tasmania: Owner Built Houses', (paper presented at a conference at the Royal Melbourne Institute of Technology, 1991).

[20] Stewart Brand, *How Buildings Learn*, Viking Press, 1994

The site

LOCATION

Most decisions about buying or renting a house, or designing a new one, are dominated by questions of location and site. We are pretty good at balancing hundreds of factors – closeness to schools, work, shops, on a quiet road, good rail links, private garden, car parking, not under a flightpath. The choice or design of the house itself tends to come after all these. This section of the book has three objectives: to extend your innate ability to select a good site, to help you to locate and shape the house on a new site, and to help in creating or improving existing spaces around the house.

Community amenities

These are the dominant factors in deciding on a house location. From an environmental standpoint, proximity to the most frequent activity is an important means of reducing car use and stress from commuting. Look at locations that have good bicycle routes and access to bus and train services. Whilst a country location may appear 'healthiest', it is quite likely that you will be highly dependant on the car, unless you work from home.

Negative factors

Thoroughly check local plans for sources of pollution and noise: power stations, incinerators, factories, flight paths. Also check out the industrial activities upwind of the site. In the UK the prevailing wind comes from the south west.

THE CLIMATE

The design of low-energy houses starts with an understanding of climate – at the regional and site-specific level.

Macroclimate (regional and national)

The western European climate is described as maritime – that is, dominated by the airflows over the Atlantic and the Gulf Stream. But there are considerable variations across the region that are important to the individual, both as a matter of personal taste or health, and from the point of view of energy conservation. Typical maritime airflows are warm and moist, producing mild, wet, and cloudy weather in winter, with occasional cold, sunny periods due to easterly winds from Central Europe and Siberia. Summers are similarly mild and often wet. A maritime climate is variable and unstable – but of course you already know that. Due to global warming, our climate seems to be changing, with more extreme weather (storms and floods) and long dry periods. It is difficult to predict trends – the only thing we can be fairly certain about is an increasing unpredictability!

Climate is unique to any particular site. There is nowhere in the world with the same weather characteristics as the British Isles. Some are similar, but you find that it is slightly sunnier in the winter, or the temperature drops much more at night. So it makes no sense to copy directly designs of houses that have worked in other climates. Elements of such designs can, of course, be included – techniques for superinsulation, ideas for solar heating devices – but all must be tested against the prevailing weather conditions, as well as the expectations of the household.

3.1

Previous page: House in Pembrokeshire, Wales by Future Systems. Photo: Richard Davies

Fig. 3.1 'Developer's vernacular': houses made (probably) from non-local materials with a high embodied energy content, poor values of insulation and poor airtightness. The large expanses of Tarmac and other impervious surfaces prevent rainwater from being absorbed locally. Houses are sprinkled around the dominating road layout; no attention is paid to solar orientation, overshadowing, privacy, views or the shape of the spaces between the houses. The development is a greenfield site, built on what used to be farmland. The gardens are tiny and have little topsoil. In our terms, a high-impact development.

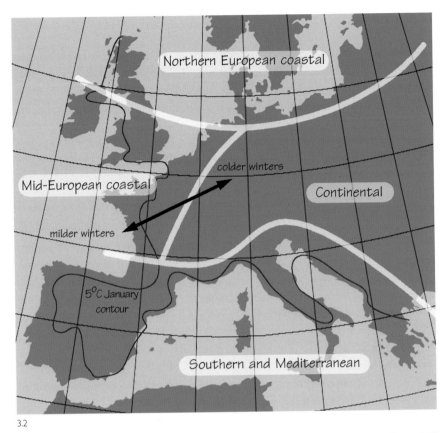

3.2

3.3

Fig. 3.2 Map of Europe showing the climatic zones. January 5°C contour to show where the mild winters are. Source: Boyle, G. (1996).

Fig. 3.3 Average solar radiation, in watts, falling on a horizontal square metre per year. This is called an insolation map and shows how much average solar energy is available in a given place. Source: Solarex.

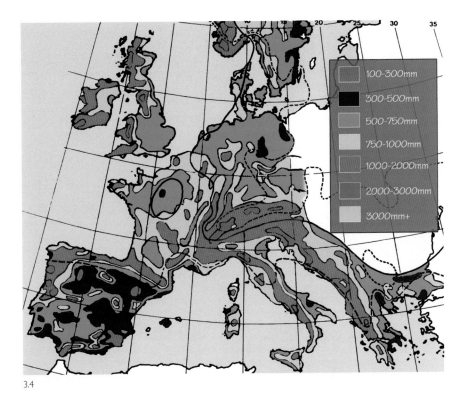

	100-300mm
	300-500mm
	500-750mm
	750-1000mm
	1000-2000mm
	2000-3000mm
	3000mm+

3.4

Even across a land mass the size of Britain the climate changes significantly. Within 80km of the west coast, the average annual rainfall ranges from 800mm to 2000mm, the average winter temperature varies by 2°C, the number of sunny days increases as we move inland – although total solar energy remains the same (West Wales benefits from clean Atlantic air). Snow falls on five days per year in south-west England, 15 in the south-east and 35 days per year in northern Scotland. It gets colder and less sunny the further north you are in Britain. It is 50% colder in Shetland than in Cornwall, and about 25% duller. However, the latitude effect can be qualified by the presence of warm Gulf Stream winds and the amount of pollution in the air.

Indeed, the mildness of the western European climate is due to the powerful influence of the Gulf Stream. There is a danger that rising global temperatures may 'switch off' the Gulf Stream, resulting in sub-arctic winter conditions in Britain.

There are four key factors in assessing the effects of climate on a particular location:

- **Solar energy** is measured in kWh, per square metre of horizontal surface, per day (or month or year). Common sense tells us it is sunnier in the south than in the north, but our weather is dominated by the seas that surround us, the prevailing winds and regional pollution, all of which produce odd patterns of sunny or overcast conditions (see figure 3.3).
- **Precipitation** (or rain) is measured in mm/day (or month or year) and it is useful to know average, maximum and minimum readings. Rain distribution is determined by prevailing winds and the height of the site above sea level. The frequency of precipitation varies quite dramatically – from 600 to 1200 hours per year. If you do not like rain, then Cambridge and the Fens is the place to live (500mm); if you do, then you'll enjoy the top of Snowdon (4000mm) (see figure 3.4).

Fig. 3.4 Average annual rainfall in millimetres.

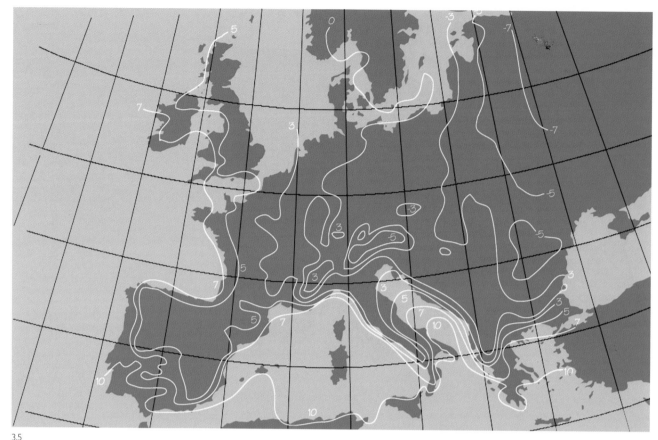

3.5

- **Wind speed** is measured in metres per second, at 10 metres above the ground, and it is also useful to know wind direction. Altitude, ground roughness, and other local variables will affect wind speeds, but generally the coasts are windier than the hinterland, and west winds are stronger (but warmer) than north and east winds.
- **Temperature** measured in degrees Centigrade(°C)or Kelvin(K). Again, average, maximum and minimum figures are useful as well as the diurnal range (over 24 hours). Figure 3.5 shows the two variables of latitude and prevailing winds. Additionally, height above sea level is significant – the uplands can be half as cold again as their neighbouring seaside.

Extreme weather events, e.g. floods, earthquakes or hurricanes, are becoming increasingly common. Information concerning their severity, and possible future trends, should help to avoid or protect a vulnerable site. In the UK flood warning information is available from the Environment Agency's website or telephone helplines and the BBC's website (www.environment-agency.gov.uk, www.bbc.co.uk).

Microclimate (the neighbourhood)

Topographic factors give rise to local variations in climate: estuaries funnel winds and sea fog inland, mountains block winds from one direction, inversion pockets of cold air form in steep valleys, north slopes see no winter sun, etc.

The microclimate around a house is also affected by prevailing vegetation and tree cover, bumps and dips in the ground, and water courses, as well as any existing structures. These features can be used to give maximum solar access (or shading)

Fig. 3.5 Average mid-winter temperature in °C (at sea level). For every 100 metres height above sea level, the average temperature drops by 0.6°C.

and wind protection (or exposure) as appropriate, to obtain the best low-energy, bioclimatic design.

Shelter from wind

Concerns over wind are mostly involved with its chilling effects during the winter months. Winter winds can do the following:

- increase infiltration and hence heat loss from the house;
- cool the outer surface of the house, especially when wet with rain, thereby increasing heat transfer from the inside to outside;
- create uncomfortable wind-swept spaces around the house;
- force driving rain and wind-blown snow into the house or into parts of its construction; and
- cause structural damage to a property.

The following techniques may be used to reduce these undesirable effects:

- wind shelter from other buildings, tree planting, fences, earthworks, and building underground;
- orientation (which way it is facing), shape, layout and height of the house; and
- an outer surface that has pockets of still air.

Wind direction and strength

First, know your enemy. A 'wind rose' is the charming term for a diagram that shows the direction, strength and temperature of the wind in an average year. Figure 3.6 shows a typical January wind rose for Britain. You will see that the prevailing wind direction is from the south-west quarter (approximately 55%), but it is a warmer wind (7°C) than the colder (2°C) north-east quarter (15%) – both should be considered in shelter design.

Average wind speeds vary according to general location, regional characteristics and the specific topographical situation of the house. In Britain, it is windiest in the west, facing the unfettered Atlantic gales. Next windiest is the east coast, facing the Continental winds. The least windy is the central strip running up through London and the Midlands and in the Highlands of Scotland.

Topography is the effect of hills and valleys. Figure 3.7 shows the basic effect of hills – a house on the leeward slope will experience about 80% of the wind speeds on the exposed face or ridge. Valleys facing the prevailing wind will tend to funnel those winds to levels similar to that experienced on a ridge. At the valley bottom and

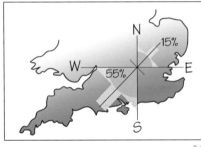

3.6

Fig. 3.6 A wind rose. The 'arms' show wind strength and direction. 55% of wind comes from the SW quarter but it is warmer than the 15% coming in from the NE.

Fig. 3.7 The effect of topography on wind speed.

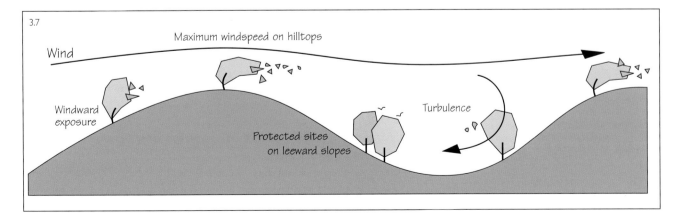

on windward valley sides the wind speeds will be about 90% of that at the ridge.

None of this is very helpful for an existing house, although it might be useful when you choose your next one. Within a specific locale, the rougher the ground, the lower the wind speed. It is possible to estimate the impact of various windbreaks upon the wind speed:

<u>Open country with no windbreaks</u>	<u>100%</u>
(coastal fringes, moorland and fens)	
<u>Open country with scattered windbreaks</u>	<u>89%</u>
(most undulating farmland with hedges)	
<u>Country with many windbreaks</u>	<u>78%</u>
(parks, woods, small towns, suburbia)	
<u>Surface with large and frequent obstructions</u>	<u>66%</u>
(city centres – high buildings, closely spaced)	

Airflow and shelter

Figures 3.8 and 3.9 show airflow around a house and around a tall building. On the windward wall there is a build up of pressure, and on the leeward wall a reduction. The roof can experience either positive or negative pressure, depending on its angle and the proportions of the house. Shelter can be provided by other buildings, planting or earthworks. The following points offer some general design principles for reducing infiltration:

- Wind infiltration into a house is usually a flow from high to low pressure areas. To reduce draughts through the house, it is helpful if the path is broken by planning the house so that no room runs right through from front to back (as well as by having an airtight structure).
- A house should be oriented to present the narrow end to the prevailing wind.
- Groups of houses should be spaced approximately six house-heights apart, and staggered for the best shelter effect. Designs should avoid forms that accelerate the wind or form 'venturi' i.e. tunnels/funnels. Houses on stilts, as in the Segal Method, should have their undercroft boarded off.
- Shelter-belts of trees are very effective. As the foliage is porous to varying degrees (depending on species and season), there is less eddying behind them than there would be with a solid wall; a more general wind-slowing takes place. Ideally the trees should be the same height as the house and 1-3 house-heights distant. It has been found that such an arrangement can reduce air infiltration by 40%.
- A solid fence of about 20% of house-height, spaced one house-height to windward, is also useful – reducing infiltration by maybe 30%. Combining fence and trees can give a reduction of 60%. A fence at an angle to the wind is not very effective; indeed funnelling can take place, which will make things worse.
- A courtyard-shaped house, groups of L-shaped houses, or a walled garden are forms that will provide sheltered external spaces, with relatively still air that may be warmed by the sun. Thus, they provide pleasant outdoor spaces as well as protecting the house from cold winds.
- The ancient techniques of jettied floors and wide eaves help protect the lower walls from the effects of driving rain.
- The house surface should be as rough as possible; this is easily done by planting wall-climbing plants (clematis, honeysuckle, Virginia creeper) on trellis. The effect is to extend the boundary layer, providing a slightly warmer layer of air

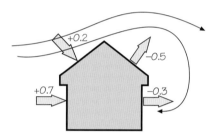

3.8

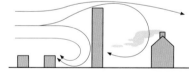

3.9

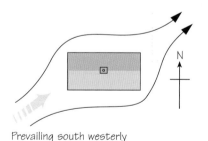

Prevailing south westerly

3.10

Fig. 3.8 Windflows around a house. The figures are pressure coefficients that vary with the slope and height of the house.

Fig. 3.9 Effects of a tall building on wind.

Fig. 3.10 Fortunately, presenting a narrow end to the prevailing wind also presents one of the large faces to the south for passive solar gain.

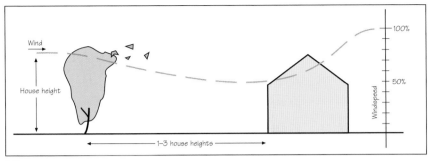

3.12

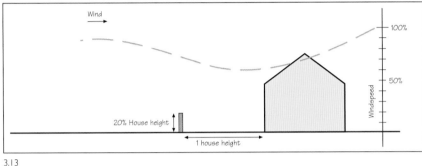

3.13

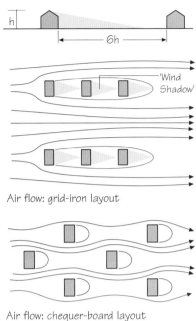

Air flow: grid-iron layout

Air flow: chequer-board layout

3.11

around the walls. Verandahs and arbours will help to provide wind protection, by breaking up wind flows

- A house can present a better aerodynamic shape to cold winds by having a low roof on the north side. Care must be taken to avoid eddies on the leeward side of the house; a glazed verandah or balcony will reduce their effect. A typical wedge-shaped passive solar house will also present less flat wall to the northerly winds.

- Earth-sheltering does just that: it shelters the house by using mounds of earth. These mounds can either envelop part of the house or provide some streamlining in the path of the wind. They are most useful, probably, on the north-east side – earth sheltering on the south-west would cut out useful wintertime sunshine.

In summary

- Site, orient, and plan new houses for maximum shelter.
- Plant shelter belts, erect windbreak fences.
- Plant creepers up walls.

External noise sources

Nearby roads and other continuous sources of background noise can be tiresome. The effects can be lessened in the following ways:

- visual screening of the source to psychologically lessen its disturbance;
- planting will attenuate noise, large-leaved vegetation is best, but will not help much in winter – but then windows are more likely to be closed at that time of year;
- planning the house to avoid windows of quiet areas facing noise sources; and
- using running water to disguise background noise in the garden.

3.14

3.15

Fig. 3.11 Spacing houses for maximum shelter.

Fig. 3.12 The effect of a shelter belt on wind speed. The line shows the dip in speed to be read off on the scale on the right.

Fig. 3.13 A fence can reduce windspeed to 60% by the house.

Fig. 3.14 Energy conserving topiary – a wind sheltering hedge with a window cut-out aligning with the house window.

Fig. 3.15 Plants protecting the wall from the wind. The Metro is probably helpful too!

3.16

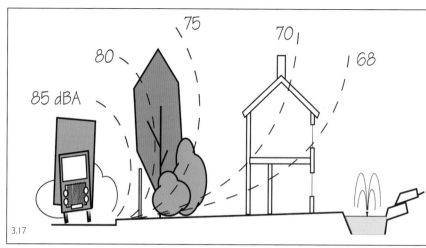

3.17

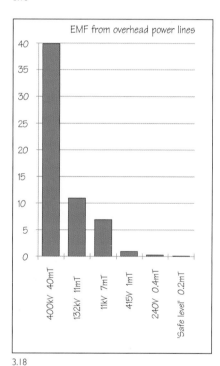

EMF from overhead power lines

40
35
30
25
20
15
10
5
0

400kV 40mT
132kV 11mT
11kV 7mT
415V 1mT
240V 0.4mT
'Safe level' 0.2mT

3.18

Electromagnetic fields (EMF)

There is considerable disquiet over the unusual electromagnetic environments found at some sites. A survey can be undertaken to measure electromagnetic radiation, which comes in three forms:

- Disturbances in the earth's magnetic field: these are caused by faults in the ground. The normal geomagnetic field strength is around 47 microtesla (mT).

- Electromagnetic field (EMF) and electrical field levels from overhead and underground electricity supplies. High-voltage power lines emit high EMF levels because the live and neutral cables are separated. This also applies to 240V overhead power cables, which are the type that carry ordinary domestic supply. Underground cables are generally shielded and are safer. Figure 3.18 shows electro-magnetic fields normally encountered under high-voltage cables and at the perimeter fence of substations. If you have worries about a particular installation, all local electricity companies have officers who will come and measure field strength for you.*

- Radio frequency fields: These are present in most locations, with TV and radio channels evident at around 100 decibels (dB) – which is not thought to be sufficiently strong to raise concern. However, the increase in numbers of powerful transmitters installed for mobile phones, as well as military sources of radio frequency fields, may have links to some cases of childhood cancers. To put it into some perspective, in Sweden a limit of a continuous level of 0.2mT (the bar marked 'safe') has been set for video display units and in schools and day centres. The Electricity Council is considering adopting a rule that no habitation should be within 50 metres of a pole-mounted transformer.

Geobiology

Or the effect of geology on living things. Dowsing will reveal underground anomalies, such as water courses or ley lines, which are thought to affect humans. A house can be placed to avoid harmful forces. The simplest form of dowsing finds water sources. It has a very high rate of success: even the author can find water pipes and drains reliably.

Fig. 3.16 A willow wall, a living sound barrier to a busy road. Earth is put between the two basket weaves of willows. Designer/builder: Ewan McEwan.

Fig. 3.17 Reducing the effects of street noise. The contour lines show typical sound levels without any reduction.

Fig. 3.18 Electromagnetic field strength from overhead electricity distribution, measured below the cables at ground level. You will see 400kV cables on steel pylons; 132 and 11kV lines on wooden poles with ceramic insulators; and 415kV cables could be strung between houses. Source: Electricity Council.

*A recent study by Sir Richard Doll for the National Radiation Protection Board (NRPB) found a small but significant risk to children of developing leukaemia, and a possible risk to adults, if they lived in close proximity to high voltage power lines (Building For a Future vol 11, no 1 and Sunday Times March 2001). This risk affects approx. 60,000 people in the UK – [Thomas Saunders, 2002]

Do-it-yourself dowsing

- Cut the hook and twisted bit off a wire coathanger.
- Straighten the wire and cut in half.
- Bend the wire 80mm down from the tip to a 90° angle.
- Hold one rod in each hand so that the wands are parallel to each other and pointing away from you.
- Slowly walk over a known buried water pipe, or hose full of water, with a clear mind, just staring at your feet and thinking 'water pipe'.
- As you cross the pipe, the wands will cross without any conscious effort on your part, and uncross as you move away.
- When you have practiced the technique, then you can try on an unknown, but provable water source.

3.19

3.20

3.21

Sustainability initiatives

Although most areas have a smattering of natural alternative activities and businesses, there are certain hot spots that attract more than their fair share of neighbourhood recycling schemes, holistic healing centres, and wholefood shops (of course you might prefer to avoid such places). Some local authorities are open to ideas of ecological building and are taking a more active role in post-Rio Earth Summit initiatives. Sherwood Energy Village is a new sustainable settlement – initiated by the Newark and Sherwood District Council – that has transformed a 91-acre former colliery into an environmental enterprise. The site comprises industry, commerce, housing, education, recreation, tourism and leisure.

Community involvement

Planning the spaces around buildings can cover a large number of topics, from designing a town or involvement in the 'Local Plan', to where to put the flower beds in your garden. Although we are dealing here primarily with the house and its curtilage, we can all influence the larger scheme of things by our comments on Local Plans and planning applications for, say, housing estates and other new developments. Some of us may be involved in a group self-build scheme or a community planning process of neighbourhood redevelopment.

There are well-developed tools and organisations that can help involvement with community planning. One tool, called 'Planning for Real', developed by the Neighbourhood Initiatives Foundation (NIF), enables community planning processes to be clear and helpful. It is a logical and enjoyable procedure for prioritising local requirements that helps individuals identify vital and unrealistic components within a community plan. It also helps determine the most useful location to place facilities. NIF helps develop the ideas, skills, and experience of a neighbourhood, allowing it to shape the future of its community.

3.22

Fig. 3.19 Dowsing the coat hanger way (the black cats have no significance – or have they?)

Fig. 3.20 Crystal Waters permaculture village – an attempt to create a sustainable development.

Fig. 3.21 A 'Planning for Real' session underway on a housing estate. Source: NIF.

Fig. 3.22 NIF logo.

There are many opportunities available to improve neighbourhoods. One of the most successful is 'Home Zones', whereby the streets can be humanised by planting, pedestrian areas and safe meeting places. Initiatives like these can grow out of established community groups, or can help galvanise local action and thereby establish the basis for future community involvement.

The desire for sustainable villages, green towns, and other community-based, low-impact developments far outstrips the supply allowed by the planning process and land costs. The lowest-impact developers of all are those who solve their housing need temporarily, setting up on waste land. Such initiatives as those made by travellers, yurt dwellers, and others should not be discouraged *per se*.

Features of a sustainable, low-impact development

Whether building from scratch or buying an existing house, the first step is to narrow your options to a handful of potential and suitable locations for your house. Then it is time to look at choosing a building in which to live. In making these decisions, you need to consider the design factors of setting the house in its landscape. Remember that whilst it is always possible to remodel a house, you are stuck with a site. The main building criterion is that it should be a sustainable, low-impact development.

Space, form, and design
- **Local context:** design the house to respect, but not mimic, local forms, and to be honestly built of mainly local materials.
- **Community involvement:** your development should have full local involvement and approval and, where appropriate, use 'Planning for Real' techniques.
- **Spaces around the house:** use pattern language (see page 39) for arranging human habitation to plan your house and garden.

Improving the biology
- **Soil structure:** organic horticulture and techniques such as green manures and composting will provide a safe and bountiful garden.
- **Biodiversity:** create wild areas, using native trees, shrubs, and weeds to attract local wildlife and blur the edges of a garden. Install bird and bat boxes.
- **Trees:** plant plenty of trees for biodiversity, future building materials, coppice crafts, biofuel, shade, wind shelter and beauty.
- **Green roofs:** make your garden larger without making your house smaller by covering the roof in soil. The vegetation that grows there will absorb some of the carbon dioxide created by your dwelling and may enable you to be self-sufficient in oxygen (to do so, each person needs 30m^2 of vegetation). Rainwater run-off will also be slowed which will improve the efficiency of rainwater storage and disposal systems.)

Towards a sustainable home
- **Low-energy:** plan the site and house to use as little fossil fuel as possible and make the house of materials that use little energy in their manufacture.
- **Renewable energy sources:** aim to replace fossil fuels with energy from the sun (passive and active solar heating, electricity from photovoltaics) and biofuels. Wind or hydro generation may be possible on some sites.
- **Water supply:** construct a garden that requires minimal water with drought-resistant species and plenty of mulches. Collect all rainwater and consider

3.23

Fig. 3.23 The opening day of Methleys Street 'home zone' in Chapel Allerton, Leeds. The measures taken were mainly traffic calming, shared surfaces and planting – reclaiming the street for pedestrians…over two-thirds of the adults interviewed thought that the home zone had made it safer for children when walking or cycling and just over half thought that children should play in the street now that it was a home zone.
TRL Report TRL586 2003 for the Department of Transport.

recycling greywater. Use soakaways for surplus rainwater so that the water table is replenished, rather than connecting to mains drainage which could worsen flooding downstream.

- **Sewage treatment:** on site sewage treatment systems can recycle nutrients and reduce your water use. There are many safe and hygienic options, such as compost toilets, reed bed effluent treatment, and greywater recycling, depending on site and context.
- **Growing food:** reduce your dependence on the supermarket and over-processed foods by enjoying organic gardening and animal husbandry. Plant edible hedges (hazel, elder, cherry, apple, etc.).
- **Recycling and re-use:** minimise refuse from your house by storing and re-using materials and composting organic wastes. When you are building, try to use all your waste on site, or use local recycling schemes.
- **Working from home:** if you cannot have a home-based workshop, smallholding, and/or office, reduce your impact on the environment by using as little fossil fuel energy as you can to reach your workplace.

Planning for a low-energy house

There are particular aspects of site design relating to a low-energy house:

- **Solar aspect:** a site should be able to 'see' the sun all year round. You will have to consider the path that the sun takes during the winter months to check that your house can make the most of passive solar gains (see figure 3.24). It is usually best in a city to have the back garden facing south: there will be less overshadowing, and you can add passive and active solar structures (a

Fig. 3.24 A 'Waldren Diagram' showing the apparent path of the sun throughout the year and angles of altitude (angle up from horizontal) and azimuth (degrees of the compass). The heavy line is the shape of the window, and obstructions such as trees and buildings have been sketched on.

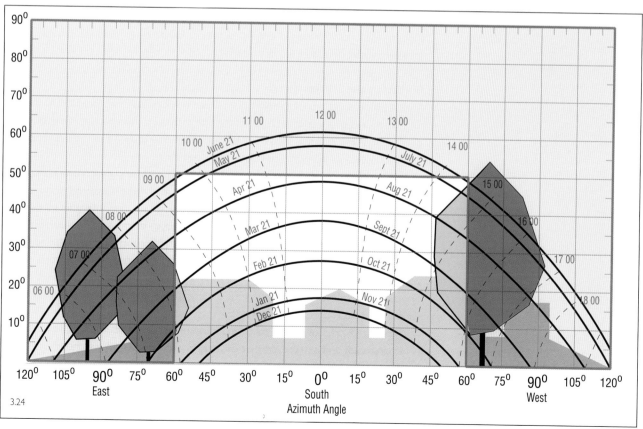

3.24

conservatory, solar panels, etc.) without too much worry over planning constraints. When moving to the country, it is all too easy to fall in love with a particularly cute cottage without considering winter sunshine. For this and other reasons (rain leaks, condensation, daylighting, cosiness), it is best to view a house during the winter.

- **Shelter from wind:** hills, other buildings and trees can either protect a house from prevailing winds, or they can funnel and concentrate them. It is notoriously difficult to predict wind movement – generally, shelter to the west and north-east is useful. If possible, visit potential sites on a blustery winter day, or study the local vernacular buildings: people had more time in the past to find the naturally calm sites (although this is not a fail-safe method, as humble houses were often put where the lord of the manor said so).
- **Growing biofuels:** try to get a large enough plot to grow biofuels. The most practical and attractive biofuel crop is timber for firewood. A hectare of coppiced trees will yield 10-25 tonnes of wood fuel per year.

Surveying the ecology and geology

Look at the soil, topography and wildlife habitats. Your house should be integrated as much as possible into the local ecology. Have a soil test done to find out if there is any toxicity in the soil (ask your local Environmental Health Office about this). Water quality tests can be undertaken by the local authority. If you are building on a brownfield site, the soil may be contaminated by years of industrial waste and may need cleaning or 'remediation'. Check for local air pollution sources. Buy as much land as you can afford, so that you can improve the site by planting trees, allowing wild areas, and organic gardening. Before you can build, you are required to check with the NRPB for any possibility of radon gas in the underlying subsoil. If your site is thought to be at risk, then a test will be necessary to determine the gravity of the problem and recommended remedies.

Gardening and soil fertility

A new house should be located on the least ecologically promising bit of the site that still meets all requirements of solar access, shelter, overshading, views, and so on. The most fertile areas should be left for vegetable growing and garden space, which can be viewed from the house and used for leisure.

The principles of organic gardening (continually recycling organic wastes, using mulches and green manures, rotating crops, valuing weeds, and using biological pest control) can be used to build up soil fertility and soil life. Your garden can be used for growing vegetables, herbs, fruit and raising animals, as well as being a decorative and useful place for play. The ambition of organic gardening is to tread a delicate path. On the one hand, we prefer to cultivate specific crops (fruits, vegetables, etc.), and in doing so, we create monocultures. On the other, we like to encourage natural soil fertility and biological pest control, which can then exuberantly swamp our monocultures.

Growing food is not just a rural or suburban enterprise. About 15% of world food is grown in cities: one in three urban households, worldwide, grow some of their own food. At Apple Tree Court, on a housing estate in Salford, the residents have dug the barren, windswept open space around the block to create vegetable plots, an orchard, and a wildlife area. Health benefits include greater physical activity, access to fresh crops, and a sense of mental well-being. The co-operative spirit

3.25

3.26

3.27

3.28

developed in the process of establishing a garden has in turn led to a community cafe, a food co-op and the establishment of a credit union. City food growing is being promoted by the National Food Alliance.

Allotments – deriving from the enclosure legislation of the 18th and 19th centuries – enable people to grow their own produce regardless of whether they have access to a private garden or not. Although plots were initially provided solely with this aim in mind, the extent and use of allotments have since varied and allotment sites now fulfil a broader range of needs for both plot-holders and the community at large. At present, there are around 250,000 plot-holders in England. During the Second World War the 'Dig for Victory' campaign saw annual food production from allotments rise to 1,300,000 tonnes per year from around 1,400,000 plots. Although the traditional image of an allotment holder is an older, retired man, the profile has started to broaden in recent years. Fewer than half of all plot-holders are retired.

Biodiversity

Nature abhors tidiness – but most humans love it. Despite our inclination towards groomed lawns and neat borders, gardens can benefit from some wildness and biodiversity in any number of ways. A ragged, overgrown edge can make a garden feel bigger, as its limits are undefined. A reed bed can double as wildlife habitat and greywater treatment system. Ponds offer both tranquillity and wildlife value. Every garden should have a tree – even a miniature one – it provides a visual focus, a shady sitting place, and a habitat for diverse wildlife.

Trees

Passions are aroused by trees – they seem to hold a special grip on our psyche. Campaigns have been waged for a single oak tree that stands in the way of a road 'improvement'. Civil protest over the relentless expansion of roads and airports centres around copses of trees. Trees and forests are evocative: tree-worship, tree-hugging, the May tree, Robin Hood's Sherwood Forest. To us, trees are curiously linked to freedom, independence, and stoicism. Ecologically, of course, trees have an important role to play. They are the major provider of oxygen and habitat for the

Fig. 3.25 'Allotments are an important feature in the cultural landscape. They combine utility, meaning and beauty with local distinctiveness.' – Select Committee on Environment, Transport and Regional Affairs, Fifth Report.

Fig. 3.26 A kitchen garden.

Fig. 3.27 A shady sitting place and water. The whole site at CAT is 'repairing the land', mostly by nature reclaiming a bit of industrial waste but also by design.

Fig. 3.28 Orchards provide food, shade, fuel, and a wildlife haven.

myriad life-forms necessary for the survival of all species and they are net absorbers of CO_2 over their lifetime. They are also useful, providing fruit, nuts and timber, as well as serving as the major energy source for most of the world's human population. So, plant as many native trees as you can. They are easy to grow and will provide shelter from the wind, shade if needed, privacy, and visual delight.

Designing a new home

*The movement
between rooms is as
important as the rooms
themselves.*

Christopher Alexander *et al*

FUNCTIONAL LAYOUT

The start to any building design is to establish the relationships between the various functions to be housed. The bubble diagram is a useful way of ordering your thoughts. Every activity bubble will not necessarily be a room – it can be a way of organising things within one huge space. The 'bubbles' can be cut out of paper and moved around to find the best relationship between them. Later, floor area and shape can be added and the whole diagram will be reworked to bring in site factors:

- solar access;
- wind shelter and buffering;
- connections to the street and garden;
- views;
- privacy; and
- protection from noise.

Having brought in the site factors, the design now has to be refined. To start with – how large should it be? The obvious major factor, apart from the area available on your plot, is cost – capital and running cost. You will use a cost per square metre of floor area. This will vary according to the type of construction and your specification, which are informed by the major themes of this book – materials, building elements and energy concerns.

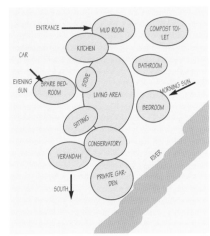

4.1

Fig. 4.2

Then there is the 'style' of the house. Unless you are constrained by particular policies relating to conservation areas and national parks, you have examples stretching over hundreds of years to choose from – styles arising from local customs and materials, fashions and fads. Thanks largely to good television programmes, such as *Grand Designs*, the idea that a house does not have to be a conventional brick box is gradually implanting itself. The ideas of the 'Modern Movement' are being rediscovered – it gave us some principles that should be central to any house design.

Previous page: The gallery at Roche Court.
Architect: Stephen Marshall of Munkenbeck & Marshall.

Fig. 4.1 The bubble diagram showing basic relationships between functions.

Fig. 4.2 The tradition of good design (Port Sunlight).

- A house with lots of daylight and sunlight falling onto surfaces, and windows framing views.
- A house that responds to its site and climate, integrating landscape and internal spaces – creating courtyards and 'outdoor rooms' and connections between the outside and the inside.
- Functional but flowing spaces.
- Honesty. The materials, form and appearance are determined by the function, the structure, and the spaces. No fakery.

'...the marketing of houses in the UK offers ample proof that "features" designed to assert status and impress passers-by are a key part of the mass house-builder's bag of tricks. Not least of the consequences of this obsession with "presenting a good front" is that many new houses are still condemned to have private gardens and living room windows that receive minimal amounts of sunlight. In Scandinavia things are done very differently....Making exposure to the sun an overriding concern of housing layout...is the most reliable way of ensuring the genuine variety of layout that most house builders now produce mindlessly through arbitrary and meaningless informality'. Richard Weston 'The extraordinary ordinariness', *Touchstone*, November 2003.

Fig. 4.3 A house by the architect Baragan demonstrating the qualities of modern design.

4.3

4.4

4.5

4.6

A PATTERN LANGUAGE

We are all full of ideas for what makes up our ideal home:

- 'A big kitchen with a huge table – the cooking mustn't take place somewhere out of the way'.
- 'The living room must have access to the garden, and mustn't be overlooked'.
- 'I want to see who's coming to the front door when I'm in the kitchen'.
- 'Lots of sunlight in the main rooms – but a cosy dark area as well'.

These sorts of random and sometimes contradictory ideas – a mixture of functional layout choices and living patterns – guide us when we are choosing or designing a new home, or altering an existing one. Not many of us have the luxury of designing a house from scratch, although a significant minority do. In the UK, about 8-9,000 houses are self-built every year[01] – presumably they have been planned by their eventual occupants. Virtually all the rest – around 160,000 – are built either as speculative developments or as Housing Association properties. Here, the house is of generic design, and the occupants fit in as best they can.

Those of us involved in self-build house design are constantly surprised by the ingenuity with which people evolve designs very different from the standard seven room layout normally provided. Admittedly, many self-builders conform to this norm out of fear that their ideal house would be unsaleable. There again, there are many people out there who will be as attracted to your ideas as you are.

Christopher Alexander's book *A Pattern Language*[1] is the result of studying those timeless ways of building that we all find satisfying, desirable, and joyful. Alexander and his team of researchers have tried to catalogue all these building experiences that we love, in order to identify what is important about these patterns

Fig. 4.4 'Modern' housing on a human scale – Jørn Utzon's courtyard housing at Fredensborg, Denmark 1963. (Photo by Kjeld Helmer Petersen, from 'Materials Form and Architecture' Richard Weston).

Fig. 4.5 Oasis of Peace, Porthmadog. Architect: David Lea.

Fig. 4.6 The Modern movement in Devon – High Cross House, Dartington. Architect: WE Lescaze.

4.7

4.8

and how they relate to other patterns. The many patterns relating to an individual house fall into the following principal groups.

Outdoor spaces as 'rooms'

We so often see houses just plonked down, more or less at random: the rest of the plot being no more than 'the bits left over'. Designers should think of the inside and outside of the house as a series of linked spaces: how does that area of garden feel when looked at from within the house? How does the house look from that area? There should be protected south-facing areas, with enclosing elements (walls, fences, hedges) apart from the house itself. Each of these external rooms should have views out, just like an internal room. The house should be low on the north side to avoid deeply-shadowed areas.

Ambiguous boundaries

Our houses generally have a distinct boundary between inside and out. We are outdoors in the foul weather; we go through the front door; and it is warm and cosy – there is rarely an in-between environment. The British climate is very changeable. We get lots of not-very-cold winter days with a bit of drizzle; the odd shaft of sunlight; some bright and cold spring days – yet we tend to stay indoors all winter, with occasional, well wrapped-up excursions. Our houses are not adaptable and do not have a variety of spaces for a variety of weathers. The edge of the house should be varied – with features such as verandahs, a semi-enclosed balcony, a sheltered terrace, a conservatory, and low, overhanging roofs with a seat, all of which provide sheltered spaces in between the house and garden.

4.9

Fig. 4.7 Patterns of 'Farmhouse Kitchen': the big table at the heart of activity; 'Sequence of Sitting Spaces', from the table to the easy chairs; 'A Window Place'.

Fig. 4.8 Courtyard – an outdoor space as a 'room'.

Fig. 4.9 The sheltering roof and sliding walls dissolve the boundary between house and garden – Ryoanji, Japan.

4.10

4.11

Create entrances and views

The British front door normally offers a not terribly interesting transition from public to private realm. It could be off to one side, with a welcoming porch, or entrance room; there could be a meandering path up to it, with a change in direction. An interesting view can be framed by a window or some landscaping feature, and some windows should overlook street life. The Japanese often frame views in gardens of some distant landscape, which, by careful stage-setting, appears to be part of their tiny garden (called 'borrowed scenery'). The British version of the same effect is created by the 'ha-ha', a ditch with an out-of-view fence, giving the impression that the garden extends into farm land. If you have a small garden, it will feel bigger if you hide one part of it from view; a tiny courtyard can seem to be of indeterminate size if it is heavily planted with obscuring vegetation.

Fig. 4.10 'Garden growing wild', a ragged overgrown edge to a garden makes it feel bigger…

Fig. 4.11 …and provides opportunities for the curious.

4.12a

4.12b

4.13

4.14

A house to suit its occupants

This might sound obvious, but most houses are designed for the mythical family of two adults and 2.2 children: a unit that is already becoming a demographic minority. The new house needs to meet the requirements of other family structures. It should give the inhabitants the spaces they require, with definite public and private rooms. Children should have their own private realms. Lay out the house to suit your style of living: the 'farmhouse kitchen' with its huge table for all activities from food preparation to homework, the bedrooms to the east if you want to be woken by the rising sun, living rooms to the west, for relaxation in the evenings. Provide a room to rent out, a cottage in the garden for an elderly parent or for teenagers, or build a garden shed or workshop. Subsequent occupiers will always be found for the most personalised designs, or the layout can be altered.

Fig. 4.12a & 4.12b Courtyard houses with 'outdoor rooms' and roofs covering part of the path to form protected entrances.

Fig. 4.13 Entrance transition…

Fig. 4.14 …to courtyard.

Design for natural movement through the house

Entrances are important, both for the visitors and the hosts. The progression from street or car to front door, to entrance room and the public realm of the house, and on to semi-public and private spaces must be carefully considered. Passages should be short, rooms should be laid out so that routes across them do not disturb the activities taking place. The main activity room can also be used as circulation space, with other major rooms leading off it. Treat the stairs as a stage – enjoy the act of moving up and down. Provide a surprising glimpse of a view, only seen when moving through the house.

Create inviting places

Avoid one-sided sloping ceilings and rooms with acute angles – right-angled or nearly right-angled junctions work best; circular rooms often lead to awkward shapes outside them. Have lower ceilings upstairs and for children's rooms, which might have 'secret places'. Provide personal spaces (which can be made private, or personalised): window seats in the sun, alcoves for beds, a seat by the front door, a sitting circle, a fireplace and seat. Consider which room you want to have a lot of daylight – it could be kitchen, study, or living room. Have some windows that open fully (French windows), have others with deep sills and have some internal windows between rooms. Ideally each room should enjoy light on two sides, with windows in more than one wall. This will give more of a sense of the surroundings and prevent glare – the uncomfortable contrast between lit and unlit parts of the room.

4.15

4.16

4.17

4.18

Fig. 4.15 'Entrance Room': a place to greet visitors from all parts of the house.

Fig. 4.16 'Staircase as a stage.'

Fig. 4.17 'Window Place': bay windows offer oblique views and more light per wall opening.

Fig. 4.18 'Light on two sides of every room': one of the most important patterns. Extension of homegrown larch near Welshpool, Powys.

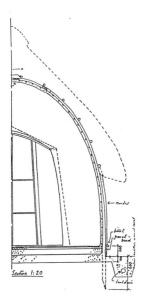

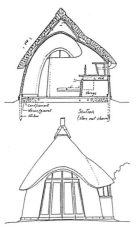

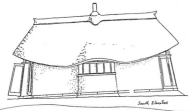

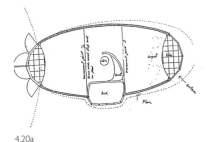

4.20a

Fig. 4.20a, & 20b Artist's studio made of materials from the site. Architect: David Lea.

Organic form

'Organic' can mean many things. In buildings, it can refer simply to non-rectangular form, such as the florid vegetation of Art Nouveau. It can suggest a deeper reverence for the earth, as found in the dynamic, earth-bound buildings by Frank Lloyd Wright. It can be a belief that architecture can have a profound effect on our growth and behaviour, as in the teaching and designs of Rudolf Steiner. Above all, it is 'full of the vitality of the natural world...its free-flowing curves and expressive forms are sympathetic to the human body, mind and spirit.'[2]

References

[01] Barlow, Jackson and Meikle, *Figures for 1999 from Homes to DIY For*, Joseph Rowntree Foundation, 2001

[1] Christopher Alexander et al, *A Pattern Language*

[2] David Pearson, *The New Organic Architecture*, Gaia Books, 2001.

4.20b

The healthy house

*'Health is a state of
complete physical mental
and social well-being
and not merely
an absence of disease'*

World Health Organisation

THE HEALTHY HOUSE

A healthy indoor environment is not only free from toxic substances, but also actively promotes thermal, visual and acoustic comfort. It is achieved through an understanding of the interaction between external climate, the building fabric and the human body. In some ways modern houses are likely to be less healthy than older ones made from naturally occurring materials, with open hearths and chimneys, and little or no draught stripping. As houses have become more airtight – for energy efficiency – so any indoor pollutants have tended to accumulate and become more concentrated. During the same period, there has been a huge increase in the number of building and household products based on synthetic chemicals, most of which have never been tested for their effects on human health.

Most of the ways in which built environments pose a threat to healthy living are to do with the materials and finishes used in construction, or the ways in which buildings are heated and ventilated (or not). In addition, we are exposed to external air and water pollutants, we eat chemically treated foods, we build on contaminated ground, we make and are harassed by incessant noise. It follows that all these stresses and contaminations may lead to health problems.

Recent years have seen a growing interest in the relation between health and buildings. The emergence of Sick Building Syndrome and the increase in such health problems as allergies, medical hypersensitivity, and asthma have added urgency to this debate. One in nine children now suffer from asthma. Most western governments, it is claimed[1], now realise that many post-1950 buildings, mainly non-domestic commercial or industrial buildings, are a direct cause of stress, depression, fatigue or the 'general malaise' typical of Sick Building Syndrome. Conversely, recent research tends to suggest that workers and students perform better, and

> Sick Building Syndrome is the name given to a cluster of symptoms such as headaches, nausea, lethargy, sore throat, eye and nose irritation, and lack of concentration, which affect people using a particular building and subside only after sufferers leave the building. Its cause is still uncertain but low relative humidity (RH), caused by poorly designed and maintained air conditioning and ventilation systems, has been implicated.

patients recover more quickly, in well designed, naturally ventilated and generously daylit schools, offices and hospitals.

As a species we have evolved to live in contact with certain materials – organic materials such as wood, wool and other fibres, and earth materials such as clay and lime. To us, they are benign (although some people are becoming so sensitised that fresh wood is an irritant). The smells that we notice – that 'new car' or 'fresh paint' smell – are sometimes an indication that our body finds them alien.

Pointers towards a healthy house
Reference to health issues will be found throughout this book, but there are several key considerations.

Site
- Select a site that is favourable: avoid wet ground, contaminated soil, persistent noise, local air pollution, radon gas and areas of geopathic stress.
- Select a site that allows you to orientate the building for sunlight and wind shelter.

Internal climate

- Provide good daylight and sunlight.
- Insulate well to provide thermal comfort.
- Build tight to avoid draughts.
- Vent pollutants and excess moisture at source (bathroom, kitchen).
- Have plenty of openable windows.
- Install controllable and easily understood heating systems. Use radiant, rather than air-based, heat delivery.

Building materials

- Use traditional, long-established materials that do not emit pollutants.
- Use materials that are durable, stable and appropriate for the job they have to do.
- Do not use materials that contain heavy metals, biocides or known toxins such as lead or asbestos.
- Make sure that mineral and other fibres are completely encapsulated.
- Use low or nil-formaldehyde-emitting materials.
- Avoid polyvinyl chloride (PVC) products and foam-filled furniture.
- Avoid surface-area finishes with a high 'fluff-factor' (for example, wall-to-wall synthetic mixture carpets) in high use rooms.
- Minimise the use of paints. Use water-based, organic or mineral paints that are micro-porous.
- Avoid timber preservatives – design the house so that these agents are unnecessary.

Building use

- Avoid harmful cleaning agents, solvents and smoke from tobacco and open fires.
- Keep heating appliances well serviced. Do not use unflued room heaters.
- Take care to minimise exposure to electromagnetic fields from equipment (televisions, video display units, microwave ovens, bedside alarms) and from the main electrical installation.

Thermal comfort

Thermal comfort is necessary for health and is linked to a sensation of complete physical well-being. This can be experienced in a huge range of activities, from walking around outside on a cold but sunny day, to lying in bed under the duvet. It is much easier to obtain a reasonable comfort level in a home than in a public space such as an office, school, or cinema. This is because we can regulate more of the factors that make us hot or cold. What factors contribute to our feeling this thermal balance – that is, feeling neither too hot nor too cold?

Figure 5.1 shows the six variables. Two of these are individual or local (activity and clothing), the other four are environmental (air temperature, mean radiant temperature, air velocity and humidity). In an office environment, you can often only change the clothing variable. In the house, however, most of the variables can be readily changed and comfort adjusted. It is significant that designs for 'green' offices are becoming much more like houses, with limited depth front to back giving good daylight penetration, openable windows to control personal ventilation and individual task lighting – in other words, more local control.

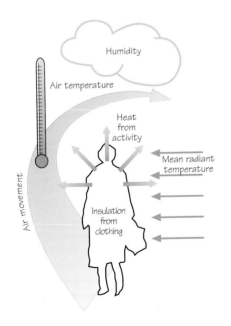

5.1

Fig. 5.1 The six variables affecting thermal comfort.

Activity

The rate at which the body converts food into heat depends largely on the activity level, and will vary from 80-400 watts. The metabolic rate, as it is called, is measured in watts per square metre W/m^2 of body area, or in 'mets', one met being the metabolic rate of a seated person ($58W/m^2$). An average man has a surface area of about $1.8m^2$.

Clothing

Clothing is our personal insulation, and is measured in 'clo'. One clo is, predictably, the insulating value of a man's suit, or $0.155W/m^2K$. Winter outdoor clothing or a duvet are about 2.2clo, summer clothing 0.6clo, shorts and T-shirt about 0.3clo, and nakedness is 0.0clo.

Air temperature

Air temperature is the one we all understand, and is measured with a dry bulb thermometer, in degrees Centigrade or Fahrenheit.

Mean radiant temperature

Mean radiant temperature is as important as air temperature, and the two are related. It is the mean of the temperatures of the surrounding surfaces weighted by area, ability to emit heat, and proximity. This relates to experiences such as feeling uncomfortably cool seated next to a large single-glazed window, when the air temperature is perfectly adequate elsewhere in the room; feeling comfortable in a cold room when the sun is streaming in; or sitting in front of a blazing fire in a deep armchair that is insulating your back. In practice, a well-insulated house can be kept at much lower air temperatures than a poorly insulated one, because all the surfaces will be warmer. Of course, lower air temperatures mean energy savings. Similarly, underfloor heating systems give relatively high mean radiant temperatures and allow lower air temperatures for the same comfort conditions.

Air movement

An increase in air speed will increase cooling of the body by convection and evaporation. Even if the surrounding air is at an adequate comfort level, an increase in air speed will increase the body's heat loss and be sensed as a cold draught. Air movement may be caused by bad draughtstripping, large cold surfaces, high rooms and the poor siting of air handling outlets. Overhead ceiling fans, although very useful for stirring up the air to ensure an even temperature throughout a room, can cause discomfort if too vigorous. Ideally air movement should be between 0.1 and 0.25 metres/second – below that air becomes stagnant; above it and it is experienced as draughts.

Humidity

High humidity is more of a problem in hot climates, where it inhibits the evaporative cooling of the body (sweating). In temperate climates, relative humidity makes little difference to the comfort of a person not engaged in strenuous activity. It is, however, important to keep it below 65% (to prevent mould and other damaging fungi growing) and above 40% (otherwise the membranes in eyes, nose, and throat become too dry).

There are several ways of modifying relative humidity:

- **Ventilation:** e.g. opening windows or turning on fans.
- **Using hygroscopic materials:** during periods of high humidity, certain materials – porous earth materials (clay, plaster) and organic materials (timber, wool, vegetable fibres) – can absorb and store liquid water in pores which will be released during periods of low relative humidity. These materials, exposed internally, can help regulate humidity levels automatically.
- **Breathing, vapour permeable constructions:** if water vapour can pass through the building fabric relatively easily, high humidity levels will be slowly lowered.
- **Electrically powered humidifiers or de-humidifiers**.

Highly hygroscopic materials

- Timber
- Cork
- Fibreboards
- Woodwool slab, preferably magnesite-bound
- Unfired clay, earth
- Lime plaster and mortar
- Coconut and other natural fibres
- Cellulose insulation

Finishes for the above should be vapour permeable (beeswax, stains, limewash)

Medium hygroscopic materials

- Wood particleboard, plywood
- Hardboard
- Gypsum plaster and plasterboard
- Cement mortar
- Fibre-cement sheets
- Limestone
- Linoleum

Low hygroscopic materials

- Bricks
- Pumice concrete blocks

Zero hygroscopic materials

- Mineral fibres
- Concrete
- Ceramic tiles
- Glass
- Plastics foams and finishes

Thermal comfort tolerance

If we were designing a heating and ventilating system for, say, a cinema, where the occupants will be sitting for a few hours at a time, unable to change their comfort factors beyond slight adjustments in clothing, it would be vitally important to be able to use predictive techniques. These have been developed, and take the form of various thermal comfort charts. Fortunately, in a house we can so easily change so many of the comfort factors that such a tight definition of comfort is not necessary. If the house is well insulated, with no draughts, low air velocity from any fans, and no large cold surfaces (temperature differences of not more than 10°C), a simple table will show the sort of temperatures that 90% of the population will find comfortable.

Activity	Metabolic rate in 'met'	Clothing in 'clo'	Comfort temperature in °C
Sleeping	0.8	2.2	18+/-3
Bathing	1.4	0.0	27+/-1
Sitting	1.0	1.5	20+/-2.5
Light work	2.0	1.0	16+/-3
Heavy work	3.0	1.0	10+/-4
Walking	1.2	2.2	14+/-4

It has also been shown that a passive solar design, where the temperature may well fluctuate somewhat, promotes comfort tolerance in its occupants, providing the temperature changes are gradual. We tend to dress more appropriately for the season, rather than expecting a year-round shirtsleeves environment, and we tend to adjust our clothing as the temperature changes.

Our comfort tolerance is even greater in unheated spaces such as conservatories – the proximity to the outdoors seems to reduce our intolerance to discomfort, to make us prepared to feel a bit colder or hotter than we would indoors. Here, the comfort range can go from 14°C (when it is less than 10°C outside) up to 32°C (when it is that temperature outside); whereas the comfort range in a heated indoor space might only be from 18-26°C. This phenomenon leads to energy savings.

Daylighting

Visual comfort is another aspect of healthy buildings. We all like a well-daylit room, especially if there is some sunlight around to give us cheer, and even more so if the lighting is coming from more than one direction. Good daylighting can also save energy, as electric lighting will be replaced by solar radiation. However, a balance must be found between the saving on electric lighting and heat loss from the windows, as they will lose heat at about six times the rate of a wall. In schools and offices that are rarely used at night, this balance tips in favour of high daylighting levels. Passive solar heating will add to the energy saving by reducing the fossil fuel demand.

In a house, which may be unoccupied through most of the day and will be reaching its highest temperatures during the hours of darkness, good daylighting is not so useful as an energy saving option. High daylighting levels can be confined to areas where it is needed for particular tasks, such as the kitchen, living room or study.

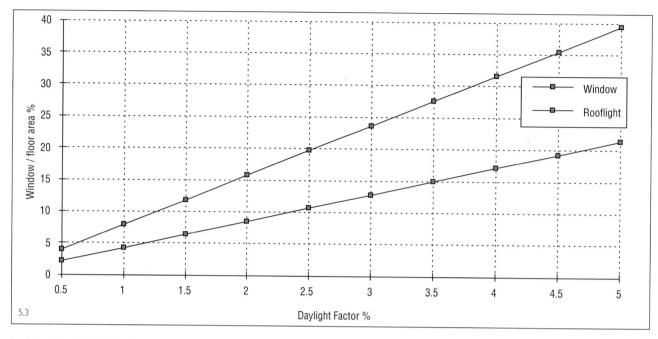

5.3

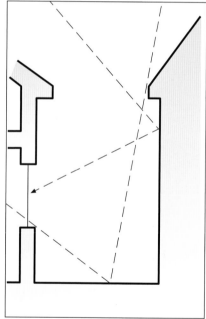

5.4

Fig. 5.3 Graph showing the relationship between daylight factor and window glass/floor area for an average domestic-sized room (of 12m²). The glass is assumed to be Low-E double-glazing; the vertical window can 'see' a sky angle of 65°; the rooflight can 'see' a sky angle of 120°; and the walls are painted a light colour. Smaller rooms, such as single bedrooms, will require slightly more glazing, and larger rooms less, pro rata. Look up the required daylight factor along the horizontal axis (e.g. 3% for a kitchen); the intersection on the 'window' line gives you a window glass/floor area of around 25% – a quarter of the floor area.

Fig. 5.4 Pale surfaces outside of windows that see little of the sky can greatly improve daylighting.

Daylight level

How big should windows be? For daylighting comfort, there isn't really an upper limit: we are perfectly happy with the levels of daylight outside or in a fully-glazed conservatory. We have to strike a balance where the daylight level is comfortable, so that we can easily read a book or thread a needle, and the room feels bright and cheery – without sacrificing too much thermal comfort or heat loss. One way to find a good level is to survey rooms that you feel are comfortable and to mimic the window sizes and positions and the room proportions and finishes. Or you can use the science of daylight factors.

Daylight factors

Daylight comes into a room from the sky vault, from direct sunshine or diffused by cloud cover, or by reflecting off surfaces in front of the window. How much comes

---

Average daylight factor for rooms in houses

$$\text{Av Daylight Factor (\%)} = \frac{M \times W \times O \times T}{A \times (1 - R^2)} = \begin{array}{l}\text{0.7 for double-glazing} \\ \text{0.6 for low-E double-glazing}\end{array}$$

where typically:

'M' is the correction factor for dirt

=   1.0 for vertical glazing

     0.8 for sloping glazing

     0.7 for horizontal glazing

'W' is the total glazed area of windows or rooflights in m².

'O' is the angle of the visible sky

=   65° for vertical glazing

     or see figure 5.7

'T'   is the glass transmission factor

'A' is the total area of all room surfaces (including windows)

'R' is the area weighted reflectance of room surfaces = 0.5

Or, with the typical factors given, window area = Daylight Factor x A x 0.75/39

in is dependant on the window size, type, angle and cleanliness of glazing, and how much of the sky vault is seen. The room depth, height and colours affect the distribution of daylight internally. The level of daylight within a room is measured as a percentage of that found outside on a horizontal surface, and is called the daylight factor. You can get a feel for daylight factors by taking measurements with a photographic light meter. Stand outside, preferably on a lightly overcast day, somewhere where you can see the whole of the sky vault and take a reading, then rush indoors and take a reading at an average point in the room, divide the second by the first and multiply by 100 – this will give you a daylight factor percentage.

When creating a new room you should aim to better the following recommended minimum daylight factors (Ref: Ecohomes 2002):

Kitchen   2% minimum

Other rooms   1.5% minimum

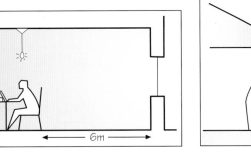

5.6

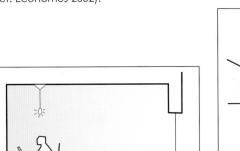

5.5

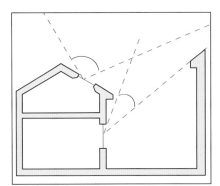

5.7

5.8

5.9a

5.9b

Fig. 5.5 Daylight is not effective at lighting rooms deeper than about 6m. Glare may also be a problem.

Fig. 5.6 All work surfaces should be able to 'see' the sky.

Fig. 5.7 The angle of sky that can be seen from the middle of each window is very important; obstructions such as other buildings, trees and roof overhangs make a significant difference.

Fig. 5.8 Roof windows are very effective at lighting rooms: they can 'see' a very wide part of the sky vault, and only need to be about half the area of a vertical window for the same daylighting.

Fig. 5.9a A 'Sunpipe' is very effective at bringing daylight to a windowless space. A 300mm diameter unit will, on most days, give a similar illumination to that of a normal light-bulb.

Fig. 5.9b The kit of parts consists of a highly reflective metal tube that connects a rooflight to a ceiling-mounted diffuser.

5.10a

5.10b

5.11

Fig. 5.10a & 5.10b Rooflights admit about twice the daylight as the same sized vertical window, for the same heat loss. A rooflight in this position will 'wash' the wall, so providing a large diffuse light source, and interesting shadows. The wall should be a light colour.
5.10a Architect's office: David Lea.
5.10b Architect and builder: Jono Hines

Fig. 5.11 A rooflight over a room which requires good daylighting for sewing. Roderick James.

All rooms should have a view of the sky from table top height (0.85m) in at least 80% of the room area.

In practice, most people prefer daylight factors of at least double the minimum (2-5%).

The daylight factors can be worked out using various methods, the simplest being average daylight factor (see figure 5.3). In most domestic rooms with windows with a reasonable view of the sky they will relate to a percentage of floor area.

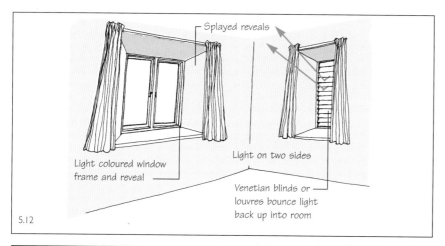

Splayed reveals

Light coloured window
frame and reveal

Light on two sides

Venetian blinds or
louvres bounce light
back up into room

5.12

5.15

5.13

5.14

Glare

This discomfort is caused by a strong contrast between a bright light source (the window) and the surrounding area. At its extreme, people in front of the window are viewed in silhouette. We feel more comfortable when people's faces are well-modelled by a variety of light sources. To avoid glare it is necessary to reduce the brightness of the window in comparison with its internal surrounding. This can be achieved in several ways:

- Window frames and surrounding walls painted a light colour.
- Splayed window reveals.
- Light from more than one direction in a room, with windows on different walls – this is the familiar pattern language of 'light on two sides of every room'.
- Shades or louvres which bounce light back further into the room and off other surfaces. The window will also not appear as such a bright light source.

Fig. 5.12 Techniques for reducing glare.

Fig. 5.13 Glare. With light from one source, people are often viewed in silhouette.

Fig. 5.14 Splayed window reveals were common in old houses with thick walls and small windows – a larger reflective surface is presented to the light. Notice also that the chunky window frames are splayed.

Fig. 5.15 A rooflight can reduce glare from the window of a highly glazed, but deep, room ('Light on Two Sides' pattern).

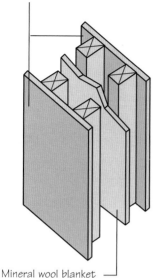

Plasterboard on timber frame

Mineral wool blanket

5.16

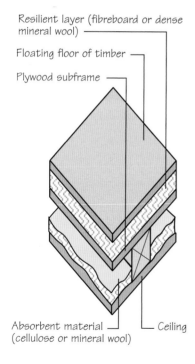

Resilient layer (fibreboard or dense mineral wool)

Floating floor of timber

Plywood subframe

Absorbent material (cellulose or mineral wool)

Ceiling

5.17

Fig. 5.16 Wall of separated timber frames.

Fig. 5.17 'Floating' timber floor.

Sound

Noise pollution is a general health hazard and another contributing factor to Sick Building Syndrome. Almost inaudible noises from, for example, badly fitted or faulty electrical equipment can be as irritating as, for example, loud noise from traffic. In the home, vacuum cleaner, washing machine, low buzzing from a fridge, loud music from a teenager's bedroom and/or the TV can add to the stress of daily life. As a general rule, if you have to raise your voice to be heard, your long-term hearing may be affected by the noise you are subjected to.

Other species too are affected by noise. Research carried out by the RSPB indicates that song birds in cities are becoming tone deaf. They cannot hear one another and so cannot learn their unique songs, instead imitating the sounds they hear most frequently – mobile phones and car alarms[2].

Sound is a pressure wave travelling through a medium of gas, liquid or solid (there is no sound in the vacuum of space). It is described by its pitch or frequency (in Hz or cycles per second), and its loudness is measured in decibels (dB). dBA, a non-linear scale that combines frequency and loudness, mimics the sensitivity of the human ear.

Typical sound levels in dBA:

- threshold of hearing   10
- inside a house in a quiet area   30
- listening to music in a room   60
- busy urban street   70

Acoustics is a complicated business, but most of us just need to know the techniques for reducing sound coming from the outside in, between rooms within a house, and from next door in a terraced or semi-detached house. A comfortable sound level in a house is around 25dBA, so that if you are next to a busy street you will require an external wall construction of 70-25 = 45dB reduction. There are plenty of wall constructions that will give a 45dB reduction, but unfortunately there will also be windows and doors in the external wall, which do not perform nearly as well. Small gaps around openings also make a significant difference, as a gap will give no reduction in sound levels. The resultant composite dB reduction of our wall with windows can be worked out using the table below. Noise reduction is only as good as the weakest part of the construction.

The two principal methods of reducing sound levels are to provide mass (weight) and to isolate materials. Thus the most successful sound reducing structures are those that have two massive parts separated from each other (like a masonry cavity wall).

Average sound transmission loss of various constructions in decibels (dB)

Walls

• Solid 110mm brickwork, plastered	45
• Solid 220mm brickwork, plastered	50
• Cavity (50mm) brick or block, plastered	55
• Separated timber frames, 32mm plasterboard and mineral wool	57

Floors

• Tongue and groove flooring, plasterboard ceiling	34
• Same, but floating boards on glass wool with 75mm min. wool	43
• Same, but with 50mm sand pugging (i.e. 50mm sand layer)	49
• 125mm reinforced concrete	45

- Same, but with floating screed   50

Note that the lightweight separated timber structures can achieve the same reductions as the heavy structures, or better.

5.18

Windows

- Any window when open   10
- Single-glazed window   22
- Weather-stripped single-glazed window   25
- Weather-stripped double-glazed window   30
- Two casements, with 150mm between them   40
- Two casements, with 300mm between them and absorbent reveals 45

Upgrading an opening by installing a second window inside an existing one is a very good energy saving and sound reduction measure.

Doors

- 50mm solid door   18
- 50mm solid door with weatherstrips   22
- Double 50mm solid door with weatherstrips and absorbent lobby   45

Upgrading an entrance opening by installing a second door inside (lobby), or outside (porch) an existing one is also a very good energy saving and sound reduction measure.

When landscaping around your house, remember that vegetation such as small trees and shrubs can help to reduce sound transmission.

Air quality

One of the legacies of the Industrial Revolution is air pollution, and whilst the more visible effects have been cleaned up, our atmosphere is now burdened with a sometimes lethal cocktail of less visible chemicals and particles. In addition, our homes are full of modern materials made of synthetic compounds unknown until recently, and the off-gassing effects of these are only gradually being understood.

5.19

Fig. 5.18 Sound.proof house. This timber framed music room uses lightweight separating constructions to achieve acoustic isolation.
Studio near Bath: Feilden Clegg Design.

Fig. 5.19 Industrial technology overshadowing earlier, renewable technology, now making a comeback due to the former's level of pollution.

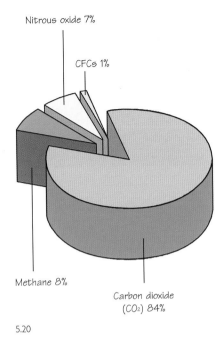

Nitrous oxide 7%

CFCs 1%

Methane 8%

Carbon dioxide
(CO₂) 84%

5.20

Outdoor pollution

Well known atmospheric pollution problems – global warming, holes in the ozone layer, photochemical smog, lead particles, acid rain – may seem like world problems that, individually, we can do little about. But most of them stem from simple, everyday actions like starting the car, turning on the central heating, throwing away materials that will be incinerated, using a household aerosol, using a photocopier.

Ozone holes

Although ozone gas is harmful in the lower atmosphere (see below), it is very necessary in the stratosphere. It is created by sunlight acting on oxygen and it protects the Earth's surface from ultraviolet radiation. Before it existed, multi-cellular life could not exist on the planet. If we lose it, we lose all. It was completely unexpected that a stable, non-toxic molecule such as chlorofluorocarbon (CFC), which is an otherwise useful insulating gas, would have such a devastating effect (each chlorine atom from a CFC molecule destroys 100,000 ozone molecules). CFC use has fallen dramatically since the Montreal Protocol, but is still produced and exported by some developing countries not covered by the agreement. In the UK, CFCs are no longer used in new building products or refrigeration systems, and their replacement HCFCs and HFCs are also being phased out in favour of simple hydrocarbons.

Acid substances

These are mostly sulphur dioxide and nitrous oxides (SOx and NOx) formed from burning fossil fuels and other industrial processes. Acidification of the atmosphere precipitates as 'acid rain' and can cause premature death in trees and whole forests.

Photochemical smog

This is caused by the action of sunlight on nitrogen oxides, dust and volatile organic compounds (VOCs) and leads to the formation of low-level ozone, which is damaging to human respiratory systems at high levels.

Atmospheric lead

This is much reduced following the advent of lead-free petrol. By far the biggest source of lead contamination now is from old paint which may flake off and be ingested by babies and children, or may be sanded or burnt off when redecorating.

> An American study carried out in Pennsylvania showed that teenage boys appearing in juvenile courts had a higher concentration of lead in their bones (11ppm), compared with non-delinquent boys of the same age (1.5ppm). Up to 38% of juvenile crime in Allegheny County, Pennsylvania, has been attributed to the effects of lead poisoning.
> From 'Neurotoxicology and Terotology' reported in the *Guardian* 7/1/03.

Indoor pollution

As well as the global effects of these pollutants, most of them affect human health directly. In addition, we are subject to gases and particles given off from building materials and appliances within the home. The effects of these are exacerbated by increased air tightness in modern buildings, as well as an astronomical increase in

Fig. 5.20 The principal greenhouse gases.

Carbon dioxide (CO₂): 84%. Most of this (80%) comes from burning fossil fuels, the rest from agriculture, burning wood and forests.

Methane: 8%. From decomposing landfill sites, agriculture and mining. Fifty times more potent, per molecule, than CO₂.

Nitrous oxide: 7%. From fossil fuel burning and agriculture.

CFCs: 1%. Although present in small amounts, each molecule is 1500 times more potent as a greenhouse gas than CO₂. Figures from 'Carbon UK 2000' [2a]

the number of synthetic substances. Tests carried out by the BRE on Indoor Air Quality found that indoor air was at least as polluted as the outside air in built up environments, and that indoor levels of some pollutants were highest in homes built after 1980[4]. Indoor air quality is becoming an essential part of the environmental assessment of any building.

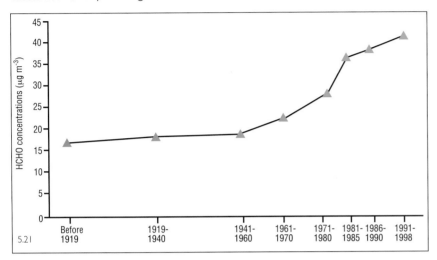

5.21

Although measured levels of indoor pollution are often very low, the effect of continuous and cumulative exposure should be borne in mind. There is also the additional risk of a synergistic reaction, taking place between two or more pollutants, which typically has a more potent effect than the sum of its parts. For example, the risk of cancer caused by asbestos or radon is statistically higher for those who smoke.

Individual response to pollutants varies widely. Either some degree of adaptation takes place or the immune system becomes overloaded, with some people becoming increasingly allergic to those chemicals that most of us adjust to. Your sense of smell is a reasonable guide to a material's harmful effects, but not always. You cannot smell radon gas, and the woodsmoke/burning leaves smell that most of us find beguiling and evocative of rural idyll, merely disguises its carcinogenic nature. Some of us find the smell of wood resin appealing; in others it causes an allergic reaction.

Some common indoor pollutants and how to avoid them:

Nitrogen dioxide *

- From incomplete combustion of fuels, particularly gas cookers and gas and paraffin heaters.
- Toxic, affecting respiration.
- Ventilate when cooking, fit a gas alarm, or avoid cooking with natural gas.*

Carbon monoxide

- Also from combustion – gas pilot lights, heaters and cookers, woodstoves, vehicle exhausts.
- Replaces oxygen in the blood stream; the effects of this include nausea, dizziness, death.
- Make sure boilers and woodstoves draw well and have their own air supply.
- Ventilate when cooking, fit a gas alarm, or avoid cooking with natural gas.
- Do not have pilot lights.

*A study of over 800 houses by the BRE found that nitrogen dioxide (NO₂) levels exceeded World Health Organisation (WHO) guidelines in 25% of homes[4].

Fig. 5.21 Increased formaldehyde concentrations in newer homes. From 'Indoor Air Quality in homes in England', BRE 2001.

Ozone
- Produced by photocopiers and electric motors.
- Eyes, nose and throat irritant.
- Ventilate if photocopying.

Radon
- Radioactive gas present in many areas due to prevailing geology.
- Damages lungs, cancer risk.
- Seal building at floor level and ventilate underfloor.

Volatile organic compounds (VOCs)
This class of chemicals are highly reactive producing a gas which may or may not be detectable. Chronic exposure can produce debilitating allergies and immune system deficiencies. VOCs include:

Organochlorines
- A wide family of plastics compounds including PVC and polychlorinated biphenyls (PCBs) found in many building and household products and paints, cleaning products, pesticides. Isocyanurate from cavity foam fillers.
- Persistent and toxic irritants, headaches, nausea.
- Avoid synthetic paints, stains and glues, PVC and solvent-based household products.

Formaldehyde
- Present in many building materials as a glue constituent. Formaldehyde vapours given off from many synthetic products.
- Present in new wood (small amounts) and combustion by-products.
- Very irritating to skin, eyes and respiratory system. A 'probable human carcinogen' (WHO). A possible trigger for asthma.
- Avoid composite wood materials (chipboard, MDF) or use zero-formaldehyde versions.
- Use solid wood, preferably well-seasoned, natural fibre carpets and furnishings, and traditional glues.

Timber treatments
- The most common preventative treatment is Chrome, Copper, Arsenic (CCA). 100,000 tonnes are used worldwide each year[5] and it has proved highly dangerous in transit[6].
- Use no preservatives or use safer preservatives such as borax.

Airborne micro-organisms
- Fungal spores and bacteria, dust mites.
- Cause allergic reactions and respiratory problems.
- Maintain proper humidity and avoid surface condensation, through insulation, trickle ventilation and airtight constructions.
- Use timber flooring and linoleum rather than carpet.

Mineral particles

- Asbestos fibres can be lethal when inhaled. There is no safe threshold. It is still present in half a million UK buildings. Asbestos removal should be carried out by specialists.
- Carcinogenic – mesothelioma is a particularly aggressive form of cancer.
- The incidence of asbestos-related diseases is still on the increase due to the long incubation period.
- Some non-asbestos mineral fibres e.g. rock or glass have been identified as potentially hazardous.
- Ensure mineral fibre insulation (e.g. rockwool) is well sealed from the internal environment.

Toxic pollutants given off during a house-fire

- Often one of the first materials to burn in a house-fire is PVC electrical sheathing or plastic foam filled furniture.
- Hydrogen chloride, dioxins and heavy metals are given off, which are often the cause of death or illness, rather than carbon monoxide poisoning or burning.
- Avoid and replace PVC and foamed plastic products in the home.

Fragrance

The upside of air pollution... Your house can be made odourless by choice of materials and good ventilation. Or it can have the natural smells of grass matting, resinous timber, wool fabrics, whatever you like. Fragrances can be added by essential oils – usually vaporised by heat. The effects of such aromatherapy are not proven, but such scents are stimulating and evocative.

Electromagnetic fields

Whenever electricity is used an electromagnetic field (EMF) is produced, which diminishes rapidly with distance from the source. There are two types: electric fields and magnetic fields. Electric fields occur whenever there is a voltage differential, and can be easily screened by trees and building materials. Magnetic fields are only present when a current is flowing, and will readily pass through most materials. The two types of field are independent of one another at low frequencies. As frequencies increase, the two interact and combine into one electro-magnetic field. In practice, the two usually occur together. The concern is mostly over magnetic fields, and whether continued exposure to them is harmful, principally carcinogenic. There is no conclusive evidence either way, but there is sufficient circumstantial evidence to suggest that avoidance can only be a good thing[7].

Magnetic fields are measured in microtesla (mT). The UK National Radiological Protection Board (NRPB) has no recommendation as to what constitutes a safe level, but Sweden has adopted a maximum of 0.2mT for computer monitors. Powerwatch, a campaign group dedicated to promoting the understanding and safe use of electricity, believes that magnetic fields should be less than 0.01mT.

Figures 5.22 and 5.23 show electromagnetic field strengths of household equipment, for distances away of 30mm and one metre. You will see that field strength drops dramatically with distance, so the advice 'don't sit so close to the TV' was instinctively correct.

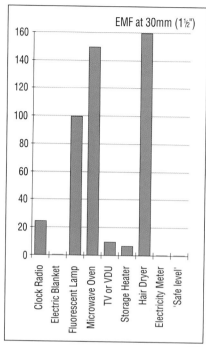

5.22

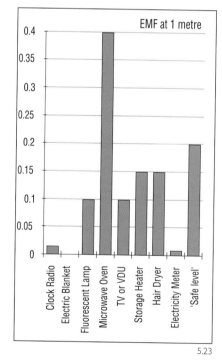

5.23

Fig. 5.22 Average electromagnetic field strength (mT) at 30mm from some household appliances. Distance from the source is very important – for example the clock radio next to your head all night may be emitting a field over ten times that thought to be safe for medium time periods (0.2mT), but at one metre distance the field is insignificant. Source: Electricity Association.

Fig. 5.23 Average electromagnetic field strength (mT) at one metre from some household appliances. Source: Electricity Association.

Five items of electrical equipment or installations give rise to concern.

- **Clock radio:** many people have a mains-powered clock radio within reach of the bed. They are lying next to this source of EMF for eight hours a day – probably not a good idea. Either switch it off at the plug at night, or move it away and operate it by remote (or just get up), or have a wind-up alarm.
- **Electric blanket:** only use it to warm up the bed before you go to sleep – do not lie in bed with it on.
- **TV or computer monitors:** get a protective screen if your VDU is not fitted with one; sit at least one metre away.
- **Electricity meter/consumer unit:** it is important that this is not sited near a sleeping person (remember, building materials will not stop magnetic radiation), partly because of the meter itself, and also because of the wires entering the consumer unit.
- **The ring main:** a faulty ring main could produce a magnetic field – and you would not be aware that anything was amiss. If one cable becomes disconnected at a socket the ring main will simply supply electricity 'around the other way' and your appliances will keep working. But there will now be an imbalance in the circuit that produces an EMF. Many people have reverted to using spur wiring or using a system that cuts off all power at the consumer unit once all appliances are switched off for the night.

References

[1] Thomas Saunders, *The Boiled Frog Syndrome*, Wiley Academy, 2002

[2] Thomas Saunders, ibid

[2a] Fawcett, Hurst and Boardman, Carbon UK, University of Oxford 2002

[3] Thomas Saunders, ibid

[4] S K D Coward, J W Llewellyn, G J Raw, V M Brown, D R Crump, D I Ross, *Indoor air quality in homes in England*, BRE Publications, 2001

[5] Brian Ridout, *Timber Decay in Buildings*, E&FN Spon, 2000

[6] CCA chemicals exported from a firm in Widnes to Djibouti (E Africa) in plastic (not metal) containers. Chemicals leaked in transit, workers unloading became exposed, 3 died and dozens injured with burns, etc. UK Government paying £1m to ship 2000 tonnes of contaminated soil back to UK. (*Guardian* 20/7/02)

[7] A recent study by Professor Richard Doll found a small but significant risk of children developing leukaemia (and a possible risk to adults) if they lived close to high voltage power lines, as do 60,000 people in the UK; *Building for a Future*, vol 11, no 1; and *Sunday Times*, March 2001

Building elements

*'Vernacular design is
always prudent about
materials and time...
it provides an economical
grammar of construction.'*

Stewart Brand

BUILDING ELEMENTS

The more closely we look at the materials that make up the fabric of our typical buildings and the equipment and furnishings contained in them, the more unhappy we get. Highly-processed and much-travelled materials bring with them a large debt of pollution and probably exploitation. We find it difficult to build in a harmless, non-destructive way. Many materials pollute air in the house, and some are carcinogenic.

As contemporary materials are rejected for this or that reason, we move towards a limited palette of materials familiar to builders in the past – to the vernacular: wood and other renewable materials, earth and lime, glass, with a small proportion of recyclable metal. This is not very surprising, since the vernacular was inevitably based on what came easily and sustainably to hand in any particular locale – it could be nothing else but low-impact building.

But in most cases, the vernacular in its raw form is too expensive and/or too uncomfortable to satisfy our needs today. So, we have to use our ingenuity to create buildings that are built of truly sustainable materials, that are benign to the occupants and builders, that are positively miserly in their use of fossil fuels and other resources, that treat their own wastes – and are also a joy to live in. As R W Brunskill explains: 'And so the term "vernacular architecture" has been adopted to define that sort of building which is deliberately permanent rather than temporary, which is traditional rather than academic in its inspiration, which provides for the simple activities of ordinary people, their farms and simple industrial enterprises, which is strongly related to place, especially through the use of local building materials, but which represents design and building with thought and feeling rather than in a base or strictly utilitarian manner.'[1]

6.1

Principles

There is no one ecologically best way to build. All forms of construction have their good and bad points: a timber frame house will be easier to superinsulate, a brick or concrete one will be better suited to utilising passive solar gain; a timber house can be built from locally grown, sustainable materials, bricks can be re-used again and again. The choice of construction and materials will be based on all the following principles, which are described in detail elsewhere:

- **Design for low energy use:** superinsulation, air tightness and ventilation control, active and passive solar energy, daylighting, efficient heating system, efficient lighting and appliances.
- **Minimising new resources:** using second-hand materials, re-using buildings for new uses.
- **Using whole unprocessed materials first:** solid timber, natural stone, earth and clay, natural fibres.
- **Using low embodied energy materials:** locally sourced, relatively unprocessed, renewable, sparing use of high-energy materials.
- **Using materials so that they can be re-used:** soft mortars for bricks and blocks, screw fixings rather than nails, no glues or composite materials.
- **Using materials for a healthy internal environment:** organic paints, natural fibres, no formaldehyde glues.

Fig. 6.1 The palette of vernacular materials, Stokesay Castle, Shropshire.

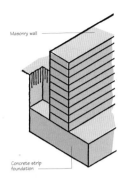

6.2

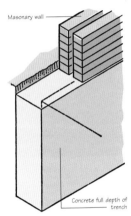

6.3

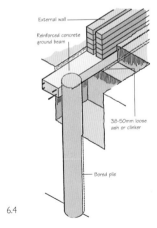

6.4

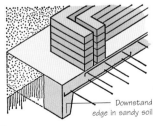

6.5

Fig. 6.2 Concrete strip foundation.

Fig. 6.3 Trench-filled concrete foundation.

Fig. 6.4 Short bored piles and ground beam.

Fig. 6.5 Reinforced concrete raft.

How to read the preference sections

These sections provide guidance to the authors' preferred construction and materials. The grades of preference are based on the above criteria and we refer to many of the other sections in this book for backup. Although presented as a definitive guide, the preferences are, of course, a mixture of science, accepted common sense and downright prejudice. They are ranked as follows:

> **1 The ultimate aim:** best ecological practice. Some of these techniques will be in use already, others need more practical research or a change in lifestyle expectations.
>
> **2 Good practice:** achievable now for little or no extra cost, but it will require a commitment in terms of money and effort from the client and designer.
>
> **3 Acceptable solution:** if particular conditions allow no better. Modifications to make standard practice environmentally acceptable.
>
> **4 Material and construction to be avoided:** if possible, these measures should be avoided for environmental or practical reasons.
>
> *Where no preference is available in given category: n/a, i.e. there may be nothing available between 1 The ultimate aim and 4 Material and construction to be avoided.*

Foundations

The function of a foundation is to spread the loads (the weight of the house, its contents and any snow on the roof) over a wide area of undisturbed subsoil, to prevent the house sinking into the ground. The base of the foundation has to be below the frost line (usually 750mm), free of organic material that could rot away and leave holes, and well away from trees.

The vernacular: Stone houses, with walls 600mm wide, have no distinct foundation. The wall is wide enough to spread the loads, usually starting 300-600mm below ground level. Occasionally, such walls have failed due to subsidence, but mostly the use of lime mortar has generally allowed for some movement. Brick walls were built progressively wider to form a base wide enough to spread out the load. More recently, concrete was used to solidify the trench bottom. Earth and timber frame buildings had stone foundations, which came a little above ground level, to prevent damage from rain splashing. Damp-proof courses (DPCs) in brick houses were two layers of slates, or lead. Land drainage around the base of the house was a major factor in keeping the fabric dry.

Current practice: Foundations are normally made by one of the following methods:
- a concrete strip with frost-resistant brick or block sub-walls up to DPC level; usually 150mm above ground (figure 6.2);
- a trench completely filled with concrete (figure 6.3);
- a thin raft of reinforced concrete, used where ground conditions are unstable (figure 6.5); and
- piles with a ground beam in exceptionally difficult ground (figure 6.4);

DPC materials now come in a continuous roll and are bitumen or (recycled) polythene based.

Preference – general

Minimise both disturbance to the site and concrete use by having pad or strip foundations, preferably of materials that are or can be re-used. Although concrete is a low-energy material per ton, it is used in large quantities and its use as mass foundations should be minimised. Recycled rubble may be used as general fill.

Reinforced concrete should be avoided if ground conditions allow, as it is difficult to re-use the materials. Concrete can be made using hydraulic lime as the binder, instead of Ordinary Portland Cement (OPC).

Preference – masonry construction

1 Local stone foundation wall. DPCs and membranes of recycled polythene or bitumen. Land drains around the house perimeter. Minimise thermal bridging between foundations and the ground floor by using edge insulation.

2 Second-hand bricks, sand/lime blocks or dense concrete blocks made with secondary aggregate, laid in a lime or lean cement mortar onto the smallest concrete strip necessary. Limecrete made from (eminently) hydraulic lime and ballast, possible with additional pozzolan (setting) material. Limecrete is a lot more expensive than OPC concrete and it is necessary to understand its particular properties to get best results.

3 Concrete blocks made from new aggregate, or new bricks, laid onto the smallest concrete strip necessary.

4 Trench-fill or reinforced concrete slab made from new aggregate. Short piles with reinforced concrete ground beams.

Preference – timber construction

1 Timber (ground) beams spanning between timber piles or recycled brick piers on compacted re-used rubble. DPCs and membranes of recycled polythene or bitumen or slate.

2 Piers as above on minimal concrete foundation. Posts set directly on a minimal concrete pad – the Segal Method – or short piles.

3 Strip foundations and plinth wall as for masonry construction.

4 Trench-fill or reinforced concrete slab made from new aggregate, unless ground conditions dictate. Short piles with reinforced concrete ground beam.

6.6

6.7

Fig. 6.8

6.9

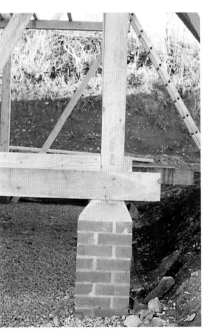

6.10

Fig. 6.6 A foundation pad of compacted stone rubble.
Photo: Duncan Roberts.

Fig. 6.7 A strip foundation of 'limecrete' – hydraulic lime and aggregate.

6.8 The minimal excavations for a Segal Method foundation.

Fig. 6.9 Timber post bearing on a concrete pad foundation with a concrete 'bucket'.

Fig. 6.10 Homegrown timber ground beams on brick pier foundations. Self-build house at Castle Caerenion, Powys.

6.11

6.12

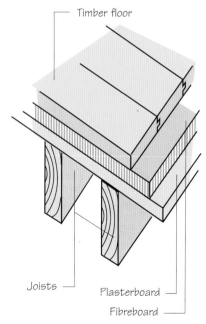

6.13

Fig. 6.11 Home-grown softwood flooring being laid over underfloor heating trays.

Fig. 6.12 A 'limecrete' solid floor at Y Faenol, North Wales.

Fig. 6.13 Intermediate (first) floor with exposed joists. The fibreboard is there to reduce impact sound.

Floors

Ground floors and floor finishes

Ground floors are part of the external, insulating skin of the house, and are either solid – bearing directly on to the ground, or suspended – spanning between foundation walls.

The vernacular: Solid ground floors usually consist of stone slabs or clay tiles and bricks laid directly onto soil or cinders. They depend for their insulation and dryness on the earth underneath them being kept dry, which in turn depends on the ground level outside being lower, and good drainage around the house perimeter. Often this construction method will have worked well for years, until linoleum or oilcloth is laid on top, trapping moisture underneath and negating the insulation value of the soil.

Suspended ground floors consist of timber joists and floorboards. The joists were often built into the external walls – a detail which could cause the ends to rot, especially if the wall became damp. The underspace was often not ventilated which again could lead to joists rotting away unnoticed. If the underspace was ventilated, the draughts into the house could often flap the carpets.

Current practice: The most common practice – because it is the cheapest on flat sites – is the solid concrete slab, usually about 100mm thick, laid on a DPC of polythene and hardcore fill. Insulation is obtained by using a 'floating' floor of polystyrene insulation and chipboard flooring or a sand/cement screed. Suspended floors are either timber joists, on steel hangers, with insulation suspended between, and chipboard or timber floorboards; or reinforced concrete joists with concrete blocks between, and finished as the solid floor. Finishes are timber boards (often a laminated veneer), carpet and vinyl flooring.

Preference

1 A suspended, well-insulated timber floor of home-grown soft or hardwood joists and floorboards. Good ventilation of the underspace and a draught-proofed floor are vital, and will ensure that radon gas (if present) is dissipated. Underfloor space sealed with a recycled polythene membrane and covered in local granular fill or recycled aggregate; or

1b a solid limecrete floor using recycled aggregate, laid on insulation. Lime can be used to stabilise earth or hemp as a floor base and finish, but should not be covered with an impermeable material such as lino.
Damp-proof membrane of recycled polythene or bitumen.
Finishes of homegrown timber, cork, natural fibres, linoleum, ceramic tiles, stone.

2 n/a

3 Precast reinforced concrete joists with concrete or expanded polystyrene block infill, insulation and screed. In situ Portland cement concrete slab. finished as above.

4 Floating chipboard floor above concrete slab. Vinyl floor finish, synthetic carpets.

Intermediate floors

The vernacular: Usually of timber joists (initially of timbers sawn on two opposite sides and laid on the flat), with timber floorboarding. Lath and plaster infill between the joists would give some privacy between rooms and prevent dust coming down through the cracks. Formal rooms had ceilings of lath and plaster attached to the underside of the joists. Garret (loft) rooms often had a floor of gypsum concrete on timber joists and reed matting, probably to give fire protection.

Current practice: Usually timber joists with chipboard or softwood flooring and plasterboard underlining. In multi-storey housing, precast concrete beam and block, or in situ reinforced concrete floors are used.

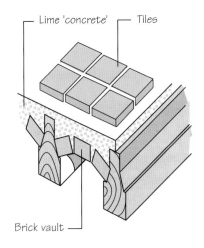

6.14a

> ### Preference
>
> 1 Home-grown soft or hardwood tongue-and-groove (T&G) timber floorboarding, on home-grown softwood joists with timber lath and lime plaster or plasterboard underlining. There are special constructions for sound-deadening and fire resistant floors (see figure 5.17). If you want to see the joists, then the flooring should rest on layers of fibreboard and plasterboard. The joists will have to be 75mm wide for fire protection. Do not build joists into wall – use joist hangers.
>
> 2 As above, but with plywood or orientated strand board floor.
>
> 3 Precast concrete beam and block.
>
> 4 As above, but with chipboard floor. In situ reinforced concrete.

Some thermal and acoustic mass can be given to an intermediate floor by laying ceramic tiles onto a plywood sub-floor, or limecrete onto a solid timber floor. Even better would be a composite floor of timber joists and brick vaults as traditionally used in southern Europe (figure 6.14a).

6.15

6.14b

Frames

In a house that has a post and beam structural frame, the walling takes no weight beyond its own. This is called 'non-loadbearing' walling. A great variety of materials can be used, usually lightweight sheets, timber supports and insulation.

The vernacular: For hundreds of years, a heavy oak frame was the preferred structure on which to build many houses – from the humblest cottage to great royal halls. A post and beam frame offers several advantages: there can be lots of windows that can be placed anywhere, without lintels, the house can be easily adapted to change, low-cost local materials can be used, and it is quick to construct. This ensured its popularity until the advent of the railways made low-cost bricks widely available. The infill walls were either of wattle-and-daub or brickwork

Fig. 6.14a Traditional floor in Barcelona. Brick vaults span between oak joists and lime 'concrete' is laid over the top and finished with ceramic tiles. Gives thermal mass to intermediate floors.

Fig. 6.14b Traditional Mediterranean solid upper floor of lime screed on clay tiles, laid on timber joists.

Fig. 6.15 Remains of old burial chamber made from huge monolithic stone blocks. An early version of post and beam frame! Carreg Samson, Pembrokeshire.

6.16a

6.16c

6.16b

Fig. 6.16a The familiar vernacular of timber framed Shrewsbury, with its fake modern imitator behind.

Fig. 6.16b The simple structural efficiency of the traditional cruck frame used in a modern house. Photo: Bl@st Architects

Fig. 6.16c A cathedral for agriculture. The Bredon tithe barn.

and were left as a decorative black and white façade, or the whole elevation was painted with limewash, or rendered for protection. Neither infill material was very good at keeping out the rain, wind or cold, and trapped water often led to timber rot. Barns and houses clad externally with timber boards, tiles or slates survive somewhat better.

6.17a

6.17b

Fig. 6.17c

Fig. 6.17a There has been a recent popular revival in English traditional timber framing, far beyond the local building technique it once was. Frames are exported to the US and Japan, and much oak is imported from France. Carpenter Oak.

Fig. 6.17b Post and beam frame built with traditional jointing, but using stress-graded homegrown larch in an engineered structure.

Fig. 6.17c The mortice and tenon: an efficient joint proved over the centuries.

6.18

6.20

6.19

Current practice: Post and beam frames are found occupying three niches:

- **Revival of traditional green oak heavy framing:** there does seem to be some sort of tribal-memory love of oak post and beam structures, reflected in the several hundred houses built each year in this manner (and the aspirations of thousands of people who would like such a house). The better designs enclose the whole structure in an insulating shell, rather than attempting the black and white look. There is some criticism of the use of over-large section, old-growth oak, but the framers also use the whole tree – curved bits for braces, and small sections for rafters.
- **Lightweight post and beam frames (Segal Method):** using homegrown timber and highly insulated walls, this way of building has become popular for ecological self-build.
- **Laminated timber (glulam) structures with steel connectors:** the contemporary building industry has problems accommodating itself to using solid timber: it comes in shortish lengths and small cross sections, it moves as it dries out and it is difficult to joint in tension. Glulam timber constructions, jointed with steel plates, overcome most of these difficulties, so that large-span, simple buildings at reasonable cost are possible. The infill walls can be anything from glass to brick.

Fig. 6.18 The cliff railway top station at CAT. The lower structure and deck are of small section-and-length homegrown green oak, the upper structure is of recycled pitch pine, and the roof is of locally grown Douglas fir and larch.

Fig. 6.19 Green oak and steel combine to form a strong structure for the CAT cliff railway stations.

Fig. 6.20 Segal Method lightweight timber frames at Seesaw self-build in Brighton.

Preference

1 Frames of home-grown durable timber from sustainable sources, or recycled timber, with traditional wood to wood joints. The timber sizes should be the minimum needed for any particular job, but sufficiently robust to prevent undue flexing of the building. Round timber straight from the forest has the lowest embodied energy, but at CAT we have always advocated minimal processing (i.e. squaring the log) in the interests of buildability. The frame should be completely wrapped in highly insulated walls and protected by 'rainscreen' cladding.

2 Laminated home-grown timber structures. The advantage of glulam beams is that small sections of timber can be combined to make a beam of greater strength than solid timber, and in very long lengths. The disadvantages are that the glues used contain formaldehyde, and the beams are usually imported from abroad. Occasionally it is possible to find a small laminated timber producer dedicated to using local, sustainable timber.

3 Timber frames of imported softwood from sustainable sources, untreated or treated with borax.

4 Timber frames of treated, imported softwood from old growth forests or tropical hardwoods.

6.21

Walls
External walls – masonry

Apart from protection from rain, wind and cold, and to give privacy, masonry walls serve to transfer loads from the floors and roof down to the foundations.

The vernacular: Solid walls are built of stone, brick or earth, with thicknesses from 600mm for stone and earth, to 225mm or less for brick. Finishes for wind-proofing and decoration are lime/horsehair plaster and limewash inside, and sometimes limewash outside. Thermal insulation is poor, particularly for solid brick. Thick stone walls are often built in two skins with rubble in between, which improves their thermal performance, and their huge thermal mass does help a little at smoothing out fluctuations in temperature (they are wonderfully cool in summer). The only forms of construction that come close to today's thermal requirements are those utilising

Fig. 6.21 Workshop with round poles forming the curved structure. Hooke Park, Dorset.

6.22a

6.22b

6.23

Fig. 6.22a Rammed earth blocks laid in lime mortar with lime render at CAT.

Fig. 6.22b Clay/straw blocks for an internal partition.

Fig. 6.23 Stone and earth walling.

earth and straw. A Devon cob house has a thermal performance that would have met the requirements of the Building Regulations until 1982. Beams spanning window and door openings, called lintels, were of oak or stone. Brick or stone arches were also used to span openings.

Current practice: Masonry walls are now of cavity construction – two skins of brick or block with space between. The cavity has the dual function of preventing damp penetration and providing a little insulation. In the rest of Europe, hollow clay blocks are used for walls and floors, and these are now being imported to the UK. Cavities are partially or wholly filled with thermal insulation to meet the current Building Regulations. The modern practice of drylining the inside face, by gluing plasterboard sheets to it, is to be discouraged: it is difficult to seal against draughts, and it effectively prevents the internal masonry from having any useful function as primary thermal mass. Instead, plaster straight on to the blocks. Lintels are usually steel with an insulation fill.

Preference

1 Walling of earth from the site (cob, pise de terre, or stabilised earth blocks) is a good ecological choice for a masonry wall. The walls are best insulated on the outside and clad in a rainscreen of timber lath and lime render, or tiles. The well-insulated, thermally massive walls will provide a very comfortable internal environment. Earthen walls must be well protected from rain and rising damp, otherwise they will return whence they came.
Straw bale walls can also bring excellent environmental benefits and need similar protection to keep out damp. The bales are built up like bricks and bound together to form a superinsulated loadbearing wall, then rendered inside and out.

OR Local stone or re-used bricks. Masonry materials should be chosen to have a low embodied energy content, preferably locally sourced, and produced with the minimum of pollution. Second-hand is best. Masonry walls should be built using soft, lime-rich mortar so the materials can be easily re-used. Lintels should be separate for each skin of the cavity wall and of stone, timber or reinforced concrete. Alternatively brick and stone arches can be used.

2 n/a

3 New clay bricks, hollow clay blocks and slabs, sand/lime blocks or dense concrete blocks made from secondary aggregate.

4 Autoclaved aerated blocks. Strong cement mortars. Cement concrete blocks made from new aggregates.

External walls – timber stud

The weight of the house is taken by many slim posts called 'studs'. These are usually spaced at 450-600mm intervals. Sheet materials are fixed to both sides and insulation put in the spaces between.

The vernacular: As large-section timbers became more difficult to obtain, the posts became smaller and closer together. The invention of the machine-made nail resulted in this becoming the dominant form of construction in North America.

Current practice: Timber stud framing is becoming more and more popular in British housing – around half of new housing in Scotland is built this way. This is due to its superior insulating capacity and speed of erection on site. Panels can be prefabricated in a factory, and a weathertight shell erected on the base within a few days. Internal work can be undertaken in all weathers, whilst the externals can

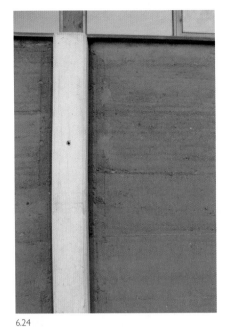

6.24

6.25

6.26

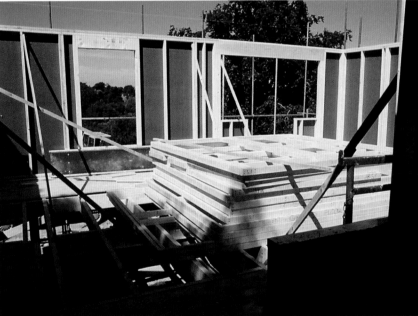

6.27

6.28

be finished as weather permits. The standard construction is of 90mm or 140mm studs with plywood external sheathing, fibreglass insulation, a vapour barrier and plasterboard. The external face is usually protected by a single thickness brick or block wall tied back to the timber frame. Recent developments in fire resistance have resulted in the upper limit for timber buildings rising to eight storeys. There are now some examples of five-storey timber stud frame flats. Post-and-beam structures are usually infilled with lightweight stud framing.

Fig. 6.24 Pisé external walls of the sports hall at Skelmersdale.

Fig. 6.25 New local bricks laid in hydraulic lime mortar can be re-used in the future.

Fig. 6.26 Early stud framing being renovated in Llanidloes, Powys.

Fig. 6.27 Stud framing. In the design of the Camelot Self-Build, Somerset, two conventional stud walls are spaced apart to achieve high insulation levels – the inner stud frames are stacked up ready for 'plating' to the outer frame.

Fig. 6.28 A minimal solution for low-energy timber houses – spaced 50 x 50mm stud walls.

6.29

6.32

6.30

6.31

Biocomposite Walls

Modern ecological houses are being built using thick insulating infill walls of 'biocomposites' – vegetable fibres bound together with lime or clay – or straw bales.

Fig. 6.29 Hemp/lime/gypsum mixture 275mm thick cast in situ around a timber stud wall.
Builder/Photo: Jeremy Light.

Fig. 6.30 A 300mm thick biocomposite construction of woodwool waste and lime cast in-situ at Bells Court in Bishops Castle.

Fig. 6.31 Experimental biocomposite coffer wall, 450mm thick, constructed by Galliers of Shrewsbury.

Fig. 6.32 Straw bale wall enveloping the timber frame of a small theatre at CAT.

External wall – finishes

The vernacular: Brick or stone walls were left unpainted, limewashed, rendered, or harled. Earth and cob was invariably limewashed, and/or mud rendered. Timber frame constructions had lime rendered panels and unpainted timber, or limewash. Some were clad in timber clapboarding, or tiles – occasionally with 'mathematical tiles' that mimicked brickwork.

Current practice: Fairface brickwork or stone, and rendered, harled or pebbledash concrete blockwork. Timber frame houses usually have a facing of brickwork or rendered blockwork, timber cladding, tile hanging, or render on lightweight lath.

Preference – masonry construction

1 Solid masonry structure, with an external insulation layer protected by a rain-screen of timber lath and lime render, or tiles. OR Insulated cavity earthen walls, rendered and limewashed. OR Insulated cavity masonry of fairface, re-used clay or stonework.

2. Solid or cavity walls of sand/lime brick or block.

3. New block or brickwork rendered with lime/sand, self-coloured or painted with mineral-based paint.

4. Hard cement render on any of the above, masonry paint with a non-breathing finish.

6.33

6.35

6.37

6.38

6.36

6.34

6.39

Fig. 6.33 & 6.34 SIPS – timber frame without the timber. The highly efficient TEK system from Kingspan.

Fig. 6.35 Wattle and daub in timber frame, under repair. National Museum of Welsh Life, St Fagans.

Fig. 6.36 Compressed earth blocks laid in a cavity wall, with 100mm cork insulation.

Fig. 6.37 Rendered with hydraulic lime and sand and finished with mineral paint. Toilet block, CAT.

Fig. 6.38 Slate waste walling, showing one cut face. Unpointed to give the simple appearance of dry stone walling.

Fig. 6.39 Contemporary tile-hanging. Walsall Art Gallery. Architects: Caruso St John.

6.40

6.41

6.45

6.42

6.43

6.44

Preference – timber frame construction

1. A rainscreen of durable timber from sustainable source. OR Tile slate and shingle hanging.
2. Lime/sand render on a lightweight lath, self-coloured or with a microporous mineral paint finish.
3. Non-loadbearing skin of brickwork.
4. Fibre/cement sheet rainscreen. Cement render on metal lath.

Internal wall and ceiling finishes

The vernacular: Lime/horsehair plaster on masonry or on timber lath, painted with limewash.

Current practice: Masonry: gypsum plaster or sand/cement render, or plasterboard glued with dabs of plaster and finished with joint filler.

Timber frame: plasterboard with either a skim coat of gypsum plaster, or joint filler.

Preference

1. Home-grown timber from sustainable sources, waxed, oiled, soaped or left raw. The area of exposed timber finish allowed under the Fire Regulations is not more than half the room floor area or 20m². OR Limewashed earth walls.
2. Lime or clay plaster on masonry or on timber lath or woodwool slab. Unfinished fairfaced brick or stone.
3. Gypsum (natural or flue gas derived) plasterboard and skim coat of gypsum plaster.
4. Medium density fibreboard (MDF) or plastics boards.

Fig. 6.40 Home-grown oak cladding and shutters at the Millennium Arboretum. Architect: Architype.

Fig. 6.41 The new Wales Millennium Centre, with its timber clad rear elevation. Architects: Percy Thomas.

Fig. 6.42 Patterns of timber shingles.

Fig. 6.43 The warmth of unpainted timber. All the timber for this farmhouse was from the farm. Blaen Camel. Architect. David Lea

Fig. 6.44 Self-coloured clay plaster applied to lath.

Fig. 6.45 New internal wall finish of oak lath and lime putty plaster (seen from the back).

6.46

Roofs

The vernacular: Timber cut rafters, that is, cut to fit wallplates and beams, supporting lath, which supports thatch, slates, or tiles. The rafters were in turn supported by various arrangements of beams, called purlins, and trusses supported on walls or timber posts. Loft spaces were always usable and the internal sloping face was plastered – partly to hold the tiles in place, which were usually hung on oak pegs, and partly to slow down the ingress of wind and snow.

Current practice: Timber is still the favourite structural material, steel and concrete generally only being used for high-rise dwellings. There are three general forms:

6.47

- Flat roof: made of timber joists with a plywood or chipboard decking covered in bituminous 3-layer felt or a single-ply plastics membrane. It is difficult to achieve a 'breathing' flat roof construction. Traditional leaking problems have been largely overcome by the use of loose fit, single-layer membranes of more durable materials.

- Pitched roof using trussed rafters: the most common house roof, of factory-made trusses, spaced at 600mm intervals, and covered in sarking felt, lath and slates or tiles. It is cheaper than even a flat roof, and performs well. Insulation is placed at ceiling level, and the whole construction is dry and well ventilated. The loftspace is unusable for anything but storage, although there are attic trusses available where the centre of the truss is left open to provide a narrow room.

- Pitched roof using cut rafters: traditional roof construction, whereby the whole of the loft is available for living space ('room-in-the-roof'). Rafters have to be deep to take the required loads and insulation, and an airspace must be left between the insulation and the tiles for ventilation, unless a vapour-porous underfelt is used.

Fig. 6.46 Masonite I-beams which will allow for 300mm of insulation in the roof slope and a clear-span loftspace. Camelot self-build, Somerset.

Fig. 6.47 Rooflights are possible in a 'cut' roof. Education office at CAT.

6.48

6.49

Preference

1. A cut roof, for more interestingly-shaped living spaces, good use of the house volume and better energy conservation. Pitched roofs are naturally rain-shedding, are safe constructions, and allow for a wide choice of finishes. Spaced rafters of home-grown timber or I-beam composite timber rafters are used to give a good depth of insulation with minimal timber use.

2. Flat or low pitch roof constructions, with a finish of soil and turf or sedum – which will replace the area of vegetation covered over by the house.

3. Pitched roof using trussed rafters.

4. Reinforced concrete constructions.

6.50

Pitched roof finishes and flashings

The vernacular: Thatch was the predominant roof finish until the advent of the railways, when slates could be delivered easily all over the country. A slate roof was prestigious, durable and fireproof and it could be laid at a shallower pitch, which gave more headroom. The conversion to slates can be seen on many vernacular houses, where walls have been raised under eaves. Pantiles and plain tiles were used in clay-producing parts of the country. Timber shingles, which are lightweight but require a steep pitch, were used on church steeples.

Current practice: Clay and concrete tiles; artificial slates made from fibre/cement or fibre/resin-filler. Natural slate when cost allows. Flexible strips fitted between roof finish and wall or chimney, called flashings, are usually of lead, aluminium, or bitumen material.

Fig. 6.48 Oak shingles on a church in Shropshire. Photo: Tom Borer.

Fig. 6.49 Clay pantiles on environmental centre in Birmingham. Architect: David Lea.

Fig. 6.50 Plain clay tiles on a sheltered housing scheme. Architect: David Lea.

Preference

1. Second-hand tiles and slates OR Thatch from locally-sourced reed or straw: very expensive and beautiful, of course* OR Cleft oak shingles and shakes. A good use for short logs, which may otherwise be used as firewood. Sawn cedar shingles are also available, but check that the timber is from a sustainable source.** Flashings of EPDM (ethylene propylene diene monomer) and Uginox (tin-coated stainless steel).

2. Durable timber (oak or larch) board on board. OR Natural UK slate.

3. New clay or concrete tiles. Imported slates. Metal roofs. Bitumen fibre corrugated sheets or shingles. Flashings of bitumen felt.

4. Fibre-cement tiles or corrugated sheets. Cedar shingles from unsustainable sources. Lead flashings.

6.52

6.51

Flat or low-pitched roof finishes

The vernacular: Lead, zinc and copper, laid to a slight fall in trays, with cappings over the tray junctions.

Current practice: Bitumen felt in three layers, asphalt, single layer membranes of PVC or EPDM, lead, zinc, and copper. The flat roof has gained itself a bad reputation for leakage. This is mainly due to the practice of gluing down the bitumen felt to the structure. As the structure expands and contracts over the seasons, the felt cannot accommodate the movement and therefore develops cracks. If the membrane is laid loose, like a tablecloth, and ballasted with heavy materials, it should be reliable. As a flat roof needs to be completely impervious to water, it is difficult to contrive a well ventilated construction. The materials used will always be highly processed.

Fig. 6.51   New 10" x 6" Welsh slates at CAT.
Fig. 6.52   Larch batten on board roofing at CAT.

*Thatch 400mm thick will have a U-value of about 0.20W/m²K, which betters the current Building Regulations requirement.
**Houses (up to a terrace of three is allowed) with thatch or shingle roofs have to be separated from their neighbours by at least 6 metres, to prevent fire spread.

6.53

6.54

6.55

Preference

1. Single-layer natural rubber or EPDM membrane, loose-laid, fixed around the edges only. A covering of earth and turf, or sedum (a sort of succulent) and other hardy planting, will ballast the membrane and prevent it blowing off. The 'green roof' will compensate a little for the use of high impact materials, by replacing the vegetation covered up by the house. The vegetation growing on 30m² of turf roof will add the same amount of oxygen to the atmosphere as one person uses. A loose-laid EPDM sheet can be re-used and is preferred to bitumen or PVC materials.

2. Tin-coated or plain stainless steel.

3. Other metal sheet roofs. Bitumen felt.

4. PVC sheet membrane.

6.56

Fig. 6.53 Hardy grasses, house leek and stonecrop at the edge of a turf roof.

Fig. 6.54 Green roof using sedum. House for the Future, National Museum of Welsh Life, St Fagans. Architects: Jestico & Whiles.

Fig. 6.55 Drought-tolerant and shallow-rooting, sedum makes an ideal finish for a 'green' roof.

Fig. 6.56 Standing seam metal roofs at the Arts centre, Aberystwyth. Architects: Smith Roberts Associates.

Earth sheltered construction

This is quite different from buildings made from earth and usually involves structures that are, in effect, tanked and reinforced concrete shells built underground. The surrounding earth will act as a huge thermal store and reduce energy usage, assuming it is fairly dry and well drained. These buildings are usually long and thin in plan, but even where the 'front' wall is highly glazed, back areas tend to be dark and permanently artificially lit.

Although this technique involves using relatively high-impact materials – concrete, steel, plastic foam insulation – it should deliver high energy savings in use. Neither Hockerton Housing Project nor the Berm House have space heating systems fitted. Monitoring on the Berm House by the then Department of Energy showed virtually no diurnal temperature change in the main rooms. Minimum air temperatures were 17-18°C and had changed by less than 1°C in all months from 1987-1995, 'with the exception of one very wet September'[2]. Hockerton Housing Project estimate their energy use as one tenth that of a comparable conventional house – 8kWh instead of 80kWh[3].

Windows and external doors

The vernacular: Glass in small panes in timber, stone or cast iron frames. Part of the popularity of post and beam timber frame houses in towns was that a high percentage of the narrow medieval street frontage could be window. (Post and beam frames allow for large openings without loss of structural integrity.) The main problem was with draughts – even the elegant sliding sash windows of Georgian times were draughty. The solution was to fit internal timber shutters, wear plenty of clothes, and eat fatty foods.

Current practice: Double-glazing in timber, PVC-u (unplasticized polyvinyl chloride), aluminium or steel frames. The standard British softwood window is generally of poor quality. It usually has too small an airspace between the glass panes, is made of preservative-treated timber, is not well draught-stripped, and does not close securely. The objections to PVC-u windows are that the production of the PVC is environmentally damaging, they have an unknown lifespan and wear badly, they are expensive (and they are really ugly).

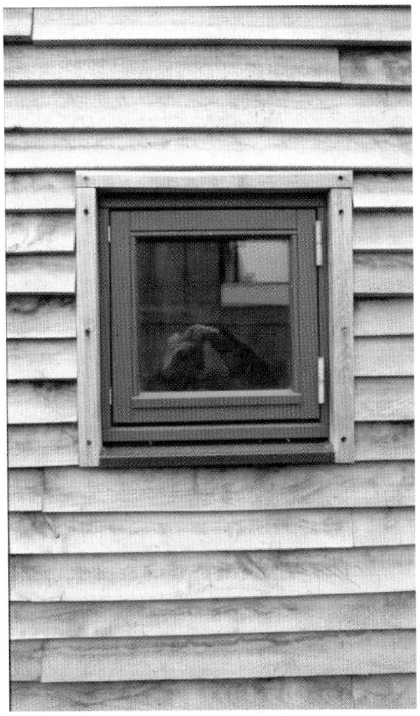

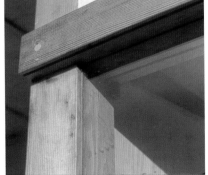

6.57

6.58

Preference

1. External joinery (windows and doors) of home-grown, durable, untreated softwood or oak, built to Scandinavian standards of air-tightness. Glazing to be a minimum of double low emissivity (low-E), with at least a 16mm airspace. A good arrangement is to have two casement windows, one double-glazed and one single.
2. Imported softwood and hardwoods from certified sources.
3. Aluminium or steel, with 'thermal breaks'.
4. Joinery of PVC-u and tropical hardwoods from uncertified sources.

Fig. 6.57 Typical Scandinavian treated softwood high performance window.

Fig. 6.58 Recycled pitch pine glazing bars.

6.59

Paint finishes

The vernacular: Limewash to external and internal walls and ceilings. Lead-based oil paint or shellac varnish to woodwork.

Current practice: Vinyl emulsion to walls and ceilings. Plastics-based external masonry paints. Preservative stains to external cladding timber. Non-lead oil gloss paint to woodwork. Health concerns over the use of volatile organic compounds (VOCs) in paints has led to a gradual reduction in their use. They have been replaced by water-based vinyls, the production of which, however, is no less damaging to the environment. Great care must be exercised in rubbing down old joinery or paint-stripping areas that may have been finished with lead paint.

Preference

1. Unpainted finishes wherever possible e.g. slate floors, ceramic tiles, clay plasters.

2. Limewash or water-based mineral paint for walls and ceilings. Organic paints and stains, wood wax, linseed oil. Mineral paints for external masonry.

3. Water-based vinyl or acrylic paints.

4. Paint with high VOC levels.

6.60

Fig. 6.59 Render on woodwool slabs, unpainted.

Fig. 6.60 Natural slate floor tiles and exposed brick walls.

Rainwater goods

The vernacular: Gutters and downpipes of cast iron, lead, or timber. Thatched houses have no gutters, but a large overhang and drainage at the foot of the wall.

Current practice: PVC gutter and downpipe systems dominate as they are light, cheap, easy to joint and fairly long-lasting. Other materials used are cast iron, aluminium, copper, zinc and galvanised steel.

6.61a

6.61b

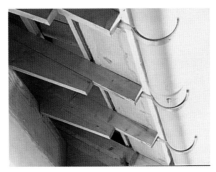

6.61c

6.62a

6.62b

Preference

1. Timber guttering, lined with EPDM or metal-faced bitumen. Downpipes of metal, which can be re-used or recycled.

2. Galvanised steel, zinc, copper or cast iron rainwater goods.

3. Aluminium rainwater goods.

4. PVC rainwater goods.

Fig. 6.61a Gutter made of home-grown larch.
Fig. 6.61b Traditional Sheffield timber gutter.
Fig. 6.61c Aluminium gutter.
Fig. 6.62a Traditional glazed clay downpipe in Spain.
Fig. 6.62b Galvanised steel rainwater pipe.

6.63

6.64

6.65

Drainage

The vernacular: Vitrified clay (earthenware) socketed pipes with hemp jointing. Unglazed clay pipes were used for land drains.

Normal practice: PVC pipes are light, flexible and cheap, and come in long lengths. Earthenware pipes are, however, tougher and require less bedding material and, with the advent of better jointing techniques, are becoming as popular on building sites as PVC. Spun concrete pipes are used for large installations.

Preference

1. Earthenware pipework. It is produced by a considerably cleaner process than PVC and can be easily reused and harmlessly disposed of at the end of its life. Inspection chambers can be in polypropylene or recycled engineering bricks.
2. Cast iron.
3. Spun concrete pipe.
4. PVC pipes.

Plumbing

The vernacular: Lead piping for water supply and drainage, later galvanised iron and asbestos cement, with brass taps. Lead – the word plumbing comes from the Latin *plumbum* meaning lead – is poisonous and has been largely, though not completely, replaced. Copper was sometimes used for drainage.

Current practice: Copper pipework jointed with lead-free solder for water supply. Underground water pipes are usually in polyethylene. Polybutylene or cross linked polyethylene internal pipework, also for water supply, is becoming popular largely due to the ease of installation. Above ground drainage is either polypropylene or ABS (Acrylonitrile Butadiene Styrene).

Preference

1. Stainless steel pipework – a high value material that corrodes little and will be readily re-used. Assuming UK source with 100% recycled content. Expensive.
2. Polybutylene or polyethylene hot and cold plumbing, and polyethylene pipework for underground services. Both materials are non-corrosive and can be recycled. Internal waste pipes should be in polypropylene or polyethylene. Make all services accessible for changes and maintenance. OR Copper – high value and readily re-used.
3. n/a
4. PVC internal waste pipes. Lead piping – must be replaced.

Fig. 6.63 Earthenware pipes.

Fig. 6.64 Polybutylene hot and cold plumbing (tradename Hep²O) is very suitable for DIY, as there are fewer joints and no tricky soldering.

Fig. 6.65 Stainless steel internal drainage pipes are made of largely recycled materials and are 100% recyclable. Blücher UK Ltd.

Electrical installations

Current practice: Copper wiring sheathed in PVC. Power circuits in ring main format. Consumer protection by miniature circuit breakers and residual-current circuit breakers.

Preference

1. Spur circuits, or 'looped back' ring circuits avoid possible problems from electromagnetic fields, if there is a fault in a conventional ring main. For extra safety a device can be fitted that shuts down the whole system when demand is zero. Avoid live wires run without a neutral wire, as can happen in two-way lighting circuits and heating controls.
   Make all services accessible for later changes and maintenance.
   Wire should be cased in non-PVC (low halogen) cable.
   Galvanised steel ducting.

2. n/a

3. n/a

4. PVC-sheathed cable in ring circuits. PVC ducts.

Landscaping and construction waste

The vernacular: Hard landscaping of stone flags and brick pavers laid in sand. Fencing between areas by brick and dry stone walls, or pleached hedges. As materials used in house construction were mostly earth or renewable materials, there would have been little waste from the building process.

Current practice: Hard landscaping is usually impervious to rainwater, being tarmac or paving with cement mortar pointing. Fencing is of treated timber or concrete posts and boards, or wire. Construction (and/or demolition) has become a very wasteful process and the detritus is usually removed from site in unsorted skips.

Preference – hard landscaping

1. Wood chippings or forest bark.

2. Stone or recycled brick or concrete flags made from recycled aggregate, set in sand with no pointing, on a porous base, to let rainwater through to the soil.

3. New concrete or brick pavers, with cement pointing.

4. Tarmac.

6.66

6.67

6.68

Fig. 6.66 Water on natural slate. Piccadilly Gardens, Manchester.

Fig. 6.67 End-grain log paving at Terre Vivante, Mens.

Fig. 6.68 Second-hand bricks, dry laid in sand – with self-seeded chamomile.

6.69a

6.69b

6.69c

6.69d

Figs. 6.69a, b, c & d Raked gravel and other natural
stone paving patterns at Kyoto, Dartington and Terre
Vivante.

Preference – fencing

1. Hedges of native broadleaf species, or willow walls.
2. Durable home-grown timber fences, drystone walls, or recycled brick walls, built using lime mortar.
3. Walls of new brick or concrete block.
4. Reinforced concrete or treated timber fences.

Preference – construction waste

1. Export no soil from site. Create no waste that cannot be dealt with on site. Bury inert waste to create landscape features.
2. Sort waste into rubble, timber and metals for re-using, recycling or separate disposal. Compost waste timber and brash on site.
3. n/a
4. Indiscriminate use of skips.

References

[1] RW Brunskill, *Traditional Buildings of Britain*, Gollancz, 1981
[2] David Olivier and John Willoughby, Review of ultra-low-energy homes – 10 UK Profiles, BRECSU, 1996.
[3] Hockerton Housing Project launch brochure

6.70

6.71

Fig. 6.70 Pletched hedge of native species. A hedge can become a wildlife refuge, a windbreak and an effective barrier.

Fig. 6.71 Soil excavated whilst constructing the house should be used on site, to form a terrace or hillock.

Self-build architect: Brian Richardson.

Resources and materials

'What you want in
materials is a quality of
forgivingness...'

Stewart Brand

RESOURCES AND MATERIALS

The search for environmentally benign building materials is not easy. There are no simple, black-and-white solutions; instead we are faced with multiple shades of grey. We have to assess the relative importance of different environmental impacts, and balance these against other factors such as cost, availability and function. But in the process of sifting through the information and reaching a solution, we are making crucial decisions about our use of global resources, and the kinds of buildings we live in. Indeed, materials selection goes hand in hand with design considerations, in determining a building's form, structure, and performance.

Environmental impacts – energy and pollution

Virtually every activity we undertake has an effect on the environment, and building is no exception. A major indicator of this impact is the amount of energy used in any given process. Building services are the biggest single source of energy consumption (and therefore CO_2 emissions) in the UK and domestic buildings alone account for 29% of total energy use. This includes all the energy used for space and water heating, cooking, lighting and appliances. The rate of domestic energy use has changed very little over the past few decades, as increased energy efficiency has been cancelled out by an increase in the number of appliances in use. It is expected to grow slightly, at around 1% per annum, mainly due to the growth in consumer electrical goods[1].

But we must also take into account the energy used to produce the materials to build the buildings in the first place. This is called embodied energy and accounts for a further 8-10% of the nation's energy bill[2].

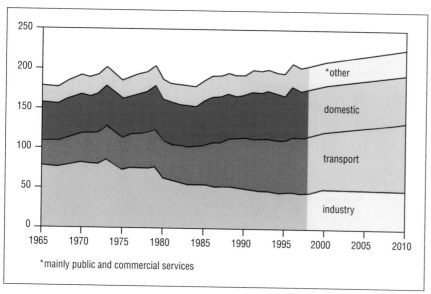

*mainly public and commercial services

7.1

Fig. 7.1 UK rate of energy consumption by final user, by sector 1965-2010.
From the Royal Commission on Environmental Pollution, Summary, 2000.

Embodied energy

We define embodied energy as the primary energy used in all the different stages of materials processing, from the extraction of raw materials, through manufacture, processing and packaging, transportation at all the different stages, installation, and, finally, demolition and disposal. Primary energy refers to the energy content of the original fuel, plus all the energy needed for its extraction and processing, including losses in conversion and transmission. Delivered energy refers to the energy used once it reaches the consumer. The aim is to include all related energy impacts of using a particular material, so that a holistic assessment can be made and alternative materials can be compared as accurately as possible.

The energy in question here is derived from fossil fuels – coal, oil, or gas – and it is the carbon content of the fuel that determines the amount of CO_2 released. Thus, significant carbon savings can be made simply by switching fuels: the reduction in CO_2 emissions in the UK over the last two decades is largely due to gas-fired replacing coal-fired power stations.

Any power produced from a renewable source can effectively be discounted from embodied energy calculations, as the energy used to produce it comes ultimately from the sun and is non-polluting. Similarly, any energy saving measures incorporated into the production or transportation process (e.g. heat reclamation on the flue of a boiler) should appear as a credit. A comprehensive assessment of embodied energy will also take into account the likely energy costs of repair and maintenance over the lifetime of the building. Thus, durable low maintenance products will score well on that parameter.

7.2

Embodied energy can be measured in kilowatt-hours (kWh) per tonne or per cubic metre of material. Different densities and functions mean that some materials will go a lot further than others – for example, compare a ton of concrete to a ton of aluminium. Some researchers prefer to calculate the embodied energy of whole building elements (e.g. wall constructions) in kilowatt-hours per square metre (kWh/m²), and this is often a more relevant way to interpret the data. Sometimes gigajoules are used instead of kilowatt-hours – one gigajoule equals 278kWh.

.Fig. 7.2 Restored 14th century moated manor house belonging to the National Trust. A very low-embodied energy house. Such vernacular buildings were built by a society entirely fuelled by renewable energy.

7.3

Recent 'eco-schemes', such as the Dyfi Eco Park in Machynlleth, have achieved 60-70% reductions on average embodied energy costs.

It is easy to quote figures for embodied energy but much more difficult to justify them, especially as there is as yet no standardised, widely accepted methodology for calculating them[3]. Some methodologies base their calculations on delivered, rather than primary energy. Figures from different sources will vary, as they include, or omit, different stages in the product's life cycle. As one postgraduate from Queen's University wrote in his thesis: 'Should we consider the energy used to cook the building worker's breakfast?'[4]. Or, when calculating the embodied energy of plastics, should we include the energy consumed by the petrochemical industry as a whole? And does the energy that goes into building and equipping a steelworks form part of the embodied energy of the steel produced?

It comes down to the question of where to draw the boundaries for inclusion and investigation, and the answer to this question is largely arbitrary. Rather than getting bogged down in the minutiae of this debate, it is probably enough for most of us to know the relative values of the most common building materials (see figure 7.4).

Fig. 7.3 A low-energy building constructed with low-embodied energy in mind.
Architects: Peter Holden.

7.5

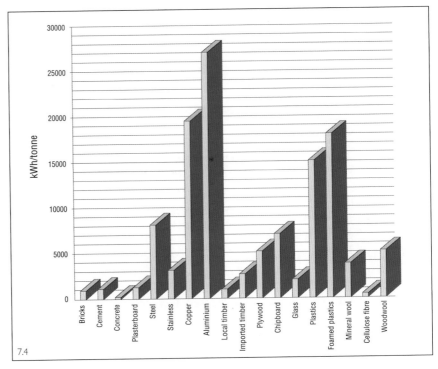
7.4

Some materials, once installed in buildings, actually save energy and this fact has been used, in the case of insulation products, to offset and justify their primary energy cost. However, it is perfectly possible to achieve high insulation standards with low-impact materials, and the reduction of overall energy use should continue to be the main goal.

It has been argued that embodied energy is relatively insignificant, compared to the energy used to service a building over its lifetime. Work done by the BRE in 1991 showed that for a typical 3-bedroom detached house with a 60 year life, the energy-in-use would exceed the embodied energy by a factor of 10. However, for a low-energy house, built to standards which exceed the current Building Regulations, the figures for the two types of energy are roughly equal, over 60 years[5]. Others have estimated that embodied energy could constitute up to 50% of the total energy use of an energy-efficient building over 25 years[6]. It is clear that

Fig. 7.4 These figures for embodied energy are compiled by the authors, using data from BRE, CIRIA, Bjørn Berge.

Fig. 7.5 Renewable insulation materials, such as sheep's wool, save energy – and have minimal embodied energy content.

Fig. 7.6 Energy consumption in use, compared with embodied energy, for a conventional house, and a low energy house.

From 'Sustainable Homes' – Hastoe Housing Association.

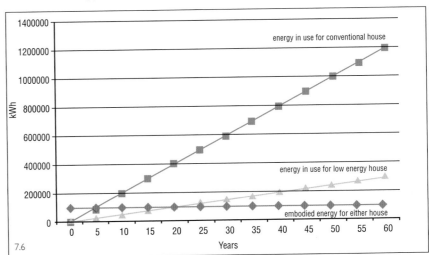
7.6

as we move towards higher standards of energy efficiency and carbon reduction, embodied energy will become the major part of a building's lifetime energy consumption.

Atmospheric pollution

Atmospheric pollution leading to irreversible climate change, is generally recognised to be the most pressing threat to the sustainability of our major eco-systems[7]. Atmospheric pollutants which cause global warming include carbon dioxide, methane, nitrous oxide and HCFC's, but it is CO_2 which is the major factor, constituting 84% of all greenhouse gas emissions[8]. The major source of carbon emissions is the burning of fossil fuels, for energy production and industrial processing.

Other noxious substances released into the atmosphere by burning fossil fuels are: oxides of sulphur and nitrogen (SOx and NOx), carbon monoxide, and hydrocarbons, and these also contribute to the problems of acid rain and low-level ozone formation.

Another issue of concern relates to the thinning of the stratospheric ozone layer, which protects people from harmful ultraviolet (UV) rays. As a result of the Montreal Protocol of 1987, the production and consumption of CFCs (chlorofluorocarbons) has been effectively banned in most western countries. This has been replaced with more 'ozone friendly' agents in materials such as foamed plastic insulation, and products such as refrigerators and air conditioning systems. Unfortunately for the environment as a whole, these replacements, although having a lower Ozone Depletion Potential than the original CFCs, are very potent greenhouse gases. In addition, because of the expense of material substitution in industrial processing, a profitable 'black market' has emerged trading in CFCs. Nations such as China which are not signatories to the Montreal Protocol are exporting CFCs, and importation of CFCs into North America is second in monetary value to the trade in narcotics[9].

As figure 7.8 shows, CFC use fell sharply from 1989-1996 but then stabilised at a lower level, rather than continued falling. Even if all CFC production were to cease now, it would take 100 years for the ozone layer to return to the level of the late 1980s.

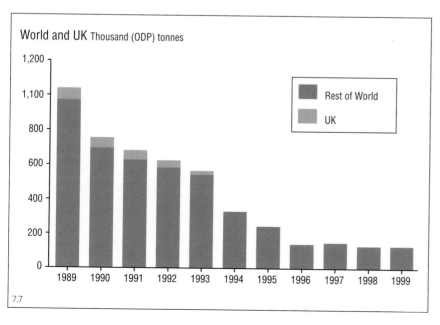

World and UK Thousand (ODP) tonnes

7.7

Fig. 7.7 World and UK consumption of CFCs: 1986-1999.
Source: DEFRA National Statistics 2002.

Other pollution

Toxic waste materials, such as synthetic chemicals or heavy metals, may leach into the subsoil or ground water as a result of industrial processing, or may even be discharged directly into rivers or on to tips. This may be due to careless control or deliberate evasion of statutory regulations. Often it is cheaper for polluters to pay the fines than to dispose of the waste safely – or reduce the amount created.

Agriculture, too, is a very polluting industry. Much of our agricultural land is contaminated by chemical pesticides and many rivers contain high levels of nitrates and phosphates, which can lead to eutrophication ('algal blooms') and affect drinking water quality.

Environmental impacts – resources and waste

Extraction

This category of environmental impacts relates to the excavation, via surface quarrying or mining, of naturally occurring, non-renewable resources, which form the basic feedstock for many manufacturing processes. Included here are metallic ores, rock, sand, clay, limestone, and gravel – used to produce metals, glass, bricks and tiles, cement and concrete, lime and plaster. Production of the most common building materials, used in large quantities in the vast majority of our buildings, depends, in the first instance, on something being dug out of the ground.

The construction industry in the UK uses about 6 tonnes of material per person per year – about half of our total primary resource consumption. For every tonne of general consumer products that we buy, approximately 10 tonnes of raw materials are consumed.

It is important to realise that, although many of these resources may be in plentiful supply at present, they are nevertheless finite and non-renewable (unless you adopt a very long time scale). Some minerals are being exploited so intensively that they are no longer abundant. Limestone in particular, with its widespread use in cement and plaster, is now in such great demand that there is pressure to open up new excavation sites in environmentally sensitive areas. The ores used to produce lead, zinc, and copper are also seriously depleted on a global scale.

Fig. 7.8 Llynclys Quarry, a limestone quarry operating for over 100 years. The subsoil for CAT's rammed earth walls was sourced from Llynclys.

7.8

Apart from the long-term effects of resource depletion, the environmental impact is mostly felt at a local level. There is bound to be loss of landscape and destruction of wildlife habitats. Huge amounts of unsightly and sometimes dangerous waste are generated, particularly in the extraction of metallic ores. Copper mining creates 50-200kg of waste for every kg of finished copper. Because we import most of the metals we use, this burden often falls on developing countries where people often do not have the means to withstand the incursions of multinational mining companies.

In the UK, the more immediate problems include dust, visual intrusion, noise and vibration, and an increase in heavy traffic. These effects are compounded where secondary production processes (e.g. brick and cement works) are sited near to quarries. This saves on transport energy costs but increases local nuisance.

Some radical environmental theorists, such as the Natural Step movement in Sweden, argue in favour of a complete phase-out of all mineral extraction. In this scenario, future demand would have to be met entirely by recycling existing stock. A recent attempt has been made to quantify the reductions in primary resource use necessary for sustainable and equitable distribution in the future. It is estimated that by the year 2050, assuming a medium estimate of population growth, the use of virgin steel will need to fall by 83%, cement by 72%, and aluminium by 88%[10].

Waste creation and disposal

Any item of waste creation can be seen as a failure, due to inefficiency in the system, especially when compared to natural systems, which recycle all waste products. Waste disposal leads to environmental degradation and possible human health hazards. Finding a sustainable solution to this problem is becoming urgent for society as a whole.

Construction waste is produced in large quantities – 70 million tonnes annually, or 1.25 tonnes per person per year. This equates to 24% of all UK waste – more than double the figure for all domestic waste. Of this, 12-15m tonnes is recycled, but mainly 'downcycled', to low-grade uses such as hardcore and landscaping fill. By contrast, the Dutch recycle over 90% of their construction and demolition (C&D) waste.

7.9a

Waste per person per year

Domestic

Building

1/2 Tonne

1 1/2 Tonne

7.9b

Fig. 7.9a Construction waste.
Fig. 7.9b Construction and demolition waste far exceeds domestic waste, but there are fewer incentives for builders to reduce, reuse and recycle.

Energy used in processing virgin and recycled materials			
	Energy needed to process (BTU/pound)		Amount of energy saved by recycling (per cent)
Material	Virgin ore	Recycled material	
Steel	8300	7500 (40% scrap)	10
		4400 (100% scrap)	47
Aluminium	134,700	5000	96
Aluminium ingot	108,000	2200-3400	97
Copper	25,900	1400-2900	85-95
Glass containers	7800	7200	8
Plastics	49,500	1350	97
Newsprint	11,400	8800	23

7.10

The key stages in any responsible waste management strategy are:

- reduce;
- re-use;
- recycle.

We should be aiming to minimise the amount of waste created by reducing consumption and by accurate ordering and specifying. Excess packaging should be avoided and adequate dry storage facilities provided on site. Incredibly, the amount of new construction materials spoiled and discarded exceeds demolition waste, and this is often the result of poor planning and sloppy site practice. It has been estimated that of all the new construction materials delivered to commercial development sites, 20% are never used.

Where non-renewable materials are used, those that have been or can be re-used or recycled should be favoured. Straightforward re-use is the best option, without the extra stage of reprocessing involved in recycling. Timber, roofing slates and tiles, and bricks and blocks in a low-cement mortar are all suitable for re-use and often provide better quality than buying new.

Once these options for minimising present and future waste creation have been exhausted, then incineration in a high temperature boiler, complying with the latest regulations on emissions control, and preferably with some means of recovering heat from the flue gases, should be considered. However, waste is rarely destroyed completely – just transferred elsewhere. Three tonnes of waste typically creates one tonne of ash, which will be sent to landfill, often containing more toxic pollutants than the original material. Hazardous waste should only be burnt in specialised incinerators, but even these can emit highly toxic PICs (products of incomplete combustion).

Environmentally speaking the least preferred option for waste disposal, but still the one most commonly used, is landfill. Unsorted waste is simply dumped in the ground and left for future generations to deal with. According to the Environment Agency, more than half of the 2264 landfill sites in England and Wales are breaching their licenses; 14% are 'nowhere near compliance' and pose a serious risk to health[11]. More than 80% of the population of England and Wales live within a few miles of a landfill site, and thousands of complaints are made every year about litter, mud, smells and flooding, as well as non-response to complaints!

Fig. 7.10 Recycling materials saves very different amounts of energy, depending on the nature of the reprocessing. But all recycling saves primary source use.

The potential exists both for reducing the overall amount of waste and for re-using or recycling a far higher proportion than is currently done. The recently implemented Landfill Tax, and new European Directives on Landfill, means that there are now greater incentives for builders and suppliers to find more cost effective and environmentally acceptable solutions for waste disposal. Unfortunately, there are also barriers to a more widespread use of recovered materials in the present-day construction industry, constrained by time and cost budgets. There are sometimes problems of quality control and the lack of a guaranteed, predictable supply of homogeneous materials.

7.11

Case Study 1

When the Building Research Establishment (BRE) built its new 'Office of the Future', it had to demolish existing buildings on the site. 96% of the waste generated in the demolition was re-used in the new building. In addition, around 80,000 reclaimed bricks were used in the external cladding, and 300m² of wood block flooring from the former County Hall in London were laid, at a cost saving of 30%.

Figures from BRE show 10-15% wastage rate on building sites, which could easily be cut to 5% saving the industry £130m a year.

7.12

Case Study 2

A DETR sponsored study conducted by Bovis – over 16 months, 2000-2001 – based on three new build commercial projects in Central London, measured all waste generated, in type and quantity. Researchers worked closely with designers, trades and their suppliers, to analyse why waste arose and the cost to the project. It was found that project costs of £65/m² of building area were attributable to unnecessary waste generation. Most of this cost came from wasted materials and the cost of re-ordering and reinstating. Waste disposal costs were only 2% of total waste costs. (Taken from *Sustain* magazine vol 2, no 2.)

Environmental assessment of materials

Life Cycle Analysis (LCA) is currently the most commonly used tool for evaluating the environmental impacts of construction and forms the basis for most environmental assessment schemes. It has been defined as a process that 'identifies the material, energy and waste flows associated with a building over its entire life, in such a fashion that the environmental impacts can be determined in advance.'[12]. Comparisons can then be made between different products or construction methods and used to justify an environmentally positive choice.

Fig. 7.11 Waste from old buildings is crushed on site to provide hardcore for new offices for the Building Research Establishment.
Photo: *Building for a Future* 6/1, the magazine of AECB.

Fig. 7.12 The Building Research Eestablishment's new energy efficient office.

One drawback of the LCA method is the tendency to focus on individual elements of construction, rather than on the interaction between them. There is also the unresolved question of the 'weighting' of different impacts, and their boundaries. This method does not remove the inevitable subjective value judgements, but should provide reliable objective data on which to base these judgements.

A study carried out for Scottish Homes in 1995 used LCA as the basis for comparison of whole house designs. Two different specifications for identical house types were developed, one low-energy (Eco-Type 1), and one conventional (the control). Subsequent analysis showed that the latter was responsible for 3.9 times the level of environmental damage caused by the former. Furthermore, it was shown that substantial savings of 30-35% could be made on running costs for management and tenants of Eco-Type 1, with only a small increase in capital costs of 1.1%.

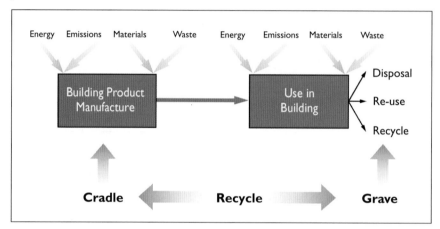

7.13

The *Green Building Handbook*[13] presents environmental assessment data for different materials in the form of tables, which are useful in giving a quick and accurate 'snapshot' of their relative merits across a whole range of environmental impacts (see figure 7.14). The tables are based on well documented research which is also included.

The *Green Guide to Specification*, produced by the BRE[14], evaluates the environmental impacts of building materials in terms of embodied energy, emissions, toxicity, wastes, resource use and recycling properties. Commonly used specifications are given an A, B or C rating and this was subsequently used as the basis for the Eco-Homes standard.

Curwell *et al*[15] offer a number of 'application sheets' for different building components and, uniquely, include assessment of potential health hazards as well as technical, environmental and cost comparisons. In the 'Health' section, different scores are allocated according to whether the material in question is likely to be disturbed, and environmental impacts are scored in four categories, attributable to: manufacturing, construction, use and disposal.

Assessment schemes for whole houses, or building elements, are described in the section on 'Finance and Legislation'.

Fig. 7.13 Table from *Rough Guide to Sustainability*
Brian Edwards, RIBA Publications, 2001.

	£	Production									Use					
	Unit Price Multiplier	Energy Use	Resource Depletion (bio)	Resource Depletion (non-bio)	Global Warming	Ozone Depletion	Toxins	Acid Rain	Photochemical Oxidants	Other	Energy Use	Durability/Maintenance	Recycling/Reuse/Disposal	Health	Other	ALERT!
Bricks																
Ordinary Clay	1.0	●					●	●	●	●						
Flettons	0.8	·					●	●	·	●						
Soft Mud/Stocks	1.0	●					●	●	●	●						
Perforated Clay	1.0	·					·	·	●	·						
Calcium-Silicate	0.9	●		●	●		●	●		●						
Re-Used	1.4															
Concrete Blocks																
Ordinary Dense Blocks	0.3	●	·	●	●		●	●	●	●						
Lightweight Aggregate	?	●	·	●	●		●	●	·	●				●		
Aerated	3.2	●	·	·	●		●	●	●	●						
Composite Insulating	1.4	●	·	●	●	●	●	·	·	●						CFCs?
Stone																
Local	3.2									●						
Imported	?	●								●						
Reclaimed	3.2															
Artificial	1.4	●		·	●	●	●	●	●	●						
Mortar Ingredients																
Ordinary Portland Cement	n/a	●		·	●		●	●	●	●			·	●		Haz. Waste
Pure Lime	n/a	●		·			●	●	·	●				●		
Hydraulic Lime	n/a	●		·	●		●	●	·	●				●		
OP Blastfurnace Cement	n/a	●		·	●		·	·	·	·			·	●		
OP Pulverised Fuel Ash	n/a	●		·	●		·	·	·	·			·	●		
Masonry Cement	n/a	●		·	●		●	·	·	●			·	·		
Sand and Gravel	n/a		·	●						●						

7.14

Fig. 7.14 Data sheet on masonry products.
From *Green Building Handbook*

	Technical	Rank	Health Impacts	Rank	Environmental Impacts	Rank	Cost
Mineral wool quilt	Non-combustible. Material compacts over time thereby reducing insulation value. Mesh support between rafters.	1	Contained fibre presents no foreseeable hazard. In the loft situation there is a risk of contamination to occupied spaces and to the unprotected persons engaged in maintenance or disturbance activities. The B score is related to the amount of disturbance and risk to exposure and in extreme cases may be elevated to 3.	0/1	Resin binders. Pollution during manufacture and disposal.	1/0/0/2	178
Loose mineral fibre (ceiling only)	Non-combustible. Sprayed application	2	Contained fibre presents no foreseeable hazard. In the loft situation there is a risk of contamination of occupied spaces and to the unprotected persons engaged in maintenance or disturbance activities. The B score is related to the amount of disturbance and risk of exposure and in extreme cases may be elevated to 3.	0/1	Resin binders. Pollution during manufacture and disposal.	1/0/0/2	100
Loose cellulose fibre (ceiling only)	Boron supplies insecticidal and fungicidal protection for long-term durability. Combustible. Available with various fire properties.	3	No hazard to occupants subject to no exposure to inhalable fibres. A definitive safety rating of this material awaits full toxicity testing. The addition of fire retardants, insecticides and fungicides will compound the problem. Blown fibre installation, lift ventilation, subsequent maintenance and loft access, and hiatuses in the ceiling expost tradesman, DIYers and occupants. The B score is related to the amount of disturbance and risk of export and in extreme may be elevated to 3.	0/1	Sight risk from boron preservative. Low embodied enregy.	0/0/0/0	n/a
Polyisocyaurate board	Combustible, but slightly better fire properties than other foamed plastics except phenolic and protected by class O lining and non-combustible covering. Adequate bending strength required to support roof fixers when boards fixed over rafters.	3	No significant risk to occupants forseen.	0/0	High embodied energy. Pollution from manufacture and eventual disposal. Older materials in existing buildings is likely to contain CFCs.	2/0/0/2	1363

7.15

Fig. 7.15 Data sheet adapted from Curwell et al [15].
Technical scoring relates to performance and durability, the higher figure being better.
Health impacts are rated according to whether the material in question is stable (first figure) or likely to be disturbed (second figure). Environmental impacts are scored in four categories, attributable to:
1.manufacturing, 2.construction, 3.use and 4.disposal.

Product labelling

The European Eco-Label – also known as the Flower, see figure 7.16 – is administered in the UK by DEFRA. It is a voluntary scheme awarded to products in selected areas, the producers of which meet strict criteria on minimising their environmental impact. Manufacturers are encouraged to produce goods to a common specification, to ensure consistency and to support the Single Market. In return, the Flower offers them a competitive advantage in a market of 370 million consumers. However, the criteria are adjusted to allow up to 30% of the market share in any product area to qualify, and some environmentally damaging materials (such as PVC in furniture) will not necessarily be excluded. (Building For a Future, 12/4/7.)

Initiated by an EEC regulation in 1992, the scheme was revised in 2000, to include services as well as products. Building related products covered under the scheme so far include: white goods, light bulbs, floor coverings, and indoor paints and varnishes.

There are a number of national schemes operating within the EU, and the Commission is trying to improve cooperation and coordination between them and the Flower. There is no national scheme in the UK.

7.16

Bedding	Gardening	Electronic equipment
Mattresses	Soil improvers	Personal computers Portable computers Televisions
Footwear	**Household appliances**	**Textiles**
Shoes	Dishwashers Refrigerators Vacuum cleaners Washing machines	Clothing, bed linen and indoor textiles
Do-it-yourself	**Cleaning**	**Paper**
Hard floor coverings Paints and varnishes Light bulbs	All purpose cleaners Dishwashing detergents Hand dishwashing detergents Laundry detergents	Tissue paper Copying & graphic paper
Services	**Furniture**	
Tourist accommodation service	under development	

7.17

In summary

As we have seen, there are no simple, cut-and-dried solutions to the complex problem of how to minimise construction-related environmental impacts. There are no building materials which are completely environmentally benign, nor are there any without some redeeming features. The process of evaluation is almost always a balance of pros and cons, and involves subjective judgements as well as objective facts. In the end, we may have to accept or 'trade off' certain impacts against products or processes that are even more damaging.

There are some general indications that we can use as a guide, such as the amount of processing involved. As with wholefoods, the nearer a material is to its

Fig. 7.16 The European Community Ecolabel logo.

Fig. 7.17 Product categories from www.eco-label.com

7.18

natural state, and the less processed it is, then the more environmentally benign it is likely to be. There is also a lot we can learn from our gut response to handling an object. Is it pleasant to touch? To smell? If it were a garment, would you wear it next to your skin?

All too often, we are at the mercy of manufacturers' claims or bland attempts at reassurance from government and industry. Accurate and impartial information available at the point of sale, or before, would help us understand the nature of the materials, with which we are in daily, intimate contact.

The following sections of this chapter offer a more in-depth examination of different classes of materials, beginning with the need to reduce our consumption overall.

Minimising new resource consumption

All building activity is environmentally damaging to a greater or lesser degree. New building should only be considered when all options for re-use of existing buildings have been exhausted. The extension of the useful life of an old building, through renovation or works associated with a change of use, is a very effective form of recycling. For a relatively low input in terms of cost and environmental resources, older buildings can fulfil contemporary requirements in terms of function and amenity, and save the resource and energy costs of building new.

Currently, a favoured approach to reviving town and city centres is to renovate grand old civic buildings, and there are many examples of change of use, e.g. warehouse to studio; church to restaurant or theatre; hospital to museum; power station or flour mill to art gallery! These conversions are often prestigious landmarks, symbolising the regeneration of a much larger area, attracting funds and awards, and carrying great popular appeal.

Some buildings of course have passed the point of no return. Where renovation is not feasible, then the possibility of recycling the site, at least, should be considered. This means a preference for development of 'brownfield' sites, which have been built on before. Previous use may have involved industrial activity that has left the land contaminated, and site 'remediation', or cleaning up the soil, can add to the costs of development. On the other hand, some environmentalists would promote development of 'greenfield' sites, arguing that building in rural areas promotes a more diverse habitat than the alternative land use – i.e. agriculture; and that some derelict sites in cities should be left as pockets of greenery and wildlife.

When building new, there are certain construction techniques that can be used to facilitate future recycling. For example, the use of low-cement or lime-based mortars and renders ensures that bricks and blocks can be re-used on demolition. Timber frame buildings, which are bolted or pegged together, allow re-use of the structural members in their full length and undamaged. Steel sections that are bolted rather than welded together are also more likely to be re-used. Labelling materials for future identification will also facilitate recovery and re-use. The use of composite or coated materials often precludes recycling, and plastics, particularly PVC, are notoriously difficult to recycle.

Future re-use calls for a design approach that treats the building as a number of separate layers, which could be detachable, allowing for easy repair and replacement without prejudicing the building as a whole. Structure, 'skin' (or cladding), services and fittings all have different life spans and different maintenance rates and therefore need to be independently accessible, according

Fig. 7.18 The Baltic Art Gallery in Newcastle converted from a former grain silo.

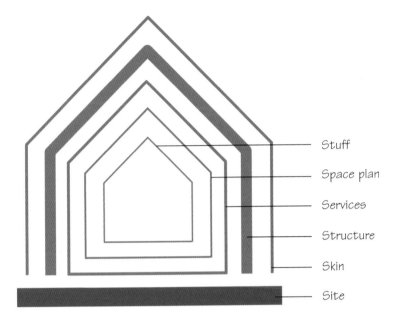

Stuff

Space plan

Services

Structure

Skin

Site

7.19

7.20

7.21

7.22

to this 'long life, loose fit' philosophy promoted by Alex Gordon in the early 1970s[16].

The ultimate in recyclable buildings comes in the flexible modular system developed by Walter Segal, in which standard-size sheets or boards are assembled together in a dry-fix 'sandwich' to form a wall panel. At a later date, this can be simply unscrewed or unbolted, and the wall moved or its components re-used. Several examples exist of Segal Method buildings that have been disassembled and re-erected in other parts of the country, or in different configurations to serve a new function.

There are some building materials which can be re-used very simply, taken out of one building and put into another with a minimum amount of reprocessing. This is the ideal way to use second-hand materials, and applies to timber in many forms – floorboards, doors, windows and decorative mouldings – as well as bricks and blocks, stone slabs, roofing slates, steel sections.

Other materials, such as glass, metals and plastics, usually require an energy-intensive process of recycling, before they can be re-used. In general, this is still worthwhile in energy terms, and of course saves on finite resources. The fact that these materials are capable of being recycled can offset, to some degree, the high energy cost of their initial production. Some metals, such as stainless steel and aluminium, are so expensive to produce that their recycling can be virtually guaranteed.

Then there are materials that can be re-used to serve a totally different purpose from the one for which they were originally produced. For example, artificial roofing slates which are now available made from old tyres, or paving made with recycled glass.

Fig. 7.19 'Shearing layers of change. Because of the different rates of change of its components, a building is always tearing itself apart'. From Stewart Brand: *How Buildings Learn*.

Fig. 7.20 This Segal-style building at CAT originally stood in a different part of the site. Following a re-organisation, it was dismantled piece by piece and re-erected in its present position.

Fig. 7.21 Walter Segal's timber houses were constructed without 'wet trades'. The whole building could be, and this one has been, dismantled and re-used elsewhere.

Fig. 7.22 The main structural frames of the top station at CAT, together with the cross bracing and railings, were all made from recycled pitch pine.

7.23

However, in order to make full use of the vast potential for recycling, we have to re-evaluate what is a fundamental cultural prejudice against anything second-hand. Goods that have been used once are generally assumed to be shoddy, inferior, and to perform less well than a brand new version. In reality the reverse is often the case, particularly with buildings and their components.

Recycling is likely to happen wherever there is particular quality or beauty, or where the cost of buying new is prohibitive (as with roofing slates). Indeed, there is a booming market in 'architectural salvage', such as Victorian fireplaces or chimney pots. However, such high cost, quality items do not represent the limit of what we can do to recycle building materials. Rather, they are the tip of the iceberg. What we need to do now is to cultivate an attitude, within the construction industry and among the buying public, that always presumes in favour of saving and re-use unless otherwise indicated.

There are a number of steps that the individual DIYer or self-builder can take to promote the use of second-hand materials and whole buildings.

- If you need to move house, then consider the option of renovating an old house rather than building new.
- If you need more space, you could look at the possibility of restructuring the space you already have. Turning two smaller rooms into one larger one, or combining different functions in the same room, such as a spare bedroom-cum-study, might well be a cost effective solution. You may be able to incorporate into your living space areas already within the house envelope, such as a loft, cellar or attached garage. Or you may have the yen and the space to build a workshop, studio or retreat in the garden, which may just take the pressure off space in the house.
- Become aware of buildings being demolished in your area, and talk to the local builders. Many a bargain has been acquired in this way. Keep your design flexible until you have explored these possibilities it may have to be altered slightly to accommodate particular salvaged items eg. a staircase.
- Design or renovate a building with an eye to how materials and components can be recovered and reused in the future.
- Consult the many websites offering recycled materials:
  - www.salvo.co.uk Good for architectural salvage. For sale, Wanted, Demolition sites & Theft alert
  - www.bre.co.uk/waste Materials Information Exchange operated in conjunction with DETR. Has noticeboards for Sale, Wanted, Unutilised materials, and forthcoming/live demolition sites.
  - www.ciria.org.uk Coming soon, register of recycling sites
  - www.ecoconstruction.org Sponsored by the Housing Corporation and developed by FaberMaunsell's Sustainable Development Group. Presents the case for recycling, as well as a searchable database
- Above all, create a market for re-used and recycled materials. Patronise your local junk yard, give them advance warning of what you need, and make it your first port of call, before the builders' merchant. You will have the satisfaction of practising very low-energy, low-resource-use building; you should get good value for money; and you could achieve a uniquely appealing and aesthetically interesting house.

Fig. 7.23 Recycling can be glamorous – paving made from crushed glass. Crystal Paving Ltd.

RENEWABLE RESOURCES

Timber

Introduction

In the construction industry, timber is to be found everywhere. It is hard to imagine a building of whatever style or period that does not use wood in some form or other. No other material can match its versatility, or meet the requirements of so many different building elements – from structural support, flooring, cladding, doors and windows, to decorative finishes and furniture. Timber is an appropriate and appealing material for DIYers and self-builders, as it is relatively easily worked and repaired. The necessary skills and tools are widely accessible and available.

It is estimated that across all the industrialised countries, timber frame accounts for 70% of all housing stock, representing some 150 million homes. Britain shows the lowest percentage of timber frame houses, but conversely the greatest potential for increasing market share.

7.24

Country	Housing Stock (millions)	Timber Frame %
Australia	6.09	90%
Canada	9.91	90%
Ireland	0.87	10%
Japan	40.54	45%
Norway	1.82	90%
Sweden	3.86	90%
USA	97.31	90%
UK	21.39	8%

7.25

7.26

Fig. 7.24 Timber framed buildings have a long life because they can be easily adapted to new circumstances. This house – now a café and shop – has undergone centuries of adaption and renovation (Bear Steps, Shrewsbury).

Fig. 7.25 Taken from *Timber Frame Housing*, Hastoe Housing Association.

Fig. 7.26 The tallest timber frame building in the UK, with restored stone frontage. Student hall of residence, Aberystwyth.
Architects: James & Jenkins

7.27

Environmental advantages

Timber frame is much more prevalent in the 'eco-housing' sector, and the environmental benefits of timber construction are many:

- Timber is the only renewable structural building material, and therefore avoids the extraction of non-renewable resources. Assuming that each tree felled is replanted, the resource will never run out, as it is the sun's (renewable) energy that makes trees grow and produces timber.

- Timber has a low embodied energy, compared with other structural building materials. A concrete block wall will take 1.7 times as much energy to construct as a timber wall. The production process for timber is relatively simple and low-energy, as are its installation, maintenance and disposal operations. If it is kiln-dried, this will add to its embodied energy costs, depending on the fuel used to fire the kiln. Most of the embodied energy of timber derives from transportation, which makes locally grown timber the best environmental option.

- As a low-energy process, the extraction and conversion of timber accounts for very little pollution. Most of this can be attributed to motorised transport, and therefore avoided by sourcing locally. (As a fuel, however, wood can be polluting if it is not burnt in the right conditions.)

- Minimal waste is created in the production and use of timber, as there are viable end uses for virtually every part of the tree. Good quality timber can easily be re-used or recycled, while poorer quality pieces or untreated offcuts can be burnt to create heat and so offset fossil fuel use. Chemically treated timber should NOT be burned as dioxins may be released. Waste timber in the form of wood chips or pellets can be burnt in Combined Heat and Power (CHP) boilers, which provide heat and power on a district scale. Plantations of fast-growing timber such as willow can be regularly coppiced to provide biofuels for power stations. In the last resort, if timber is sent to landfill, it will simply biodegrade.

- The use of untreated timber in buildings poses no health risks to the user and can help to regulate the humidity of the indoor environment. Wood is warm to feel and inviting to touch, and for many it has an immediate aesthetic appeal. There is very little health risk for carpenters or others working with wood, although prolonged exposure to some wood dusts is thought to be harmful.*

- Because growing trees absorb carbon dioxide, harvested timber can be seen as a 'carbon sink', locking up the CO_2 which the tree has absorbed, until it is burnt or rots away. One kilogram of dry timber contains about 50% carbon, which binds in 1.8kg of CO_2. If the forests that are harvested are then replanted, timber becomes a carbon-neutral material. The growing tree will take up as much CO_2 as the harvested one will eventually release. (Nevertheless, we should beware of over-emphasising the importance of 'carbon sinks'. The amount of CO_2 absorbed by our existing forests is less than 1% of our annual CO_2 emissions. As well as absorbing CO_2, forest eco-systems will also give off CO_2, from decomposition of organic matter. Different temperatures and management systems will affect the carbon balance of a particular forest[17]. Using forests as carbon sinks can only be a temporary and partial solution, and any 'carbon credits' generated should not be used to justify continued excessive fossil fuel use.)

Fig. 7.27 In this environmental centre in Iceland, timber has been used for the structural frame, floor and wall finish, decorative musical instruments, and as fuel in the woodburning stove.

*Wood dust (unspecified) a newly declared 'known human carcinogen', USA National Institutes of Health, Environmental Building News, vol 12, no 3.

- Forests will also trap air pollution, prevent soil erosion, store and filter surface water, and support a multitude of plant and wildlife species. The leisure space and amenity value that well managed woodland represents is important for tourism and an invaluable national resource.
- In general, it is easier to achieve higher insulation values, and therefore lower energy use, with a timber construction than with a masonry one. It is difficult to increase the cavity depth in a masonry wall substantially, without extra-long ties or additional structural support. As the Building Regulations call for higher standards of energy efficiency, so contractors and developers are turning to timber frame construction to minimise extra works and cost.

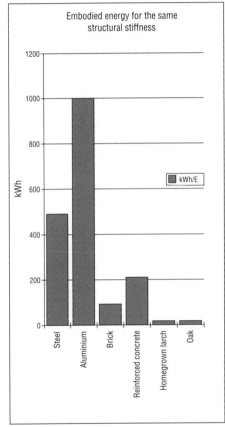

7.28

Structural and performance advantages

- Because of its unique cellular structure (longitudinal fibres combined with cross sectional cells), timber is strong in tension, compression and bending. It has a good strength-to-weight ratio, better than steel for example, which means it may take less energy to install.
- Contrary to many people's expectations, timber performs well in fire as it burns steadily at a predictable rate. In the process charcoal is formed on the surface of the timber, which serves to insulate and protect the core. It is possible therefore to make precise calculations of the dimensions that structural timbers need to be, in order to hold the building up for half an hour, or an hour, to allow the occupants to escape. By contrast, steel structures behave unpredictably in fires, appearing to be unaffected and then failing suddenly.
- Recent experience in areas most affected by natural or climatic disasters, such as earthquakes and hurricanes, suggests that framed buildings withstand extreme conditions better, all other things being equal. Timber frame buildings in particular are able to absorb sudden shocks or loads without permanent damage, owing to the elasticity of the material and flexing around the frame joints.
- Timber buildings are inherently durable and easy to maintain. In the UK there are many examples of ancient timber frame buildings still standing, from the 15th century onwards. The oldest building in the UK is an 11th century stave church in Essex, and the oldest building in the world is the Horiuji temple in Japan, built in 607 AD out of cypress. In this century too, timber buildings age well compared with their conventionally built equivalents. A study carried out by the Building Research Establishment on 120 timber frame houses built between 1920 and 1975, found their performance to be 'similar to traditionally built dwellings of the same age and, given proper maintenance, likely to remain so for the foreseeable future.'[18]

With such an overwhelming pedigree, you may wonder why timber frame construction is not used more. Unfortunately, for various historical and cultural reasons, timber buildings in the UK are often seen as inferior, temporary and less solid and reliable than their masonry counterparts. In addition, there were some much-publicised failures in timber frame system housing in the 1980s – due not to the nature of the material, but to defects in construction practice.

Fig. 7.28 We have a natural urge to self-build. At this visitor centre, children need little encouragement to build dens – copying each other's styles and stealing materials from abandoned dens.

Fig. 7.29 Embodied energy vs stiffness.

7.30

7.32

7.33

7.31

Fig. 7.30 Stave church builders in Norway developed a sophisticated structural system that has enabled this church at Heddal, Telemark, to survive for 750 years.

Fig. 7.31 Nijo-jo temple in Kyoto, Japan, 400 years old.

Fig. 7.32 Maximum ecological diversity – the native oak habitat supports more species of wildlife than any other.

Fig. 7.33 Local green oak self-build. Engineered frame using traditional jointing.

However, in this area of materials analysis, there are no simple certainties or solutions. Nor is there any one material that is completely environmentally benign. A rigid adherence to timber specification and use can cause environmental and other problems, although these can be minimised by careful selection and good practice.

The potential disadvantages of timber can be grouped under four main headings:

- The origin of the timber or where it is sourced from (transportation issues).
- Any additional treatment that is deemed necessary prior to use.
- Guarantees of sustainable forest management and harvesting practice.
- Natural limitations to the length and strength of timber members.

Home-grown hardwoods

About one-third of the six million cubic metres of timber produced annually by British forests is hardwood such as ash, beech, birch and oak, the majority of which is used for furniture. There are, however, two species generally considered suitable for structural purposes: oak and sweet chestnut. These are the traditional materials used in timber-framed houses in Britain, and they are very strong and long lasting. Buried in the ground, a 50x50mm post of oak or sweet chestnut heartwood will last 15-25 years, which classifies oak as 'durable' according to the Timber Research and Development Association (TRADA) classifications.

Usually, these hardwoods are worked on and incorporated into a building while still in their 'green' or unseasoned state. As they dry out, many timbers have a tendency to warp or twist. Oak is especially susceptible to this (hence the wavy beams characteristic of many old buildings). However, this drawback can be overcome by the use of ties and braces at frequent intervals.

7.34

7.35a

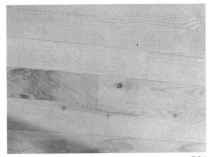

7.35b

7.36

7.37

The high tannin content of oak and sweet chestnut can lead to corrosion in ferrous metals and lead, so care should be taken when specifying fixings and flashings. The traditional mortice and tenon joint with its oak peg is often the best solution to jointing a post and beam. As the timber shrinks on drying, so the joint is pulled together. Run-off from exposed oak timbers can cause brown staining, on concrete foundations for instance.

Because of their inherent quality and longevity, as well as their relatively high financial cost and limited availability, these woods are highly likely to be re-used. There is no question of their needing chemical timber treatment – indeed the structure of the heartwood is so dense that no preservative would penetrate very far.

In some areas of the country sufficient home-grown oak is not always able to meet the demand for long, straight, large section timbers and as a consequence, a lot of French oak is currently being imported to meet the demand for high-quality framing timber. However, it is still possible to specify small lengths and sections of local oak for joists, floorboards, or laminated for joinery items such as window frames.

The use of home-grown hardwoods is being promoted at a regional level by bodies such as Coed Cymru in Wales, who work with timber producers to encourage good forest management and a sustainable supply, and to research and develop new markets for the end products. Recent investigation and research has highlighted the need for higher value uses to be found for home-grown timber, to the value of £75m per year[19].

The higher value that is placed on timber as a building material, compared with its value as fencing or firewood, should ensure replanting and stimulate the cultivation of good quality mature trees, which in turn creates a more diverse and balanced woodland habitat.

It is, however, vitally important that replanting of hardwood species is maintained and promoted, so that they continue to be a renewable resource. In Wales, there is currently no replanting of oak as a crop, although natural regeneration is encouraged.

Fig. 7.34 Creating a great structure from small-section green oak. The gridshell at the Weald and Downland Museum. Buro Happold engineers. Architects: Edward Cullinan Architects.

Fig. 7.35a A building product to suit the resource. 100 x 25mm oak boards from local thinnings.

Fig. 7.35b Home-grown timber production using small scale machinery brings much-needed cash into the countryside.

Fig. 7.36 Home-grown ash flooring – a high quality material at a reasonable price. Being 'tongued and grooved' all round boards, this flooring can be cut from small trees and thinnings.

Fig. 7.37 Oak shingles on a small oak framed structure.

7.38

7.40

7.39

Home-grown softwoods

These timbers, mostly spruce and pine, are used in the main for pallets, packaging and fencing, and for paper and chipboard manufacture. The poor quality of timber that is acceptable for such end uses goes hand in hand with a system of forestry oriented exclusively towards short-term financial return. Here, trees are planted close together in vast monocultural plantations where few other species can thrive. They are left unthinned and then harvested while the trees are still immature by clear-felling whole areas at a time, leaving a barren desert of stumps. The acidification of the soil resulting from such dense conifer plantations means that few other plants can start to grow before the new rotation cycle begins. However, blanket spraying of plantations – often with organophosphates – to treat disease or suppress growth before planting remains common practice.

Where home-grown softwood is used in the construction industry, it is mainly for carcassing – studs, joists and roofing timbers – and is assumed to be relatively poor quality and non-structural. Chemical preservatives are relied upon to give it any sort of useful life. But it is possible to look beyond this scenario when searching out suitable timber for structural use.

European larch and Douglas fir are excellent framing timbers which grow well in our climate. The heartwood of larch is classified as 'semi-durable' by TRADA. Both these softwoods are naturally dense, resinous and therefore relatively rot- and insect-resistant. In our experience at CAT they can be used without the need for chemical timber treatment, which cuts down on both cost and environmental impact. Once seasoned, they are also suitable for use in doors, window frames and floorboards.

By specifying and using timber grown in the UK, we not only get a higher quality product, but also one with very low embodied energy: one-seventh that of imported timber and by far the lowest of any of the mainstream structural building materials.

Imported timber

In the UK, we import 87% of our timber requirements, mainly from Canada, Sweden and Russia. Only 10% of the 6 million cubic metres of sawn softwood used yearly by the UK construction industry is home-grown. Indeed, timber is one of the most widely traded commodities in the world, second only to oil.

Fig. 7.38 A conifer plantation is clear felled, leaving a blighted landscape of stumps and brash.

Fig. 7.39 The 'clear felling' of dense spruce forest can lead to soil loss on poor land. Lake Vyrnwy, Wales.

Fig. 7.40 A larch plantation, thinned to produce construction timber, also creates a valuable wildlife habitat.

7.41

The energy costs of transporting such a heavy, bulky material are enormous, ranging from 0.1GJ per tonne from Sweden to the UK, to 2.4GJ per tonne from Papua New Guinea[20]. (Multiply these figures by 278 for kWh.) The financial costs of timber transportation can likewise be considerable. An increase in local timber production and marketing could not only save on the costs of imports – some £5 billion a year of the UK trade deficit in 1997[21] – but also reduce the environmental impact of timber, and promote an important rural industry.

Environmental costs in the producing countries include tropical deforestation (2.5m hectares of tropical forest were lost in 2002) and loss of livelihood for indigenous peoples. It is true that in tropical areas, more trees are felled for agricultural development geared for export, than for timber harvesting. Nevertheless, the extraction of valuable trees for export (an extremely wasteful process, involving the felling of huge numbers of 'non-commercial' trees) serves to open up virgin areas for further clearance. Remaining small pockets of trees are often not ecologically viable[21a].

Importation of illegally felled timber is a major impediment to establishing sustainable timber industries in producer countries. Illegal harvesting deprives governments of up to US$15bn a year in lost revenue. Many countries in Europe import large quantities of illegally harvested tropical timber, and furthermore it is almost impossible to identify it on the open market. Even if it is identified, it is not necessarily illegal to import it.

The UK is one of the worst offenders, and knowingly supports the illegal timber trade in Indonesia, by importing large quantities of tropical plywood, door blanks and paper pulp – a trade worth around £128m. The illegal timber industry in Indonesia inevitably brings with it corruption and human rights abuses[21b].

Friends of the Earth, which has produced the table (figure 7.42), is calling on the EU to make it illegal to import and sell illegally harvested timber. The EC has responded by developing an Action Plan to establish systems that can be used to differentiate between legal and illegal timber imports.

Fig. 7.41 Roof trusses for the Environmental Information Centre at CAT are made in the workshop from local larch.

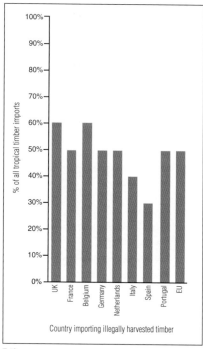

7.42

7.43

Fig. 7.42 Graph showing % of all illegally harvested tropical timber imports by country. Figures from FoE, published in *Sustain* magazine, vol 2, no 2.

Fig. 7.43 Stacked timber seasoning naturally at Parnham House School of Furniture Making, Dorset.

In the temperate and boreal areas at northern latitudes, where most of our softwoods are produced, the amount of forest cover is actually increasing, due to the replanting policy of the timber producers and their desire to safeguard the availability of their product well into the future. However, these new forests are still, on the whole, monocultural conifer plantations, which induce an acidic soil and are, ecologically speaking, deserts. In Scandinavia this form of forestry threatens more than 200 species of plants and animals with extinction[22].

Timber seasoning

When timber is first felled it has a moisture content of 20-25%. The process of seasoning timber involves drying it out until the moisture content falls to a stable 8-12%. The drying can be done naturally over a longer period (air drying) or artificially but more quickly (kiln drying). The advantage of using dry, seasoned timber is that it will not shrink, twist or warp. This is particularly important for timber used internally, for finishes. Seasoned timber is also more resistant to rot or insect attack.

Timber used for structural or carcassing purposes can stand being less well seasoned, or even 'green' – the term used for freshly felled, unseasoned wood. The danger here is the shrinkage and possible twisting that occurs as the timber dries out in the building, and the construction method and design should take account of this. Some very hard timbers such as oak can only be worked easily when green. Locally produced timber is often supplied green, whereas imported timber will be at least partially seasoned.

Clearly, timber that has been kiln dried will have a higher embodied energy than air-dried or 'green' timber. Some UK timber suppliers are using woodchip boilers to heat their kilns, fuelled by waste from the milling process. It is possible to use solar kilns, which involves seasoning timber in a greenhouse or polytunnel, and is basically an accelerated form of air-drying[23].

Timber treatment

The assumption that all structural softwood used in buildings needs to be chemically treated to protect it from insect or fungus attack, has become established for a number of historical reasons and now needs radical re-evaluation.

As the harvesting of timber became subject to the requirements of mass production, so chemical treatments were relied upon to make up for deficiencies in the quality and seasoning of available timber. Similarly, the skill in detailing timber buildings to ensure good drainage and ventilation became eroded, in favour of the routine use of chemical treatment to ensure durability. The recent trend towards well-sealed buildings, designed to minimise heat loss and reduce unwanted air infiltration, carried an increased risk of condensation occurring in hidden spaces such as the roof or wall cavity. The effects of this could be (and in some cases were) catastrophic and major timber frame designers and developers welcomed the supposed security of the long-term guarantees offered by the timber treatment companies.

But what if such guarantees of longevity simply do not hold up? Hutton and Rostron Environmental Investigations, a highly reputable company that investigates buildings and materials failure, believes that extensive remedial chemical treatments for rot and/or insect attack are neither necessary nor appropriate. Such treatment 'provides little more than temporary protection of structural timber, and the long term guarantees commonly offered are entirely speculative.'[24]

In fact, such guarantees are usually valid only if the structure is kept free from water penetration. Furthermore, as the London Hazards Centre argues, 'the adoption of chemical timber treatment as the norm is directly encouraging bad design practices...and gives a false sense of long term security which may encourage inadequate maintenance.'[25]

By contrast, the only sure way to avoid timber decay is to use good quality, well-seasoned timber, to ensure that the building design provides protection or ventilation of all timbers, and to institute regular inspections of all vulnerable timbers and adjacent building fabric. It is very important that any timber liable to wetting, is able to dry out. As a rule, rot-producing fungi will only attack timber that has a moisture content of more than 20% over a sustained period.

Where rot or insect infestation has already occurred, the affected timber must be replaced (plus one metre either side), the source of moisture identified and put right, and the supply of adequate ventilation ensured. This approach cures the problem at source, rather than relying on a chemical fix to reverse an invasive attack that is already established. Without this approach, the problem will recur, even on treated timber. Non-durable softwood used externally will need some protection from the effects of ultraviolet rays in sunlight. This can be in the form of an organic, microporous paint or stain.

7.44

7.45

7.46

There are three main types of timber pre-treatment against rot and insect attack:
- **Pressure impregnation with water-based preservatives:** in this method, a partial vacuum is created in the treatment vessel, which draws air from the timber cells, and the timber is flooded with the treatment solution which is drawn deep into the wood. The solution is then drained and a final vacuum applied to remove surplus chemicals. The main formulation used in this context is a mix of chrome, copper and arsenic (CCA), first produced in 1933. As from June 2004, the updated EU Marketing and Use Directive prohibits the use of CCA treated timber in residential constructions or where there is a risk of repeated skin contact. However, some timber treatment companies intend to support the continued use of CCA in certain situations alongside 'new generation products' such as 'Tanalith-E', marketed as a 'green' timber treatment and based on copper and triazole – an 'organic biocide'. (www.archtp.com)

Fig. 7.44 Toxic chemical containers left lying around a builders' yard.
Photo: Keith Hall, Association for Environment Conscious Building (AECB).

Fig. 7.45 Hutton and Rostron use specially trained dogs – Rothounds – to locate active dry rot which might otherwise be overlooked. This minimises the intrusive nature of the investigation and searches may be carried out in furnished or inhabited buildings.

Fig. 7.46 Timber boarding cladding the curved shapes of the Weald and Downland Museum.

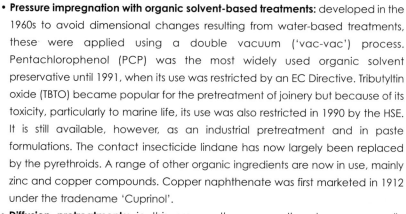

- **Pressure impregnation with organic solvent-based treatments:** developed in the 1960s to avoid dimensional changes resulting from water-based treatments, these were applied using a double vacuum ('vac-vac') process. Pentachlorophenol (PCP) was the most widely used organic solvent preservative until 1991, when its use was restricted by an EC Directive. Tributyltin oxide (TBTO) became popular for the pretreatment of joinery but because of its toxicity, particularly to marine life, its use was also restricted in 1990 by the HSE. It is still available, however, as an industrial pretreatment and in paste formulations. The contact insecticide lindane has now largely been replaced by the pyrethroids. A range of other organic ingredients are now in use, mainly zinc and copper compounds. Copper naphthenate was first marketed in 1912 under the tradename 'Cuprinol'.

- **Diffusion pretreatments:** in this process the preservatives become equally distributed in the treatment solution and the free water within the timber cells. Because it relies on a high moisture content, it is more applicable to green timber. It is a time-consuming process, involving storage for up to four weeks. Borax based compounds are usually used in an aqueous solution. They are active against a wide spectrum of fungi and insects, and have a low mammalian toxicity. Doubts have been expressed that borates will easily leach from timbers, but research has suggested that this is only likely to be a problem if the timber is in prolonged contact with water[26].

Once timber is chemically treated the process is irreversible and a natural, healthy material is turned into a toxic product, and destined to become toxic waste. Tests conducted in the USA on soil under CCA treated decks or verandahs showed arsenic levels 80 times greater than the surrounding soil and 35 times greater than the legal limit[27]. Subsequent studies have shown an increased cancer risk for children using playground equipment made from treated timber, because of exposure to arsenic[28].

Although CCA treatment is being phased out in the United States, the chemicals persist in the environment, and the EPA (Environment Protection Agency) are testing a variety of sealants to encapsulate treated timber in use. There are also problems of disposal. Wood treated with chlorine-based compounds will give off highly toxic dioxins if burnt. Even when burnt in the latest high-temperature incinerators, designed to minimise emissions, the residue is a highly toxic and leachable ash, which inevitably ends up in landfill. Most pretreated timbers will have a service life of only a few decades, and with 30 million cubic metres of treated timber used annually, the scale of this particular toxic waste problem is likely to increase sharply in the near future. Currently disposal to landfill, though not ideal, is judged the best environmental option[29].

If timber preservatives are thought to be necessary, then probably the safest option is to use boron based compounds with their relatively low toxicity. The LD50 (the lethal dose required to kill 50% of a given population) is 4500-6000mg/kg for borax, compared with 27mg/kg for PCP and 88mg/kg for lindane. Boron and permethrin are approved for use on roof timbers where bats are likely to roost.

Wood preservation through heat treatment is being pioneered in Finland and one UK timber supplier is importing Finnforest 'Thermowood' profiled cladding boards[30]. The timber is treated in special kilns at temperatures of 200°C, which reduces equilibrium moisture content by 50%. The result is stable and durable timber with a high resistance to fungus attack. The enhanced durability applies to sapwood and heartwood, with surface coatings lasting up to five times longer.

Timber certification

Even with renewable resources, we need guarantees of sustainable production, including replanting first and foremost, but also the promotion of biodiversity, soil and water quality, and the rights of local people. Timber certification by bodies such as the Forest Stewardship Council (FSC) offers guarantees of sustainable production for consumers, as well as an acceptable future in international timber trading for producer countries. Founded in 1993, the FSC is a non-profit organisation, representing timber traders, environmentalists, indigenous peoples organisations, community forestry groups, forest workers unions, forestry professionals and retail companies.

There are three other major international timber certification schemes – PEFC (Europe); CSA (Canada) and SFI (North America) – but these have been developed, and are still controlled, by the forest industry itself. FSC certification is the only 'third-party' process, in which the certifiers are separate from the forest owners and managers. A recent report by FERN* concludes that the FSC, though not perfect, offers the only 'independent and credible' certification scheme. Other widely respected NGOs such as World Wildlife Fund, Greenpeace, Friends of the Earth and the Woodland Trust, support the FSC's work.

The FSC publishes a set of criteria – Ten Principles of Forest Stewardship – on which its certification scheme is based, and which incorporates environmentally appropriate management, social benefit and economic viability. Genetically modified organisms are prohibited and the use of chemicals is minimised. Regular inspections of certified forests are carried out by independent organisations accredited by the FSC, which is represented in 28 countries.

The FSC relies on consumer demand to provide the incentive for forest products manufacturers to seek certification. Their label is now on thousands of 'Home and Garden' products in UK supermarkets and DIY stores, including items such as garden furniture, doors and flooring. For construction timber, it is worth doing a 'product search' on the FSC website (www.fsc-uk.org). There are now nearly 40 million hectares of FSC certified forest worldwide, and over one million hectares in the UK, representing more than 70% of all UK commercial forestry.

The UK Government has pledged that all its departments will source timber from sustainable sources 'identified under independent certification schemes such as that operated by the Forest Stewardship Council.'[31]. It was subsequently confirmed that this applied also to 'wood used temporarily during construction works, as well as wood fixed as part of a finished structure'. Failure to follow this policy has led to actions by Greenpeace, to protest at the use of non-certified hardwood doors and illegally harvested Indonesian plywood in government buildings[32].

Timber technology

There are drawbacks to using natural materials like timber, such as limitations on the length available and a tendency to distort as it dries. This has been addressed by developments in the field of timber technology, such as composite beams (see page 124).

7.47

7.48

Fig. 7.47 Timber can be heat-treated to make long-lasting cladding out of non-durable timber species – thus avoiding chemical treatments. Thermowood from Finnforest.

Fig. 7.48 The logo of the Forest Stewardship Council, which means that the timber has been sourced from sustainably managed forests.

*FERN is an NGO promoting conservation and sustainable use of forestry within the EU. The report 'Behind the Logo' is available at www.fern.org

In summary

- Use reclaimed timber where appropriate.
- Use home-grown certified timber, either hardwood or semi-durable softwood, and be prepared to spend some time searching out suppliers.
- If your source of home-grown timber is not certified, try and satisfy yourself that the forestry management practices used to produce your timber are acceptable. Encourage your supplier to seek certification.
- If using imported timber, try to source FSC certified. Scandinavian timber has the lowest transport energy costs.
- Support retailers committed to supplying sustainably produced products, such as B&Q, Do It All, and Homebase.
- Reduce consumption and wastage, by careful ordering and site practice, and by innovative use of smaller section timbers (e.g. spaced studs – chapter 6 page 74).
- Use no chemical treatment. Instead, choose well-seasoned durable or semi-durable wood. Ensure adequate ventilation and regular inspections.
- If you decide that some treatment is necessary, use boron based products.
- Avoid pre-treated joinery items such as windows and doors.
- If you are having a property surveyed, try to find a genuinely independent surveyor who is sympathetic to non-invasive and non-chemical treatments.
- If you are concerned about a particular pesticide or want more information, contact the London Hazards Centre or the Pesticide Action Network: www.pan-uk.org

Timber products

Composite boards

These are sheet materials, usually measuring 2400x1200mm (8'x4') in varying thicknesses, made from small pieces of wood or very thin layers of wood glued together. They have a wide variety of uses including concrete formwork, sheathing and sarking, flooring and flat roofs, through to finishing joinery and furniture. They can be invaluable for covering large areas and provide an extremely economical alternative to solid timber. In some instances their manufacture uses the waste products of felling and their use in construction means there is less demand for virgin timber in low grade applications.

However, they do take more energy to produce (about 15 times that required to produce rough sawn timber) and there are health hazards associated with the glues and binders used in their manufacture.

Plywood

This is made by soaking the whole log and peeling off thin layers or veneers, which are then dried and glued together using formaldehyde or, more recently, isocyanate resins. The finished sheet can contain as few as three veneers (3-ply) or as many as 15, and the grains of adjacent layers are laid at right angles to each other. WBP (weather and boil proof) board used to refer to the type of glue and meant it was suitable for external use. This classification has been superseded by new European standards and there is now no direct equivalent to WBP. Instead, the bonding classes for veneer plywood are specified according to their end uses. Class 1 is for dry conditions, Class 2 for humid, and Class 3 for external.

There are numerous grades of plywood.

- Shuttering ply is the cheapest grade. It is used for formwork and made with poor quality softwood, but it is often the best environmental option where a good quality finish is not important (as softwood is usually home-grown).

- Middle-of-the-range ply, often used for shelving, counters and internal doors, is usually made from tropical hardwoods and has a characteristic reddish colour. It is closed grained and knot-free. The bulk of the tropical hardwood we import is in this form (over one million cubic metres annually) and should be avoided completely. There is no justification for using tropical hardwoods in board manufacture, and in environmental terms it is scandalously expensive. Importing and using this plywood makes a substantial contribution to the destruction of the tropical rainforest.

- Marine ply is top of the range plywood. It is usually made from non-sustainably harvested tropical hardwoods such as mahogany or gaboon, and resorcinol glues, which prevent it from delaminating even in very wet conditions. Also available in this price range – and a good 'eco' alternative – are decorative boards finished with an oak, beech or birch veneer.

- Blockboard or laminboard is basically a variation of plywood used largely in furniture and shopfitting. Between the two outer veneers – either hardwood or good quality softwood – is a core of small section softwood. The same synthetic resin glues are used.

7.49

Oriented Strand Board (OSB)

Commonly known as Sterling Board after one major manufacturer, this is made from wood shavings or 'strands', oriented in a random fashion to give maximum strength, and glued together under heat and pressure. It makes efficient use of low-grade timber and is used mainly as an alternative to shuttering ply. It can also be used for flooring, in a tongue-and-grooved (T&G) pre-sanded version.

7.50

Chipboard

Suitable for internal use only, chipboard is made from small particles (or 'chips') of wood, bound together with urea-formaldehyde glue. Although chipboard manufacture ought to be an appropriate end-use for forestry waste, most manufacturers insist on using the whole log and even on logs of a minimum diameter. Chipboard manufacture can cause extremely unpleasant air pollution, with local residents complaining of skin irritation, breathing difficulties and an increase in cases of serious asthma.

Because the particles of wood are so small that they cannot impart much strength to the board, correspondingly more glue is necessary, and this will typically form 7-10% of the board's weight. A low-formaldehyde chipboard, marketed as Kucospan, is being imported from Germany, but it is expensive.

Chipboard is widely used for furniture and internal doors. Moisture resistant chipboard is available (chemically teated), as is flooring grade, tongue and groove chipboard. It can be covered with melamine and this forms the basis for very many kitchen units and shop counters.

7.51

Fig. 7.49 Softwood shuttering plywood.

Fig. 7.50 Oriented strand board ('Sterling Board').

Fig. 7.51 Birch veneered chipboard, common in much modern furniture.

7.52

7.53a

753b

Fig. 7.52 Breathable timber frame sheathing made of bitumen-impregnated softboard.

Fig. 7.53a & 7.53b Tectan® boards, made from Tetra-Pak cartons, can be used to make office furniture.

Fibreboards

There are two basic types of fibreboard.

- Medium Density Fibreboard (MDF) is manufactured with urea-formaldehyde as the bonding agent, which accounts for 14% of the board's weight. It is commonly used for internal finishes, where off-gassing from formaldehyde-based glues is most dangerous due to lack of ventilation. Workers involved in the cutting and shaping of MDF for furniture, fittings and theatre sets, are thought to be at particular risk from inhaling dust. There is now a zero-formaldehyde MDF (Medite ZF) available, but it is more expensive.

- Softboard, mediumboard, and hardboard are all made by felting wood fibres and then bonding them into a sheet using heat, pressure and the wood's own resins. No synthetic glues are needed and the use of this type of fibreboard is associated with a very low environmental impact. Softboard can be used as pinboard and to increase the insulation value of a wall. Impregnated with bitumen, it can be used for sheathing timber-framed walls, providing racking resistance* temporary weather protection and vapour permeability. Medium board can also be used for sheathing, but do not confuse it with MDF, which is much more common. Hardboard can be used for internal flush doors and as a smooth, high quality finish over shuttering ply for desks, counters, shelves, etc. As 'Masonite' it can be used structurally, and in its oil-tempered version it is moderately moisture resistant.

The Trade Association for the Fibreboard Industry, FIDOR, have a full range of information and can help with technical problems.

Alternative fibreboards

Non-wood fibres such as flax, hemp, or sugar cane fibre can be used for board manufacture. Boards made from flax shiv are currently imported from Belgium at the rate of 50,000m³ a year for use as the core material in internal doors.

Stramit or strawboard, which has been made in this country since the 1940s, is still being used for self-supporting internal partitions, doors and wall/ceiling panels. It has National House Building Council (NHBC) and British Standards (BS 4046) approval.

Tectan® board is made in Germany from pre- and post-consumer-waste from drinks cartons. It consists of 75% paper, 20% polyethylene and 5% aluminium. The waste is shredded and heated to a point where the polyethylene melts and acts as a bonding agent. No toxic glues are used.

Re-use/disposal

The more durable boards, such as plywood, can be re-used several times over. This is made easier by screwing rather than nailing boards together, and by the use of release oil on formwork. If they are burned, harmful gases such as hydrogen cyanide from isocyanate resins may be produced. If dumped on a landfill site, the timber will biodegrade but the constituents of the glues will remain in the ecosystem.

*Racking resistance is needed to keep frames and panels square and stop them 'parallelogramming' – it can be done by sheathing material or triangular braces.

Synthetic resins

Common to the manufacture of most of these boards is the use of a synthetic resin binder, which turns relatively weak and flimsy materials into strong, rigid sheets. Often this resin is a form of formaldehyde, which is a known animal carcinogen and a probable human carcinogen according to the World Health Organisation (WHO). As a constituent of internal fixtures or finishes, it can off-gas inside a building where the amounts may be small, but the exposure can be long term and constant. It is a major source of indoor VOC emissions.

Recommended maximum exposure levels vary from two parts per million (2ppm) for occupational exposure in the UK, to 0.1ppm for the general population, as advised by WHO. There are no recommended maximum levels for exposure to formaldehyde in domestic situations in the UK, although it is acknowledged by the Department of Health that homes with new carpets or furniture could have levels of up to 0.3ppm – or three times the WHO general population limit[33].

Painted or melamine covered boards will off-gas much less. Unsealed boards in warm spots, such as near a cooker or immersion heater, are particularly dangerous. Urea-formaldehyde contains more of the hazardous 'free' formaldehyde, which has not chemically bonded with the timber. Phenol and resorcinol formaldehydes tend to be more stable.

Over recent years, the industry has begun to respond to health and safety concerns by reducing the quantities of formaldehyde used. An alternative binder, methylene bisphenyl di-isocyanate (or MDI), is beginning to replace formaldehyde. It is now used in over 20% of OSB production worldwide, and in some MDF production in North America and Europe. It is a very efficient binder and so accounts for only 3% of the board's weight. However, it is more expensive and has been associated with respiratory problems and skin irritation suffered by workers in the industry.

The production processes for these glues are energy-intensive and polluting, and the raw materials, mainly oil or gas, are non-renewable resources.

In summary

- Use sheet materials only when the use of solid timber would be extravagant or inappropriate. For decorative internal finishes such as floors, skirtings, doors and shelves, natural wood is always preferable to composite boards for reasons of health and aesthetics.
- Use plywood or OSB rather than chipboard or MDF. Plywood probably contains the least glue and so is the best environmental option, although it cannot be made from waste products.
- Seek out and experiment with non-wood fibreboards.
- Maximise the use of the naturally bonded wood fibreboards.
- Avoid all tropical hardwood ply. It is possible to find a plywood for all applications made from softwoods or temperate hardwoods. Always assemble and install with a view to facilitating re-use.
- Avoid chipboard and MDF as much as possible, unless you are prepared to search out, and pay for, the low to zero formaldehyde versions.

7.54

7.55

7.56

Composite/laminated beams

We have probably all seen examples of laminated beams, dramatically arching across a school hall or sports stadium, spanning a distance that would be impossible with conventional timber. They are made from small sections of softwood, glued side by side and end to end with staggered joints, and engineered to carry high loads over long spans. Knots and other defects can be avoided and in any case will not run through the full depth of the beam. Though mostly manufactured by Glulam (the name that has become synonymous with this type of beam), UK-made laminated beams using local timber are available. All of them are usually custom-made to specific requirements.

In so far as they allow timber to be used in this way, as an alternative to steel or concrete, composite beams are a sensible use of resources. The energy cost for the production of a Glulam beam is one-sixth that of a steel beam and one-fifth that of a concrete beam of equal strength. Moreover, value-added uses for short-length, small-section timbers are important for the viability of small-scale timber growers in particular, and the forest industry as a whole.

There are, however, health problems associated with the off-gassing of formaldehyde-based glues, as discussed above. Concern over the effects of using synthetic glues has led to an increased interest in 'mechanical lamination' (i.e. bolting). However, it has been suggested that in the case of a Masonite I-beam, any VOC off-gassing is less than that from natural timber.

Parallel Strand Lumber (PSL) is a more recent product of timber technology and has been used for posts or columns as well as beams. Made from timber strands, with the grains aligned, and the ever present formaldehyde glues, it can be formed into virtually any length (up to 20m), dimension or shape required. Its manufacturers claim a strength-to-weight ratio superior to natural timber, steel or concrete. Although it is supposedly capable of being drilled, nailed and jointed in the normal way, promotional photographs invariably show steel plates used to connect the members at every junction.

Laminated Veneer Lumber (LVL) is made from fast growing trees such as aspen and yellow poplar. Veneer sheets are peeled from logs and glued together with heat and pressure in a process similar to plywood manufacture. Here, however, the wood grains in the veneer sheets are parallel to each other, and lengths up to 24m can be achieved with a width of 1.2m.

Fig. 7.54 Glulam beams spanning the first floor office of Dulas Engineering, Dyfi Eco Business Park, Machynlleth.

Fig. 7.55 These 10m long beams were made locally by laminating together small sections of homegrown larch.

Fig. 7.56 Masonite timber I-beam system for wall studwork, floor joists and rafters.

Photo: Masonite, Byggsystem.

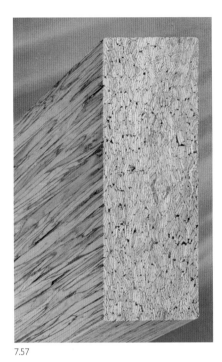

7.57

7.58

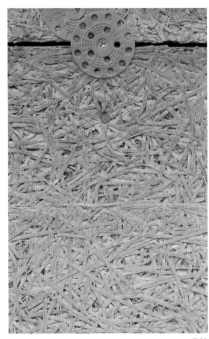

7.59

Plywood beams such as 'Kerto' from Finnforest are much stronger than conventional laminated beams. Presently these are not available with FSC certification.

Timber I-beams, similar in profile to the structurally efficient steel I-beams, are beginning to be widely used in low-energy buildings in this country. One version, called Masonite, is made from small section softwood (usually 50x50mm) at each end, and a connecting web of very strong and dense hardboard with extra long fibres. The formaldehyde content of their glues is said to be low and Masonite beams have been awarded the German Blue Swallow label for minimising environmental impact. Another version uses LVL for the flanges and OSB or plywood as the web. This is used in the Silent Floor joisting system, which claims an absence of creaking noises in the finished floor as, unlike ordinary timber joists, these manufactured I-beam joists are free of warps or twist.

Pre-fabricated timber I-beams can be used for rafters, studs and joists, where the structurally efficient profile can be used to span greater distances, as well as increasing the insulation zone and minimising cold bridging.

All these examples of timber technology have a uniformity and dimensional stability, which is difficult to achieve with natural timber, even when seasoned. Their length is not limited to the height of a tree and their long lengths can increase the strength of a beam by eliminating the need for joints and connections. They are an efficient use of timber, using 35% more of the tree for high-grade products than is possible with ordinary sawn timber.

Cement/wood fibre boards

Woodwool boards, made from wood shavings coated in a cement slurry, can be used for roof decking, infill walls and as a render-carrier, internal partitions, acoustic linings and permanent shuttering. Unfortunately, woodwool/cement boards are no longer made in the UK. A similar product called Heraklith, bonded with magnesite

7.59b

Fig. 7.57 Piece of Parallam Parallel Strand Lumber.

Fig. 7.58 'Silent Floor' timber I-joists, using Laminated Veneer Lumber and Oriented Strand Board.

Fig. 7.59 This building board, made from woodfibres bound together with magnesite, is a strong, breathable, sheathing and render carrier. ('Heraklith').

Fig. 7.59b Laminated Verneered Lumbar (LVL) is a high strength engineered product made from softwood layers. Beams can be up to 600mm deep and 26m long, and is therefore ideal for long spans with minimum deflection. Finnforest Kerto-S shown.

7.60   7.61

instead of cement, is available but imported from Austria. Cement-bonded fibreboards are available for use in high-moisture areas.

Cork

A product of the oak *Quercus suber* which grows on the Iberian peninsula, cork is formed from the bark of the tree, which can be stripped every ten years once the tree is 25 years old. Once stripped, the bark is slowly replenished without harming the tree, so cork is a renewable resource. The stripping process is very low-energy and is carried out mostly by small local producers, who have lost a large part of their market with the advent of plastic corks for wine bottles.

Its main use in eco-buildings is as a waterproof insulation, replacing foamed plastics in cavity walls, 'warm' roofs and under solid ground floors. It is lightweight, durable, and non-flammable, with an attractive grain when used in flooring and veneers. When buying cork tiles, check that they have not been treated with a polyurethane varnish, or backed with vinyl. Cork is a major ingredient in the manufacture of linoleum.

Cellulose fibre

A major constituent of all trees and plants, cellulose fibres are used extensively in the building industry, often as an alternative to asbestos. In fibre-cement sheets, (e.g. Minerit, Masterboard) they provide a cheap, weatherproof surface for cladding. They can be mixed with bitumen to form a corrugated roofing sheet sold as Onduline, which provides a cheaper alternative to corrugated iron, although it has a shorter life. Combined with resins, cellulose fibres are used to make artificial slates.

Cellulose fibres can also be reclaimed from paper products, and from this source comes an insulation material with good environmental credentials. Warmcel is made from unsold newspapers, books, and surplus telephone directories. These are simply shredded and treated with borax and gypsum, as a flame and insect

Fig. 7.60 Cork oak tree growing in Spain. The bottom of the trunk shows where two previous layers of bark have been removed.

Fig. 7.61 Cork slab – a renewable, benign, insulation material. Waterproof and strong, it is ideal for cavity walls and placed under floor slabs. Suppliers include Alumasc, British Cork Mills.

retardant, before being compressed into bales for ease and economy of transport. It is a very low-energy production process and uses recycled materials as the main feedstock.

Because it is a loose-fill material, rather than a board or quilt, Warmcel has the additional performance advantage of filling every nook and cranny with insulation, thus ensuring its effectiveness by avoiding gaps which could form cold bridges. As a result, it was found to be a more effective insulant than rockwool, in tests carried out by Gwalia Housing Association in South Wales.

The drawback is that in most cases it has to be professionally installed. This is done using a machine with rotating blades, which break up and aerate the material before pumping it out through a long flexible hose to wherever it is needed. Where the area to be insulated is horizontal (e.g. roof space or floor), the Warmcel is simply allowed to settle. With vertical spaces such as walls or sloping roofs, the material can be pumped into the closed cavity through small holes under pressure. In the case of a new-build, it can be sprayed directly into wall cavities between timber studs before the plasterboard is fixed, but only up to a maximum depth of 200mm. This is a tricky operation and needs the skills of a trained operator. For small areas of loft or underfloor insulation, you can buy it pre-fluffed and simply cut the bag open and tip it out. Warmcel can only be used in spaces that are protected from moisture and is therefore not suitable for cavities in masonry walls.

Warmcel is manufactured by a South Wales company called Excel, which is extending the use of cellulose to include applications such as brake linings, cement and lime renders, and special road surfaces.

Animal fibres

Animal hair, such as horse and goat hair, has been used for centuries as a filler and binder in plasterwork and render, which was applied much more thickly than is common today. It is still used for the same purpose in modern lime and clay-based plasters.

Wool

Wool has traditionally been used in carpets, and is still regarded as the best quality, though the most expensive carpet. It is soft but hardwearing, dyes well, and provides good thermal and sound insulation. Most of the wool used in British carpets comes from native sheep. Wool carpet is usually treated against moth, with additives such as naphthalene and permethrin.

Sheep's wool is currently attracting much interest as a natural alternative to conventional insulation materials. Wool is renewable, healthy, recyclable and biodegradeable, and fortunately there is now a UK wool insulation product on the market, called Thermafleece, which has BBA approval. This guarantees it as stable, rot-proof and durable, remaining an effective insulant for the life of the building. Produced in batt form, it is easy to install and safe to handle. It has a low thermal conductivity (k = 0.038 W/mK) which compares well with other fibrous insulants, yet has a much lower environmental impact.

The various stages of wool processing are simple and low-energy, and most of them have remained essentially unchanged for the last 200 years. To make an insulation quilt of uniform density, the fleeces need to be scoured and carded (washed and 'combed'), and then bonded together with some kind of adhesive. This is usually a plastic of some kind – PVA or polyester – which melts on heating. One

7.62

7.63

7.64

Fig. 7.62 Trained operator spraying Warmcel into timber stud wall.

Fig. 7.63 Cellulose fibre insulation (Warmcel) is ideal for filling suspended timber floors – as it leaves no gaps.

Fig. 7.64 Natural insulation materials – clockwise from top right: sheep's wool, cellulose fibre, flax quilt, and cork slab.

7.65

7.66

German producer uses latex as the bonding agent. Modest temperatures (120-180°C) are used for scouring, drying and bonding. Treatment against fire, insect and bacteria is usually applied in the form of boric salts and a non-volatile larvacide.

Wool has certain natural properties which offer significant performance advantages. It has a natural 'loft' or springiness, which helps prevent slump, and the fibres have microscopic hooks which key well with rough sawn timber. The coarser wool from mountain sheep has a hollow core and so is a better insulator, which gives this lower-grade product a market advantage for this particular application. Wool is naturally resistant to fire, with a high ignition point (560°C) and gains added fire protection from the presence of water and keratin. Indeed, it tends to melt away from the fire source and self-extinguish. Wool is highly hygroscopic. It can absorb up to 40% of its dry weight in moisture, without significantly affecting its thermal performance, and this makes it particularly suitable for use in 'breathing' construction. Also, 'this can give a latent heat advantage whereby, in winter, absorption of water vapour has a warming effect and in summer, evaporation will have a cooling effect.'[34]. In addition, when latent heat is generated, it may help prevent interstitial condensation by maintaining the temperature above dew-point.

The most serious environmental impact of wool production, and indeed the whole process of sheep rearing, is the still prevalent (though no longer compulsory) use of sheep dip, to treat scab and other parasitic diseases. The chemicals used in dipping were originally organochlorines, now replaced with organophosphates (OPs). These chemicals can be ingested, inhaled or absorbed through the skin. There is some evidence to link OPs with nervous disorders and suicidal depression and it is worth noting that the suicide rate among sheep farmers in this country is twice the national average. Organophosphates are now in turn being replaced with permethrin and other pyrethroids, which have a lower mammalian toxicity, but are highly toxic to aquatic life.

Plant fibres

All of these plant-derived fibres have the ecological advantage of being renewable and biodegradable. They require minimum processing and are sometimes the waste product of another production process.

Jute

Jute is grown in the Ganges delta and yields several crops a year. It began to be imported from India in the early 19th century. Its long fibres must be soaked in water and beaten before use. Together with hemp, it is used to make hessian, the traditional sacking material, used as wall coverings and as a backing for carpets and linoleum. Combined with cellulose fibre, it forms an insulation board marketed as Homatherm. Jute is softer and less hardwearing than sisal.

Coir

Coir fibres come from the husks of coconuts. Tough and durable, they are used to make floor coverings (the old coconut matting of the 1960s and 70s) and rope. In this country, coir is most commonly found as doormats. The husks must be soaked for up to 12 months before the fibres can be extracted, and this has caused some damage to underwater creatures in Indian estuaries, because of the anoxic conditions created in the process.

Fig. 7.65 Carded or combed wool is processed into a wool hank or 'carded sliver'.

Fig. 7.66 Carded slivers of sheep's wool being placed into a timber-frame wall.

7.67   7.68a   7.68b

Sisal

This very long and tough plant fibre comes from the leaf of the Mexican plant *Agave sisalana*. The leaves can grow up to one metre long and are used in cord and matting. However, there is concern about the intensive methods of cultivation, leading to soil erosion, and the effect of sisal dust on factory workers.

Seagrass

This is grown in seawater paddy fields and is used to produce a floor covering that is naturally water and stain resistant (which means it cannot be dyed) and totally antistatic. It is part of an interrelated ecosystem in which mangrove, coral reefs and seagrass flourish by their mutual dependence. Care must be taken that harvesting procedures and rate of extraction do not interfere with or disrupt this system.

Hemp

Hemp is in the process of being rediscovered as a useful crop. Coarse fibres from the stem of the *Cannabis sativa* plant were traditionally used for rope, and the original Levi jeans were made from hemp. New uses for this versatile plant are now being promoted in the areas of textiles, cosmetics, biomass and as an alternative to cellulose or glass fibres in a variety of products from paper to car bodies.

7.68c

Innovative uses of hemp in building materials (e.g. particleboard and insulation) rely on the non-fibrous inner core of the stem, known as 'shiv'. Mixed with hydraulic lime, hemp shiv forms a biocomposite material, which can be cast in situ for infill walls and solid floors. Until recently this was marketed in France as Isochanvre, for which the hemp was treated with a caustic soda solution to produce a 'mineralised' fibre – it was claimed to be resistant to fire and vermin attack, with superior thermal and acoustic performance. Initial tests carried out at CAT and Queen's University Belfast, indicate that untreated, UK grown hemp (marketed as Hemcore for horse bedding) performs at least as well.

Fig. 7.67 Jute matting.
Fig. 7.68a Coir floor covering,
7.68b Sisal,
7.68c Seagrass.

7.69

7.70

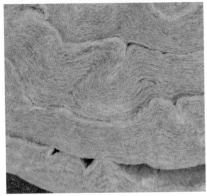

7.71

However, there remains the question of just how good an insulator any compacted material can be. With a conductivity or k-value of around 0.1W/mK, a hemp/lime wall would need to be at least 350mm thick to meet current 2002 Building Regulations. For 'superinsulation', it would need to be double that thickness.

Isochanvre has been used in an experimental scheme of four houses for the Suffolk Housing Society – two houses built with hemp/lime, and two (otherwise identical) houses built with conventional brick-and-block. Aspects of the construction process were monitored and, for four months following completion, comparative temperature and humidity levels were recorded. Results were published by the BRE in 2002[35] under the following headings:

- **Structure and durability** – hemp houses were found to be at least equal to conventional houses.
- **Thermal performance** – heating fuel consumed was roughly equal for both housing types, even though SAP and U-value calculations suggested that the hemp houses would be less well insulated. Hemp houses showed internal temperatures 1°-2°C higher than the brick houses, for the same amount of heat input.
- **Acoustic performance** – hemp houses did not perform as well as conventional, though they did meet the sound resistance requirement.
- **Permeability** – both forms of construction appeared to give adequate protection against water penetration, though the hemp houses generated less condensation.
- **Waste minimisation** – little difference was found between the amount of waste produced by each construction method.
- **Construction costs** – were higher for hemp construction than conventional, and higher for the first hemp house than for the second (due to unfamiliarity with the process). The hemp houses were found to cost £526/m², compared to £478/m² for brick houses.

Flax

Different varieties of the plant *Linum usitatissimum* can be used to produce linseed oil or flax fibres. The longer fibres are reserved for linen production and the shorter fibres can be used for low-grade textiles, papermaking or insulation.

Flax insulation has been used by Groundwork Bridgend in two housing schemes, as part of a study to assess the local market, introduce natural fibre insulation to the social housing sector, and eventually set up a production facility using UK grown hemp and/or flax. In the meantime, the French product used by Groundwork – Natalin – is available in the UK through Natural Building Technologies.

A particle board made from flax shiv is produced in large quantities in Belgium and imported into the UK mainly for the core of fire doors.

Fig. 7.69 Hemcore hemp fibre, produced for horse bedding.

Fig. 7.70 Hemp/lime houses built near Bury St Edmonds, for Suffolk Housing Society. Architects: Modece.

Fig. 7.71 'Natalin' flax insulation.

7.72

7.73

Reed

Matting can be produced by binding together fibres from materials such as reed, usually with galvanised wire. A plaster coat can be applied for an internal finish. Alternatively, reeds can be used as the basic reinforcement of a clayboard, fixed to timber studwork and finished with a clay plaster. Reed is the traditional material in the UK for thatched roofs, being more durable than straw. However, the life spans of both are reduced by artificial fertilisers, which produce 'enlarged and spongy cell growth.'[36a]

Cotton

Cotton is the most widely used plant fibre for clothes and furnishings, and the cotton industry worldwide is a massive one. Cotton is soft and absorbent and comfortable to wear in all seasons. Its basic constituent is cellulose, produced by the hairs that grow round the seed pod of the plant *Gossypium*. The seeds are separated out from the fibres and used for cooking oil and cattle fodder. The coarser fibres can be used for bedding, rayon, and papermaking. Although potentially a naturally derived and healthy product, the intensive farming practices of cotton production have led to much environmental degradation. Insecticides and fungicides are sprayed regularly on to crops during the growing season, and defoliants are used after harvest and before the new crop is sown. The high demand for irrigation can lead to local water shortages.

7.74

Most chemicals are removed from the cotton during the treatment process or on first washing, but some can remain and affect sensitive skin. In particular, formaldehyde resin is used to treat garments that are advertised as being crease-resistant, easy-care or non-iron, and this cannot be washed out. Compulsory additives to retard the spread of flame can also affect health. Virtually all cotton is chemically bleached and, if coloured, the dyes and fixatives used are chemically derived.

It is possible to buy unbleached and/or organically grown cotton. Some treatments are relatively harmless, such as those that pre-shrink or improve colour-fastness – 'mercerised' and 'sanforised' cotton come into this category.

Fig. 7.72 Reed mat used as a render carrier for lime render in an oak frame.

Fig. 7.73 Reed mat as a base for clay plaster.

Fig. 7.74 A thatched roof. The original low-energy, breathable, renewable roof construction – it insulates very nearly to today's standards.

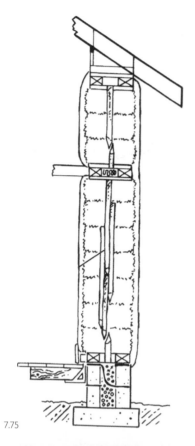

7.75

7.76

Fig. 7.75 Typical wall section for a loadbearing straw bale wall.

Fig. 7.76 The complete renewable walling system. Straw bale walling is low-cost, fast and provides excellent thermal insulation.

Fig. 7.77 A straw bale house built with a mortared bale matrix (Canadian method) by Rene Pelletier, Quebec, 1993. Copyright Barbara Jones.

Fig. 7.78 Straw bale house built for a private client in Ireland by Amazon Nails.

A note on artificial fibres...

Some would argue that the production of artificial fibres is a relatively clean process (with the exception of viscose)[36]. Given the environmental pollution caused by conventional cotton production, this may be a case where 'natural' is not necessarily best. Sometimes artificial fibres are added to natural fibres to increase their strength and durability, e.g. a wool / nylon mix carpet. Acetates and rayon are synthetic fibres that are made from digested wood and plant fibres. Nylon, polyesters, acrylics and polypropylene are based on petroleum derivatives.

Straw

Straw is a by-product of grain production, but has very few agricultural uses apart from animal bedding. There are obvious advantages in finding some constructive application for all this waste material, especially as a replacement for non-renewable or scarce resources.

Compressed Agricultural Fibre (CAF) boards, marketed as Stramit, have a long history of use in construction. The fibres are bonded together at moderate temperatures (200°C) without the use of synthetic adhesives. The UK plant uses 80,000 tonnes of straw per annum to produce 200,000m² of board, of which about one-quarter are exported as archery targets. Otherwise, they are mainly used for internal partitions, as in the Easiwall system, which is held together with metal clips and needs no vertical studs.

Straw bale housing was first developed in the late 1800s, on the treeless plains of Nebraska. Today, this method has become credible and respected for its cheapness, ease of building, and superior insulation properties. Straw bale building is an easily learned and accessible technique, which lends itself well to self-build. A straw bale wall provides reasonably thermal insulation' largely due to its thickness (450mm). With a U-value of 0.2 it performs nearly twice as well as the standard laid down in the current (2002) Building Regulations.

Walls made of straw bales can be fully load bearing or, alternatively, bales can be used as an infill between timber frames. The bales are stacked like giant building blocks, with staggered joints, and pinned to the foundation and to each other with coppiced hazel rods. The walls are then plastered inside and out, ideally with a lime render. Straw bale building is cost-effective, with potential savings of over £4,000 on a normal 3-bedroomed house, compared to brick-and-block construction, and more if self-build labour is used. In addition, straw bale houses are cheap to run, with potential savings of 75% on normal home energy demands.

To date in the UK, several straw bale buildings have received planning permission, including an architect's house and office in Islington, a three-storey building in

7.77

7.78

Ireland, a 95m² farm dwelling in South Wales, and a theatre space at CAT. 'No straw bale building in the UK or Ireland has ever been refused planning permission or building regulation approval on the grounds of it being made of straw, or on the question of durability.'[37]

There is no reason why a well-built and maintained straw bale house should not last at least 100 years. In the USA, there are a dozen or so houses nearing their century and showing no signs of decay. Rodents can be kept out by keeping the render in good repair and avoiding any gaps or cavities. Fireproofing is partly afforded by the two-coat sand/lime render that surrounds the straw. In addition, the high silica content of straw (3-14%) inhibits fire spread and there is very little free oxygen in a compressed bale to support a flame. Fire tests carried out in New Mexico found that a 450mm thick bale, plastered on both sides, survived fire penetration for more than two hours and even an unplastered bale survived for 34 minutes.

The main danger to the integrity of a straw bale building is damp. If bales get wet at any time, during construction or occupation, then they must be cut out and replaced or they will eventually rot away. Like earth buildings, details such as a high plinth wall and overhanging eaves are essential for protection against excessive weathering. 'The key to durability is good design, good quality work, and maintenance.'[37]

Oils and resins

Paints and stains

All paints and stains are either water-based or solvent-based. Where a solvent is used, it can either be chemically produced, such as white spirit, or derived from naturally occurring plants, such as citrus peel oil. Natural or organic paints and stains use plant-based solvents, fillers, and dyes – renewable resources that will biodegrade on disposal. The production process is simple and uses relatively little energy.

All solvents are designed to evaporate – this is how paint dries – and therefore the constituents are easily inhaled. Although some people do have an allergic response to the solvents in natural paints (plant-based turpentine is still toxic when inhaled), this is far less prevalent and serious than exposure to the petrochemical solvents in conventional paints. It is important to ventilate the work area when using any solvent.

Organic paints are available for plasterwork, wood and metal; stains for internal and external woodwork; and waxes for floors and furniture. The plant-based solvents will react with the natural oils and resins in untreated wood, creating a chemical bond and a breathable finish, rather than an impervious coating that is liable to crack and flake.

Marketed by small producers or imported from Europe, these products tend to be more expensive than the bottom-of-the-range chemical equivalents. But their use is absolutely integral to the achievement of a healthy, allergen-free internal environment.

Some paints that claim to be natural actually contain synthetic ingredients. It is worth looking for a full declaration of contents, as given by manufacturers such as Auro and Aglaia.

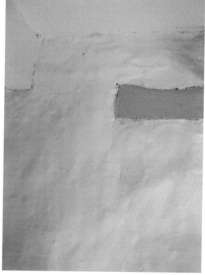

7.79a

7.79b

Fig. 7.79a Breathable internal mineral paint bonds to the plaster. Keim Paints.

Fig. 7.79b Layers of age – generations of limewashes coloured with earth pigments, on a Welsh cottage wall.

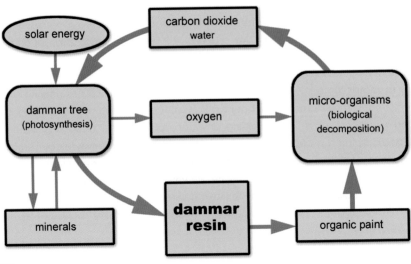

7.80a

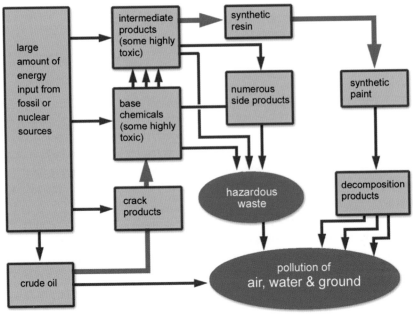

7.80b

Glues

Adhesives can be produced from animal products – bone, hide, or casein (made from soured milk) – and vegetable products, such as starches, gum arabic and tragacanth. These glues tend to be water-soluble and only suitable for interior use. Pitch and latex rubber are also naturally occurring adhesives.

In summary

- Wherever possible, use animal and plant fibres, sustainably and organically produced, for furnishings, floor and wall coverings.
- Use organic paints and stains for all internal and external decoration and preservation of timber.

Fig. 7.80a & 7.80b Paintwars: the ingredients of organic paints can be recycled or will biodegrade naturally, unlike synthetic paints.

- Seek out and try out ways of building using radically different, benign materials, e.g. straw bale, wool insulation.
- Think again before gluing down things such as floor coverings. Gluing it means that the item cannot be re-used.

Earth materials

Introduction

All the following, widely used, bulk building materials are gained by digging something out of the ground. Used in their raw state, without further processing, they have a low embodied energy per tonne. However, the large quantities needed to construct a building, together with their high density, means that masonry materials are often the greatest single contributor to the total embodied energy costs of that building.

The loss of non-renewable resources must be the greatest ecological impact, but the local and immediate effects of quarrying are often more apparent. These include noise, dust, vibration and increased heavy traffic, as well as disturbance of wildlife habitats and effects on water quality and availability. These damaging effects can be mitigated by the producer, through the institution of a responsible environmental management programme including site restoration, and by designers and builders by avoiding over-specification and extravagant use.

Proposals for new, opencast quarrying have been resisted by many communities: in much the same way that new road construction has become a focus of protest among environmentalists. The promise of newly created local jobs rarely seems to materialise, and there is perhaps even more concern at the prospect that the site may convert to landfill once quarrying is exhausted.

While a limited amount of surface extraction may be environmentally acceptable – and is certainly necessary to a modern construction industry – most environmentalists agree that reductions in resource consumption of 80-90% over the next 50 years, are necessary to achieve a sustainable rate of use, together with equal rights of access to that resource[38]. The work that has been done on 'environmental footprinting' points to an over-consumption of the earth's resources by a factor of three. In other words, we would need three planets to fulfil our current demands in a sustainable way, which, of course, we don't have.

Rock

Stone

Through the ages, people have built out of stone if they were fortunate enough to live near to an outcrop of granite, slate, flint, limestone, or sandstone. Once dug out of the ground, virtually no extra processing was required, apart from cutting and trimming the blocks.

Old stone buildings were generally very durable and strong with massively thick walls, which acted as a heat store and buffer against extremes of temperature before the days of insulation. The stones were resistant to water penetration, yet stone walls were generally able to 'breathe' through the mortar joints or through the gaps in a dry wall construction. Many are still standing, and in our major cities, they form the noblest of the older civic buildings, often extending to five or six storeys high.

7.81a

7.81b

7.82

Fig. 7.81a Cotswold stone is locally quarried and easily shaped to form a timeless roof finish.
Architect: David Lea.

Fig. 7.81b Huge Lancashire sandstone slabs forming the simplest of roofs.

Fig. 7.82 Stone wall in a derelict former convent on Iona, Scotland.

7.83a

7.83b

7.83c

7.84

Fig. 7.83a, b & c Ashlar stone walling. The precise narrow joints, the textures and the colours make ashlar the perfect surface for both ancient and modern buildings. Photo: David Lea.

Fig. 7.84 Locally sourced, cut and tapered slate blocks forming an arch over the water intake for the cliff railway at CAT.

Fig. 7.85 Slate pillars with a minimal amount of lime mortar, support the roof and form an entranceway.

7.85

Nowadays, building with stone in the structural sense is rare. At most, it is used as a cladding, often at the request of the local Planning Authority, concerned to replicate the 'vernacular'. Occasionally the cladding is real stone, skilfully laid with fine mortar joints, but more often any 'stone' used will be a synthetic, reconstituted product, made of crushed stone mixed with a resin binder or cement.

Pre-cut, polished pieces of slate or granite are now sold as counter tops, fire surrounds or flooring. Their high price reflects the quality and precious nature of the raw material, as well as the labour that goes into the extraction and processing. Transport energy costs can be very high owing to the density and weight of stone.

Slate

Although slate was used in big blocks for walls in areas where it occurred naturally, its traditional use in building has been as a superior roof covering. Its environmental impact is similar to that of stone, although there is a much higher wastage rate for slate. Only good quality slate can be used for roofing and the main geological areas for slate extraction are in North Wales and Cumbria.

Although a small slate industry remains in these areas, its relatively high price often prohibits the use of new British slate, (unless it is specified for use in a conservation area or historic building). Instead, artificial or imported slates are more commonly used. It does seem insane that slates from Spanish or Chinese quarries can be imported and sold for about half the price of home-produced ones, but sadly this is the case. As imported slate is generally of inferior quality, it is better to find second-hand Welsh or Cumbrian slate through specialist suppliers, if you are about to roof or re-roof a building.

Roofing slate is extremely durable and can be re-used many times. In most cases when a roof leaks, it will be the fixings or flashings that have failed, rather than the slates themselves. If you are stripping an old slate roof, take great care to remove the slates intact. You should be able to save most of them and either re-use them or sell them on.

Avoid fibre-cement artificial slates, which have a short life and an unpleasantly homogeneous appearance. Asbestos-cement artificial slates are in use on many

7.86

buildings re-roofed in the last 40-50 years, and constitute a present and future health hazard. Other artificial slates are made from slate dust and resin.

Aggregate

The term aggregate covers sand, gravel, broken stone, and brick fragments. Coarser aggregate is used mainly for concrete and hardcore, while sand is used in mortar for brickwork, external rendering and glass production.

In a conventionally built brick and block house, the masonry material composed of clay, sand, gravel and cement, can form up to 80% of the weight of the whole building. At the current rate of new building, this will lead to three cubic miles (12 km^3) of aggregate being extracted annually. As the more accessible sites in non-sensitive areas become exhausted, so pressure is growing from the construction lobby for permission to extract from sites in National Parks and other protected areas.

One way to curtail this burgeoning demand for aggregate is to encourage building developers to make greater use of structural timber frame, if necessary with a brick or rendered block outer skin. This system, while looking exactly the same from the outside as a conventional masonry house, uses a lot less aggregate and also makes it easier to comply with the latest Building Regulation requirements for thermal insulation.

Aggregates may be sourced from the waste products of other industrial processes. These are known as 'secondary aggregates', but they also have a cementitious effect and can replace up to 50% of the cement content in a concrete mix. The most common sources are pulverised fuel ash (PFA) from coal-fired power stations, or ground, granulated blast furnace slag (GGBS) from the steel producing industry. These have been used in projects like the Channel Tunnel and Thames Barrier, and have certain performance and cost advantages.

The use of secondary aggregate in structural concrete or concrete blocks is often promoted as an environmentally beneficial choice, since it replaces a precious finite resource and limits the effects of quarrying, as well as solving a waste disposal problem. The Government has set targets for increased use of secondary

Fig. 7.86 The strength and precision of natural slate make it perfect for complex roof shapes.

7.87

7.88

7.89

Fig. 7.87 Recycled glass as aggregate for mortars and renders.

Fig. 7.88 Lime render using ground recycled glass to replace sand in the mix. The mix, known as Glaster is produced by TyMawr Lime, Brecon.

Fig. 7.89 Rockwool quilt being unrolled in a loftspace.

aggregates as a percentage of total aggregate use, and has introduced the 'Aggregates Tax' to discourage the extraction of primary resources.

There is concern, however, that these materials may contain pollution from the original processing, or present health risks from other sources. Toxic ash from municipal incinerators has been widely distributed to the building trade, for use in breeze blocks and roads.* The use of secondary materials is also questionable, to the extent that it relies on by-products from industrial processes, that are unsustainable.

Lytag

A lightweight aggregate ('Lytag'), made from pelletising and sintering PFA, provides a source of structural lightweight concrete. With densities of 1500-1900kg/m³, and a compressive strength of 20-70N/mm², it has good durability and better thermal performance than OPC concrete. It can also be used for insulating floor and roof screeds, offering improved acoustic, as well as thermal, insulation and using only half the cement of a conventional mix.

There is considerable scope for recycling demolition waste as aggregates or hardcore fill, as well as road construction. Sorted, uncontaminated material can be crushed and then sieved to produce the required grading for engineering fill. More mixed, less processed rubble can be used for general fill and landscaping.

Marine dredging for aggregates, which can threaten the aquatic ecosystem and lead to coastal erosion, should only be allowed under strict environmental guidelines.

Mineral wool

Rockwool, one of the most commonly used insulation products, is one version of mineral wool and is one of the few products known almost exclusively by its brand name. It is made from volcanic rock heated up with coke to 1500°C, and then spun at high speed in a drum pierced with small holes to produce long thin fibres. These fibres are then bound together in a batt or roll with formaldehyde-based resins.

The use of formaldehyde is one health hazard associated with the production and use of mineral wool. Another comes from the possible inhalation of the fibres, now thought to be small enough to be as carcinogenic as asbestos. Workers in the industry have been found to have a risk of lung cancer 25% above normal, 30 years after first being employed. In the US, mineral fibre insulation products carry the warning: 'Possible cancer hazard by inhalation'.

Installing Rockwool may cause skin rash, or irritation to eyes, nose, throat and lungs. Even for casual DIY use, protective gloves and masks should always be worn. If it becomes damp, mineral wool may offgas aliphates, aromates and ketones into the building which in turn may cause ear, nose and throat irritation[39]. Additives in mineral wool make it susceptible to mould growth. It has been suggested that mineral wool should only be installed in areas that are normally inaccessible and from which air infiltration into the building is impossible[40].

Despite these risks, Rockwool is popular because it is relatively cheap and easy to install. The raw materials are abundant and in terms of its overall environmental impact, it is probably a lot better than the plastic sheets and foams that are its main commercial rivals. But it is not as benign as cellulose fibre insulation, or some of the newer products based on wool, flax, or hemp.

*(Guardian 5/7/01). Fly ash containing dioxins (167,000 times more toxic than cyanide) was mixed with bottom ash containing heavy metal residues and sold to Ballast Phoenix in Lincolnshire by the Edmonton incinerator. BBC TV's 'Newsnight' tested a breeze block made using 30% ash from the ballast company site and found dioxins 10-20 times greater than the permitted level.

The Rockwool Company claims to take environmental concerns seriously. It publishes its own environmental policy statement in which it is claimed that over the lifetime of a building insulated with Rockwool, CO_2 emissions are reduced by 300-1500 times the amount released during manufacture. Independent experts monitor the emissions of gases and particulates from the production process. The headquarters is an energy efficient building, overlooking a pond reclaimed from an old slurry pit, and the company has sponsored a tree bank nursery on its factory site. In the last few years it has installed two fly-ash filters and a plant for recycling waste materials.

7.90

Vermiculite

This is a form of mica or lightweight volcanic rock, mined from open quarries. The process of 'exfoliation' involves heating the rock to the point where steam is generated inside the material (800-1100°C), thereby trapping air and producing a lightweight, granular, loose-fill insulation. Like perlite, it can also be used as an insulating aggregate for lining old chimneys. It is heat-resistant and can be used to insulate around metal flues and other high temperature equipment.

Perlite

This is a type of volcanic rock with a high silicium dioxide content, usually expanded for use as insulation, either loose or in concrete blocks and slabs. It is pulverised and heated to temperatures of 900-1200°C, which increases its volume between five and twenty times. Small amounts of silicon or bitumen may be added to prevent the material absorbing moisture. It can therefore be used in cavity wall construction. When exposed to even higher temperatures naturally it becomes pumice. The largest deposits are found in Iceland, though it is also present in Greece, Hungary and the Czech Republic.

Unfired earth

Earth is one of the most immediate and locally available materials it is possible to build with. It is also one of the cheapest and lowest impact construction methods. Most construction activity begins with clearing earth away from the site of the building, and in many cases, this excavated material could be used in the construction, although it is the subsoil rather than the topsoil that is required. Over 70% of the earth's landmass is either pure clay or laterite (a clay with some iron content) and over one-third of the world's population lives in houses built from earth[41].

There is archaeological evidence to show the existence of entire cities built of earth, such as Jericho and Babylon, some 10,000 years old. And we are not talking here of mud huts or primitive housing, but imposing temples and monuments – including the Tower of Babel, which was seven storeys high. Earth buildings dating from the 7th century BC have been excavated in China, and the greatest earthen construction of all, the Great Wall, was begun over 5000 years ago.

Different construction techniques were introduced into different countries by invaders who then settled. The conquering Roman armies introduced rammed earth building to the South East of France, in the area of the Rhone valley where the capital of Roman Gaul, Lugdunum, was situated, and where the foothills of the Alps provided earth of a suitable composition. When the Moors invaded Spain from the south, they brought with them a kind of mud brick construction known as adobe,

Fig. 7.90 Expanded perlite is an excellent mineral insulation for cavity walls and under slabs.

7.91

7.92a

7.92b

7.93a

7.93b

Fig. 7.91 One of several pisé houses built in Wiltshire in 1919 – at a time of dire materials shortages – for the Ministry of Agriculture. From 'Building in cob, pisé and stabilized earth', Clough Williams-Ellis 1919.

Fig. 7.92a & 7.92b Pisé is a traditional construction technique of southern France that is undergoing a strong revival.

Fig. 7.93a This Nepali 'gompa' is a multi-storey monastery built of rammed earth, painted in pigmented limewash.

Fig. 7.93b Rammed earth construction is still used today in Nepal, in areas where there is little timber and no cement.

more suited to heavier clay soils, and this technology in turn accompanied the Spanish invasion of South America. From there it spread north to Mexico and the south-western USA, where it survives today in the form of the much-cultivated 'Santa Fe' style. In Australia, the first earth buildings appeared during the gold rush period of the 1850s and in the vast treeless deserts of Central Australia earth construction was often the most practical option.

In 19th century central Europe earth building flourished. It was revived after the first and second World Wars – in the UK by pioneering architect Clough Williams-Ellis. The tradition of cob building in Devon, or 'clom' in parts of Wales, is now being rediscovered by 'eco' developers and particularly by self-builders.

Environmental advantages

In general, earth construction involves a very low external energy input, and creates virtually no pollution. Historically of course, the energy required to dig up and treat sufficient earth for a house, was all provided by humans and animals. Nowadays, mechanical extraction and mixing is the more likely method, but assuming the earth is sourced fairly locally to the site, it is still a very low-energy form of construction.

The transportation of large amounts of earth is potentially an energy-intensive and polluting process. However, the distances involved are rarely that great and the overall energy cost is certainly much lower than the conventional alternatives of cement, sand and aggregates.

All earth buildings tend to have a high 'thermal mass', as earth is a dense material, particularly when compressed. This means that it can absorb and store solar energy, and re-release it in the form of heat when the building cools down, usually in the evening. Earthen elements therefore have the effect of modifying temperature extremes internally, and are more comfortable and energy efficient than many conventionally built houses. Being hygroscopic, they can also regulate humidity levels, which is thought to be an important factor in achieving good indoor air quality.*

Earth is not a particularly good insulator, but its performance can be improved by adding organic fibres or lightweight mineral aggregates. On the whole though, it is not suitable for external walls without additional insulation.

On demolition, the components may be recycled or, if left, will simply revert to earth.

Rammed earth

Rammed earth, or pise de terre, consists of moist, loose subsoil compacted between shuttering, or formwork, in layers of 100-150mm depth. The mechanical compaction compresses this depth to about half, and forces the clay molecules to bond with the various aggregates in a physical rather than a chemical process (as with cement). The forms are then moved along or upwards to form a whole wall.

Knowing the exact composition of the soil and the correct amount of water to be added, are critical for the success of this method. At CAT, researching suitable sources of earth for our Environmental Information Centre (AtEIC), we had tests carried out on various samples to determine the following:

- Clay content: our best samples were only 8% clay, and as rammed earth was thought to need a clay content of between 15% and 30%, we added a further 8% pure powdered clay.
- Particle size distribution: ideally, a good sample should have an even distribution of different size particles, from fine silt through to small aggregate. In our case the largest diameter aggregate was 6mm – everything bigger was screened out before construction.
- Compressive strength: our best samples showed a compressive strength of 2.29 Newtons/mm^2 – well in excess of what is needed to support a lightweight, two-storey building.
- Optimum moisture content: this was found to be 8%, which meant adding very little water before ramming. Our main problem was keeping the earth dry!

*The oldest European earth building, dating from 1270, is a library in central France used for storing antique, moisture-sensitive books.

When building our rammed earth walls, we used a modified version of the 'Californian' system, described in David Easton [41]. The shuttering was phenol-faced ply (to give a smooth finish) laid on edge so that the maximum width of a panel was 2.4 metres, and the panels butted together every 1.2 metres up the wall. The wall panels were cast as separate units with a 150mm gap in between. This allowed space for a series of sash cramps holding the plywood sheets against an end board the width of the wall. Great care was taken to ensure that the shuttering box, was vertical and square. Sitting on the sash cramps either side of the ply were 200x50mm walers, at 300mm centres to stiffen the sheets and prevent them from bowing. The whole construction was dismantled and reused for successive panels, and columns.

7.94a

7.94b

7.94c

7.95

Figs. 7.94a Scaffolding showing endboard and walers held in place by sash cramps.
7.94b, The position of the wall under the king post allowed builders access to the top of the rammed earth panel.
7.94c One panel freshly stripped of its shuttering, then set up for the next panel to the right.
Fig. 7.95 The finished product.
Architect: Pat Borer, Consultants: Simmonds & Mills.

7.96a

7.96b

7.97

7.96c

Where stabilisers such as lime or cement are considered necessary, these should be kept to a minimum. Where they are used routinely, as with most modern earth construction in Australia, some of the environmental benefits are eroded. Because of the relatively dry mix, shrinkage of rammed earth elements is much less than for other earth building methods, and the strength is correspondingly higher. In CAT's AtEIC building, the rammed earth walls and columns are loadbearing and support the weight of the roof. Over a period of up to two years a rammed earth wall will dry out and become as durable as sandstone, as long as it is protected from damp.*

Fig. 7.96a Rammed earth wall forming part of the visitor centre at the Eden project, Cornwall.

Fig. 7.96b The powerful elliptical walls of this 'Chapel for Reconciliation' contain materials from a church demolished to make way for the Berlin Wall. Rammed earth: Martin Rauch. Architect: Peter Sassenroth.

Fig. 7.96c A beautifully textured wall built from chalk found on site. The Kindersley Centre. Architects: Alex French Partnership.

Fig. 7.97 Five-storey apartment block, built of compressed earth blocks, at Domaine de la Terre, near Grenoble, France.

*The tallest earth building in Europe is in Weilburg, Germany. Built in 1828, it has seven storeys and rammed earth walls tapering from 750mm to 400mm thick.

7.98

7.99

7.100

Fig. 7.98 Devonshire Cob house: Keppel Gate, built 2003 by Kevin McCabe. www.buildsomethingbeautiful.com

Fig. 7.99 Curved rammed earth wall with cement mortar coursing and edges, Domaine de la Terre, Grenoble, France.

Fig. 7.100 Rammed earth walls on stone plinths finished with clay plaster, in Morocco. David Easton [41].

Cob

This is the main form of earth building to be found in Britain, in parts of East Anglia, the East Midlands and West Wales – but particularly in Devon, where hundreds of Devonshire cob houses are still standing, the earliest dating back to the 15th century. In this method the sub-soil is mixed with straw and water, and then pounded or trodden until it reaches a suitable consistency. It is then laid in horizontal layers and again trodden down to form free-standing mass walls. The use of timber shuttering was a late development, from the 1820s onwards. Especially in wet climates like the British one, cob walls need to be laid on raised stone foundations and protected with overhanging eaves.

Mud brick or adobe

This method of earth construction has been common throughout Asia, North Africa, and South America for thousands of years. Adobe or sun-dried earth blocks can be made from most types of sub-soil, and they will tolerate heavier clays than are suitable for rammed earth. Enough clay is required to bind the mix together, but not so much that the block cracks on drying.

The earth is trodden to a paste, often by animals, then mixed with chopped straw, pushed or thrown into moulds, and left to dry in the sun. The blocks are then laid with a mud and lime mortar, rendered with a mud and dung mix, and/or limewashed. Mud bricks have the advantage of being simple to make and therefore appropriate for unskilled labour. They can be produced all at once, or in small batches, as and when time permits. The quality can be checked, and any suspect bricks rejected, before they are built into a wall.

Compressed/stabilised blocks

Stabilised or unstabilised mixes can be compressed in a machine such as a CINVA Ram or an 'Elephant Blockmaker': both are able to exert a large amount of pressure on the mould. Blocks are produced in standard sizes and allowed to dry, under cover, for several weeks. They can then be laid in a lime or clay-based mortar and rendered with the same. Stabilised earth blocks are made stronger and more durable by the addition of small amounts of lime or cement (5-10%). Bitumen may also be added as a water repellent.

7.101

7.102

7.103

7.104

Lightweight earth

The original 'Leichtlehm' or 'Light Earth' was developed in Germany, in the 1920s, using straw in clay slurry. Recent developments in earth construction have incorporated lightweight mineral aggregates or plant fibres, in an attempt to increase the thermal performance of earth walls to meet stricter Building Regulations. (Even then, earth walls have to be very thick – about 800mm – to meet current required U-values.)

These mixes can be extruded into moulds for block production, or into cotton hoses to create earth 'sausages', and used for infill walls in a frame construction.

Fig. 7.101 Vaults, arches and domes of compressed earth bricks in a Berlin kindergarten. Architect Gernot Mincke.

Fig. 7.102 Vaulted ceiling made from compressed earth bricks, Terre Vivante environmental centre, France.

Fig. 7.103 Manufacturing compressed earth blocks using a three-worker 'Elephant' press.

Fig. 7.104 Compressed earth blocks, stacked for drying.

7.105

7.106

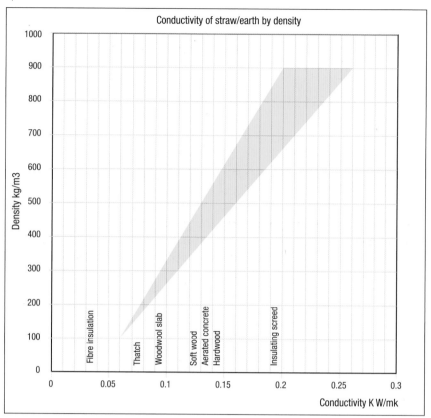

7.107

7.108

Fig. 7.105 'Light earth' – a German product made of earth, straw and recycled glass beads. The damp mixture is tamped between shuttering set around a timber frame.

Fig. 7.106 Lightweight loam extruded into cotton hoses, and packed into a timber frame, Germany. Architect Gernot Mincke.

Fig. 7.107 Table showing a direct relationship between density and conductivity in straw/clay walls. The more compacted the material, the less good it will be as an insulator.

Fig. 7.108 Straw fibres coated with a clay slurry and packed between timber studs, Scotland. Architect: Chris Morgan.

Lightweight, insulating earth can also be sprayed between timber studwork to create prefabricated panels.

In this country, cob is a form of light earth construction, though using more earth than straw, while a straw/clay mix has recently been used for a small domestic building by Gaia Architects in Scotland.

Lightweight Expanded Clay Aggregate (LECA)

This is made from clay heated to 115°C, in a rotary kiln, to form a granular material with a hard ceramic shell surrounding a honeycomb core. It is available in pellets from 4mm to 20mm diameter and is 75% less dense than traditional aggregate. It is used in the production of lightweight concrete blocks and for insulating under solid ground floors.

Clay plasters

Usually a mix of clay (5-12%), fine sand and fibres, this can be used instead of standard gypsum plaster, to create a self-coloured wall finish with a slightly rough and rustic texture. It is best applied to a clay/reed/hessian backing board, which can be fixed to the inside of a timber frame. Unlike gypsum, it is very slow to 'go off' and can be reworked indefinitely. It will wear away through abrasion and should be used with care in public areas with heavy traffic.

Turf roofs

For low pitched roofs (5°-15°) turf sods, or just plain seeded earth can be used as the roof finish. This is laid on top of a tough, waterproof membrane, which is itself laid loose over a deck of boards and restrained at the edges. It is possible to use a cheaper membrane such as ordinary builder's polythene or roofing felt, but this will give a much shorter life, as the polythene will eventually degrade and roots will penetrate the felt.

Many claims of eco-friendliness are made for these 'green roofs', but in fact they rely on a high-energy, high-impact, plastic or synthetic rubber membrane for a reasonably long life. The turf itself is not a good insulator, so you will still need insulation between or under the rafters in the normal way and the rafters themselves may need to be increased in depth to accommodate the extra weight.

However, there are some microclimatic benefits, particularly in cities, from any area of green growth. The attenuation of rainwater runoff can help to avoid flooding in vulnerable areas subject to sudden high rainfall. Grass roofs can accommodate bulbs and wild flowers. They do not need mowing, as the growth will be self-regulating due to the limited depth of soil. If you have had to remove topsoil in order to build, it can be satisfying to put that soil back on top of the building, thus closing the circle and allowing the building to blend in with its landscape.

There are a number of green roof 'systems' on the market – mostly unnecessarily complicated and expensive. Many of them use sedum instead of grass as the vegetation. This has the advantage of being shallow-rooted and drought-tolerant, and generally looks 'tidier' than the slightly rough and shaggy appearance of turf sods. It's probably not worth buying lawn turf as the roof will eventually become colonised with the tougher 'couch' grass, more able to withstand greater exposure and less depth of soil.

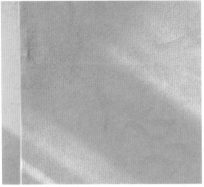

7.109

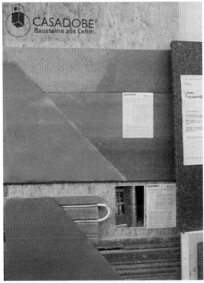

7.110

7.111

Fig. 7.109 Clay plaster, coloured with earth pigments.

Fig. 7.110 Some clay and earth products available for walling.

Fig. 7.111 Food store at CAT recently re-roofed with an elastomeric membrane and finished with a mix of turf and sedum (see Fig. 7.112).

Fig. 7.112 From John Willoughby and David Olivier 'Review of Ultra Low Energy Homes', Report for BRECSU 1996, Profile no 9: Birchdene Drive Self-Build scheme. Architects: Architype Ltd.

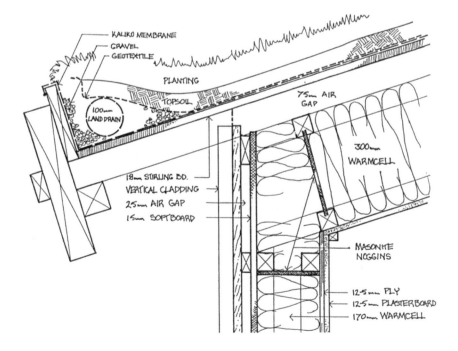

7.112

7.113

7.114

7.115

Fig. 7.113 Old terracotta (literally 'fired earth') floor tiles.

Fig. 7.114 Fired clay bricks, whilst having a high embodied energy content, are long-lasting and durable. Lime mortars should be used to ensure they can always be re-used.

Fig. 7.115 Fired clay 'Roman tiles' are shaped to shed the rain easily.

Fired clay

Bricks and tiles

When clay is heated in kilns to high temperatures (up to 2000°C), it gains very good compressive strength and weather resistance, but at the environmental expense of the energy used and pollution created in the firing process. However, the average energy used in brick production has fallen from 945kWh/tonne in 1976 to 764 kWh/tonne in 1986, since when it has remained fairly constant[42]. Some types of kiln are more energy efficient than others – for example, the continuous rather than the intermittent kiln. At least one brick producer is using methane to fuel its kilns, collected from landfill sites occupying the quarries created by clay extraction[42a]!

Fired clay is used to produce bricks, roof tiles, drainage pipes, and glazed tiles for walls and floors. In France and Spain, hollow clay bricks, blocks and tiles are widely used. Fired expanded clay pellets can also be used as insulation, usually under solid floors. (See LECA above.)

Different clays are required to produce the many different types of brick and tile available today. Some is to be found on the earth's surface – in river beds for instance. Some fire clays are only found underground and need to be mined. Whether clay is quarried or mined, a policy of site restoration should be practised, and potential purchasers could enquire whether this is the case.

Most bricks and tiles nowadays are made by mass production techniques, and the once small, local brickworks have been centralised into a few large production facilities. The link between brick buildings and the colour and quality of the local soil has been lost. Ironically, 'handmade' bricks, with their variations in shape and colour, are becoming popular for quality bedpoke projects. Reclaimed bricks are now available relatively easily and these offer the same aesthetic advantages, as well as financial saving. Otherwise, use ordinary perforated clay bricks from a local supplier.

7.116

7.117

The embodied energy of bricks could be minimised by builders using low- and medium-fired bricks (or even unfired bricks) in internal partitions and non-loadbearing walls. For every 100°C increase in the firing temperature, another 0.2MJ of energy is used per kilogram of bricks[43]. However, in general the only bricks that are widely available are vitrified or well-fired bricks, sold for all-purpose use.

When laying bricks, use a hydraulic lime mortar (or keep the cement content as low as possible), in order to maintain the inherent porosity and vapour-diffusing properties of the brickwork, and to facilitate re-use.

Calcium silicate bricks and blocks

Bricks made from calcium silicate, using only silica, sand, lime and water, are widely used in Europe (70% of Dutch housing). They are also made in the UK and come in a variety of colours and finishes. These bricks are not fired, but cured by steaming at high pressure for 4-12 hours, which gives them a relatively high embodied energy count. However, they are high-strength, durable and can be made frost-resistant. Pulverised Fuel Ash may be used as a part replacement for the sand.

Lime

Historically, powdered lime has been used extensively for the fertilisation of crops, and disused limekilns can still be found beside many former harbours, up and down the coast, where the limestone was imported. Lime is still in great demand for a whole range of uses in industry and agriculture as well as construction. This demand is fuelling the pressure to excavate hitherto unexploited sources of limestone, often from areas of outstanding natural beauty such as the Peak District and the Yorkshire Dales.

Originally meaning 'sticky material', lime was the ultimate binder of other materials in construction. Before the advent of cement, lime was mixed with sand and fillers, such as coarse hair or fine gravel, for use as mortars and renders. Nowadays, hydrated or 'bagged' lime – an inferior version of 'pure' lime – is often used as an additive to cement mortar or render to make the mix more plastic and pliable. Lime is also a basic ingredient of Portland cement, plasterboard and plaster finishes, and some bricks and blocks.

7.118

Fig. 7.116 Powerful and simple – just bricks.
Architect: Louis Kahn.

Fig. 7.117 Perforated hollow bricks and blocks – one of the commonest constructions on the European continent – offer better thermal insulation than plain bricks, and use less material.

Fig. 7.118 Sand-lime blockwork has better environmental credentials than cement concrete. A Dutch thin-bed panel system is shown that offers speed and economy.

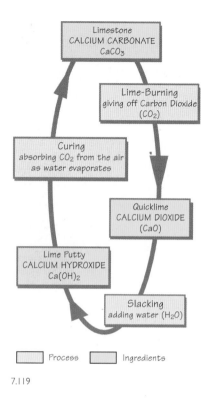

7.120

7.121

7.119

7.122

Fig. 7.119 The Lime Cycle shows how lime mortars and renders turn back into calcium carbonate, absorbing the CO_2 given off in the firing.

Fig. 7.120 Roughcast render is a very durable finish. Porthmadog. Architect: David Lea.

Fig. 7.121 Locally grown oak lath clads the inside of this timber frame house – ready for plastering. Lampeter. Architect: David Lea.

Fig. 7.122 The straw bale theatre at CAT with a lime render made up of 1 part hydraulic lime to 3 parts sand.

The manufacture of lime involves heating crushed limestone or chalk to high temperatures (800-900°C) to produce quicklime or calcium oxide. The quicklime, which is caustic and unstable, is then slaked or hydrated by adding water, to form calcium hydroxide or lime putty. In the production process, large amounts of CO_2 are given off from a chemical reaction within the kiln, but unlike cement, pure lime mortars will reabsorb all of that CO_2 as they dry out and harden over a number of years, converting back into calcium carbonate or limestone. On demolition, bricks and stones in a lime-based mortar or render will separate and clean up much more easily, and are therefore more likely to be re-used.

Lime is less dense than cement, so although it is more expensive, less will be needed to make a standard mortar mix. To produce 1m³ of mortar requires 240kg of cement (1:6) or 200kg of lime (1:3). There is no doubt that cement is the stronger material, but is often used in strengths that are unnecessarily high.

Lime putty

Lime putty is made by adding water to quicklime, enough to make a thick creamy paste, and is the basis for all lime renders, plasters, mortars and washes. It is unwise to try and do this yourself as the procedure can be dangerous – buy it ready-made from one of the specialist suppliers. Don't be tempted to make do with the 'bagged' hydrated lime that is commonly available in builders' merchants. It is a poor substitute and will not perform well in pure lime applications.

Lime putty must be made with freshly slaked lime, covered with water, and allowed to mature for at least six weeks (the longer, the better). For mortars, plasters and renders, the putty must be thoroughly mixed with sand (in the proportion 1:3 lime:sand), plus other aggregates and fillers as required. Animal hair (cow or goat is traditional, though yak hair is now often used) can be added to form a matrix of fibres which binds the mix together. This is a slow and laborious job by hand, but it can also be done in a drum mixer. No water is added. This 'coarse stuff' (as it is called) is ready for use after it has been stored in plastic, or wet sacks in airtight bins, for a minimum of two weeks.

It is obvious from this description that the use of pure lime products is labour intensive, needs planning for well in advance and is not conducive to the quick-build, fast track approach of the modern construction industry. On the other hand, it will be used and appreciated by those lovingly restoring old buildings in an authentic way, and by ecologically-minded builders looking for a low-energy, 'soft' finish that will breathe and move with the building itself.

Hydraulic lime

Hydraulic lime is produced as for pure limes, but using certain limestones containing impurities of silica and alumina. It has the practical advantage of a quick initial chemical set (like cement) on the outer surface, followed by a much slower process of carbonation (like lime). It is therefore easier to integrate its use with the demands of modern construction practice, where 'time is money'.

However, this convenience comes at an environmental cost, with hydraulic lime needing firing temperatures of about 1200°C – somewhere in between pure lime and cement – and absorbing only about 50% of the CO_2 given off in the production process. Hydraulic lime has about half to two-thirds the strength of Ordinary Portland Cement (OPC) and uses about 30% less embodied energy (Lime Technology UK).

7.123

Limewash

Limewash is available ready-made, but you can make it yourself by adding water to lime putty till it is the consistency of milk, and then passing it through a fine sieve. Pigment can also be added, diluted in water, and the limewash then sieved again. For external application, tallow or raw linseed oil may be added (a walnut-size lump of tallow or one tablespoon of oil to two gallons of limewash) and the mixture heated until the additive is blended in. Pumice added at one part to twelve will aid faster curing. Three to five coats are usually required, and regular reapplication is necessary throughout the building's life. Wet the previous coat with a fine mist spray before applying the next. Limewash is a natural antiseptic and deters insects.

Lime/hemp mix

See under 'Hemp'.

Cement

Cement, composed of lime and volcanic ash, was first used by the Romans 2000 years ago. What we think of as cement, today, was first developed in the 1750s during the building of the Eddystone Lighthouse, but it did not appear in common use until the 1870s. It is known as Portland cement because Joseph Aspdin, who took out a patent for it in 1834, thought it looked like Portland stone. It has the considerable advantages of quick setting times, high compressive strength, and durability.

Cement is the second most widely used material in the world, second only to water, and globally the amount used is equivalent to 1 ton/person/year. It has replaced lime as the main setting agent in mortars, renders and concrete. The widespread availability of cement and steel has led to the prevalence of structural concrete in 20th century buildings. But, however available and cheap it may be, cement is a material that should be used sparingly or not at all, mainly because of the environmental damage caused by extraction and processing of the raw materials.

The main ingredients of cement – limestone, silica, and alumina – are crushed and then burned at high temperatures (1500°C). CO_2 is emitted from fossil fuels used to fire the kilns, and is also released by the chemical reaction, which takes place inside the kiln. In the UK the cement industry is the biggest CO_2 producer after the electricity generating industry, and in some developing countries, cement production can account for up to two thirds of total energy use. Globally cement production is responsible for 8-10% of all CO_2 emissions – almost as much as the

7.124a

Fig. 7.123 The rich colours of natural earth pigments. Limewash at St. Fagan's Museum of Welsh Life.

Fig. 7.124a Concrete can be beautiful: Falling Water, Bear Run, Pennsylvania. Frank Lloyd Wright, 1936.

7.124b

7.124c

Fig. 7.124b Sagrada Familia cathederal in Barcelona. Begun by Gaudi, still being finished.

7.124c Mosaic bench in Parc Guell, Barcelona, by Gaudi.

international aviation industry. In addition, heavy metals are emitted during the firing and other associated atmospheric pollutants are SO_2, NO_2 and dust. Pollution to watercourses can occur, with the highly alkaline wash-out water being toxic to fish.

There are other performance-related reasons to minimise cement use. By its nature, cement is extremely hard and brittle when set, and this can lead to cracks in mortars and renders if there is the slightest movement in the building. Cement mixes should be no stronger than they need to be for structural reasons, but ignorance of this fact, or lack of confidence, leads to the very common practice of using too 'strong' a mix. A high-cement mortar will typically be stronger than the bricks or blocks themselves, which makes future separation and re-use difficult. Cement products in general are not easy to dispose of, although some can be recycled to lower grade uses. Cement mortars and renders should never be applied to lime- or earth-based substrates.

Like lime, cement is a dangerous material to handle. In a wet mix, it can cause skin burns that go unnoticed at the time. If the dry dust is inhaled, the silica content can cause scarring of the lungs or silicosis. The various additives used to hasten the setting process or plasticise the mix, may cause dermatitis and eczema.

The cement industry has responded to a report compiled for the World Business Council for Sustainable Development, by publishing the Cement Sustainability Initiative[44], which pledges improvements in several areas including climate change emissions. It is clear, nevertheless, that from an environmental viewpoint we need to limit our use of cement and explore the viability of alternative materials.

Secondary liquid fuels

Partly to cut fuel bills, and presented as an environmental improvement, many cement producers are now using Secondary Liquid Fuels (SLFs) to heat their kilns. These fuels are the (often hazardous) waste products from other industries, such as old tyres and industrial solvents. Known as 'coincineration' this practice is covered by permits issued by the Environment Agency. Cement kilns, however, are not covered by the stringent EU Waste Incineration Standards that apply to municipal incinerators.

There is strong concern about the emissions, from such fuels, of dioxins, furans and heavy metals to the atmosphere and to landfill, where the ash from the kilns is dumped. It is possible that the cement itself is contaminated. The Environment Protection Agency in the USA states that cement kilns burning chemical waste are the highest emitters of dioxins. American studies have shown that cement from waste burning plants contains twice the normal chromium content.

It is obviously worth the waste-producing industry paying the cement works to take the waste off their hands; meanwhile the cement industry is being paid to use SLFs, and saving on fossil fuel bills (35% of manufacturing costs). With economic incentives like this, it may be that health and safety issues are being disregarded.

In a new development, Castle Cement are considering using Agricultural Waste Derived Fuel (AWDF) to replace up to 40% of coal used at their Ribblesdale works. AWDF is slaughterhouse waste that has been sterilised and ground. As a result, they would anticipate a reduction in NOx emissions.

Concrete blocks

There are three basic types of concrete blocks:

- Dense concrete blocks are made from cement, sand and aggregates steam-cured under pressure. Secondary aggregates such as PFA may be used to partly replace the cement and aggregate content, and this is an increasingly common practice. This type of block is relatively cheap and probably the most widely used material for external walls in this country.
- Lightweight concrete blocks use expanded clays and shales such as pumice, sintered or fired PFA, vermiculite, or perlite. Breeze-blocks use furnace clinker. The lighter weight goes some way towards reducing their transport energy costs.
- Aerated concrete blocks are made from cement, sand and lime, with a small amount of aluminium sulphate added, which reacts with the lime to form hydrogen. The blocks are then autoclaved, or steamed under pressure to increase their strength. The aggregate used may be PFA.

Lightweight and aerated blocks are more expensive than dense blocks, but have better insulation qualities. Whether this justifies the extra energy used in their manufacture is a moot point. On disposal, they can be used as insulating filler in foundations and road building.

Gypsum-based products

Gypsum is a naturally occurring rock, that is crushed and heated to produce calcium sulphate hemihydrate, the main constituent of finishing plasters and plasterboard. Masonry walls usually have a two-coat plaster finish, or plasterboard stuck to the blockwork with 'dabs' of wet plaster. Timber frame walls are usually lined internally with plasterboard, which then has a thin coat of 'skim' plaster applied to seal the joints and provide a surface that can be decorated. Most plasterboard now contains some or all recycled industrial gypsum (see below), but this is not suitable for 'wet' plaster applications. Gypsum can be recycled and used as 5-15% of new material.

An alternative to ordinary plasterboard can now be found in a board that mixes recycled industrial gypsum with cellulose fibres. These gypsum fibreboards are stronger, and more fire and water resistant (but heavier) than conventional plasterboard. They have a plaster rather than a paper finish, which does not require skimming. The joints between the boards, and the nail heads, must be filled and smoothed off before decorating – a laborious but relatively unskilled job which can save the cost of a professional plasterer. Some jointing compounds contain formaldehyde. Given that some sanding is necessary to achieve a smooth finish, it is best to avoid such compounds altogether.

Secondary materials

These are industrial by-products, which are often available in large quantities and are difficult to dispose of. If they can be used to replace a virgin resource (e.g. cement in a concrete mix) this would reduce mineral extraction, energy costs and the environmental impact of disposal. The Government, in trying to discourage the use of primary aggregates, has imposed a tax on all newly quarried materials and has published a target of a 25% increase in the use of secondary aggregates, based on 1997 levels, by 2006. As far as the construction industry is concerned, there are three main sources of secondary materials:

- Recycled industrial gypsum is used in the manufacture of most makes of plasterboard to replace natural gypsum. Usually this comes from spent flue gas desulphurisation kits (FGD gypsum) used in power station chimneys to extract pollutants from the exhaust gases. There is also phospho-gypsum: a by-product of artificial fertiliser manufacture.
- Ground Granulated Blastfurnace Slag (GGBS) is a by-product of steel manufacture and can be used to replace between 30% and 60% of the cement component of concrete. It has been in use since the 1920s, is covered by a British Standard and was used in the construction of the Humber Bridge and Channel Tunnel. GGBS cement is also resistant to sulphur attack.
- Pulverised Fuel Ash (PFA) comes from coal-fired electricity generation, and is the residue left once the coal has been burned. In common with GGBS, it is a pozzolan, which means that, like cement, it causes other materials to harden. Both PFA and GGBS have greater durability and strength than OPC mixes, and show a reduced risk of shrinking and cracking. However, longer curing times for PFA cement can be a problem. Lytag is a pelletised form of PFA, used as an insulating aggregate, produced to BS 3797.

In a holistic assessment of the environmental impact of using such secondary materials, it is important to realise that they are themselves products of polluting processes in non-sustainable industries, and that these negative factors should be set against their environmental benefits. There are also potential health hazards associated with the use of these products. Concrete blocks made with GGBS cement have been found to contain high levels of dioxins. Heavy metals left over from the original incineration process may leach from secondary materials in cement powder and products. It has been suggested that industrial gypsum may contain heavy metals and radioactive particles, particularly phospho-gypsum from European sources[45].

7.125

Fig. 7.125 The Hauer King House built in 1996. A completely glazed façade faces a small courtyard garden. Architects: Future Systems.

Glass

Sheet glass

The main raw material for glass is silica (from sand), mixed with lime and soda to improve workability, and heated to about 1500°C. Sheet glass has been made since Roman times by a variety of methods. But it was not until the late 1950s that the float glass method was developed and quickly replaced cast glass. Float glass is formed by floating the required thickness of molten glass on a pool of molten tin that hardens as it cools. Emissions from glass production include chlorides, fluorides and particulate matter.

Glass is a unique material that presents us with a design paradox. On the one hand, it is relatively energy-intensive to produce. On the other hand, it is an energy saving material, allowing buildings to make use of passive (and active) solar heating and reducing the need for electric lighting. It allows daylight to pass through it, lighting and warming the interior of a building, while at the same time trapping heat by absorbing most of the infra-red radiation. Put simply, this is the greenhouse effect that we have all experienced sitting by a window or in a car on a sunny day.

In general, glass is a poor insulator, and windows can be areas of enormous heat loss. The exact effect of any area of glazing on overall energy use depends on size (of window and building), orientation, location and climate. In the case of domestic buildings in the UK, specify the best performance windows you can afford, taking low-E double-glazing as the minimum standard for energy efficiency.

7.126

Sealed double- (or triple-) units are becoming the standard form of new glazing. Each pane of glass is separated from the next by a layer of air, or an inert gas such as argon, which improves the thermal and acoustic insulation. Plastic or metal sections separate the edges of the panes, which are then sealed with a silicone mastic. Older multiple-pane units may be contaminated with polychlorinated bisphenyls (PCBs) from the sealants, and this causes problems on disposal. In Norway, the national directorate of public construction, Statsbygg, has set up a treatment plant to dispose of contaminated window frames with minimal environmental impact.

Glass was the first everyday material to be recycled on a mass scale. Recycled glass is mainly used for bottle production, which involves heating the glass almost to the original temperatures. A preferable alternative would be for all bottles to be sterilised and re-used – as milk bottles still are. But while the recycling process may not save much energy (only 8%), it does save on the extraction of raw materials, and it has engendered a culture of recycling, which is very important. Waste from the production process is normally re-used. Glass waste from the construction industry can only be recycled into low-grade glass or aggregate.

Glass is inert, non-polluting and can last indefinitely if protected from impact. It can be wired, toughened, or laminated to improve its strength on impact and ensure that it breaks safely (like a car windscreen). Such glass must be used in vulnerable areas such as on roofs, low level windows and doors. Modern glass can be turned from transparent to opaque by passing an electric current through it[45a]. Amazingly, the compressive strength of glass is similar to that of stone, and since the 1990s glass has been used as a loadbearing structural material. Research and development work is currently looking into ways of improving the insulating and climate-responsive properties of glass.

Fig. 7.126 Extension to Reichstag in Berlin.
Architect: Norman Forster.

7.127

7.128

Fig. 7.127 A durable, strong, water and heat-proof insulation material – foamed glass.

Fig. 7.128 Mineral paint, made from a form of glass, bonds with the substrate to form a long-lasting and benign finish. Keim Paints.

Glass fibre

Glass is used to produce a glass fibre insulation quilt in much the same way as volcanic rock is used in the production of Rockwool. The energy used and pollution produced during manufacture, as well as the health risks arising from close contact with it, are virtually the same as for Rockwool. Current best practice provides for a completely closed process, whereby harmful by-products such as phenol, formaldehyde, and ammonia, are re-introduced into the manufacturing process.

Glass fibre will not biodegrade and has been measured at low concentrations in the air above landfill sites. As it has been in widespread use for only 40 years, and therefore relatively little has already been disposed of, there is concern that it may become a serious atmospheric pollutant. Glass fibres are also used as reinforcement in boat hulls and car bodies, bonded with resin; and in roofing tiles, bonded with cement.

Foamed glass

Also an insulating material, foamed glass is made by heating ground glass (mostly recycled) with carbon, forming CO_2, which is then trapped in closed cells within the material. It is mixed with bitumen, which makes it difficult to recycle as glass. It comes as a rigid slab, has good insulating properties, is non-combustible, dimensionally stable, and extremely durable. It is waterproof and vapour-proof, and so is particularly suitable for insulating flat roofs, including turf roofs, and for earth-sheltered construction.

In situations that are inaccessible and prone to damp, the extra expense may be justified. While it has a high embodied energy (because the glass, once made, is then reheated), it is probably preferable to foamed plastic – a more common waterproof insulation. Cork is a better environmental choice.

Inorganic paints

Silicate paints (e.g. Keim, BEECK) for use on mineral surfaces, are water-based and use potassium silicate as a binder, along with quartz, feldspars, and inorganic mineral pigments. They were patented in 1938 by AW Keim. The ingredients are related chemically and physically to all mineral building materials, have similar coefficients of expansion and so will not crack or chip. This high-performance paint system penetrates the mineral substrate and forms a chemical bond with it. The crystallisation process forms insoluble silicates, which are resistant to acid and alkali attack and are the basis of the paint's extreme longevity.

Keim paints has been given the maximum BBA rating of a 15 year life expectancy, but European experience has shown that it can last for over one hundred years without maintenance or fading. This degree of durability has obvious environmental and financial advantages, and it has been specified by cost-conscious Housing Associations on the basis that there will be a net saving after only ten years. It is widely used by English Heritage and the National Trust on some of our most famous buildings, such as the Brighton Pavilion.

Keim Ecosil is an interior silicate-based paint that gives a dense matt finish. It is generally applied as a two-coat system, and it is claimed that the cost is equivalent to vinyl silk emulsion. Due to the micro-crystalline structure it forms with the substrate, it can be used as an anti-condensation coating that still allows vapour permeability.

7.129

In summary

- When using large quantities of non-renewable resources, seek a manufacturer/supplier with an environmental management system in place.
- Buy as locally as possible, to cut transport energy costs.
- Use secondary aggregates to replace primary resource extraction.
- Use second-hand slates, tiles and bricks where possible.
- Explore the possibilities of building with earth and lime.
- Use dense, rather than lightweight or aerated concrete blocks.
- Minimise cement content of mortars and renders.
- Find alternatives to insulating with mineral wool or glass fibre.

Metals

In 1894, an English explorer in Greenland was taken to Cape York by an Inuit and shown a huge metallic meteorite half buried in the ground. For the previous hundred years, the Inuits had been chipping bits off this lump to fashion a variety of tools. There were still 37 tonnes of it left. Thus it may have been that Stone Age people discovered the value of metals and the Bronze Age began. Indeed, so great was their value to existing civilisations that the meteorites were seen as gifts from the gods.

More mundanely, we usually obtain the metals we use today from metallic ores extracted from the ground. They are generally high cost materials requiring an energy-intensive manufacturing process. Extraction can accelerate methane release, and the high temperature smelting process releases large amounts of CO_2 and acid gases. Global reserves of some metallic ores (lead, zinc, copper) are seriously depleted, with only a few decades of supply left. The many surface treatments such as galvanising, may also be responsible for toxic emissions.

Fig. 7.129 Detail of decorated façade of house in Walenstadt, Switzerland, painted with Keim mineral paints in 1890.

Metals	Using virgin ore	50% recycled stock	100% recycled stock
Aluminium	165-260	95	30
Copper	80-127	55	
Steel	21-25	18	6-10
Zinc	47-87		

7.130

In the UK, we import most of the raw materials necessary for metals production, often in a semi-processed state. Thus, the (often high) environmental and social impacts of extraction and processing are borne by the exporters, many of which are developing countries, ill equipped to resist the incursions of multinational companies on their homes, health and livelihoods – or demand redress when irreversible damage is done. For example, 90% of bauxite reserves, used to produce aluminium, occur in countries with low/medium industrialisation, while 90% of processed aluminium is used in highly industrialised countries[46].

Metallic ore extraction typically creates many more tonnes of waste than useful product. For aluminium, the ratio of waste to product is about 50:1; for copper it varies between 50:1 and 200:1. The waste spoil created is often toxic to varying degrees and disrupts existing ecosystems and any productive value the land may have had.

In addition to their high energy cost and environmental impact, metals are toxic to humans to a greater or lesser degree, as are their associated dust, fumes, sludge, particles and residues. They will accumulate in the body, so that constant minor exposure can lead eventually to toxic levels. It has been suggested by one expert in the field[46] that use of chrome, nickel, copper and zinc should be minimised and that the use of mercury, cadmium and lead should be banned.

Any metal that comes into contact with water can leach its trace elements into the water and run-off areas. Pollution caused by metals is irreversible since they do not decompose. Indeed, the increasing extent of metals recycling is only postponing the pollution that is the inevitable result of production. Promoters of 'healthy' buildings feel that extensive use of metals in the home is potentially dangerous, because of their ability to disrupt natural electromagnetic fields and affect the ion balance of the air.

However, the value of metals to the development of human society is beyond dispute, and scientists and technologists are still exploring and extending the properties of metals and their alloys. In very many areas of life, from medicine to industry, metals are indispensable and irreplaceable. In the construction industry, their use covers a wide spectrum, from structures, roofs and windows, to impregnation materials and pigments in plastics, ceramics and paints. Metal fixings and jointing elements such as screw, nails and bolts, are such an integral part of most building and DIY activity, that it is hard to imagine doing without them. Due to their high conductivity they enable the distribution of electricity, and in this function they are effectively irreplaceable.

Environmentally, their main redeeming feature lies in their high intrinsic value, which means that they tend to be used sparingly and strategically, in the smallest possible quantities, to make best use of their particular physical properties. It also means that, wherever possible, they are recycled, and so scrap metal forms a proportion of the feedstock for the manufacturing process. It has been suggested

7.131

Fig. 7.130 Primary energy use for metals production, in MJ/kg. (Figures from Bjørn Berge).

Fig. 7.131 Designed by Brunel and completed after his death in 1864, the Clifton Suspension Bridge demonstrates the tensile strength of wrought iron. Telford thought that his bridge over the Menai Staits, completed in 1825, had a maximum safe span of 168m, but Brunel showed that this could be increased with the Clifton bridge to 192m.

that metals recycling is a major source of dioxin emissions[47] but this is disputed by the industry[48].

Where metals are recycled, at least part of the primary energy cost of their initial production is saved and re-invested. In the UK, between 60-90% of all metals are recycled, thus saving on the environmental costs of disposal as well as production. Manufacturers are also making progress in recycling alloys and coated products.

This progress has led some to argue that sustainable production of metals would be possible if they were comprehensively and indefinitely recycled using renewable energy sources. Indeed, some American writers have suggested that in terms of resource depletion and ecosystem impact, steel is environmentally superior to timber as a construction framing material. While most environmentalists would treat this claim with some scepticism, the industry is certainly working to promote the environmental credentials of its product and has greatly reduced its energy consumption over the last 20 years. Unfortunately, heat recovery from the smelting process remains a largely unexplored potential.

The environmental impact of metals can be kept to a minimum by substituting where possible with materials that are less damaging, and by promoting the use of metals with a high recycled content, such as stainless steel.

Steel

It was during the Industrial Revolution that the use of steel became widespread in construction and civil engineering, initially in the form of cast and wrought iron, and then as steel frames and steel reinforcement for concrete. Steel is still the most commonly used metal in the construction industry, although the vast majority of steel consumption is for motor vehicles and domestic white goods.

The steel industry is the one of the biggest energy users of all the major industries, although the energy content per kilogram is relatively low, compared to other metals. The main constituents of the production process are scrap steel (mostly industrial rather than post-consumer waste), pig iron, and metallised ore, heated to 1700-1800°C. Large amounts of coal and water are used. Much of the pig iron is imported from Brazil, where areas of forest are destroyed to produce charcoal as a smelting fuel. Sources of iron ore are becoming increasingly scarce, and what reserves there are left (estimated at about 100 years' supply) have to be transported over longer and longer distances for processing. All the iron ore used in Britain is imported, mainly from Brazil, Canada, and Australia.

7.132

Where Britain's dioxin comes from (Source: AEA Technology/Environment Agency)	
Metal recycling	8-30%
Per- and tri-chloroethylene production	5-23%
Pesticides production	1-17%
Municipal waste incineration	20-40%
Accidental fires	1-20%
Sewage sludge incineration	1-4%
Landfill of municipal waste	1-10%
Pentachlorophenol use	7-25%

7.133

Fig. 7.132 Sublime minimal use of steel. Barcelona Pavilion. Mies van der Rohe.

Fig. 7.133 Adapted from *New Scientist*, 4/10/97.

7.134

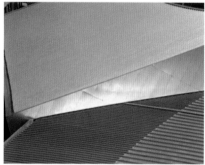

7.135

7.136a

7.136b

Fig. 7.134 Reduced environmental impact from using recycled steel beams in the BedZED scheme. Architect: Bill Dunster.

Fig. 7.135 Stainless steel seamed roof at CAT. Probably the best eco choice for metal sheet roofing.

Fig. 7.136a & 7.136b Metal roofs are light and strong and can offer sculptural possibilities not possible with other roofing materials.
7.136a Architect: Daniel Liebeskind.
7.136b Architects: Smith Roberts Associates.

As well as large amounts of CO_2, sulphur dioxide, dust, cadmium and fluorine compounds are major atmospheric pollutants associated with steel production. Arsenic occurs naturally in iron ore, and is commonly released in the recycling process. Zinc coating or galvanising are responsible for the release of organic solvents, cyanides, chrome, phosphates and fluorides, mainly in the rinse water.

Steel is eminently suitable for re-use rather than recycling, which, in any case, is less financially attractive than for other metals. Current estimates for recovery rates from demolition sites in the UK, are 10% for reuse and 84% for recycling. Existing steel sections can be reclaimed and repaired relatively easily, especially if they are bolted rather than welded together.

Stainless steel

Stainless steel is produced in a similar manner to steel, but heated to even higher temperatures, with the addition of 5% chromium – mined mainly in Russia and Zimbabwe. The principal feedstock is recycled steel and no new ore is used. Its manufacture causes emissions of chromium, nickel, vanadium, and molybdenum.

Stainless steel will resist corrosion in most situations, and thus is very durable. However, it does tend to lose its corrosion resistance under high tensile loads – which, according to one source[48a], is a little-known problem, likely to give rise to possible structural problems in the near future.

Because of its high value, stainless steel is virtually guaranteed to be continually recycled. It is inert and sterile, and is often the most suitable internal surface for allergy sufferers.

Aluminium

First produced in America in the 1880s, the use of aluminium in the construction industry is increasing rapidly. Bauxite is the ore from which aluminium is produced and it is in abundant supply. Over 8% of the earth's crust is bauxite, and only oxygen and silica are in greater supply. There are large bauxite reserves in South America and Australia. However, most of the refining and production takes place in countries with access to cheap supplies of electricity, like Norway, Iceland and Canada. This involves transportation over huge distances.

The production of aluminium consumes more energy than any other building material – about 100 times as much as imported timber weight for weight. On the other hand, having low density, a tonne of aluminium goes a very long way. The electrolytic reduction process, which is an essential part of its manufacture, requires large amounts of electricity, which is inefficiently converted from other energy sources. High energy use for aluminium production has led to the installation of many hydroelectric schemes throughout the world. While these may seem promising as replacements for fossil fuel fired power stations, the environmental impact of flooding valleys to create the large reservoirs necessary for these schemes, as well as the forced movement of indigenous populations, has given rise to mass opposition.

If aluminium is not produced utilising hydroelectric power, (which is about 35% of all aluminium produced), it releases twice as much CO_2 per tonne as steel. Other pollutants include sulphur dioxide, polyaromatic hydrocarbons (PAHs), fluorine and dust, which are released into the atmosphere and local watercourses. Dioxin emissions can result from smelting recycled aluminium.

Aluminium is easily recycled with no loss of quality, and the high cost of its production ensures that most of it will continue to be. Recycling aluminium uses only 7% of the metal's original energy cost (compared to steel's 30%) and so is well worth it, in energy and financial terms. However, re-use of aluminium products is limited by the fact that they are thin, easily damaged and often bonded to other materials. Polyester powder coated aluminum cannot be recycled, and this treatment is becoming increasingly necessary for roofing and cladding sheets to protect the metal from acid rain.

Aluminium is sometimes used to treat domestic water supplies; it is also commonly used for saucepans and other cooking utensils. Aluminium in water or food has been linked to the onset of Alzheimer's disease. (The Alzheimer's Society, www.alzheimers.org.uk, cites circumstantial evidence but no proof of a causal relationship.)

Copper

Copper and its alloy, bronze, have been found in ancient buildings such as the Pantheon in Rome. An extremely conductive material, copper is necessary for all forms of electrical cables. It is also widely used for water and gas piping, and occasionally as roofing sheet or rainwater goods, and is very durable and corrosion resistant. Its other main alloy, brass, is used in light fittings and timber treatments.

Copper ore is quarried or mined in the Congo, Zimbabwe, Canada, the USA and Chile, and 'entails a heavy assault on the natural environment[49]'. The smelting process releases large amounts of sulphur dioxide and other acid gases. An alternative process involves dissolving the ore in sulphuric acid before extracting the copper, but this is liable to cause groundwater contamination and is more expensive. Leaching of heavy metals from mines and spoil tips can lead to highly polluted rivers and watercourses, while copper mining creates large amounts of heavy metal-contaminated solid waste.

An estimated 60-70% of copper is recycled, which can reduce the energy costs of production by up to 80%. However, as with other metals, CO_2 emission is not proportionally reduced, as most recycling plants are electrically powered.

Like many metals, copper is toxic to human and aquatic life, but it does not accumulate in the food chain. It has been suggested that higher levels of copper in drinking and waste water may be due to the corrosive effect of acidic groundwater, particularly in soft water areas. However, public water supplies are treated to give a pH of 5.5–8.5, and this level of acidity should not corrode copper pipes[50]. Plastic coated copper, mdpe (medium density polyethylene), or polybutylene should be used for underground pipework or for burying in concrete screeds. Copper saucepans should be cleaned thoroughly to prevent the build-up of toxic verdigris.

7.137

7.138

7.139

Fig. 7.137 Aluminium glazing bars, part of roof-integrated photovoltaic array.

Fig. 7.138 Copper gutters, long life and attractive.

Fig. 7.139 Copper can be easily worked to form complex cladding shapes.
Architects: Okada & Tomiyama. Photo: Shinkenchikusha.

7.140

Lead

Lead has been used in buildings for 4000-5000 years and was used by the Romans for roofs and water pipes, as well as drinking vessels. Indeed, the fall of the Roman Empire has been attributed to lead poisoning. Lead is a potent and cumulative poison, capable of being stored in the body for decades via ingestion, inhalation, or skin contact.

In the 19th and 20th centuries lead was used extensively for water supply pipes, but most of these have now been replaced as older properties are renovated and people become aware of the risk. Lead solder is increasingly being replaced with a lead-free variety. Until relatively recently, lead was also used as a drying agent and pigment in paint, and the removal of any paint over 40 years old can be hazardous if dust or fumes are inhaled. There are regular cases of lead poisoning among children caused by the ingestion of particles of flaked-off paint, and there seems to be more danger of lead poisoning from within the home, via old paints and water supply, than from vehicle exhausts. One American study showed that teenage boys appearing in juvenile court had higher levels of lead in their bones (11 parts per million or ppm), compared to non-delinquent children of the same age (1.5ppm). Indeed 38% of juvenile crime in Allegheny County was attributed to the effects of lead poisoning[51].

Nowadays, the use of lead tends to be restricted to inaccessible areas such as roofs. However, it is important to note that water run-off from a roof with lead flashings or valleys (probably the majority of older roofs) should not be used for drinking or on the garden. Fruit and vegetables can absorb lead in growth, either dissolved in water or as atmospheric particles. For this reason the move towards lead-free petrol is welcome, although there are, of course, many other grossly polluting effects of vehicle exhausts.

The production process is similar to that of copper, involving burning off impurities from the ore, smelting, and finally electrolytic refining. Polluting emissions include lead oxides, zinc, mercury, cadmium, chromium, copper, and acid gases. Lead has a high scrap value and is virtually 100% recycled.

Worldwide reserves of the ore galena, or lead sulphide, are very low. Although most lead has a high recycled content, this is still a serious situation with only decades' worth of supply left.

There is a very good case for phasing out lead completely from all new constructions. Alternative materials are available, and nowhere is lead indispensable.

Zinc

Zinc is used mainly for galvanized coatings, but also for pure zinc roofing sheets and flashings. It is also used as a pigment in paints and in timber treatment against rot. Modern galvanising techniques use roughly half zinc and half aluminium. Galvanised coatings will extend the life of steel sheet and nails, but the latter are relatively fragile and easily chipped. Compared with aluminium, copper, or stainless steel, galvanised steel has a shorter life.

Most of the zinc used in this country is imported over long distances, from Australia, Peru and the US. The mining of zinc ore releases cadmium, while the enrichment process emits lead, antimony, bismuth, and arsenic, mostly in the form of soil and water pollution. Large quantities of waste contaminated with heavy metals end up in huge tailings lagoons, which poison the land for the foreseeable future.

Fig. 7.140 A church tradition – zinc standing seam roofing.

Zinc is often extracted from the same ore as lead, and reserves will be depleted within decades at the current rate of consumption. The recycling of zinc is possible but, whether as an alloy or a galvanised coating, it can be difficult and expensive.

In summary
- Use timber rather than metal for structural purposes.
- Where sheet metal is used, favour stainless steel.
- Avoid metal/plastic composites.
- Make sure that any scrap metal you create goes for recycling.
- Restrict the use of aluminium, as far as possible.
- Use no lead. Make sure all lead water pipes are replaced.

Fossil organic materials
In this section we are dealing with the many products derived from the carbon-based, fossilised reserves of the earth, in the form of coal, oil, or gas. Made up of organisms that lived many hundreds of thousands of years ago, these finite resources are irreplaceable. Taking into account known reserves and current levels of consumption, oil will last for only another 40 years, and gas for another 60 years[52]. However, all the indications are that the rate of use of these resources will in the future be limited by the pollution created by their extraction and use, especially CO_2 pollution, rather than by their actual depletion[53].

The petrochemical industry, based on the extraction and exploitation of crude oil, accounts for over half of all toxic emissions to the environment. It is a major source of CO_2, nitrous oxide, sulphur dioxide, and volatile organic compounds (VOCs). Solid wastes from oil refineries include polynuclear aromatics and heavy metals. In addition, the extraction and transportation of the raw material are potentially hazardous operations, and any leakage or spillage can have seriously damaging, long-term environmental consequences.

Ultimately, all the by-products of this processing must share in the huge environmental debt that is being incurred by this grossly polluting industry, and by our generation's profligate use of resources which have taken millennia to create.

Plastics
The original meaning of the word 'plastic', as an adjective, is the ability to be shaped or formed. In fact, the term 'plastic' can be used to describe any material that, when heated, becomes soft and malleable, and which can be cast or moulded to assume a different shape on cooling.

As a noun it refers to a large group of synthesised organic (carbon-based) compounds produced by polymerisation. The building blocks of plastics – monomers – are combined into long chain-like polymers. Depending on the different processes of polymerisation, a huge variety of materials can be produced with some or all of the following properties:
- hard as stone;
- soft as cotton;
- strong as steel;
- clear as glass;
- elastic as rubber.

Synthetic plastics are a relatively recent phenomenon, dependent as they are on the extraction and refining of petroleum. They will probably be seen by future

7.142

archaeologists and historians as the artefacts most typical of the second half of the 20th century: the 'Plastics Age'.

Plastics that already exist in nature include peat and pitch, amber and shellac. Plastics can be made from any biomass, such as wood, cotton, sugar cane, and rubber latex. It is only the cheapness and availability of the by-products of a massively powerful multi-national industry that makes plastics derived from oil and gas the norm. In the future, as our fossil reserves are depleted, we may well have to turn to organic, renewable resources to develop new kinds of plastics, which would biodegrade naturally. One bio-plastic – polylactide or (PLA) – is already used for medical sutures, but has a high financial cost. Bio-plastics are used extensively in the car industry.

Plastics were first synthesised in 1872 and the first commercial products, such as Bakelite – made from carbolic acid and formaldehyde – appeared in the 1920s. Vinyl floor tiles were first used in 1933, PVC windows in the 1950s, and single ply roofing membrane in the 1960s. The advantages of lower costs, faster installation, lighter weight, improved thermal performance, and moisture resistance were perceived as truly revolutionary.

There are now more than fifty different kinds of plastics. About 80% of these are thermoplastics – that is they can be heated, cooled and then re-heated indefinitely. Thermosetting plastics, once set, cannot be softened by heat and therefore cannot be recycled in the usual way, although they can be ground up and used as a filler. The potential for the recycling of thermoplastics is limited at the moment, due to the combination of different compounds in any one item and the lack of information on product composition.

In chemical terms, thermoplastics are not solids but visco-elastic liquids, and like any fluid they will evaporate or off-gas, especially when subjected to the environmental stresses of air, light, pressure or heat. The softer thermoplastics, which contain plasticiser, tend to be less stable. The impact on healthy buildings and indoor air quality has become more significant with the increased use of plastic finishes and furnishings. From hard plastic chairs to soft (foamed plastic) sofas; from vinyl wallpaper and tiles to synthetic fitted carpets and laminated plastic work tops – we are increasingly surrounded by plastics products and their volatile components.

The embodied energy of plastics should include the high energy costs of the industry whose by-products form the principal feedstock for plastics production. Hence all petrochemical-based plastics have a high embodied energy.

On the positive side, most plastics are cheap, versatile and relatively durable. Their maintenance requirements are relatively low, although they can break down in UV light and are degraded by ozone and other pollutants. As mastics, they play an important part in sealing the building fabric against air infiltration. They are lightweight which reduces transport energy, and can be very effective insulants.

Polyethylene (PE) and Polypropylene (PP) are thermoplastics, which in their pure form can be recycled relatively easily. These are single polymer plastics, and in the case of polyethylene terephthalate (PET), it can be recycled indefinitely. PET is already widely used in bottles and other containers. Although exposure to the constituents during manufacture can be damaging, in use there are no emissions from the finished product. They can be incinerated relatively 'cleanly'.

Fig. 7.142 Social housing project for young people in Shoneberg, Berlin. The restored building is completely PVC-free. Architect: Alexander Rudolphi. Greenpeace (1996).

Type of Plastic	Code	Uses
Thermoplastics Polyethylene Terephthalate (PET)	1	Bottles, carpets and food packaging. Recycling possibilities include being re-spun into fibre for carpets, bedding and clothing, especially fleece jackets.
High Density Polyethylene (HDPE)	2	Bottles for food products, detergents, piping, fuel tanks and toys.
Polyvinyl Chloride (PVC)	3	Window frames, flooring, wallpaper, bottles, packaging film, insulation, credit cards and medical products. Recycling includes products such as sewage pipes, flooring and shoe soles.
Low Density Polyethylene (LDPE)	4	Cling-film, bin-liners and flexible containers.
Polypropylene (PP)	5	Yoghurt and margarine pots, vehicle battery cases, cereal packet linings, milk and beer crates, automotive parts and fibres. Recycled into new crates and plant pots.
Polystyrene (PS)	6	Dairy product containers, tape cassettes, cups and plates. Recycled into desk accessories.
Thermosets Polyurethane (PU)	N/A	Coatings, finishes, gears, diaphragms, mattresses and vehicle seats.
Epoxy	N/A	Adhesives, sports equipment, boats, electrical and automotive components.
Phenolics	N/A	Ovens, toasters, handles for cutlery, automotive parts and circuit boards.

Fig. 7.143

Polyvinyl Chloride (PVC)

PVC dominates all plastics use in buildings. It is unique because of its facility for integrating additives, particularly plasticisers. This chemical versatility is why PVC can be soft (wall coverings) or hard (drainpipe). Although in fact it represents only 25% of total plastics production, it has a wide range of uses in the building industry, including rainwater goods, underground drainage, doors, windows, cladding, flooring, and sheathing for electrical cables.

One of the main constituents of PVC – chlorine – is highly toxic to plants and animals. Its manufacture is energy-intensive and specific emissions include mercury. When materials containing chlorine are burned, they may emit dioxins – known carcinogens and considered to be the most toxic man-made chemical ever. These highly persistent poisons are soluble in fat rather than water, and so accumulate in the food chain and human fatty tissue. They have been linked with cancer, immune system damage and hormone disruption. In accidental fires, emissions from burning PVC of dioxins and concentrated hydrochloric acid can kill more quickly and effectively than fire or smoke.

The intermediate components of the production process – ethylene dichloride that is then converted to vinyl chloride monomer (VCM) – are carcinogenic and mutagenic, and there is a danger that significant amounts of these chemicals will be released during production and transportation.

Additives used as stabilisers, plasticisers, pigments, fillers, biocides, flame retardants and lubricants can make up over 50% of the final content of PVC. The heavy metal cadmium is used as a stabiliser for external PVC. Phthalates such as DEHP are widely used plasticisers, which can leach out during use or disposal. These chemicals are now almost universal environmental contaminants (found even in Antarctica). They are oestrogen mimics or feminising agents and have been

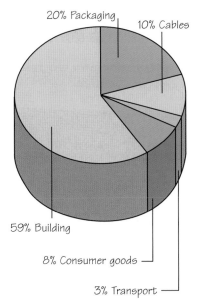

20% Packaging   10% Cables

59% Building

8% Consumer goods

3% Transport

7.144

Fig. 7.143 The arrows indicate that the item has been recycled, and the number one indicates that it is made from PET.

Fig. 7.144 PVC consumption by application share in western Europe (1998).
Source: Autochem, *Building for a Future.*

7.145a

7.145b

7.146

Fig. 7.145a Polybutylene plumbing – arguably a better
environmental choice than copper. Hep₂O.

Fig. 7.145b District heating can only be efficient and
cost-effective through the use of plastics plumbing.
Polyethyene (PE-X) pipes insulated with CFC-free
polyurethane foam. Calpex.

Fig. 7.146 Plastics insulation foams now use non-ozone-
depleting gases to achieve their high performance.

implicated as possible causes of low sperm counts and male infertility, as well as
hermaphroditic fish in polluted watercourses. They are commonly used in children's
soft plastic toys and several companies, including Lego, have announced a PVC
phase-out. Even unplasticised PVC (PVC-u) may contain up to 12% plasticiser by
weight.

Internationally, use of PVC is becoming more and more restricted. Countries such
as Germany, Austria, Japan, the Netherlands, Sweden, Norway and Denmark have
laws limiting the use of PVC in buildings.

However, perhaps the biggest environmental threat of the life cycle of PVC
occurs at its disposal. Partly because of the multitude of additives it is difficult to
recycle, although there is one plant in Germany that can recycle PVC. However, the
quality of the recycled product is questionable, there is no cost saving, and the
recycling process itself releases toxic pollution. It can also be seen as merely
delaying the ultimate problem of disposal.

Incineration remains a hazardous procedure, even with the use of flue scrubbers
to remove some of the worst pollutants, and the very high temperatures ideally
involved. When disposed of in landfill sites, PVC will not biodegrade, and may form
hydrogen chloride when exposed to solar radiation. There will also be leaching of
dioxins, phthalates and heavy metals into soil and groundwater.

Alternative materials exist for virtually every application of PVC in buildings (see
database on the Greenpeace website). It is possible to build 'PVC-free'.

Foamed plastics

Two main plastics are used to make these insulation products.

- Polyurethane foams, and the similar isocyanurate foams are available as blocks
  or sheets. They have superior insulating properties and are moisture resistant. In
  the event of fire, hydrogen cyanide gas is released. Polyurethane is no longer
  permitted for use as cavity wall insulation or in furniture.
- Polystyrene foam can either be expanded (EPS) or extruded (XPS). The
  manufacture of both types causes emissions of styrene and benzene. EPS
  comes in the form of little white beads, bonded together and is blown with
  pentane (Berge, Anink et al, Wooley et al). XPS products are often coloured
  (baby pinks and blues) and have the advantage of being waterproof. The
  blowing agents used in these products were originally CFCs (ozone depleting
  chemicals); then, as a result of the Montreal Protocol, replaced with HCFCs
  (now due to be phased out in Europe in 2004) or HFCs. These have less ozone
  depletion potential (ODP) but are still potent global warming gases. Although
  some major producers are switching to more benign blowing agents (zero
  ODP), there is, according to one expert 'a risk of complacency over this
  issue.'[54]. CFCs are still being produced in countries such as China, and
  illegally imported into Western Europe and the USA, particularly for use in air
  conditioning systems.

Recycling of foamed plastics demolition waste is largely impractical as plastics
foams are often bonded on to other materials. If bonded to steel they are likely to
be burned off to enable the steel to be recycled.

Elastomers

Natural elastomers such as rubber latex are extracted from plantation trees in
tropical countries. In the 19th century, rubber was vulcanised by combining it with

sulphur under heat and pressure, thus making it stronger, more elastic, and durable. It can be recycled – ground into granules for use as filler.

Artificial elastomers such as EPDM (ethylene propylene diene monomer) are used in the building industry as high quality roofing membranes. EPDM polymers are extracted from monomers and cause minimal environmental damage. It makes a long-life material which can be re-used indefinitely, provided the membrane is not mechanically fixed or glued to the decking, and is often used in the construction of turf or flat roofs.

7.147a

Bitumen

Bitumen is composed of various mixtures of hydrocarbons and is usually produced as a by-product of the distillation of crude oil. Naturally occurring deposits do exist, in asphalt lakes, where crude oil rises to the surface and the lighter elements evaporate. Bitumen gained from this source has a low embodied energy.

Its main property is as a waterproofing agent, used to impregnate other materials. The term asphalt usually refers to bitumen mixed with a mineral aggregate (which was traditionally crushed limestone) used for road surfaces. Organic fibres (such as jute, wool or paper) or inorganic fibres (such as glass fibre or polyester) are used as reinforcement in the manufacture of bituminous roofing felt and shingles. In the past, some bitumenised roofing felts included asbestos fibres.

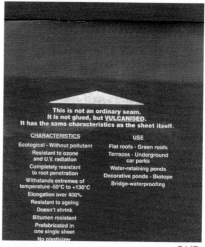

7.147b

Bitumen should not be confused with tar, which in the past was used as a roof covering. Tar contains a high proportion of polycyclic aromatic hydrocarbons, which are carcinogenic. Bitumen has replaced tar as a superior product, which does not shrink or crack and is less polluting and toxic. Skin contact should be avoided with either material.

Mastic Asphalt, or bitumen modified with a polymer such as polypropylene, has a longer lifespan, with increased strength and flexibility. Styrene-Butadiene-Styrene (SBS) is also used in this context, but is more polluting in its manufacture than polypropylene, and must be protected from ultraviolet light.

When used for roads or paths, bitumen can be extensively re-used as part of the maintenance cycle. Bitumen roofing products, which are inherently short-life, have little capacity for re-use, although they have been recycled into pavement patching materials in the USA.

7.148

In summary

- Avoid the use of PVC altogether.
- Choose alternative products to replace plastic items in general. If buying plastics, make sure they are recycled or recyclable, and recycle if possible.
- Reject products that come with an excessive amount of plastic packaging.
- Use string bags or cane baskets for shopping. Use ceramic containers to store food and drink.
- Campaign for proper recycling facilities in your area.
- Use recycled or naturally occurring bitumen where possible, and take care not to pollute watercourses.
- Favour plastic products which are clearly marked with their type, to aid recycling
- Use thermoplastics (which can be recycled) rather than thermoset plastics.

Fig. 7.147a & 7.147b EPDM (synthetic rubber) is the least environmentally damaging of the plastics roofing materials. Very strong and long-lived – essential for a roof garden or turf roof. Prelasti Ltd.

Fig. 7.148 Recycled polythene decking. University College London. Foster Associates.

Paints and coatings

Most of the myriad ingredients for synthetic solvent-based paints come from the petrochemical industry. These include bonding agents, solvents, fillers and additives such as pigments, drying and anti-foaming agents. The further processing involved in paint manufacture creates notoriously large amounts of toxic waste in proportions typically of 1:10 (one litre of paint creates ten litres of waste), rising to 1:30 for some specialist paints.

The solvents used are not only toxic in themselves, but on drying give off VOCs, which are environmental pollutants as well as human health hazards. These organic hydrocarbons react with nitrous oxides in the atmosphere to form low-level ozone. A German study in 1989 found that the synthetic paint industry emitted nearly as many VOCs into the environment as did all motor vehicle exhausts.

The average can of paint will also contain fungicides, heavy metals such as cadmium (used as a pigment), and polycyclic aromatic hydrocarbons (PAHs). Titanium dioxide, used in most shades but particularly in 'brilliant white', forms up to 25% of the content by weight. According to NIOSH (National Institute of Occupational Health and Safety) in the USA, titanium dioxide may cause lung fibrosis and is considered an occupational carcinogen. Fillers such as talc can cause lung damage when inhaled.

Disposal of paints, equipment and cleaning fluids can release heavy metals into the environment.

Different kinds of synthetic paints

- Alkyd paints refer to most conventional oil-based paints, which use alkyd as the bonding agent. Organic solvents, typically toluene or xylene, can form 50-70% of the content and will off gas VOCs. The maximum VOC level for gloss paints is 400 grams per litre.
- High gloss paint contains more solvents than the less glossy or satin finishes.
- High solids paint contains fewer organic solvents (typically 10-50% less VOCs), has better covering properties and represents a best choice of synthetic solvent-based paints.
- Acrylic paints use water as the main solvent and acrylic resin as the bonding agent. Organic solvents are still present, but reduced to about 10% of the content. Acrylate monomers can cause eczema through skin contact. Ammonia and volatile components are emitted, especially just after application, though the emissions reduce with time. The maximum VOC level for matt paint is 30 grams per litre, though some 'Low VOC' paints contain as little as 3g/l.

Microporous paints or stains are vapour-permeable, allowing the wood underneath to breathe. While avoiding many of the health problems associated with synthetic solvents and VOCs, water-based or low-solvent paints rely on a complex chemistry, and contain many harmful additives in the form of emulsifiers, biocides, and anti-corrosion agents. Their processing is, if anything, more environmentally damaging than the manufacture of conventional paints[55].

Health hazard

If the constituents of most paints were used together in an industrial situation, then protective clothing and breathing apparatus, forced ventilation, and mechanical extraction would be normal procedure. As it is, the lack of restriction on the sale and use of all paints fosters the assumption that they are basically harmless and necessary precautions, such as ventilating the indoor space, are often ignored.

Professional painters have a lung cancer rate 40% above the average and may suffer from chronic complaints such as dermatitis or asthma. Prolonged exposure to hydrocarbon solvents can lead to tremors, loss of coordination, depression and even brain damage. In Denmark, this is known as 'Solvent Dementia' and is a recognised industrial disease for which compensation is payable. By the end of 1992, over 4,500 claims had been met. Use of spray paints, where the solvent forms an easily inhaled mist, is especially dangerous.

Traditionally, one of the most dangerous contaminants of paint was lead, used universally as a drying agent. Most paints are now lead-free, but care should be taken when stripping old paints not to inhale dust or fumes.

The European Eco-label process has established criteria for assessing paints and varnishes. VOC content has been determined as the most serious environmental risk, with limits also set on embodied energy and titanium dioxide content.

In summary

- Use and specify organic paints and stains, based on naturally occurring solvents and pigments.
- For masonry use a silicate paint.
- If you choose to use a conventional gloss paint, use a high solids version.
- Use acrylic paints for protecting the health of decorators, but bear in mind the high environmental cost.

References

[1] *Lower Carbon Futures*, Environmental Change Institute, 2000

[2] 'Opportunities for Change', DETR, 1998

[3] But see BRE Methodology for Environmental Profiles of construction materials, components and buildings, CRC Ltd, 1999

[4] Quoted in Woolley et al, *Green Building Handbook*, E&FN Spon, 1997

[5] 'Embodied Energy in Residential Property Development', *Sustainable Homes*, PP3/99

[6] *A Green Vitruvius*, James & James, 1999

[7] IPCC

[8] Fawcett, Hurst & Boardman, 'Carbon UK', Environmental Change Institute, 2002

[9] Curwell, Fox, Greenberg & March, *Hazardous Building Materials*, Spon Press, 2002

[10] McLaren, Bullock & Yousuf, *Tomorrow's World*, Earthscan Publications, 1998

[11] *Guardian,* 21/12/02

[12] quoted in Brian Edwards' *Rough Guide to Sustainability*, RIBA Publications, 2001

[13] Tom Woolley and Sam Kimmins, *Green Building Handbook*, volumes 1 and 2, E&FN Spon, 1997

[14] Howard, Shiers and Sinclair, *The Green Guide to Specification*, BRE 1998

[15] Curwell, Fox, Greenberg & March, *Hazardous Building Materials*, Spon Press, 2002

[16] Stuart Brand, *How Buildings Learn*, Viking, 1994

[17] 'Swedish Research for Sustainability', no2/01

[18] S.A. Covington, I.S. McIntyre, A.J. Stevens, *Timber Frame Housing Systems, 1920-1975*. Inspection & Assessment, BRE Report 282, 1995

[19] 'Timber 2005', BRE Publications 1995

[20] Wooley & Kimmins, op cit, vol 1

[21] 'Sustainable Timber, Sustainable Homes', TRADA Technology Ltd, 1999

[21a] 'Partners in Crime' report by Greenpeace, 2003, from www.saveordelete.com

[21b] *New Scientist*, 8/11/03

[22] Bjørn Berge, *The Ecology of Building Materials*, Architectural Press, 2000, p166

[23] R.A. Plumptre & D.L. Jayanetti, 'Solar Heated Timber Drying Kilns', TRADA Technology Ltd and Overseas Development Administration, 1996

[24] Avril Fox & Robin Murrell, *Green Design*, ADTP, 1989

[25] Fox & Murrell op cit

[26] Brian Ridout, *Timber Decay in Buildings*, E&FN Spon, 2000

[27] 'New Ground', article in *Organic Gardening*, April 1997

[28] *Environmental Building News*, vol 12, no 3

[29] *Environmental Building News*, vol 6, no 3

[30] www.vincenttimber.co.uk

[31] *Sustain*, vol 2 issue 1

[32] *The Times*, 11/4/2002, and *Building For a Future* vol 13, no 1

[33] Ross Holleron 'Can the Wood Composite Industry Survive Without Formaldehyde?' paper for MSc Architecture, CAT/UEL, 2003

[34] BBA Agrement Certificate No 02/3950

[35] www.bre.co.uk/pdf/hemphomes.pdf

[36] Keith Hall & Peter Warm, *Greener Building*, AECB, 1998

[36a] Bjørn Berge, *Ecology of Building Materials*, Architectural Press, 2000, p356

[37] Barbara Jones, *Building with Straw Bales*, Green Books, 2002

[38] McLaren, Bullock & Yousuf , op cit

[39] Bjørn Berge op cit

[40] David Pearson, *The Natural House Book*, Gaia Books 1989

[41] David Easton, *The Rammed Earth House*, Chelsea Green Publishing, 1996

[41a] 'Review of ultra-low-energy homes – 10 UK Profiles', David Olivier and John Willoughby, BRECSU, 1996

[41b] Hockerton Housing Project Launch Brochure

[42] 'Environmental Impact of Materials: vol A', CIRIA 1995

[42a] Robert and Brenda Vale, *The New Autonomous House*, Thames & Hudson, 2000, p144

[43] Bjørn Berge op cit

[44] www.wbcsdcement.org

[45] Anink, Boonstra & Mak, *Handbook of Sustainable Building*, James & James, 1996

[45a] Richard Weston, *Materials, Form and Architecture*, Laurence King, 2003

[46] Bjørn Berge op cit

[47] Fred Pearce, 'Errors of Emission', *New Scientist*, 4/10/97

[48] figures from Corus, published in *EcoTech*, May 2003

[48a] Richard Weston, op cit

[49] Bjørn Berge op cit

[50] Cath Hassell, 'LCAs for copper versus plastic plumbing', paper for MSc Architecture, UEL and CAT

[51] *Guardian*, 7/1/03

[52] CIRIA, 1995 op cit

[53] McLaren at al, op cit

[54] Curwell et al

[55] Hall & Warm, *Greener Building*, AECB, 1998

Energy conservation

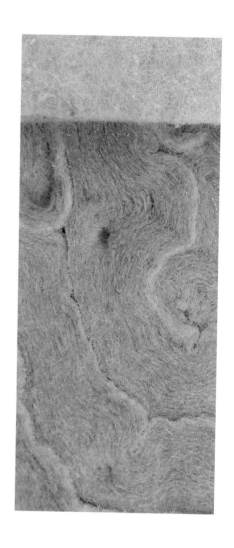

Why conserve?

Climate change

It is now pretty much accepted that some degree of climate change is in process and that mean global temperatures are set to rise by 2-3° over the next century. This will affect our lifestyles, surrounding habitats and possibly our health and economic prosperity. In particular it will probably mean:

- warmer, drier summers and milder wetter winters;
- increases in precipitation coupled with local water shortages and water table variations;
- an increase in 'extreme weather events' e.g. storms and hurricanes;
- rising seas and loss of small low-lying islands;
- higher UV radiation and an increase in airborne pollutants;
- an increase in wind activity.

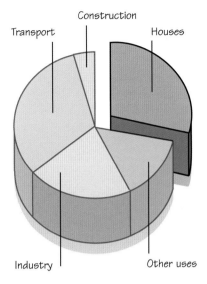

8.1

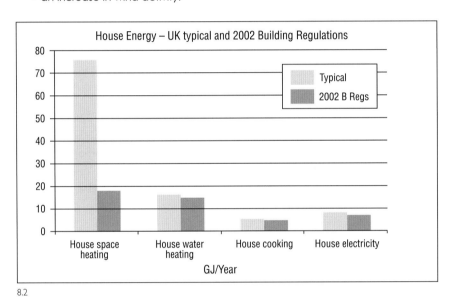

8.2

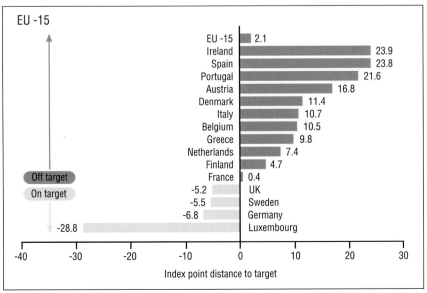

8.3

Fig. 8.1 Distributed energy use in Britain.

Fig. 8.2 End use energy proportions for an average UK house and one built to the current 2002 Building Regulations.

Fig. 8.3 EU greenhouse gas emissions distance to Kyoto. Protocol target, by country: 2001.

The impact on new building will probably be to restrict building on flood plains or near the coast and to require changes in structural performance to withstand the onslaught of 'extreme weather'. Demand for cooling buildings is likely to increase and the challenge for 'eco-construction' will be to find alternatives to conventional air conditioning systems.

The main driver of global warming is the release into the atmosphere of unprecedented amounts of carbon dioxide, mainly from burning fossil fuels for heat and electricity. Another problem is that known reserves of fossil fuels are likely to run out in the next 40-60 years at current rates of use. Although new reserves will continue to be discovered and exploited, extraction will probably become more difficult and expensive. And to make matters worse, the pollution caused by burning fossil fuels may be an even greater immediate threat to our health and survival.

Some change to the existing climate is inevitable and irreversible. Most people recognise the urgent necessity for action to limit the damage. International agencies and national governments have set targets for reduction of carbon emissions. In practice, this means reducing consumption of fossil fuel generated energy. And the most effective way to do that is to conserve energy and reduce our overall demand.

There are those who believe that the problem can be solved by increasingly sophisticated technology – the 'technical fix' – and this is important. Hence the support for wind turbines and solar panels. But a more holistic and lasting solution involves examining the effect on climate change of all our actions: buying food, going on holiday, and heating our homes – in other words our 'carbon footprint'. Reducing that will involve lifestyle changes as well as buying the latest A-rated fridge. Best results are achieved by combining modest lifestyle changes with the best technical solution.

Other benefits could flow from severely limiting fossil fuel consumption:
- reduced air pollution would alleviate many health and respiratory problems caused by photochemical smog;
- a reduction in the emissions that cause acid rain, would help preserve forests and other habitats;
- less motorised traffic would mean less congestion, noise and environmental degradation in our towns and cities;
- energy conservation in the housing stock could lead to urban regeneration, the elimination of fuel poverty and more comfortable homes.

Heat loss and heat gain

Since heating our houses ('space heating' as it is called) is still the largest proportion of domestic energy use in temperate zones, (see figure 8.2) it makes sense for any householder to tackle this first. As well as helping to save the planet, you will also save money and be more comfortable .

For the temperature to remain steady in the house, heat loss must equal heat gain.

The heat losses are threefold:
- through the fabric of the house (walls, roof, floor, windows and doors);
- through ventilation (to give us the fresh air we need);
- through infiltration (unwanted air movement through cracks in the construction).

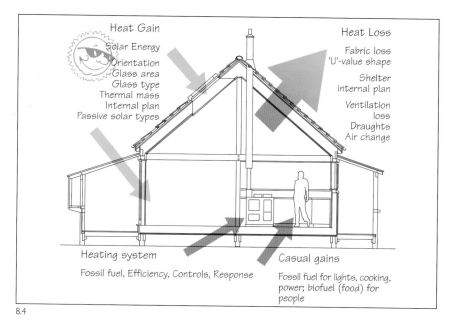

8.4

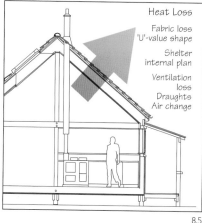

8.5

8.6

The rate of heat loss (watts) is determined by three factors:

• outside and radiant air temperature;

• inside air temperature (rate of heat loss is very sensitive to this – a reduction in the set temperature of 1°C will reduce heat loss by 5%);

• the heat transmission value (U-value) and area of the external fabric.

In this section we are looking at ways to minimise heat loss from the house, so it is helpful to understand a bit about the physics of the process.

Figure 8.5 shows the factors influencing heat loss, which we must try to minimise. Figures 8.4 and 8.6 show the three potential heat gains:

• from solar energy (passive and active solar heating);

• from casual heat gains – heat given off from activities in the house (from people, lights, cooking, hot water, TV, etc.);

• from the heating system (boiler, stove, etc).

A combination of all three of the following measures is the best approach to reducing our reliance on fossil fuels for heating:

1   Conserve first – lots of insulation and draughtproofing.

2   Harvest heat from the sun.

3   Use fossil fuels as efficiently as possible.

Casual heat gains

Average casual or incidental gains to a typical four person house are as follows:

Casual gains	Watts
Body heat from four people	320
Water heating	90
Cooking	100–140
Lighting and appliances	100–250
Total	450–730

As more efficient lights, appliances and cookers are deployed, so the internal gains decrease – but overall primary energy use also decreases (a boiler provides heat more efficiently than an electrical appliance). The human body gives off metabolic heat at between 80W (at rest) and 350W (heavy work): buildings such as

Fig. 8.4 Heat loss and gain into the house. If the gains are more than the losses – on a sunny, warm day, or when you have a big party (which generates heat from biofuels, or food as we call it) – the house will heat up. On a winter's night when the boiler is turned off, the heat loss will be larger than the gain, and the house will cool down. The rate at which it cools down depends mainly on how well the house is insulated. Heating design is the art of keeping these factors in balance to provide the appropriate comfort conditions.

Fig. 8.5 Heat Loss.

Fig. 8.6 Casual heat gains.

low-energy schools obtain most of their heat from hundreds of active children. Techniques for maximising solar gain are discussed in the section 'Energy from the Sun'.

Air temperature

The greater the difference between indoor and outdoor temperature, the faster heat is lost from a house. It is in the nature of energy that it moves from a high state (high temperature heat, light, electricity, gravity, chemical energy) to a low state (low temperature heat).

We use electricity to make light, this light radiates out and is absorbed by objects, which heat up slightly. So all light degrades to heat. Similarly, when an object falls from a high to a low place (kinetic energy), the impact creates heat. When we use the chemical energy in food to move about, heat is given off. Low grade (temperature) heat is the ultimate fate of all actions and all matter.

Energy can be changed from one form to another with very high efficiencies when going from a high to low state (electric heating is 100% efficient at point of use), but with low efficiencies in the other direction (electricity can only ever be produced from heat at an efficiency of about 30%). With energy conservation in houses (insulating and draughtstripping) we are trying in general to keep the inside air warmer than the outside air and to slow down the flow of heat. Of course, the flow of heat from inside to outside can never be completely stopped. Without heat input, the house will end up at the same temperature as its surroundings. Energy conservation, then, is just a slowing-up of the natural process, which allows us to make do with less fossil fuel heat input.

To this end, we need to know two things about the outside air temperatures: the likely minimum temperature and the seasonal average in heating degree days. (For hotter climates you would need to know maximum temperatures and cooling degree days.)

Minimum temperature

The combination of internal heat gains (from your activities, solar gains, and the heating system) need to offset the heat being lost at the lowest external temperature likely to be encountered. The absolute minimum temperature is likely to occur on a mid-winter night, when you should be tucked up under the duvet. These temperatures, say -13°C, will occur infrequently. It is not worth sizing the boiler to be able to cope; it will be hopelessly oversized most of the time. In the UK, it is usual practice to take a minimum temperature of between -1° and -3°C and ensure that the system can cope with this, assuming that the sun is not shining. This design temperature is, of course, entirely dependant on location. In Helsinki and Ottawa, it is -27°C; in Boston, Budapest and Vienna it is -15°C; in Rome, Canberra, London and Christchurch, New Zealand it is -1°C; in Sydney, Auckland and Hong Kong it is +7°C.

To find out the size of the boiler needed, you will have to work out the specific heat loss of the house. This is done by finding the areas and U-values of the external envelope, adding the ventilation and infiltration heat loss, and multiplying this total by the temperature difference between inside and outside.

8.7

Seasonal average – degree days

How cold is it over the whole of the winter (the heating season)? If you know this, you can work out how much fuel is needed for the year. The unit of measurement is the 'degree day'. A house has certain inputs of heat, apart from the boiler: solar gains and internal casual gains. For much of the year these will be enough to offset the heat loss, and no additional heat will be required. For each house – with its particular insulation value, passive solar gains and internal gains – there will be a certain 'base temperature'. When the outside temperature falls below this base temperature by one degree for one day, that is called one degree day.

Figure 8.7 shows variation in degree days across the UK. The moderating influence of sea-borne winds are evident, giving north-west Wales the same temperature climate as the Isle of Wight. The pocket of warmth around London is due to heat given off from buildings and cars, and trapped by air pollution. The winter temperature is around 2°C warmer than the surrounding countryside. Britain's mild, cloudy climate means that although its minimum temperatures are modest, its winters are very long and overcast compared to those on the Continent. Rome has the same design temperature of -1°C, but half the degree days of central England. Degree days for north Scotland are greater than for Munich and closer to that of southern Sweden.

Fig. 8.7 Annual degree days at sea level. Values increase by two degree days per metre of elevation above sea level.

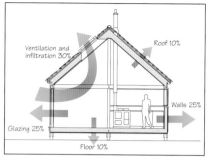

8.8

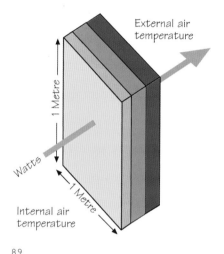

8.9

Fabric, ventilation and infiltration losses

Fabric losses – the U-value

Heat is conducted through the fabric of the house and lost to the outside air by radiation and convection. The U-value is a measure of how many watts (rate of flow of energy) pass through one square metre of construction for every degree difference in temperature between the inside and the outside. So a U-value of 6.0W/m²K (that of a single-glazed window) will mean that six watts will be escaping through each square metre of glass when the temperature difference is one degree. If it is 20°C in the house and 0°C outside, then the heat loss is 20x6=120W per square metre. Double-glazing roughly halves the heat loss, and so has a U-value of 3.0W/m²K. The lower the U-value, the better the insulation.

Location	Construction	U-value (W/m²K)
Roof	Uninsulated loft	2.00
	with 100m insulation	0.30
	Room in the roof 200mm (2002 UK)	0.20
	Loft with 250mm insulation (2002 UK)	0.16
	Superinsulated 300mm insulation	0.12
Wall	Solid brick 225mm	2.20
	Uninsulated cavity brick	1.30
	Uninsulated cavity lightweight block	0.96
	Cavity of timber frame wall with 50mm insulation	0.45
	with 100mm insulation (2002 UK)	0.35
	Superinsulated 250mm insulation	0.14
Floor	Timber floor uninsulated	0.83
	with 150mm insulation (2002 UK)	0.25
	Superinsulated 250mm insulation	0.14
	Solid floor uninsulated (average house)	0.70
	with 100mm insulation (2002 UK)	0.25
	Superinsulated 200mm insulation	0.15
Timber window	Single-glazed	4.80
	Double-low-E 12mm airspace (2002 UK)	2.00
	Double-low-E Argon fill 16mm airspace	1.70
	Triple-low-E Argon fill or double super low-E	1.30

8.10

Terms used for U-value

W = watts, the rate of energy loss
m² = square metres
K = temperature in degrees Kelvin, each degree being the same as the familiar degrees Celsius or centigrade.

Fig. 8.8 The proportions of heat loss from a typical house.

Fig. 8.9 U-value is the rate of heat loss in watts per square metre of construction multiplied by the temperature difference.

Fig. 8.10 Some typical U-values.

Ventilation and infiltration losses

The other way that heat escapes from our houses is via air movement – in well insulated houses more heat can be lost through ventilation and infiltration than through the fabric. Ventilation losses and how to combat them are discussed in subsequent sections.

Working out the heat load

Although there are many computer programmes available for energy assessment, you can do a basic calculation by hand – either by getting a copy of the UK Government's Standard Assessment Procedure (SAP) and Carbon Index Calculator or by using the simple table shown overleaf. Life will be easier if you use a spreadsheet programme on a personal computer; it saves a lot of arithmetic and you can instantly see the result of changes in U-value, window size, and so on. SAP worksheets can be downloaded free from http://projects.bre.co.uk/sap2001/

You need to know three things:

- the areas of all the different construction elements (walls, roof, windows) in square metres;
- the U-value of each construction element – from the table above;
- the house volume (floor area times the overall internal height).

Now make the following calculations:

1   Multiply each element area (m²) by its U-value – which gives the specific heat loss for this element.

2   Calculate the infiltration heat loss by multiplying the volume by 0.33, and then by the number of airchanges experienced in the house. This will be approximately 4 for an old, undraughtstripped house, 1 to 2 for an average modern house and 0.6 for a very tight, superinsulated house.

3   Add up all the heat losses together and you have a total, which is in the units of watts per K. K refers to the difference between the inside and outdoor temperature in degrees Celsius. As you are trying to find the maximum heat loss (so that you can size a boiler and radiators), the specific heat loss total must be multiplied by a likely temperature difference. If you want it to be 21°C inside, and the external minimum temperature is normally taken at -1°C, the difference is 22°C. This then gives you a peak heat loss in watts. You should add 10% to this figure (to cover the initial heat-up period – heating the house from cold) and divide the answer by 1000 to give the required boiler (or stove) output in kW (multiply by 3400 to get BTU/hour).

4   To get an approximation of your annual space heating bill, multiply the specific heat loss by degree days (take as 2000), multiply by 24 (hours in a day), and again divide by 1000 to get kWh per year. Then divide by boiler efficiency and multiply by fuel cost to arrive at your annual space heating fuel bill. The same kWh/year number can be used to estimate the weight of carbon given out by your boiler in a year.

Element	Area m² x W/m²K			U-value = Loss		Specific Heat	
Glazing							
North	1.00			x	3.0	=	3.00 W/k
East	2.50			x	3.0	=	7.50 W/k
South	14.00			x	3.0	=	42.00 W/k
West	2.50			x	3.0	=	7.50 W/k
Roof	1.50			x	2.2	=	3.30 W/k
Floor	45.00			x	0.82	=	36.90 W/k
		Less window area	Net area				
Wall	145.00	20.0	125.0	x	0.45	=	56.25 W/k
Roof	45.00	1.5	43.5	x	0.25	=	10.88 W/k

Infiltration

Airchange rate		House volume m³			
1	x	225	x	0.3333	= 74.99 W/k

Total Specific Heat Loss		=		242.32 W/k
Design Temperature Difference				22 °C
Peak Heat Loss		=		5331 Watts
(Specific Heat Loss x Temperature difference)				

Approximate Annual Heating
(Specific Heat Loss x Degree days x 24 hours/1000)

242.32	x	2000	x	24	/	1000	=	11631 kWh per year
			Divide by boiler efficiency			0.70	=	16616 kWh per year
			Multiply by fuel cost (gas) in £/kWh			£0.02	=	£332.32 per year

Carbon Dioxide Emissions

Annual delivered energy		16616 kWh per year
Carbon dioxide emission factor	x	0.187 kg/kWh
Carbon dioxide emission	=	3107 kg
		3.107 Tonnes

8.11

> **Ventilation** is the intentional use of windows, ventilators and fans to replace stale air with fresh air.
> **Infiltration** is the unwanted leakage of air through cracks in the house fabric and around windows and doors.

Fig. 8.11 A spreadsheet to calculate heat loss and annual heating energy.

Ventilation and infiltration

We need ventilation, for comfort and life support; we do not need infiltration. The basic approach is to seal up a house as tightly as is possible, and then to have plenty of opportunities to ventilate as needed: gentle background ventilation supplied from a conservatory; stack effect extract from steamy, smelly areas (see figure 8.19); a heat recovery ventilation system – there are many options. During the summer there should be secure background ventilation, as well as the option of throwing the windows wide open.

It seems alarming to suggest that we seal up a house as well as we possibly can, but the truth is that it is impossible to achieve a hermetic seal. Ventilation is only really necessary when we artificially create a very humid climate by cooking, washing, or bathing. It is also desirable, from time to time, to rid the house of cooking smells or other odours and, possibly, smoke.

British houses are poorly constructed compared to the average house in Northern Europe, Canada or the northern United States. In a conventionally constructed new house the air leakage rate is likely to be equivalent to all the air in a house being replaced by fresh, cold air every hour! All that cold air needs warming up in the winter and this is often the biggest heat loss. Masonry brick and block constructions that have been traditionally plastered are usually less 'leaky' than timber frame or dry lined construction.

BUILDING A LOW-ENERGY HOUSE (1)

This series of case studies runs throughout this section of the book, showing the effect of various insulation, efficiency and solar heating measures. It starts with a typical poorly insulated house – found in their thousands across the country – and gives the SAP rating and U-values for the building elements. The chart shows useful energy to the house split into the sources of solar gain, casual gains and heating plant.

House	1 (control case)
SAP	42 (out of a maximum of 100)
Description	A two-storey detached house of 90m² with 20m² of single-glazing distributed randomly on the four faces.

Element	U-value	Description
Walls	1.00	Brick/cavity/block or timber frame with no insulation
Roof	0.60	Tiled pitched roof with 50mm insulation
Floor	0.82	Uninsulated solid or suspended
Glazing	4.70	Single in timber frames

Window/floor	22%	Proportion of window to floor area
Ventilation	1.40 ac/hr	
Heat loss	1.84W/m³ of internal space	

Heating sources	per year (kWh)
Casual gains	3175
Solar gains	1675
Heating system	24155
Water heating	5520

Boiler efficiency	60%

Gas heating	Cost (£/p.a.)
Space heating	410
Water heating	85

CO₂ emissions	5.55 tonnes per year

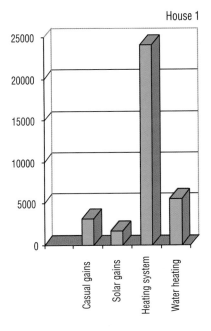

Heating supply in kWh/p.a. to the typical house – House 1.

The sections below deal with reducing unwanted air leakage and controlling ventilation, and are followed by a section on breathable constructions.

Airtightness

Most of us will be aware of the benefits of draughtproofing. It is one of the most beneficial energy saving measures available, both in financial and comfort terms. We are all familiar with the legion of DIY draughtstrips available for doors and windows and how effective they are – at least until the glue fails and they drop off. Less obvious is the air leakage that infiltrates through and around the house construction. To create a low-energy house, great care must be taken to build an airtight structure – there is little point in having thick insulation, only to lose heat through air infiltration. Having achieved airtightness, it is then important to have adequate and controllable ventilation to deal with excess humidity and unwanted odours – 'build tight...ventilate right'.

All new houses should be pressure tested for air infiltration – by fixing a large fan to a temporary front door and de-pressurising the house to several times atmospheric pressure. It is then very instructive to walk around the house with a small smoke generator and observe the air flowing in through all the cracks in the construction: under the skirting boards, through cracks between window and wall, through the loft hatch, even through the telephone socket. Airtightness performance is measured in cubic metres of air movement per hour, per square metre of external surface area of the house, at an applied pressure difference of 50 pascals. In most houses the surface area equates to the volume of the house and the figures are therefore roughly in airchanges per hour (ac/hr). The current UK Building Reulations calls for an air infiltration rate of not more than 10m³/m²/hr for non-domestic buildings over 1000m² (10ac/hr @ 50 pascals) and a 'best practice' target is 5ac/hr. However, the German 'Passivhaus' standard, which results in houses with only 10-15% of the heating demand of conventional houses, calls for an airtightness of 0.6ac/hr, and many have bettered this. The following list outlines the major air leakage paths:

8.12

8.13

8.14

Fig. 8.12 The procedure for slightly de-pressurising a house to check for air leakage involves fitting this giant fan into a doorway.

Fig. 8.13 Once a pressure difference between inside and outside of 50Pa has been achieved, a smoke gun shows exactly where and how air is getting into the house.

Fig. 8.14 High performance, wind and rain-tight Scandinavian timber window, with secure espagnolette ironmongery and double- or triple-low-E glazing.

Fig. 8.15 Possible paths for air infiltration in an old house. Illustration: Duncan Roberts.

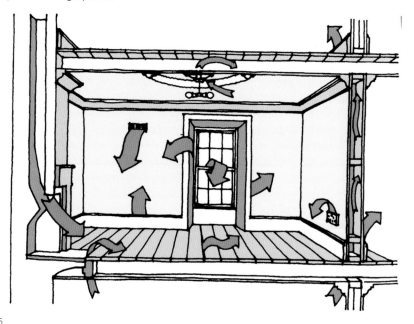
8.15

- Window and door openings: modern joinery is pretty well draughtstripped, but many casements distort and therefore do not seat properly. Most handles and catches are too feeble to close the window or door tight against the seals. Scandinavian-type 'espagnolette', multi-point ironmongery is best.
- Window/door to wall junctions: there are frequently gaps in construction particularly around windows and doors.
- Dry lining: it is common practice in new houses to dry line the walls by gluing plasterboard sheets on to the inside face of masonry walls, with 'dabs' of plaster. This leaves a small cavity behind the plasterboard which often connects with outside air. As well as ruining the insulating value of the wall construction, air can infiltrate at every junction.
- Suspended timber or concrete floors: the main air leakage will be where a suspended ground floor abuts the walls. At the first floor there may also be leakage around joist hangers, or more so if joists are built in.
- Pipes through floors and ceilings.
- Electrical fittings.
- Loft hatches.

In summary

- Seal all unwanted air paths, that continually lose heat.
- Control ventilation when and where you need it.
- Use well draughtstripped joinery with substantial closing ironmongery.
- Pressure test your house to find air leaks.
- Apply plaster direct to masonry walls rather than dry lining.
- Fill joints around windows and doors with sealant/mastic (on the inside).
- Insulate with blown or sprayed cellulose.

Porches and lobbies

These unheated spaces between the warm inside and the cold outside (buffer spaces) act as airlocks every time we venture out. This stops cold external air directly entering the warm interior. The general principle used to prevent wind and wind-driven rain from entering a building is to provide a loose-fit rainscreen that absorbs all that energy, a sort of sacrificial layer. The inner line of defence – in this case a well draughtstripped door – will then have a much easier job to do.

Ideally, porches and lobbies should be cheap, unheated and as large as can be afforded; the more outside wall, window, and door they protect, the better insulated the house will be. A lobby consists of a partition and inner door protecting the inside from draughts coming through an external door.

As the air in buffer spaces is always warmer than external air, it is very useful if ventilation for the house can be taken from these spaces, particularly if they are glazed. It is not that easy to ensure this replacement of house air with buffer space air – wind pressure can easily interfere with this – but if it works, such an arrangement (called ventilation preheat) is a very effective energy saving measure.

Ventilation

Trickle ventilation

Fresh air is needed to reintroduce oxygen, to remove human contaminants (smells, smoke, CO_2), and to restore the humidity to a comfortable level. In living rooms and

8.16

8.17

Fig. 8.16 Solar ventilation preheat is a better energy saving device than ventilation heat recovery. Ventilation flow through the conservatory can be helped by passive stack ventilation or a small fan. This photo depicts a good arrangement – the buffer space door is at 90% to the house door, encouraging the occupant to close one door before opening the other.
Architect: Architype.

Fig. 8.17 A porch added to an old stone house to improve sound insulation and prevent heat loss.

8.18

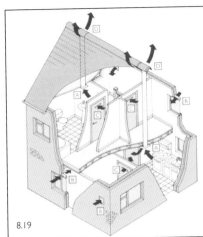

A — Stack ventilation ducts are installed in those rooms where most moisture is generated, i.e. the kitchen and bathroom.

B – Air inlets are installed in walls or windows of all other rooms.

C – Air transfer grilles are installed (through doors etc.) to permit air flow through all rooms.

D – The stack effect creates an air flow through the vertical ducts, thus extracting moist polluted air. During cold weather conditions this causes fresh air to be drawn in through the inlets, which is automatically distributed throughout the whole house.

8.19

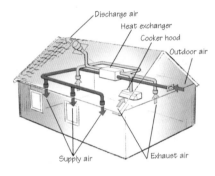

8.20

bedrooms it will normally be sufficient to have – and the Building Regulations require it for new build and renovation – a draught-free, closeable ventilator, usually in the form of a trickle ventilation slot built into a window head.

Passive stack ventilation

We must be able to ventilate well those areas of a house that cause most of the airborne pollution: the kitchen and bathroom. Since warm air rises, if these rooms contain pipes (of 100-150mm diameter) running from the ceilings to a roof opening, ventilation will be automatic and increase with the polluting activities. This is called passive (no fans) stack ventilation. Ideally, replacement fresh air will come via a conservatory or other buffer space (ventilation preheat), or through other rooms. To prevent ventilation when it is not required, stacks should be fitted with humidity-controlled valves so ventilation will only occur when there is a potential dampness problem.

Electric fans are also sometimes fitted if it is judged that passive ventilation alone would not always be adequate. The fan should be controlled by a humidity-sensitive switch.

Whole house mechanical ventilation with heat recovery (MVHR)

In a well-insulated house, most of the heating effort goes towards warming up the ventilation air. Originating from countries with very cold winter air temperatures, such as Sweden and Canada, an MVHR system will extract stale air and smells from areas of high humidity, such as the kitchen and bathroom. This warm air is passed through a heat exchanger. Fresh air is drawn from the outside through the heat exchanger and picks up around 85% of the heat that would have been lost. The warmed fresh air is then introduced into the living rooms and bedrooms. The house needs to be constructed as tightly as possible to avoid air leakage paths.

Such systems can be built into any house, with the heat exchanger, fans and controls usually fitted into a kitchen cupboard above the cooker. Whole house ventilation provides a high standard of draught-free comfort, and in very low-energy houses it can serve as the heating supply as well with a heating element installed in the supply duct. Electrical demands tend to be high (usually two 60W fans) to overcome the air resistance of all the small ducts threading through the house – sometimes more primary energy is used to generate the electricity to run the fans than is saved via the heat exchanger.

Fig. 8.18 Low-energy, through-the-wall heat recovery ventilation, for a bathroom or kitchen (Baxi UK Ltd).

Fig. 8.19 A passive stack ventilation system. Willan Building Services Ltd.

Fig. 8.20 Whole house heat recovery ventilation system. The fresh air intake (blue) can terminate in a conservatory or other solar preheater. Care must be taken to ensure that the air doesn't take a short cut between the living rooms and conservatory.

BUILDING A LOW-ENERGY HOUSE (2)

Ventilation and draughtproofing

House	No. 2
SAP	49
Description	As previous house with the following additions: all openings draughtstripped, lobbies on external doors, no open flues.

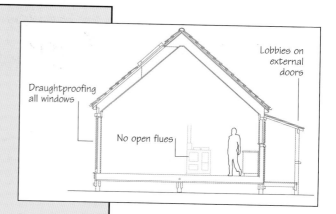

Element	U-value	Description
Walls	1.00	Brick/cavity/block or timber frame with no insulation
Roof	0.60	Tiled pitched roof with 50mm insulation
Floor	0.82	Uninsulated solid or suspended
Glazing	4.70	Single in timber frames, draughtstripped

Window/floor	22%	Proportion of window to floor area
Ventilation	0.70 ac/hr	
Heat loss	1.59W/m³ of internal space	

Heating sources	per year (kWh)
Casual gains	3110
Solar gains	1640
Heating System	19975
(House 1	24155 – for comparison)
Water Heating	5520

Boiler efficiency	60%

Use of gas	Cost (£/p.a.)	Savings (£/p.a.)	Cost of implementation (£)
Space heating	339	71	200 (DIY)
Water heating	85		

CO₂ emissions	4.77 tonnes per year
CO₂ savings on House 1	0.78 tonnes per year

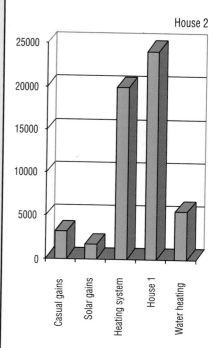

House 2

Heating supply and energy conservation measures to House 2 in kWh/p.a.

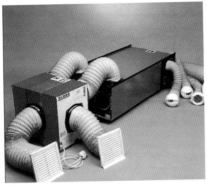

8.21

8.23

8.24

8.22

Systems are now available that use larger diameter ducts and low resistance heat exchangers to reduce fan power to a minimum (two 10W fans). Unnecessary airflow is reduced by installing humidity-sensitive extraction grilles, so that extraction only takes place when there is a potential problem. The source of fresh air to the heat exchanger can be taken from a conservatory or from the loft-space, where the air is warmer than that outside, and advantage can thus be taken of passive solar gains.

An alternative to the whole house system is to have individual humidity-controlled heat exchange fans in the kitchen and bathroom. These fans are designed to extract more air than they provide back into the rooms, so drawing some air from the rest of the house. They save approximately twice the primary energy they consume in their fans.

Insulation

This section deals with the external fabric of a house – the roof, walls, ground floor, doors and windows – and ways to reduce the flow of heat through them. A house with good insulation will not only use less fossil fuel – therefore emitting less pollution and being cheaper to keep warm – but will also be more comfortable in winter and cooler in summer. Ideally, every house should be superinsulated, a term used to describe levels of insulation thought to be the optimum for a cold climate. The following list provides a rough guide to minimum levels of superinsulation:

Roof	300-450mm
Timber walls	200-300mm
Masonry walls	150-250mm
Solid floor	150mm
Suspended floor	200-250mm
Windows	At least double-glazed low-E, gas-filled

Many houses have been built or upgraded to higher levels than these with no disbenefit; the basic rule is that where insulating is easy, put more in. The costs of insulating are dominated by the costs of materials required to contain the insulation or to keep it dry. Bulk insulation materials are cheap and have very good energy and financial paybacks. So, for example, if an unused loft space is being insulated with loose blown cellulose, the cost of an extra 150mm is almost marginal compared to the cost of getting the installer set-up on site. The most cost effective solution is to

Fig. 8.21 The kit of parts for whole house ventilation (plus lots of ducting). The system should have large diameter ducts and low-wattage fans, otherwise it can use more primary energy than it saves.

Fig. 8.22 The new generation of whole house heat recovery ventilation systems use low-wattage fans, larger ducts to give improved efficiencies. (Vent-Axia Air Minder).

Fig. 8.23 Still the most insulated house in Britain, the Low Energy House was built at CAT in 1976 to demonstrate the effectiveness of superinsulation. It has a maximum heat load of just over 1kW (one bar of an electric fire), is cocooned in 450mm of insulation, and has quadruple-glazed windows. Despite over the top insulation and some novel heat pump technology, the energy conservation measures have paid for themselves more than three times over. Architect: Peter Bond.

Fig. 8.24 The Low Energy House under construction. The cavity is so wide in the masonry walls that wall ties would be ineffective, so each wall is independent, with internal stiffening piers. The walls only come together at openings.

Fig. 8.25

TYPE OF INSULATION MATERIAL	CONDUCTIVITY (λ) measured in watts per mK
	.01 .02 .03 .04 .05 .06 .07 .08 .09 0.1 0.11
ORGANIC: Derived from natural vegetation Renewable source Reclaimable upon demolition	CORK slabs, tile and granular fill — ◇ at .04
	EXPANDED RUBBER pipe sections, etc. — ◇ at .04
	WOOD FIBRE insulation board — ◇ at .045
	HEMP loose fill — ◇ at .045
	HEMP/LIME rigid construction — ◇ at .095
	SHEEPS WOOL Felted quilt — ◇ at .035
	FLAX Felted quilt — ◇ at .035
	WOODWOOL rigid slabs — ◇ at .085
	CELLULOSE loose fill in shredded paper pellet form — ◇ at .035
INORGANIC: Derived from naturally occurring minerals Non-renewable but plentiful source Reclaimable upon demolition	MINERAL FIBRES rockwool, slagwool & fibreglass, & quilts — ◇ at .035
	PERLITE & VERMICULITE loose fill, aggregate for concrete — ◇ at .045
	AERATED CONCRETE air-entrained in situ concrete blocks — ◇ at 0.1
	FOAMED GLASS glass in cellular form — ◇ at .04
FOSSIL ORGANIC: Derived by chemical industry from fossilised vegetation Difficult to reclaim upon demolition (check for use of CFCs or urea formaldehyde in manufacture)	EXPANDED POLYSTYRENE 'bead board' — usually white — ◇ at .04
	EXTRUDED EXPANDED POLYSTYRENE semi-rigid smooth-skinned closed cell boards, usually tinted — ◇ at .03
	POLYURETHANE FOAM closed cell semi-rigid boards and foam fill — ◇ at .025
	UREA & PHENOL FORMALDEHYDE FOAM ditto — ◇ at .035
	POLYISOCYANURATE FOAM ditto — ◇ at .025

insulate all the elements (walls, floor, roof) equally. It is sometimes necessary to trade off: if insulating the walls of a historic building is undesirable, then putting 450mm in the loft will partly compensate.

The materials used to insulate, as well as the form of construction, should be chosen with care. The ideal is to insulate with renewable, benign materials wherever possible, and to arrange the construction layers so that water vapour from the warm, more humid inside can gently escape to the cold outside without causing damage on the way: breathable constructions.

A well insulated house feels much more comfortable than a poorly insulated one. It will probably heat up quicker and it will have warmer surfaces with fewer convection currents due to cold surfaces.

Fig. 8.25 Insulation materials grouped by source, showing their conductivity (the smaller the number, the better). The first choice should be organic materials from renewable sources, then the non-renewable but plentiful inorganic materials, and finally those from fossil organic sources.

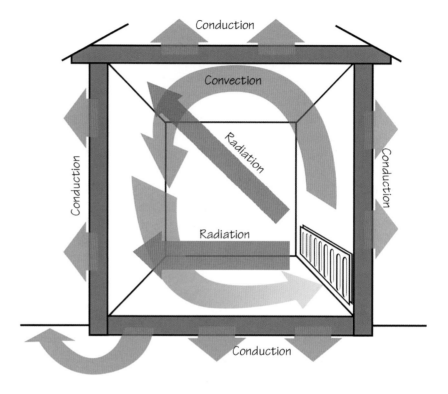

8.26

Insulation – how does it work?

Heat moves about by conduction, convection or radiation.

- **Conduction:** materials have different conductivities – heat will be conducted quickly from a gas flame to all parts of a metal saucepan, but the wooden handle remains cool. Air is a poor conductor of heat, therefore, all insulation materials have lots of airspace separated by the minimum of material in them.

- **Convection:** if the airspaces in the insulation are too large, heat will be transferred across by convection currents. The air heats up on the warm side, gets less dense, rises and is replaced by colder air; a circular pattern of air movement is set up, moving heat from one side to the other. The airspaces must be small enough to suppress convection currents. Gases other than air can be used which are less conductive, but in the past these have had damaging side-effects (CFC, HCFC).

- **Radiation:** heat is also transferred by infrared radiation (similar to light, but at a wavelength we cannot see). This radiation can be reflected by shiny surfaces such as metal foils. Foil-backed plasterboard will partly reflect radiant heat back into the room.

Fig. 8.26 Heat movement by conduction, convection and radiation.

Insulation – how thick should it be?

There is no one easy answer. But there are a number of points to consider.

- **Energy payback:** the amount of energy used to manufacture insulation (embodied energy content) must be compared to the energy savings made over its lifetime. The energy payback for insulation is very short (usually the first winter). The optimum insulation thickness (in terms of energy of manufacture versus energy savings) has been calculated at around 600mm for an average cold climate with design temp of -1°C.
- **Financial payback:** there are a large number of variables which make it impossible to give a generalised figure – which fuel is being used, how quickly its cost is rising, probable future interest rates, where the insulation is being put, whether the house is old or newly built, whether the insulation is fitted by the homeowner or a professional contractor, what pattern of heating is used and what the external climate is like. The benefits of adding insulation reduce as the insulation gets thicker – the first inch is very beneficial, the next slightly less so. Figure 8.28b shows total costs against insulation thickness flattens off at around 350mm.

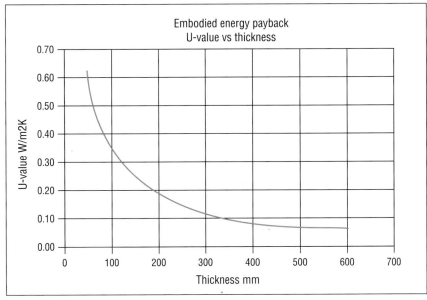

8.27

- **Installation considerations:** the overriding concern in deciding on insulation thickness will probably be how much it can be easily fitted in. An unused loft space can easily have thick layers of insulation installed; however, to internally insulate many existing house walls is difficult and inconvenient. Add a little rather than none at all. In new houses, constructions can be adapted to take the optimum levels of insulation as above or more.
- **Type of insulation:** all insulants that contain air have much the same insulating value; the differences are in the conductivity of the separating matrix (fibres, plastics foam). Some of the newer plastic foams, such as polysiocyanurate, are claimed to have lower conductivities.

There is another form of insulation consisting of several layers of aluminum foil on bubble polythene sheet. This can be useful in renovation work as it doubles as a vapour barrier.

Fig. 8.27 The optimum thickness of loft insulation – in simple energy packback terms – is around 600mm (24").

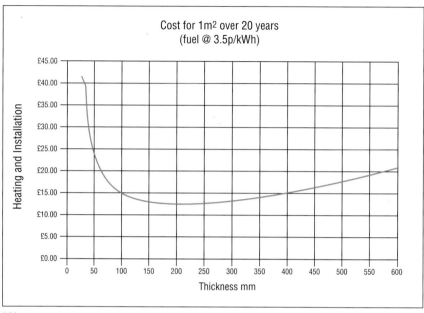

8.28a

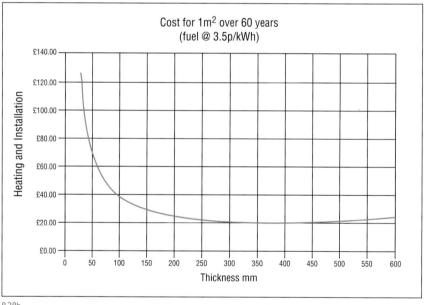

8.28b

Fig. 8.28a & 8.28b The optimum thickness of loft insulation – in terms of financial payback – depends on installation costs, the price of fuel and the time period. Currently 250-400mm (10"-16") seems reasonable.

CONDENSATION AND BREATHABLE CONSTRUCTIONS

When warm, moist air reaches a cold surface, condensation takes place. We have all seen this on the mirror or windows or gloss-painted surfaces in our bathroom. If the bathroom remains unventilated, mould can grow on the damp surface, damaging both the paintwork and our health. There is said to be a high vapour pressure in the bathroom. Water molecules are whizzing around trying to find a nice cool resting place but are prevented from escaping by the impermeable surfaces, such as glass, tiles and gloss paint. If the structure of the room is well-insulated, there will be no surface condensation, as the surfaces are near room temperature. Instead, the water vapour will make its way through the construction until it reaches a cold layer near the outside of the insulation, where it will condense (this is known as the dew point). This unfortunate process is called interstitial condensation. If it is allowed to accumulate within the structure, the dampness will give rise to mould or fungal growth and can rot structural timbers.

This process happens all the time with masonry (bricks and blocks) constructions, but the materials that are used do not support mould growth, so no damage is done. However in a timber frame wall, floor or roof, great care must be exercised to prevent interstitial condensation. A *World in Action* television programme in 1982 highlighted faulty timber frame constructions where condensation damage was extensive. Much adverse publicity for timber framing was generated.

Timber frame constructions should be free of problems if a few rules are rigorously applied:

- The construction must have higher vapour resistance materials on the inside than on the outside. Some materials, such as glass and metal sheet, are virtually impermeable to water vapour. Others have a high resistance, such as polyethylene, aluminium foil and bituminous roofing felt. Most building materials, such as plasterboard, insulation fibres, fibreboards, and bricks, have a low vapour resistance. The rule of thumb is to have five times the vapour resistance on the warm side of the construction than on the cold side. It is good practice to introduce a specific material whose job it is to provide the required vapour resistance – this is called the vapour check layer.

- The construction must be airtight on the inside. It is not much good having a vapour check layer if moisture-laden air can bypass it through holes made for electrical wiring or gaps between the floor and wall. The best practice is to have no services penetrating the vapour check, instead, lay them in an internal services zone.

- The construction must prevent outside air from entering the insulation. Cold air leaking in around the insulation will drastically reduce its effectiveness. Gaps in the insulation can mean that the house is separated from outside air by only a sheet of plasterboard.

- The outer layer of the construction should be protected by a ventilated rainscreen – for example, tiles on a roof, timber boarding, masonry, or render on lath.

In the last few years constructions have been designed using a material on the outside which has an extremely low vapour resistance – for example, using fibreboard as sheathing on a timber frame wall rather than the conventional high-vapour resistance plywood. This means (following the 5:1 rule) that the inner layer

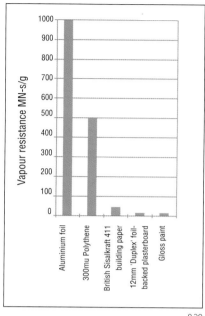

8.29

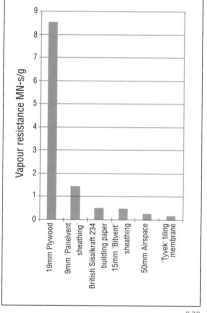

8.30

Fig. 8.29 & 8.30 Vapour resistance of check materials (top) and sheathing materials (bottom).

glass	10,000
metal sheet	10,000
aluminium foil	1,000
300mu Polythene	500
200mm Expanded polystyrene insulation	60
Bitumen tiling felt	50
British Sisalkraft 411 building paper	42
gloss paint	15
12mm 'Duplex' foil-backed plasterboard	15
19mm plywood	8.5
100mm brick or blockwork	5
6mm oil tempered hardboard	3.9
25mm timber (wet)	3
25mm timber (dry)	1.5
9mm 'Panelvent' sheathing	1.4
200mm 'Warmcel' insulation	1.4
200mm mineral fibre insulation	1.4
12mm cork	1.25
50mm woodwool slab	1
12mm plasterboard	0.75
emulsion paint	0.5
British Sisalkraft 234 building paper	0.5
15mm 'Bitvent' sheathing	0.45
50mm airspace	0.25
'Tyvek' tiling membrane	0.14

Fig. 8.31

can have a lower vapour resistance than the commonly used polythene. It is felt that the overall lower vapour resistance of this arrangement, commonly called 'breathable construction', will lead to a more healthy internal environment without excessive vapour pressures. In practice, the amount of vapour movement through a breathable construction is tiny compared to the moisture transferred to the outside by even a small amount of ventilation (a minimal 0.5ac/hr will remove around 25 times the moisture diffused through the breathable walls).

The concept of a breathable construction – a very low external vapour resistance balanced by a higher internal vapour resistance – should result in inherently safer timber frame buildings. However, unless the principles outlined above are followed, the construction could fail in its job of providing a well-insulated, trouble-free envelope.

Although we have been discussing the timber frame wall, which includes its close relative – the timber frame room-in-a-roof – most common building constructions 'breathe':

- **A conventional loft:** this has a highly ventilated, rain-protected space above the insulation. Loft hatches must securely latch down onto draught seals and ideally all services should be within the house. The insulation should fill all gaps (apart from those required for eaves ventilation) and cover the ceiling joists.
- **A masonry wall with cavity fill:** condensation will take place on the inner face of the external leaf, which will not damage the type of waterproof insulation that is used (the outer brickwork is usually rain-soaked anyway).
- **A suspended timber floor:** as with the loft, it is important that the floor is airtight, especially around the junction with the walls but ventilated underneath. Floorboards should be tight fitting or glued together.

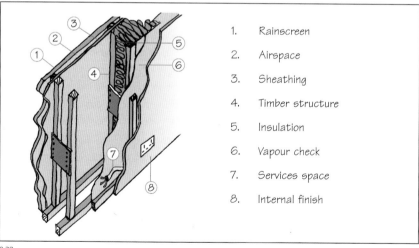

1.	Rainscreen
2.	Airspace
3.	Sheathing
4.	Timber structure
5.	Insulation
6.	Vapour check
7.	Services space
8.	Internal finish

8.32

The breathable timber frame wall used at CAT

A timber frame wall, or a roof construction that follows the line of the rafters (room-in-a-roof), is designed as an integrated whole, with the different materials performing many functions and requiring specific characteristics. The layered make-up of materials we use has many variants as described below, working from the outside to the inside.

Fig. 8.31 Vapour resistances of building materials (MN-s/g).

Fig. 8.32 The CAT breathable timber-frame wall.

Rain screen
- **Function:** to protect the insulated wall (or roof) from driving rain, snow and sunlight, and to lessen heat loss by wind chill and convection. Aesthetic appeal and durability are variables to be decided on an individual basis.
- **Materials:** tiles, shingles and slates, timber boarding, lime/sand render on woodwool and masonry.

Airspace
- **Function:** to separate the rainscreen from the insulated wall. The airspace will be ventilated top and bottom, unless the vapour resistance of the rainscreen is very low, as in a dry stone wall.
- **Materials:** the airspace is formed by 50x25mm battens of durable timber nailed through the sheathing into the studs.

Sheathing
- **Function:** to prevent cold outside air infiltrating the wall. To provide containment for the insulation materials. To make the wall stiff (racking resistance). To provide a temporary waterproof finish during construction; but also a low-vapour resistance.
- **Materials:** 15mm 'bitvent' or 18mm 'sarkit' bitumen-impregnated fibreboards; 9mm 'panelvent' medium board; 'Gutex Multiplex' medium board, nailed all round to the timber structure.

Timber structure
- **Function:** to support the weight of building materials and other loads. To space apart the inner and outer layers and provide a 200-350mm void for insulation.
- **Materials:** homegrown durable timber studs, spaced apart with hardboard web pieces, or any offcuts.

The timber sizes will depend on wall height and loading – a non-loadbearing 2.4m high wall will use two 50x50mm timber studs, while a loadbearing one will require one layer to be 100x50mm studs. Alternatively, Masonite ı-shaped studs and rafters can be used, which are particularly useful in room-in-a-roof constructions.

Insulation
- **Function:** to slow down heat loss. Some insulation materials are also highly hygroscopic, absorbing water that will be released later when conditions allow.
- **Materials:** Warmcel cellulose fibre, which has the thermal benefit of being blown or damp-sprayed into every gap open to it. This gap-filling property has been found to increase its effective insulation value by 25% compared to mineral fibres. Sheep's wool is a benign and renewable insulation material, now produced in this country and certified with BBA approval. Flax based insulation, currently being imported into the UK, is another good environmental choice. All these materials are highly hygroscopic.

Vapour check
- **Function:** to slow the diffusion of water vapour through the construction down to a safe level. To provide an airtight layer, preventing saturated air reaching the cold parts of the construction. To contain the insulation.

8.33a

8.33b

- **Materials:** use Paneline medium board or British Sisalkraft's 410 building paper, made of reinforced kraft paper containing a thin layer of bitumen. The vapour resistance is not too high and they are strong and easy to handle. The advantages of using a paper vapour check are that it is easy to seal around any openings and fold into difficult junctions. However, it is vulnerable to tearing and puncture. Other options are hardboard, plywood/OSB, or foil-backed plasterboard.

Services space

- **Function:** to avoid wiring and pipes penetrating the vapour check layer (VCL). Services will also be easier to lay and maintain, and electrical wiring will not overheat, as can happen when it is surrounded by insulation.
- **Materials:** the services space is formed by 50x25mm battens nailed over the VCL into the studs – this void will be deep enough for electrical outlet boxes and 15mm plumbing.

Internal finish

- **Function:** to provide a durable, attractive and highly-hygroscopic finish.
- **Materials:** there is a large range to choose from – plasterboards finished with gypsum plaster; clayboards and reedboards (Claytec) finished with fine clay plaster; (Claytec, Terrafino), woodwool slab (Heraklith); or wooden lath finished with lime putty render' and timber boarding. Timber has the useful characteristic that its vapour resistance increases as it gets wetter – that is, when conditions get more humid.

Roofs

Loft

A cold loft roof, where tiling is supported on a pitched roof structure and insulation is at ceiling level, is the cheapest and most common form of construction in Britain. If carefully built, it should be trouble-free.

It is very easy and cost-effective to install a thick layer of insulation (300mm minimum). A ventilation slot must be left at the eaves. A loft hatch should be insulated to the same thickness and draughtproofed, both to prevent cold loft air

Fig. 8.33a & 8.33b The Tradis system of pre-insulated 'breathing wall' cassettes, give benefits of high performance, airtightness and speed of erection.

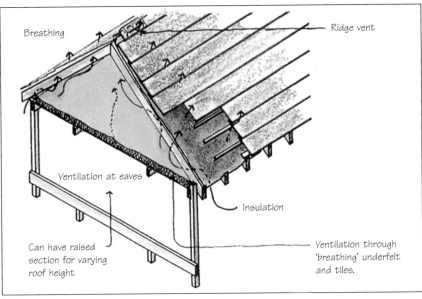

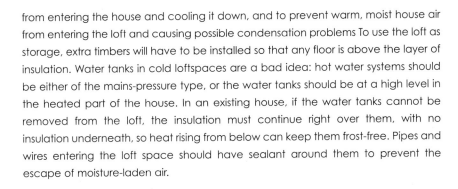

Breathing

Ridge vent

Ventilation at eaves

Insulation

Can have raised
section for varying
roof height

Ventilation through
'breathing' underfelt
and tiles.

8.34

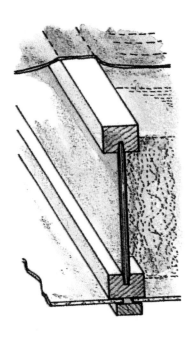

8.35a

from entering the house and cooling it down, and to prevent warm, moist house air from entering the loft and causing possible condensation problems To use the loft as storage, extra timbers will have to be installed so that any floor is above the layer of insulation. Water tanks in cold loftspaces are a bad idea: hot water systems should be either of the mains-pressure type, or the water tanks should be at a high level in the heated part of the house. In an existing house, if the water tanks cannot be removed from the loft, the insulation must continue right over them, with no insulation underneath, so heat rising from below can keep them frost-free. Pipes and wires entering the loft space should have sealant around them to prevent the escape of moisture-laden air.

Room in the roof

To make full use of available space in a house, rooms are often created in the roof. This is the preferred low-energy construction as it is likely to be more airtight. Such rooms are of interesting shape, and are naturally warmed by virtue of being at the top of the house. High levels of roof insulation can be difficult to achieve. The conventional pre-fabricated trussed rafter roof used in most new houses, cannot be insulated in this way, though 'attic trusses' go some way towards it. A free air space of 50mm must be left between the insulation and the tiling felt, unless this felt is of a low-vapour resistance type (e.g. 'Tyvek/Permo'). The most economical way of achieving a good thickness of insulation in the roof slope is to have two layers of timber: the first to support the roof finish; the second to support the insulation and ceiling finish. Insulation can then fill in between the timbers, providing a thermal break between the timbers. Relative to insulation, timber is a cold bridge to the outside and should be made discontinuous if possible. Timber I-beams (Masonite) can be used in new constructions. In an existing traditional roof, with rafters supported on roof beams, the second layer of timbers (ceiling joists) can either be hung off the rafters using hardboard, ply or timber 'hangers', or nailed crosswise to them, or they can span between the roof beams. This technique can also be used for upgrading flat roofs.

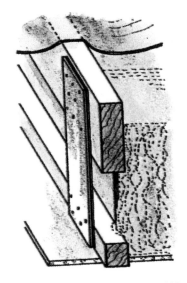

8.35b

Fig. 8.34 Ventilated cold loft.
8.35a Top: Manufactured composite I-beam rafter
Bottom Fig. 8.35b: Composite deep rafter made from
two slender timbers plated together.

8.36

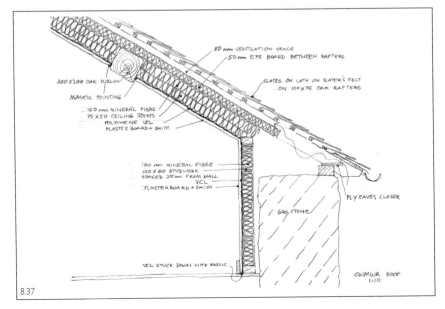

8.37

Fig. 8.36 When insulating an old purlin roof like this, fix a layer of 70x50cm ceiling joists parallel to the rafters but set as an independent structure spanning between the purlins (horizontal roof beams). In this roof the joists were set so that the oak purlins just showed proud of the plasterboard finish which gave 175-200mm of insulation thickness.

Fig. 8.37 Insulating a traditional purlin attic. New ceiling joists supported on the purlins and the studwork dry-lining, with insulation filling the whole roof void.

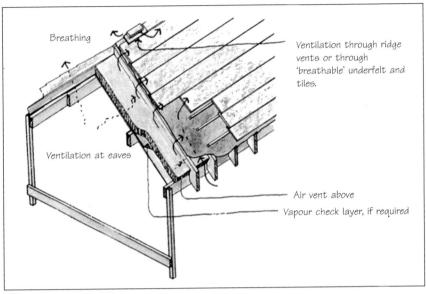

Breathing

Ventilation through ridge vents or through 'breathable' underfelt and tiles.

Ventilation at eaves

Air vent above

Vapour check layer, if required

8.38

Upside down and warm roof

An 'upside down' roof is a technique for insulating a flat or sloping roof using waterproof insulation on the outside of the structure. It is a useful way of upgrading an existing roof when internal room height is at a premium.

On a flat roof the insulation is simply laid over the waterproof membrane and held from blowing away by concrete paving slabs, pebbles or turf. The insulation material must be waterproof – and is therefore expensive – such as cork, foamed glass or closed cell plastics foam.

Where the insulation is sandwiched between a vapour control layer and the roofing membrane, or, on a sloping roof where the tiling battens are supported by the rigid insulation and fixed through to the rafters by special screwnail fixings, it is called a 'warm' roof, as the main timbers are on the warm side of the insulation.

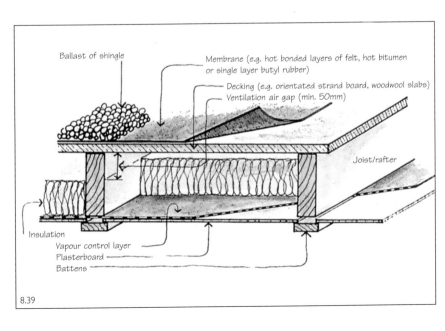

Ballast of shingle

Membrane (e.g. hot bonded layers of felt, hot bitumen or single layer butyl rubber)

Decking (e.g. orientated strand board, woodwool slabs)
Ventilation air gap (min. 50mm)

Joist/rafter

Insulation
Vapour control layer
Plasterboard
Battens

8.39

Fig. 8.38 Ventilated insulation in the roof plane.
Fig. 8.39 Flat ventilated roof construction.

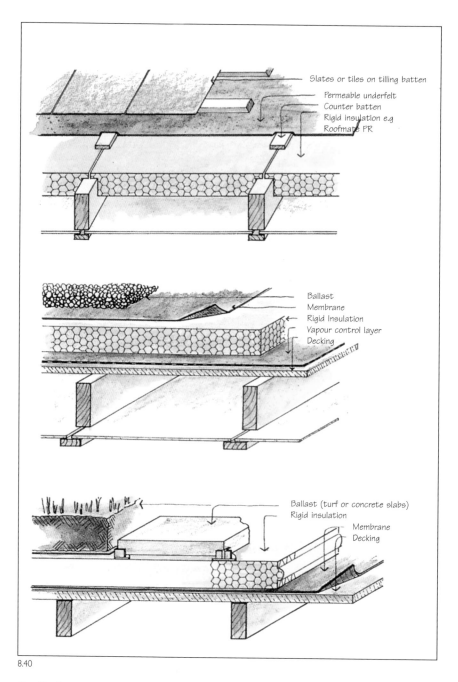

Slates or tiles on tilling batten
Permeable underfelt
Counter batten
Rigid insulation e.g
Roofmate PR

Ballast
Membrane
Rigid Insulation
Vapour control layer
Decking

Ballast (turf or concrete slabs)
Rigid insulation
Membrane
Decking

8.40

Our Preference

Room in the roof construction with spaced rafters or ɪ-beam rafters and at least 300mm insulation.

Fig. 8.40 From top to bottom: unventilated warm pitch roof, unventilated warm flat roof and upside down flat roof.

BUILDING A LOW-ENERGY HOUSE (3)

Insulating the roof

House	No. 3
SAP	51
Description	As previous house but with the following additions: 300mm loft insulation

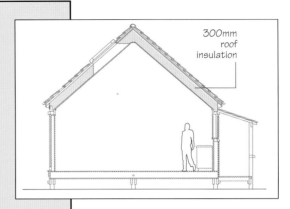

Element	U-Value	Description
Walls	1.00	Brick/cavity/block or timber frame with no insulation
Roof	0.13	Tiled pitched roof with 300mm insulation
Floor	0.82	Uninsulated solid or suspended
Glazing	4.70	Single in timber frames, draughtstripped

Window/floor	22%	Proportion of window to floor area
Ventilation	0.70ac/hr	
Heat loss	1.50W/m³ of internal space	

Heating sources	per year (kWh)
Casual gains	3025
Solar gains	1570
Heating system	18590
(House 1	24155 – for comparison)
Water heating	5520

Boiler efficiency	60%

Use of gas	Cost (£/p.a.)	Savings (£/p.a.)	Cost of implementation (£)
Space heating	316	94	300 (DIY)
Water heating	85		

CO₂ emissions	4.5 tonnes per year
CO₂ savings on House 1	1.04 tonnes per year

Note: Cost of energy saving measures are for DIY on old house or new-build extra cost, and are very approximate.

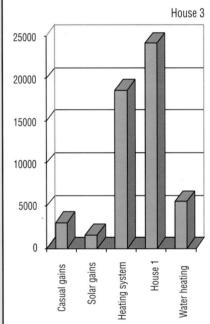

House 3

Heating supply and energy conservation measures to House 3 in kWh/p.a.

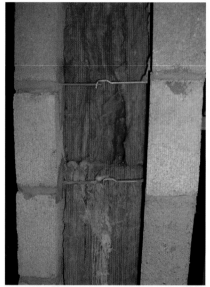

8.41

8.42

Fig. 8.41 A low-energy cavity block construction. 200mm of mineral fibre and two-piece stainless steel wall ties.

Fig. 8.42 Cavity wall with 150mm of mineral wool insulation, stone outer face and aerated concrete block inner skin. There is a danger of 'cold bridging' at the door opening (CAT restaurant building).

Walls

Masonry – cavity walls

Masonry walls (brick, block and stonework) built within the last 60 years have generally been of two skins with a 50mm cavity between. This was done principally to reduce dampness, but the air space also provides some thermal insulation. If this cavity is filled with insulating material, the heat loss is further reduced. This insulation must, however, be waterproof and installed in such a way as to prevent dampness crossing the cavity. On very exposed sites the cavity should be left unfilled or only partially filled in new constructions. In existing walls, the insulating materials – mineral wool or expanded plastics beads, for example – are blown into the cavity through holes drilled in the outside wall. These holes are then filled with matching mortar. In new walls, insulation slabs are built into the cavity as work progresses. Many houses have now been built with a 200-300mm fully-filled cavity, using long cavity wall ties (which should be made of plastics to reduce cold bridging). If the cavity is wider than this – for example the Low Energy House at CAT with 450mm – the walls have to be structurally independent with piers added for stiffness. Generally, cavity filled walls are a breathable construction. Care must be taken to avoid cold bridges at openings, where the two masonry skins come together in conventional construction, by filling the cavity with rigid insulation.

Our Preference

- Fit 250mm insulation in new walls and cavity wall ties of polypropylene.
- Do not return masonry at reveals.
- Use separate lintels.
- Fill existing cavities with blown mineral wool.

Masonry – solid walls

To improve the performance of solid masonry walls (brick, block, stone or cob), insulation can be fitted to the inside or outside face using dry lightweight materials: timber, insulation, plasterboard, tiles and so on.

If fitted externally, the inside is undisturbed. Protected from the elements, the original wall will act as a heat store, and cold bridges are avoided. This can be a breathable construction, but will be more expensive than internal insulated dry-lining, and the external appearance of the house will be changed.

If fitted internally, the outer appearance remains the same. It will be cheaper than external insulation, and can be done on a room-by-room basis as funds allow. However, the rooms will become smaller and there will be disruption to the occupants. It may also be difficult to fit insulation around existing features such as mouldings. Internal walls that abut external walls will act as cooling fins (thermal bridging), and there will be very little heat storage.

There are two basic techniques. The first uses a timber framework fitted with insulation and finished with plasterboard (internal), or timber cladding, render or tiles (external). Ideally, the area between the internal insulation and the existing wall should be ventilated (by air bricks). If not, every effort must be made to provide a well-sealed vapour check on the warm side of the insulation. The second technique uses proprietary composite materials glued and nailed to the existing wall and finished in plaster or render. Insulation thickness will depend on cost and

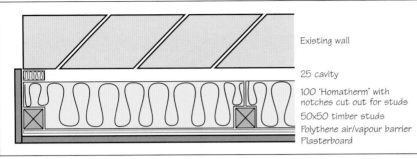

Existing wall

25 cavity

100 'Homatherm' with notches cut out for studs

50x50 timber studs

Polythene air/vapour barrier
Plasterboard

8.43

8.44a

8.44b

8.45

convenience: a common upgrading technique is to use an insulation/plasterboard composite, 65mm thick, glued to the inside face of the existing wall and finished with plaster. The insulation level of the finished wall can bring it to the standard required by current Building Regulations.

Our Preference

- Insulate externally or internally with studwork and at least 100mm insulation.

Fig. 8.43 Internal wall insulation using benign materials. This eco-renovation uses Homatherm cellulose boards.

Fig. 8.44a Cellulose insulation being damp-sprayed onto internal insulation studwork.
Photo: John Willoughby.

Fig. 8.44b Many different materials can be used. This construction has mineral fibre and a vapour barrier of 'radiant insulation' reflective film. Optimistic claims are often made for radiant insulation, but there would seem to be no advantage in using the material over another layer of fibre or foam insulation.
Photo: John Willoughby.

Fig. 8.45 Externally insulating a stone wall at CAT using a proprietary system of mineral wool batts and expanded metal lath. After fixing, the lath is finished with a cement/lime/sand render.

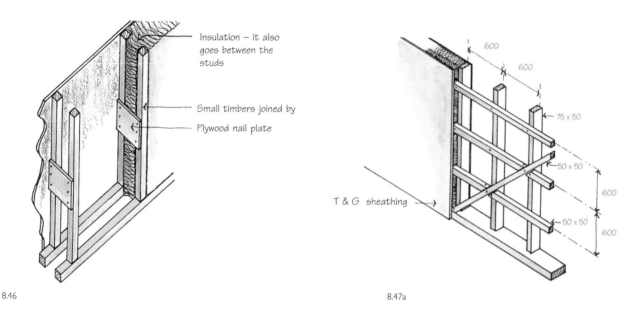

Labels in figure 8.46:
Insulation – it also goes between the studs

Small timbers joined by

Plywood nail plate

8.46

Labels in figure 8.47a:
600
600
75 x 50
50 x 50
600
T & G sheathing
50 x 50
600

8.47a

8.47b

Fig. 8.46 Spaced stud timber frame wall. For an insulation thickness above 100mm it is more economical to use two small section studs spaced apart with nailplates. As well as saving on timber, the insulation can be placed between the studs, so improving the overall insulation level by avoiding a cold bridge (timber has only a quarter of the insulating value of most insulation materials).

Fig. 8.47a Layered stud timber frame wall. Another way to reduce the cold bridging effect of the timber in a stud wall is to put two layers of timbers at right angles to each other.

Fig. 8.47b A simple way to acheive good U-values with a conventional stud frame, is to shaethe the frame with a rigid insulation board. This one is 'Pavatex Diffutherm' made of waste wood.

Photo and system: Natural Building Technologies Ltd.

Timber frame walls

In a timber frame wall, the weight of the house and its occupants is taken by vertical posts. The spaces between these posts (there is usually one every 600mm or so, and they are commonly called studs) can be readily filled with insulating materials. The greater thickness of insulation that can be contained within a given wall depth compared to a masonry construction explains the popularity of timber framing in cold countries (of course such places also have a lot of trees). Most timber stud frame walls have about 150mm of insulation, which will give a better heat resistance than currently required under Building Regulations. Superinsulated houses have 250-350mm thick walls and use a spaced stud, layered stud or I-stud technique to reduce the thermal bridging effect of the timber. Recent timber frame wall designs have also concentrated on control of water vapour diffusion through the construction, principally to avoid damaging condensation occurring within it.

The heat storage of timber frame houses is of low capacity; they heat up and cool down quickly, making little use of solar gains.

Straw bale walls

These walls do not require extra insulation. A 450mm thick bale will give a U-value of 0.2W/m²K.

Our Preference

• Fit 250-350mm insulation.

• using spaced or I-beam studs, breathable materials and rainscreen cladding.

BUILDING A LOW-ENERGY HOUSE (4)

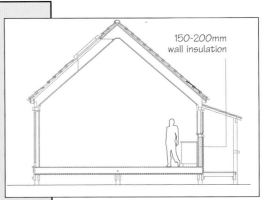

150-200mm wall insulation

Insulating the walls

House	No. 4
SAP	65
Description	As previous house, but with the following additions: 150mm wall insulation.

Element	U-Value	Description
Walls	0.20	Cavity masonry or timber frame with 150mm insulation
Roof	0.13	Tiled pitched roof with 300mm insulation
Floor	0.82	Uninsulated solid or suspended
Glazing	4.70	Single in timber frames, draughtstripped

Window/floor	22%	Proportion of window to floor area
Ventilation	0.70ac/hr	
Heat loss	1.09W/m³ of internal space	

Heating sources	per year (kWh)
Casual gains	2740
Solar gains	1400
Heating system	12200
(House 1	24155 – for comparison)
Water heating	5520

Boiler efficiency   60%

Use of gas	Cost (£/p.a.)	Savings (£/p.a.)	Cost of implementation (£)
Space heating	207	203	700
Water heating	85		

CO₂ emissions	3.31 tonnes per year
CO₂ savings on House 1	2.24 tonnes per year

Note: Cost of energy saving measures are for DIY on old house or new-build extra cost, and are very approximate. Wall insulation in an old house would be considerably more than shown.

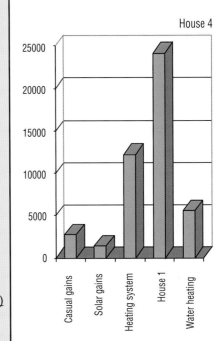

House 4

Heating supply and energy conservation measures to House 4 in kWh/p.a.

8.48

8.49

Floors

Solid floor

Until recently there was no requirement under the Building Regulations to consider floors as heat loss elements in a house. This is because dry earth is a reasonable insulator, so most heat loss occurs at the edge of a floor where the path length to the cold external air is short. However, where there is a high water table, and now that standards have improved, the floor must be insulated to balance the rest of the construction. The plan shape of the floor dominates the heat loss, a long thin plan having much more external 'heat loss edge' than a square one.

Extra insulation material should be placed around the edge of the floor extending vertically to overlap the wall insulation, and the floor finish or concrete slab should be supported on inert insulation (cork, foamed glass, perlite, expanded clay beads). An existing solid floor can be upgraded using rigid insulation and a 'floating' finish of boards or sand/cement screed. Natural timber floorboards can be supported on battens with insulation inbetween. Of course, when renovating existing buildings, the rooms will get lower, and all the doors will have to be adjusted. A solid floor will require a vapour check to prevent condensation occurring within the insulation. Some solid floors are now being made of a composite insulating material, such as hemp and lime.

Our Preference

- Use natural timber floor on timber battens on a recycled polythene or bitumen/paper damp-proof membrane, with 100-150mm cellulose or other renewable insulation, and vapour check under floorboards.
- or • For thermal mass and/or underfloor heating, use stabilised earth or limecrete on cork, perlite or foamed glass, with recycled polythene vapour check and DPM.
- or • Construct solid floor of hemp/lime.

Suspended floor

A suspended floor consists of timber (or concrete) joists spanning between walls, finished with floorboards (or concrete blocks and screed), over a ventilated space. A timber floor is preferred, as it uses a renewable resource instead of concrete, and can be insulated easily. Care must be taken to avoid air-infiltration paths around the skirtings or between floorboards. Loose fill insulation is carried between the joists on netting or on a low-vapour resistance board. In new constructions, counterbattens can be fixed over the joist tops to provide a useful zone for services and a thermal break (there is only solid timber where the two layers cross). Superinsulated houses have around 225mm of insulation in the suspended floor.

Our Preference

- Use timber joists and counterbattens with 225mm cellulose or other renewable insulation, natural timber floorboards and good underfloor ventilation.

Fig. 8.48 Limecrete floor with underfloor heating and lightweight expanded clay (LECA) used as an insulation and aggregate (Ty Mawr Lime).

Fig. 8.49 Superinsulated timber floor. 50x50mm counter joists over the normal joists limit the timber thermal bridging. Insulation is supported on fibreboard fitted between the joists.

BUILDING A LOW-ENERGY HOUSE (5)

Insulating the floor

House	No. 5
SAP	75
Description	As previous house, but with the following additions: 150mm solid floor or 200mm suspended floor insulation

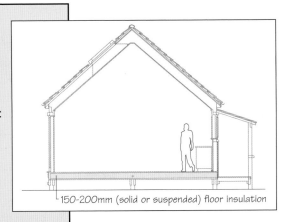

150-200mm (solid or suspended) floor insulation

Element	U-Value	Description
Walls	0.20	Cavity masonry or timber frame with 150mm insulation
Roof	0.13	Tiled pitched roof with 300mm insulation
Floor	0.20	Insulated solid or suspended
Glazing	4.70	Single in timber frames, draughtstripped

Window/floor	22%	Proportion of window to floor area
Ventilation	0.70ac/hr	
Heat loss	0.83W/m³ of internal space	

Heating sources	per year (kWh)
Casual gains	2460
Solar gains	1245
Heating system	8435
(House 1	24155 – for comparison)
Water heating	5520

Boiler efficiency   60%

Use of gas	Cost (£/p.a.)	Savings (£/p.a.)	Cost of implementation (£)
Space heating	143	267	950
Water heating	85		

CO₂ emissions	2.61 tonnes per year
CO₂ savings on House 1	2.94 tonnes per year

Note: Cost of energy saving measures are for DIY on old house or new-build extra cost, and are very approximate.

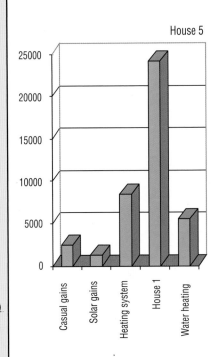

House 5

Heating supply and energy conservation measures to House 5 in kWh/p.a.

8.50

8.51

Fig. 8.50 This Norwegian timber window is triple-glazed and gas-filled, with two low-E coatings, giving it a U-value of 1.0 W/m²k (which is better than a cavity brick wall). Photo: David Olivier.

Fig. 8.51 High-performance glazed timber door, fitted with ultra efficient U= 1.1W/m²k glazing. (Ecoplus system from The Green Building Store).

Doors and windows

New or replacement doors and windows

In a new house or house conversion, deciding on the size and position of windows and doors is a trade-off between solar gain, daylight, view and heat loss. Glazed openings will lose proportionally much more heat than any other element in a well-insulated house. However, taken over the whole heating season, a high-performance south-facing window should gain as much energy from the sun during the day as it loses at night. Heavy curtains or shutters will improve this equation. High efficiency glazing, in the form of double- or triple-glazed units with low-E coatings and inert gas fillings, is becoming much less costly as more people buy the units. All replacement windows are now required by the UK Building Regulations to be fitted with low-E double-glazing. Usually, such glazing is better insulated than the frame that holds it, so it is better to have large areas of glass in fewer openings. Double sash windows – two well-sealed coupled windows – that give better sound insulation than a double-glazed unit, and better thermal and airtightness performance than a triple unit, are more widely available .

Some double-glazed units, with high-performance low-E coatings, have mid pane U-values as low as 1.1W/m²K – five times better than single-glazing. With advanced glazing there is a significant heat loss through the metal spacer used to separate the sheets of glass. 'Thermal break' glazing spacers that reduce this heat loss around the window edges are also becoming more widely available.

Frames should be made of wood, which is a reasonable insulator, and fitted with efficient draughtstripping and positive, multi-point closing systems that allow for secure ventilation. Cavity wall insulation should continue right up to the window or door and not be 'closed' with masonry. Windows and doors should be fixed using adjustable plates to cope with movement and shrinkage, and should be stained or painted with an organic microporous finish.

Insulated shutters, well fitting, heavy, lined curtains and reflective roller blinds improve night-time heat loss considerably.

Upgrading existing doors and windows

Large areas of single-glazing and rattly, draughty windows and external doors will often be the major source of heat loss and discomfort in old houses. However, many old windows and doors are very attractive, often using slender glazing bars unobtainable today, and it is good environmental practice to re-use and retain rather than replace. There are five ways to improve them:

- **Fix secondary glazing to each casement:** a sheet of glass or clear plastic can be fitted to the opening bit of the window. Draughtstrip everything. There are many DIY systems to do both these jobs. Some casements (e.g. sash windows) are impossible to draughtstrip properly. Condensation may occur on the inner side of the old window.
- **Fix secondary glazing over the whole window opening:** this will cure the draught problems but should not be done to all windows as there will be no ventilation or means of fire escape.
- **Fix new inward opening windows:** these can be fitted up against the inside face of the old ones. In houses with thick walls, the new windows can fold back against the window reveal. Doors can be fitted with something similar, either to form a walk-in lobby, or just as a sort of air-lock shutter to be closed in cold weather.

8.52   8.53

- **Fit heavy, lined curtains or blinds:** reflective materials are available for the lining of curtains. Blinds should fit well around the opening. They should seat upon the floor or window ledge, be fitted into a pelmet at the top, and well overlap the window. The sides can be Velcro®-ed to the wall. The idea is to make it as airtight as possible to restrict convection currents.
- **A low-E plastics film:** this can be applied to a single-glazed window to produce similar thermal performance to double-glazing. Courtaulds LLUMAR low-E is a good example.

Fig. 8.52 Double casement window. The inner casement
can be left open in the summer.

Fig. 8.53 Simple, lift-on insulating shutters of 25mm
expanded polystyrene coverd in paper.

Energy efficiency

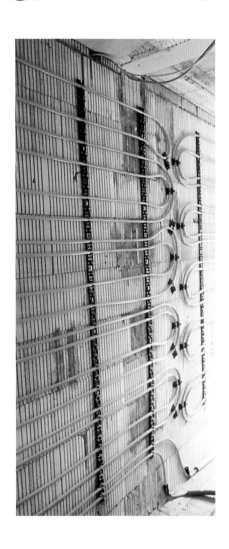

ENERGY EFFICIENCY

A low-energy house incorporates superinsulation, air-tightness, controlled ventilation with preheat, and passive solar features. The majority of its heat comes from solar and casual gains – 'free heat'. The low-energy aim is to reduce space heating fuel use to a minimum (preferably zero), then use fuel in the least polluting, most efficient way possible.

Heating – biofuels

Biofuels are produced from growing plants and are infinitely renewable. You would think that all plant-derived fuels are sustainable, as the energy to make them comes from the sun, but some are the product of unsustainable practices, such as straw produced using heavy fertiliser inputs, or wood from old forest growth which can never be replaced.

Biomass fuels are appropriate only where there is a local, reliable supply – it does not make sense to transport them over long distances.

Wood

For most households, the only practicable biofuel is wood. However, most of us live in smokeless zones. Hot-burning dry wood gives off very few particulates, but it is illegal to burn wood if smoke is still visible 15 minutes after lighting.

Wood is by far the cheapest and most convenient form of solar fuel, and there are plenty of forestry thinnings and other sources of waste wood available. A lot of undercover storage is needed to dry the timber: a low-energy household might need three tonnes of dry hardwood per year for heating, cooking and hot water, which would take up about 5m³. To be autonomous, this same household would need about a hectare of coppice woodland and a lot of human effort (coppicing yield is 10-25tonnes/ha).

The best way to burn wood is fast and furious. Slow, smouldering fires of damp or unseasoned, green wood release a smelly, carcinogenic cocktail of pollutants which produce more acid rain and smog-forming emissions than any fossil fuel. Burning wood gives off CO_2; but growing wood absorbs the same quantity, so assuming the felled tree is replanted, the net effect on global warming is zero.

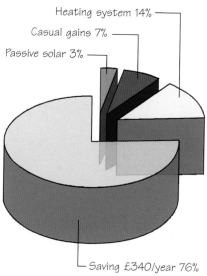

Heating system 14%
Casual gains 7%
Passive solar 3%

Saving £340/year 76%

9.1

9.2

9.3

Fig. 9.1 Energy pie for a house built to 2002 Building regulations standards, showing the saving over the UK average house.

Fig. 9.2 Native deciduous trees can be coppiced to provide a sustainable fuel harvest, and a valuable wildlife habitat.

Fig. 9.3 A modern, efficient 10kW woodstove. As the fire is raised up and insulated from the floor, the stove can be fitted over timber flooring.
('Stolla' by Austro Flam).

9.4

9.5

Wood chips and pellets

Chipped or pelleted wood from forestry, tree surgery or packaging (e.g. pallets) is a fuel which uses primarily waste materials or small-diameter timber unsuitable for other uses. It is an efficient way of burning wood, as the fuel feed can be controlled more easily with smaller size 'units' of fuel. Chips from forestry waste generally have a high moisture content and this will reduce the efficiency of the burn.

Anaerobic digestion

This is a process producing methane gas from a slurry of organic waste. The 1970s 'hippie' dream of having a methane digester attached to every house that converted sewage into cooking gas was never realised, except in tropical latitudes. However, treating assorted biological industrial wastes by anaerobic digestion is a quietly booming industry: the gas by-product is used to fire brick and glass works or to provide heat for other industrial processes. Many sewage works produce methane gas for their own use. Gas is also produced at landfill sites by decomposing rubbish, and several small power stations generate using landfill gas as a fuel. Supported under the Non-Fossil Fuel Obligation (NFFO), these 'energy-from-waste' schemes are currently producing more electricity than wind generators.

Energy crops

There are many schemes afoot that make use of specially grown crops as biofuels. These biofuels are burnt in power stations, or digested to produce gas or to make oil fuel for engines. Some schemes use native and naturalised vegetation such as bracken, cordgrass, or knotweed; others use fast-growing willow cut on a very short rotation, miscanthus, sunflowers, or oil seed rape. As with all agriculture, the growing practices must be scrutinised for biological diversity, use of fertilisers and pesticides, the ratio of fossil fuel used to biofuel obtained, and so on. A coppice of native broadleaf hardwoods is a very biologically diverse habitat, and it looks nice.

The conversion efficiency from solar energy to a good yield biofuel is only about half of a percent – but with such a large energy source and 'solar collector', the yields are still pretty high – around 50,000kWh/ha.

Fig. 9.4 A 500kW woodchip boiler was installed in the village of Llanwyddyn to provide space and water heating for a school, community centre and up to 40 houses. The wood comes from local forests, is chipped and stored off site and delivered straight to the hopper on a weekly basis. This system is owned and run by Dulas Wood Energy as an 'ESCO', [Energy Supply company], selling heat rather than fuel to the local community.

Fig. 9.5 Wood pellet stove with hopper containing fuel. House for the Future, Museum of Welsh life, St. Fagans.

Six biofuels are presently being used or developed:

- **Landfill gas:** this is a mixture of methane and CO_2, with a yield of approximately 1000kWh per tonne of municipal waste. It is a short term solution – we should not really be dumping so much biodegradable material in the first place.
- **Biogas from sewage:** anaerobic digestion of sewage can produce about 2500kWh per tonne of dry matter. The process is not very efficient in cold climates since the ideal temperature for the bacterial process to occur is 35°C, and therefore much of the gas produced has to be put back into the system as heating. This is why the house-sized methane digester is a non-starter in temperate climates.
- **Fermentation of energy crops:** potatoes, corn, sugar beet, and other crops can be fermented to make ethanol, which may be blended with petrol for internal combustion engines.
- **Biodiesel:** oil from energy crops (rape) can be blended with conventional diesel to make a greener fuel.
- **Agricultural wastes:** about seven million tonnes of surplus straw are produced every year. The energy content of this is equivalent to about 1% of UK primary energy use. Some small new power stations have been set up to burn straw bales and animal manure.
- **Wood chips and pellets:** see above

9.6

Fossil fuels

To achieve a reduction in fossil fuel use, energy conservation is the preferred option, followed by the use of renewable energy sources supported by highly efficient use of the cleanest fossil fuel. Fossil fuels can be ranked in the following order, according to cost and the level of CO_2 pollution (cleanest first)*:

Fuel	Cost (pence/kWh)	CO_2/kWh
Wood Pellets	4.66	0.03
North Sea Gas	1.51-2.17	0.19
Oil	1.77	0.27
Bulk LP Gas	2.93	0.25
Coal	1.80	0.29
Anthracite	2.05	0.31
Smokeless fuel	2.4	0.31
Electricity (standard)	7.12-8.27	0.41
Electricity (off peak)	2.85 / 7.30 / 11.49	0.41

Preference

- Conserve energy whenever possible.
- Use renewable energy to meet heating needs.
- Use gas heating with efficient appliances.
- Use oil heating with efficient appliances.

Fig. 9.6 There is great potential in growing crops specially for biofuels. Oil from sunflower and rape crops is already being used in France, South Africa and Brazil as a diesel substitute. The annual sunflower crop from one field produces enough oil to work the tractor on a further ten fields.

Thanks to John Willoughby for the above information.

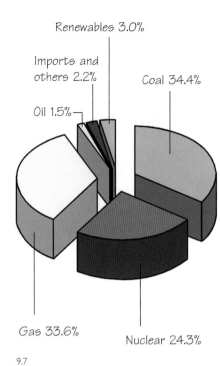

Renewables 3.0%

Imports and
others 2.2%

Coal 34.4%

Oil 1.5%

Gas 33.6%

Nuclear 24.3%

9.7

Electricity

Electricity is not a fuel as such, but a means of circulating energy. Such a seemingly clean, convenient resource in the home, it is actually the most polluting form of energy, due to its (means of) generation at the other end of the National Grid.

Electricity generation involves a series of conversions from chemical energy to heat, to mechanical energy, to electrical energy. At each stage in the process, some energy is lost, as dictated by the laws of thermodynamics. This results in an overall conversion efficiency from primary source to end use of around 35%. Thus, despite the valiant efforts to clean up emissions from power stations, electricity will always be many times more polluting than any other energy source.

This inherent inefficiency is reflected in the CO_2 emission per unit of delivered energy: for gas heating it is 52kg/GJ and for electricity 113kg/GJ – over twice as much. It follows that we must be as miserly as we possibly can be with electricity, only using it where no other fuel is possible, e.g. for artificial lighting, electronics and electric motors. Even then, around 50% of the CO_2 emissions of a superinsulated house are from electricity use.

Added to this burden of pollution is the legacy of nuclear waste and emissions. The Chernobyl accident amongst others demonstrated the life threatening potential of fission reactors. No long-term solution has been found for the safe storage of nuclear by-products, which continue to emit radioactivity for thousands of years. Economically, the privatisation of the electricity industry exposed the nuclear option to the glare of market finances. It was found to be very expensive (even if disposal costs are ignored), and is now propped up by state intervention.

There are two approaches to using less electricity: avoidance and efficiency.

Avoidance

- Do not use electricity for space heating/water heating.
- Have good daylighting to reduce electric light use and habitually switch off un-needed lights.
- Use task lighting to illuminate locally (angle-poise lamp, etc.).
- Use a gas stove (or wood stove) for cooking (and/or eat lots of salad or raw foods).
- Habitually switch off un-needed electrical appliances (TV, computer, cooker hood, fax machine, etc.). It is estimated that the load from all the UK appliances left on stand-by is equivalent to the output of one power station – a video consumes 90% of its lifetime total electricity on standby.
- Dry clothes outside or on an airer.
- Use a sustainable biological energy system (that's you) for domestic chores wherever possible.

Efficiency

- Fit compact fluorescent light bulbs instead of tungsten incandescent – it will also save you money.
- When replacing electrical appliances, look for those with the lowest electrical consumption (A rating).
- Keep fridges and freezers full and site them in a cool room, with good ventilation to the rear.
- Wash only full loads of dishes and clothes, and use hot water from your domestic hot water system rather than integral heaters.

Fig. 9.7 The various fuels used to generate electricity are used in these following proportions[1].
Contribution to national electricity supply %.

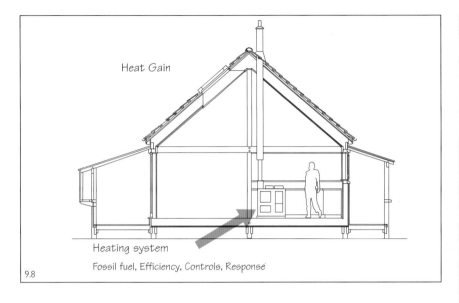

Heat Gain

Heating system

Fossil fuel, Efficiency, Controls, Response

9.8

9.9

Heating systems

The following considerations govern the choice of a space heating system:

• Fuel type and environmental concerns

Solar heating is the first choice as it is non-polluting. Biofuels come next, as their CO_2 output can be balanced by that taken to grow them. These are followed by gas – the cleanest fossil fuel, then oil, coal, and finally electricity. Systems fuelled by gas and oil will always be able to respond faster than those using solid fuel (wood and coal). They can also run at higher efficiencies without the danger of becoming blocked with the products of combustion. Slow-response systems are best used in a house with a high thermal mass that can absorb excess heat into the structure for later use.

• Comfort

Our perception of comfort varies greatly, depending on such variables as our metabolic rate, clothing, the season, convection around us, the temperature of surrounding surfaces, whether it is sunny or whether we have control over the heating system. Certainly any heating system needs to be responsive to our needs and to the weather. Gentle heat radiation is more comfortable than hot air.

• Boiler and system efficiency

Usually, boiler efficiency varies with the demands being put upon it. It is important to size boilers properly – oversized boilers never reach their full potential or optimum efficiency since they are always running at part load. Systems must be well controlled to take advantage of solar and other gains.

• System cost

In a low-energy house very little heat is required; a simple, single heat source may suffice (although many people still put a radiator in each room for reassurance). In a less well insulated house it is usually effective to invest in good controls and a very efficient boiler.

Fig. 9.8 Heating systems.

Fig. 9.9 Designed for combined solar water and space heating. The system prioritises domestic hot water, with any spare heat going into the heating system. Imported from Germany by the Green Shop, Bisley, Gloucestershire.

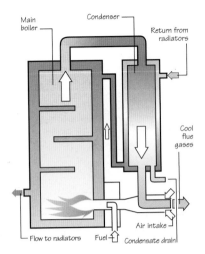

9.10

A heating system will consist of five elements.

- **Heating plant:** the boiler, solar panel, or electric element.
- **Heat storage:** a conventional central heating system will only have storage for domestic hot water; a solar inter-seasonal system will have a huge heat store.
- **Heat distribution:** the method of circulating heat energy around the house to where it is needed.
- **Heat emitters:** steel radiators, underfloor heating pipes, warm air.
- **Controls:** thermostats, timers and programmers.

Heating plant

The key factor in evaluating a heating plant is the overall conversion efficiency from the primary fuel source – coal, oil or gas – to useful heat in the house. As we have discussed elsewhere, the use of other energy sources in solar heating systems is limited to the running of pumps or fans.

In domestic heating systems there are three classes of boilers:

- **Natural convection:** maximum efficiencies of around 75%.
- **Fan-assisted flue:** maximum efficiencies of around 80%.
- **Condensing:** maximum efficiencies of around 95%.

And two types of system:

- **Boiler and hot water cylinder**
- **Combination ('combi') boiler**

Efficiency over the whole year will be less than the figures quoted above; for much of the time the boiler will be running on part load – not working very hard, yet still losing heat from the flue, pipework and casing. This is known as 'seasonal efficiency'. Efficiency also depends on the type of fuel used, as boilers using dirtier fuels have to run with higher flue temperatures to prevent them clogging up.

Gas boilers and room heaters (including LPG) and Oil boilers

Type	Seasonal efficiency %
Coal effect fire in fireplace	25
Old style gas fire room heater	50
Ducted system (to each room)	72
Ducted system with flue heat recovery	85
Natural convection boiler > 20 years old	55
Natural convection boiler < 20 years old	65
Combi boiler	65
Fan-assisted flue boiler	68
Modern gas fire room heater	70
Condensing boiler	90-97

Fig. 9.10 Schematic of condesing boiler showing the condenser around the exhaust flue.

BUILDING A LOW-ENERGY HOUSE (6)

<u>Low-E double-glazing and condensing boiler with optimising controller</u>

House	No. 6
SAP	99
Description	As previous house, but with the following additions: Double- low-E glazing argon fill, Insulating all thermal bridges, Condensing boiler and optimising controller.

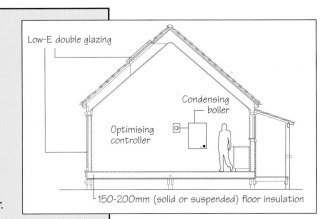

Element	U-Value	Description
Walls	0.20	Cavity masonry or timber frame with 150mm insulation
Roof	0.13	Tiled pitched roof with 300mm insulation
Floor	0.20	Insulated solid or suspended
Glazing	2.20	Double low-E in timber frames, draughtstripped
Window/floor	22%	Proportion of window to floor area
Ventilation	0.60ac/hr	
Heat loss	0.61W/m³ of internal space	

Heating sources	per year (kWh)
Casual gains	1940
Solar gains	990
Heating system	4030
(House 1	24155 – for comparison)
Water heating	3900

Boiler efficiency   85%

Use of gas	Cost (£/p.a.)	Savings (£/p.a.)	Cost of implementation (£)
Space heating	69	341	3000
Water heating	60	25	

CO₂ emissions   1.48 tonnes per year
CO₂ savings on House 1: 4.07 tonnes per year

Note: Cost of energy saving measures are for DIY on old house or new-build extra cost, and are very approximate. The condensing boiler price is the extra cost over conventional. Low-E glazing cost has been taken as £1500 – it would be less in a new house and more in an old one. All cold bridges have been eliminated.
In reality it is sensible to install the high-efficiency heating system at an early stage in any house upgrading. The savings will be even larger on a poorly insulated house.

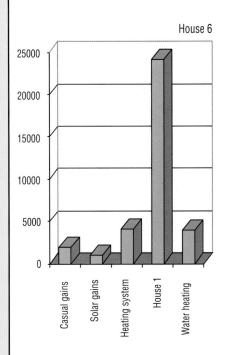

House 6

Heating supply and energy conservation measures to House 6 in kWh/p.a.

9.11

The sections below provide some typical efficiencies for four different types of plant system.

Condensing boilers have extra heating coils built into the flue through which the return water (from radiators and cylinder) passes. As the flue gases pass over these relatively cool pipes, condensation forms, recovering the latent heat of condensation from the water vapour formed as part of the combustion process. For this to happen, the return water ideally needs to be as cool as possible – but even when this is not the case, the boiler still works at high efficiencies due to its high heat-exchanger surface area. The cooled flue gases no longer have any buoyancy with which to escape through a normal flue, so there needs to be a fan blowing them out. Flue gases are cool enough for the flue to be made of plastics. The condensate has to be led to a drain (unfortunately it is not clean enough for use as distilled water in your car battery). Condensing boilers are 20% more expensive than the conventional equivalent, but are generally cost effective. The extra cost of a condensing boiler is recovered very quickly (three years) and they will be compulsory from 2006.

'Combi' boilers are powerful boilers that dispense with the need for a hot water cylinder by instantaneously heating water on demand for domestic use. Their large output means that they will have plenty to spare for space heating. The water supply is at mains pressure. However, the hot water supply may drop off if there is more than one demand at the same time (e.g. shower and washing machine). It is difficult to add a solar water heating system (which needs a storage device) to an existing combi, although there is now one make of boiler available which is designed to take solar heated water. 'Short cycling' of the boiler's firing system is inefficient and may be a problem when the hot water tap is turned on for short periods.

Combis have the advantages of not incurring cylinder losses, being capable of supplying endless hot water and operating at mains pressure for problem-free showering. Many combis have a small hot water tank in them to cope with initial demand, then supply hot water continuously at a lower rate. To an extent, such a design overcomes some of the disadvantages of combis – they are often too powerful for space heating demands and frequently run at an inefficient part load. This is especially critical in superinsulated houses, where perhaps a better solution is to have a small standard boiler and a large, mains pressure heat store, ensuring the boiler always works hard and efficiently.

All gas and oil boilers are now assessed under the SEDBUK scheme (Seasonal Efficiency of Domestic Boilers in the UK), and have to achieve a certain seasonal efficiency standard. SEDBUK shows the average annual efficiency achieved in typical domestic situations, making reasonable assessments of variable factors, such as patterns of use, climate, degree of control, etc. (See www.boilers.org.uk – a very good website which also gives information on boiler sizing, estimated fuel consumption and energy efficiency ratings.)

Micro-CHP (Combined Heat and Power) boilers have been developed for domestic use. Fuelled mainly by gas or oil, they produce heat and electricity. Usually sized for their heat output, electricity generation is an additional benefit (usually 1-5kW) which can be exported to the electricity grid if appropriate. The overall efficiency is 85-90%. Given the rate of boiler replacement, the market potential for micro-CHP is large and it is a technology identified by the Government for support and subsidy. It has been estimated[2] that by 2025 over 50% of households in the UK will have their own generator attached to a domestic boiler – in which case the

Fig. 9.11 The biomass CHP unit at BedZED, Surrey, designed to generate as much electricity as residents consume.

electrical output would be at least equal to that of the UK's nuclear power stations. Concern has been expressed over the increase in electro-magnetic fields (EMFs) produced by a generator within the home.

Solid fossil fuel boilers and room heaters*

Type	Maximum efficiency %
Open fire in grate	32
Open fire with backboiler	55
Closed room heater	60
Closed room heater with backboiler	65
Modern autofeed in heated space	65

*This includes coal and smokeless fuels such as anthracite and Furnacite.

Wood-fuelled boilers and room heaters

Type	Maximum efficiency %
Open fire in grate	32
Open fire with backboiler	55
Log burning room heater	30-60
Log burning room heater with backboiler	40-60
Wood pellet room heater	85-90
Wood pellet boiler	85-90
Log-batch boiler	85-90
Wood chip boiler	85-90

Solid fuel also includes dry wood, burnt in an open fire or specially designed boiler. While heating efficiency of these systems is less than optimum, wood scores quite well in terms of primary fossil fuel use – fossil fuels only being used for processing and transport. Wood is therefore virtually a CO_2 neutral fuel.

Wood chip boilers are designed to burn chips from forestry waste efficiently and cleanly. Commonly, the chips are delivered to the boiler from a hopper, using an auger mechanism. Ideally, they should have a maximum moisture content of 25%, but some boilers can tolerate a moisture content of up to 40%. Wood chip boilers are usually sized to provide hot water on a small industrial or district heating scale (40kW+).

Wood pellet stoves and boilers use small wood particles and dust, compressed into pellets. These have a very low moisture content and thus a high calorific value. As a result, wood pellet boilers and room heaters are very controllable and responsive devices, based on a small continuous feed. Auto ignition makes them convenient to operate, and they need feeding every few days (according to the size of the hopper) and de-ashing every few weeks. They are suitable for small domestic and district-scale systems.

Log-batch boilers are fuelled by split logs cut to a specific length. They are designed to burn a full load at high efficiencies and maximum output. The heat is then stored in a large well-insulated hot water tank, from where it can be used for space or water heating systems. Because of the storage tank and intermittent firing regime, log-batch boilers are versatile and can be used in systems of all sizes from single domestic to community scale.

All three types of boiler mentioned above, with autofeed burners and forced draught in the flues, can achieve efficiencies of 85-90%. The viability of wood-fired heating systems will always depend on reliability of supply and the availability of sufficient storage volume for fuel.

Electrical heating

Type	Efficiency %
Off-peak storage heaters	75
Off-peak fan-assisted storage radiators	80
Panel, convector or radiators & boilers	100
Air source heat pump	200-250
Ground source heat pump	300-400

Electric heating has very low installation costs and can be quite responsive. However, unless the electrical source is renewable energy from hydro, wind, or photovoltaic solar electric panel, the overall efficiency of electrical systems in primary energy terms needs to be divided by three; this represents power station efficiency. Houses which use natural gas for heating, hot water and cooking will be responsible for far less carbon emissions than all-electric houses. This is because the 'carbon intensity' – the amount of carbon released (in kilograms) per kWh of energy produced – is 0.12 for electricity, and only 0.05 for gas[3].

Heat Pumps are devices for moving heat energy from one place to another, and from a lower to a higher temperature. The low temperature source may be air, water, ground or waste heat from industrial processes or domestic ventilation systems. Typically, a heat pump would boost the source temperature from, say, 5°C to 50°C, and this would give a coefficient of performance (CP) of 3. This means that for every unit of electricity that is put in, the heat output is 3 units. If the end temperature is less (e.g. 35°C for an underfloor heating system) then the CP will be greater, and the whole system more efficient; if, however, the end temperature needs to be greater (e.g. 60°C for domestic hot water) then the CP will be less. Similarly if the supply temperature is lower (as is the case with air systems in cold weather) then the CP will also drop. Most heat pumps run on electricity, which itself is generated at efficiencies of only 0.35.

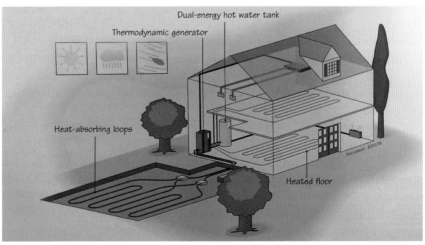

Fig. 9.12 How a ground source heat pump works.   9.12

Heat storage

Most central heating systems have little storage apart from that for domestic hot water. There are exceptions, such as electric night storage heaters. Also woodburning ceramic tile stoves (Kakkleoven), which are fired up once or twice a day by burning dry timber at high temperatures, store heat in the high-mass walls of the stove and then release it slowly over several hours. Similarly, log-batch burners need large water stores (750-1500 litres) to improve their efficiency. For super-insulated houses where it is difficult to get sufficiently small boilers, it is possible to use a very small boiler to charge a heat store at high efficiencies with minimal cycling; central heating and hot water demand can be met instantly by drawing on this heat store. Phase change materials (which release or absorb heat when changing state e.g. from gas to liquid) may be added to solid floors (e.g. in a passive solar design) to increase their effective storage potential. There are, of course, always heat losses associated with storage.

Heat distribution

In Britain, heat distribution is commonly achieved through the pump-driven circulation of water through small-bore pipes of copper or plastics, although it is possible to have a thermosiphon-driven system. Distribution to the hot water cylinder may be by thermosiphon or, more commonly nowadays, by pump.

Using air rather than water as the heat distribution medium is not as popular in Britain as in the US (where bungalows with basements allow space for the bulky ductwork) and in the rest of Europe. UK experience has been that they are frequently uncomfortable and noisy, although in fact there is no reason why they should be. An air-based system often makes sense in a very low-energy house, which usually requires so little heat it is hard to justify radiators in every room. The house may have some sort of air-handling anyway (ventilation heat recovery or solar ventilation preheating), so warmed-up ventilation air may be the answer, and high efficiencies can be reached.

Heat emitters

Air-based systems

In air systems, the distribution medium is also the emitter, so it merely needs to be introduced into the rooms in a draught-free way. Even warm air feels cold when blown hard enough (try blowing across the back of your hand at different rates; the experience goes from hot to cold), so the air must be circulated at low velocities, preferably from diffusers at high level. The room fills with warm air from the top down.

Water-based systems

Water-based systems require separate emitters.

- **Steel panel radiators:** a confusing name, as the majority of heat is given off in air convection currents, not heat radiation. Their heat emission is 1300-2500W/m², depending on the number of fins on the back. Low temperature versions are available to prevent scalding, as the water supply temperature will be about 80°C.
- **Underfloor heating:** hot water pipes are embedded in the concrete floor screed or run in insulated channels in a timber floor. As the whole of the floor area is now a radiator, at about 90W/m² the water temperature can be quite

9.13

9.14

9.15

9.16

Fig. 9.14 Underfloor heating in new solid floor, retrofit to existing timber floor and new floating foor.
Source: KEE Radiant Floor Heat Ltd.

Fig. 9.15 Wall heating, like underfloor heating, gives increased comfort levels which lead to energy savings.

Fig. 9.16 A boiler energy manager, including weather compensator, reduces unnecessary boilder cycling, improves seasonal efficiency, and reduces running costs.

low (30-45°C). Comfort conditions are improved as we are more sensitive to radiant heat, so it is possible to have the house temperature 2-3°C lower than with conventional radiator use. This lowering of air temperature for the same comfort conditions itself saves energy, as heat loss is dependent on the difference in air temperature between inside and out. Underfloor heating systems also tend to have reduced draughts and better distribution of heat vertically and horizontally. Solar space heating systems often use this heating method because the solar collectors will run more efficiently at low temperatures.

- **Fan convectors:** hot water can be piped to a finned heat exchanger with a fan (like a car radiator). Fan convectors are very useful for a quick heat-up, often being fitted at skirting level in kitchens, where there is little room for radiators.

If you choose radiators as your emitter, you need to size them appropriately. Calculators for sizing radiators are available from plumbers' merchants, but these can be inaccurate for low-energy houses. Simple radiator calculating computer programmes are available free from radiator manufacturers (e.g. Potterton Myson 'Heatloss Manager'), or you can calculate it yourself by hand. Allowance must be made for 'heat-up' – that is, the radiators and boiler must be oversized to cope with heating up the house from cold.

Controls

Good control of the heating system is vital, especially for a well-insulated house where changes in the weather can quickly result in overheating and waste of heating fuel. The basics of control are temperature and timing.

- **Temperature:** thermostats keep the house at the required temperature. Thermostatic radiator valves can be fitted, but they are not usually accurate enough for low-energy houses. Electronic thermostats should be finely sensitive; ordinary thermostats require a rise or drop in room temperature of one or two degrees before they turn on or off. Typically, they are then set higher than required and energy is wasted.
- **Timing:** programmable clocks switch on the heating between certain times, as required and to fit in with occupancy patterns.

Additional control features might include the following:

- **Optimum start:** rather than a set boiler start time in the morning, optimisers can calculate the latest possible time to start up, given the weather conditions and heat loss from the house.
- **Step switching:** the heating can be set to various temperatures throughout the day to reflect the need for heat (lower when people are active, higher when sitting in front of the telly).
- **Zoning:** a house can be split into two or more zones (e.g. bedrooms and living rooms), each of which can have their own timing and temperature regimes.
- **Weather compensating:** often used in larger buildings, weather compensating controls adjust the flow temperature of the heating circuit, so that in warmer weather it is lower and in cooler weather it is higher. These are often used with underfloor heating systems and they match condensing boilers well as the low flow-temperature helps keep the boiler in condensing mode for longer.

Reliable programmers are available to do all the above and are a vital part of the heating system of a low-energy house.

Our Preference

- Auto-ignition pellet burners or log-batch burners offer excellent control with weather compensating and optimising programmers.
- Wood-burning appliance with heat storage, such as a tile stove (Kakkleoven)
- Condensing gas- or oil-fired boiler with underfloor heating

Hot water

A superinsulated house could be using so little fuel for space heating that more energy is consumed in heating up water for domestic use. The following list shows typical hot water use for a four person household:

Function	Annual hot water use in m³
Washing hands	4
Washing hair	4
Washing face and hands	7
Washing machine	10
Dish washer	11
Shower	16
Bath	44

There are five areas where energy can be saved:

- **Hot water use:** as above.
- **Distribution losses:** 'dead-legs' of hot water – the water left in the pipe between the tap and the hot water cylinder.
- **Cylinder losses:** heat given off from the hot water storage tank.
- **Primary circuit/control losses:** heat given off from the pipework between boiler and cylinder.
- **Boiler type:** between a quarter and a half of the energy wastage from hot water may usefully heat the house in winter; but as houses become better insulated, more and more of this heat will be unnecessary. It is better to minimise wastage in every area of energy use and supply the needs as efficiently as possible when required. About 50% of a household's hot water can be supplied by solar panels.

Using less energy

Lowering water temperatures

Storing water at a lower temperature will reduce heat losses from the hot water cylinder and wastage in the pipes. If you do not use large amounts of hot water – for instance, if you take showers instead of baths – then the storage temperature should be reduced to 55°C (the minimum required to kill off Legionella bacteria). Using cold water for hand and face washing is a matter of personal taste, but remember that using small amounts of hot water frequently is very wasteful, because of 'dead-legs' – those pipe runs with hot water just sitting there losing heat.

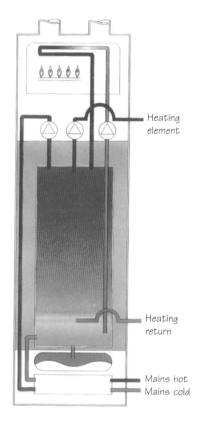

Heating element

Heating return

Mains hot
Mains cold

9.17

Fig. 9.17 An integrated thermal store.

Showers

A shower uses about half the amount of hot water of a bath. Set against this is the probability that we use the shower more frequently than the bath. Taking a power shower is likely to use as much water as a bath. Installing an electric shower may seem convenient and sensible, but it does carry with it the burden of electricity's poor conversion from primary fuel to end use. On the other hand, if you normally heat hot water in the summer by electricity anyway (having let the boiler go out), then an electric shower makes sense. Power showers aside, any sort of shower has a good financial payback, and reduces overall water use.

Mean machines

When replacing washing machines, choose the most efficient one you can afford. Most manufacturers are now producing eco-friendly models and the A-E energy efficiency rating must be displayed on all new machines for sale. (Remember low water usage is also low energy usage.) Make sure the appliance can accept hot water directly from your system and that it will mix in the cold to obtain the temperature you require – this reduces the use of the machine's electric heater, which is an inefficient and costly way to heat water. Where a machine will only accept system hot water at or below the required temperature, start it on a hot wash, and then lower the thermostat when the drum is partially filled.

Water heating systems

Hot water cylinder losses

Typical annual losses for a four person household from a hot water cylinder with different insulation thickness are given below:

Insulation	kWh loss p.a.	Cost of gas £	Cost of electric £
None	3800	95	304
25mm foam	630	16	51
40mm foam	420	10	33
Add 50mm jacket to above	330	8	25
150mm foam	104	2.5	8.3

Cylinders are now readily available that can run at mains pressure for invigorating showers and reliable hot/cold mixing, but at the expense of higher flow rates /energy.

Plumbing losses

Plumbing losses are a consequence of dead-legs and losses in the pipework between boiler and cylinder. The reason that washing hands uses such a surprisingly high volume of hot water is due to dead-legs. In new systems, ensure that the run from cylinder to kitchen sink and washbasins is as short as possible. Uses that are infrequent, but of larger volume, such as showers and washing machines, can have longer runs.

Boiler to cylinder runs should also be short and well-insulated, although the crucial factor is the controller that operates the boiler. Ideally, a system is fitted with a cylinder thermostat operating a three-port motorised valve, and a timer that prevents the boiler firing just to offset cylinder losses at a time when there is no demand. Folklore says that 'it is better to keep the cylinder hot all the time, as you use more energy heating it all up than you do just keeping it hot'. Not true. It is best to use all the hot water for your morning shower and heat up what is needed for the evening just before you need it: cold water cannot lose any heat, and boilers work more efficiently heating from cold.

Mains pressure systems

There are a number of advantages to using a mains pressure system:

- no cold water tanks and pipes in the loft;
- balanced powerful supply to shower;
- less and smaller pipework;
- choice of location for showers (not determined by the pressure head from tanks);
- BUT higher cost.

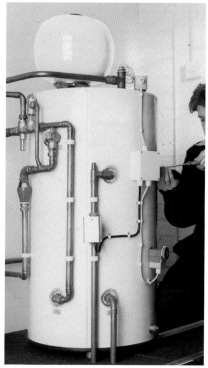

9.18

There are three types of mains pressure system:

- **Unvented (pressurised) hot water cylinder:** this is a conventional cylinder, but with a sturdier construction and a pressure vessel to cope with expansion.
- **Thermal store:** in this system, the mains cold feed runs through a cylinder of water kept hot by the boiler. The right temperature is achieved at the tap either by altering the flow rate or by mixing with cold water. Thermal stores are generally cheaper than unvented hot water cylinders, but they can suffer from a slow supply rate (this is OK for showers, but a bit slow for bath-filling). As the heat store water is directly connected to the boiler, recovery times are fast.
- **Integrated thermal store:** this is the same as a straight thermal store, except that central heating can be supplied from the store (as well as for instant heating of the house). The boiler can be smaller, and is therefore more likely to be run at full load more often, resulting in better efficiency. It is difficult to insulate these stores effectively and there are higher losses, due to keeping the store at a constant (high) temperature.

Our Preference

- Use less hot water by habit and install a shower (not power shower).
- Adjust boiler/cylinder thermostats to 55°C.
- Insulate the hot water cylinder well.
- Minimise heat losses from the system.
- Install a mains pressure system with good controls and an efficient boiler.
- Install solar water heating panels.

References

[1] Source www.dti.gov.uk 2002

[2] James Meek, Science Correspondent, writing in *The Guardian* 2/9/2000, and on www.envocare.com

[3] 'Lower Carbon Futures' published by the Environmental Change Institute, University of Oxford, 2000

Fig. 9.18 Unvented hot water cylinder.

Energy from the sun

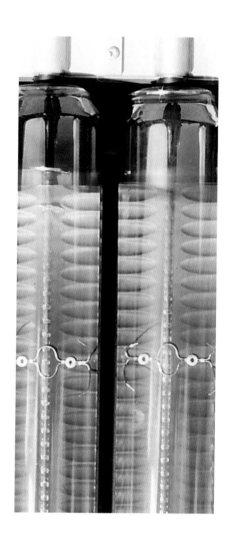

ENERGY FROM THE SUN

The sun provides almost all of the world's energy needs – warmth, wind, rain and photosynthesis. An unimaginable wealth of energy falls on the earth's surface, dwarfing human fossil fuel use. After providing for life on earth, most of this energy is converted into heat radiation, which disappears back into space. This renewable energy generation system was in perfect balance for millennia, until we over-used the capital stores of fossil fuels and discovered the greenhouse effect. If we are to minimise our fossil fuel and increase our reliance on solar energy, we need to understand how it works.

THE RESOURCE

Figure 10.1 shows what happens to the solar energy hitting the Earth. Some is reflected off snow, clouds and white sun-hats; most hits darker objects and is turned into heat; some evaporates water to form rain; a little is used up generating winds and their watery equivalents: waves and currents; and some is used by green plants in photosynthesis. A little of this plant energy goes into the fossil fuel reserves, which we use at a much greater rate than they are formed.

Solar energy devices merely intercept some of this solar radiation energy, turn it into something useful like hot water, space heating, or electricity, before it continues on its normal journey back out into space. Using technology in this way spends the Earth's 'income', rather than its 'capital'; living sustainably entails living within our means.

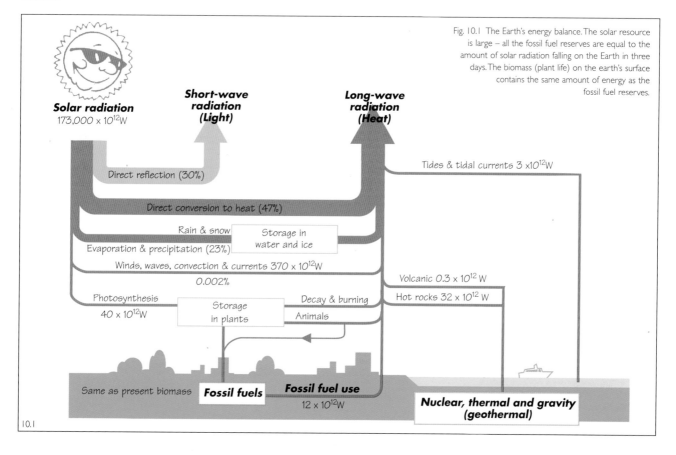

Fig. 10.1 The Earth's energy balance. The solar resource is large – all the fossil fuel reserves are equal to the amount of solar radiation falling on the Earth in three days. The biomass (plant life) on the earth's surface contains the same amount of energy as the fossil fuel reserves.

Solar radiation 173,000 × 10^{12}W

Short-wave radiation (Light)

Long-wave radiation (Heat)

Direct reflection (30%)

Direct conversion to heat (47%)

Rain & snow Storage in water and ice

Evaporation & precipitation (23%)

Winds, waves, convection & currents 370 × 10^{12}W

0.002%

Photosynthesis 40 × 10^{12}W

Storage in plants

Decay & burning

Animals

Tides & tidal currents 3 × 10^{12}W

Volcanic 0.3 × 10^{12} W

Hot rocks 32 × 10^{12} W

Same as present biomass Fossil fuels

Fossil fuel use 12 × 10^{12}W

Nuclear, thermal and gravity (geothermal)

10.1

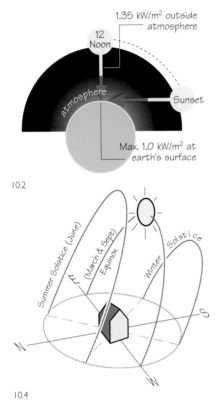

10.2

10.4

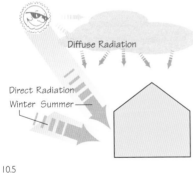

10.5

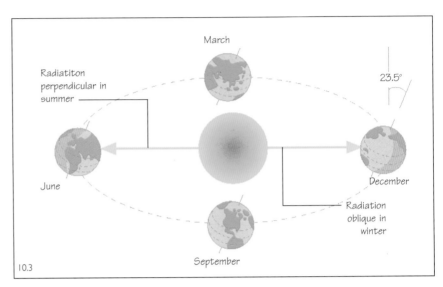

10.3

Fig. 10.2 Solar energy is absorbed by the atmosphere. At sunset, the shorter wavelengths (blue end of the spectrum) of light are absorbed more strongly than the longer (red end), resulting in sunsets.

Fig. 10.3 The tilt of the Earth relative to its orbit around the sun gives us seasons. In June the northern hemisphere is at a more perpendicular angle to the sun.

Fig. 10.4 The apparent path of the sun. At noon the sun is at an angle of about 60° in summer in Britain, and about 15° in winter. At the equinoxes (March and September 21st) the sun rises due east and sets due west (wherever you are in the world) and day and night are of equal length (hence 'equi-nox').

Fig. 10.5 Diffuse radiation comes from the whole cloudy sky vault. Summer direct radiation comes at higher angles than in winter so wintertime solar collectors, such as windows, need to be more vertical than all-year-round collectors, such as solar water heaters.

Compared to our fossil fuel use, the solar energy resource is vast, as the following terrifyingly large numbers show. The sun provides a pretty constant 173,000 terawatts (173,000x10^{12}W), whereas world fossil fuel use is only 13 terawatts. So, the solar energy falling on the earth is 15,000 times larger than our fossil fuel use. To try and imagine it, the amount of solar energy falling on an area of 7500km² – about the size of London and its suburbs – is the same as current world fossil fuel use. The solar energy falling on the Earth in one hour is equal to the annual world fossil fuel demand.

The intensity of solar radiation falling on a satellite orbiting the earth is about 1.35kW/m². By the time this energy has made its way through the atmosphere it has dropped to a maximum level of about 1kW/m². This is the most you get. In British latitudes it occasionally reaches this level in summer when the sky is clear and dark blue (the whiter the sky, the more water vapour is present: hence the dark blue skies in desert movies).

Solar geometry

The apparent path of the sun through the sky has two variables, which are brought about by the Earth's spin and its journey around the sun. As the Earth's axis of rotation is inclined at 23.5° to its solar rotation axis, we experience a change of sun angle during the year, depending on our latitude. Anywhere in the world, the sun angle at noon in mid-summer compared to in mid-winter will vary by twice 23.5° (47°). Of course, at the equator, a difference of 23.5° either side of straight overhead is hardly noticeable, whereas at the Arctic Circle the sun's angle varies between 47° and 0° above the horizon. Britain lies between latitudes 50° and 59° North. If we take 52° as an example, the sun will be at a maximum horizon angle of about 62° at mid-summer noon and a minimum horizon angle of 15° at mid-winter noon.

This is very useful information if we wish to collect winter sun into the house and yet keep out the summer sun – windows, overhangs and shading devices can be designed accordingly. The path of the sun during the day is important when deciding on the position of rooms and windows.

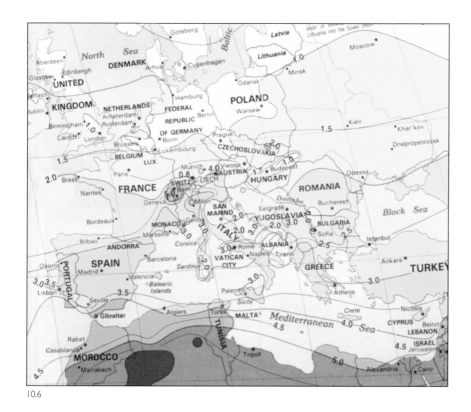

10.6

Solar geography

The final important factor is to know the weather condition – how cloudy and how dusty it is – above your site. Solar energy arrives in two forms: direct (sunshine) and diffuse (as illumination through clouds). Whilst in June the solar radiation falling on the atmosphere above Scotland is about the same as that above Gibraltar (about 11kW/m²/day), the cloudiness of our atmosphere cuts it down to two-thirds.

Sunshine is directional and can be reflected or focused, whereas diffuse radiation comes from the whole hemisphere of the sky. The ratio of these two forms varies throughout the year and will determine the angle of any sort of solar collector, depending on the job it is trying to do and when the energy it captures is needed. For example, collecting solar energy in the winter requires a collector at a steeper angle as the winter sun is lower (a vertical window will do nicely); whilst, as most solar energy is available during the summer, a solar water heater will be at a flatter angle in order to be at right angles to the higher summer sun. It will also pick up diffuse radiation better at approximately 30° from horizontal, which, conveniently, is around the average roof pitch in the UK

The effects of both latitude and weather can be seen in figure 10.6. As you would expect, available solar energy decreases as you go north, but the clean winds off the Atlantic and North Sea result in, for example, North Wales having the same annual solar energy as the Isle of Wight. However, the amount of direct sunshine will be much less. The pockets of dullness around London and downwind of Manchester are the result of dust pollution.

Fig. 10.6 Daily average wintertime solar radiation over Europe in kWh per square metre.
Source: Solarex.

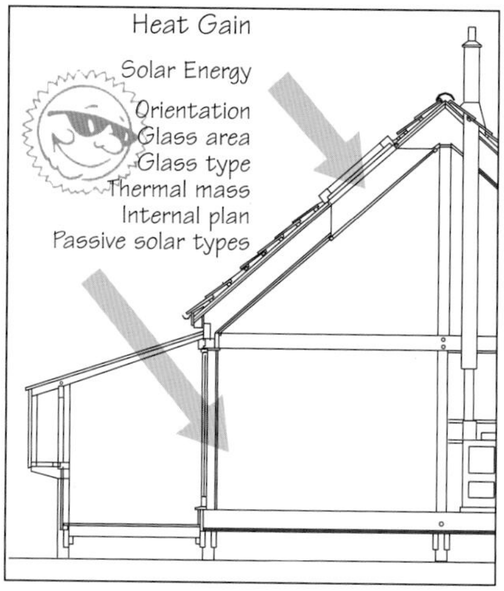

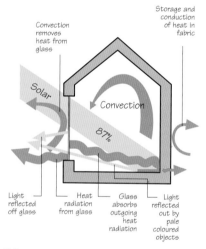

Heat Gain

Solar Energy
Orientation
Glass area
Glass type
Thermal mass
Internal plan
Passive solar types

10.7

Storage and
conduction
of heat in
fabric

Convection
removes
heat from
glass

Solar

Convection

87%

Light
reflected
off glass

Heat
radiation
from glass

Glass
absorbs
outgoing
heat
radiation

Light
reflected
out by
pale
coloured
objects

10.8

The shift of the seasons

All temperate climates experience a seasonal shift – the external temperature lags behind the solar seasons because of the time it takes to heat up and cool down water and earth. Thus, solar mid-summer (June 22nd) occurs some months before our warmest period, usually August; March 22nd has the same amount of sun as September 22nd, but is far colder.

The nature of solar heating

To get the most out of solar energy devices, be they buildings or solar panels, we have to understand the nature of the sun's radiation. When the sun is overhead, most of the energy is in the wavelength band of visible light; not surprisingly, our eyes have adapted to this spectrum. Plants make use of a similar spectrum, with a touch more ultraviolet, whereas solar panels can also make use of the invisible infrared energy. At sunrise and sunset the solar energy has to travel through a much thicker layer of air which contains dust particles and water vapour that absorb the blue end of the spectrum, giving a red-shift to the spectrum. When solar radiation hits a surface, say our body, most of the visible light energy, the ultraviolet that has got through the ozone layer and the infrared, is turned into heat by exciting the molecules of our skin, whereupon it will absorbed by the body and given out again as heat radiation.

An interesting phenomenon is associated with glass and some other glazing materials. Glass (as we well know because we can see through it) is more or less transparent in the visible spectrum of solar energy. The transparency of window glass is about 87% – in other words 13% of the visible energy gets absorbed and heats it up. The 87% meanwhile passes through and illuminates objects on the other side. Objects that are pale in colour will reflect the light out again; others that are dark will absorb the energy and get warm. Heat travels around by conduction, convection and radiation. If this warmed material is not touching the glass, then conduction can only take place through the air, which is a poor conductor. The air next to our warmed material will heat up, get less dense and rise, and be replaced by cooler air: this is a convection current. Heat radiation is predominantly in the infrared spectrum, and at these wavelengths glass acts as if it were opaque and absorbs the heat. This is the original greenhouse effect – the basic physics behind passive or active solar heating systems.

Other materials act in peculiar ways. You will come across references to 'low-E' coatings and 'selective surfaces'. These depend on a shiny surface's ability to reflect infrared radiation (a chrome kettle remains hotter longer because the shiny surface suppresses heat radiation; it does not emit much heat). In a low-E window, the shiny layer is so thin that light can mostly pass through, whilst it reflects heat back into the room. A selective surface on a solar panel appears black, so it absorbs visible light energy, whilst its shine prevents heat radiation escaping.

Fig. 10.7 Heat gain from solar energy.

Fig. 10.8 The greenhouse effect, the basis of solar collectors.

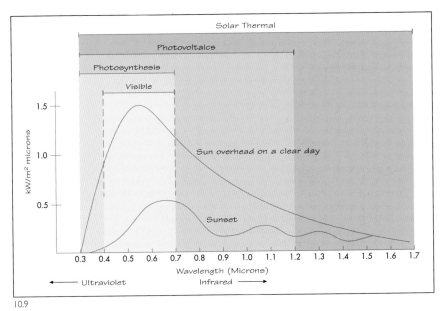

10.9

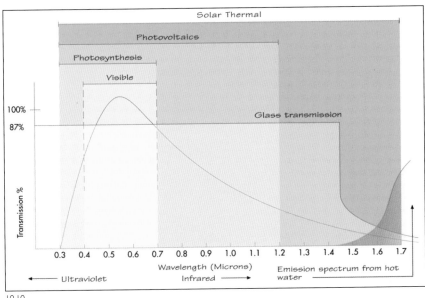

10.10

SOLAR SPACE HEATING

The ancient science

Throughout history, societies have made use of solar design. Even before the Roman invention of glass in the first century AD, the Greeks were planning and building cities whose layout was based on what we now call passive solar design. In the Greek courtyard design, the principal rooms were sheltered from cold north winds, and openings were designed to let in the low winter sun but provide shade from the summer sun. The resulting layout is remarkably similar to a modern solar courtyard design. Rows of such houses were spaced far enough apart to prevent overshading. The same idea continued unchanged in Chinese (and later Japanese) city planning right up to modern times. By the fourth century AD, the Romans were very short of heating fuel, and their public baths had large south-facing windows of mica or glass

Fig. 10.9 Solar radiation (kW/m²) across the wavelength spectrum. Our eyes are adapted to use the big bit we call the visible band. Bees can see further down into the infrared (and some flowers have infrared markings that bees can see, but that we can't), and plants also make use of the ultraviolet end. Solar heating devices can use the whole spectrum.

Source: European Passive Solar Handbook CEC.

Fig. 10.10 Transmission of glass. It lets through about 87% of the solar radiation, but at long wavelengths becomes opaque and absorbs the heat radiation.

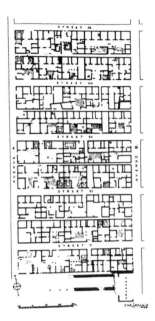

10.11a

10.11c

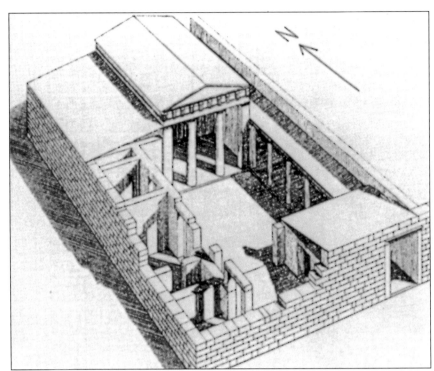

10.11b

10.11d

Fig. 10.11a & 10.11b Olynthus new town, Greece 500BC. The principles of passive solar design were well understood 2500 years ago. All the houses have courtyards facing south designed to allow in low winter sun.

Fig. 10.11c Traditional courtyard houses with massive earth walls in the Himalaya were already good examples of passive solar design – they have been improved by the recent introduction of glass.

Fig. 10.11d Herculaneum 89BC. The Romans used passive solar heating for their baths and some housing, exploiting the properties of glass for the first time.

to help heat them. Romans also started recycling bathwater and placing winter rooms directly over their baths to make use of the rising heat .

In the 19th century, a combination of the need for portable engines in their colonies, together with an uncertain coal supply, led the French to develop sun-powered motors. In the early 20th century, the high cost of coal in the American South-West prompted the invention of solar power plants and pumping sets. The first solar water heater for domestic use (the Climax) went on sale in Baltimore in 1891.

The modern era of domestic solar heating began in 1938 with an experimental house at the Massachusetts Institute of Technology (MIT). Its 40m² solar roof and 4000 litre heat store kept the house at 22°C all winter long. The promise of cheap fuels and free nuclear electricity killed off MIT's research in the 1960s, as it did the promising solar industries in Japan, Israel and South Africa. A decade later, the oil crisis brought another flurry of solar excitement (and with it the birth of CAT) that abated once more in the 1980s.

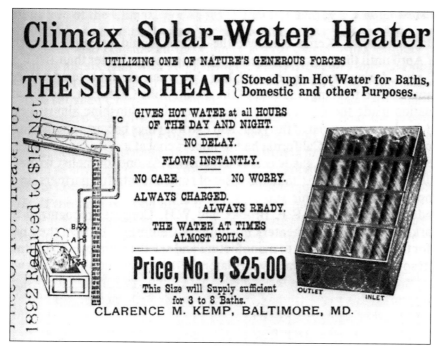

10.13

10.12

Against the trend established over the last 2000 years, current interest in solar power is not spurred on by a fuel crisis. Fossil fuels have never been more abundant and cheap. There are probably enough reserves to last hundreds of years, if we wish to pay the price of extraction. What we have discovered, however, is that there is another natural limit to growth: that the earth can only take so much pollution.

General principles

All above ground buildings benefit in some way from solar energy. The sun warms the external surfaces and immediate surrounds; sunlight enters windows and other solar collectors to give us heat and light. This is passive solar heating: the house is both solar collector and heat store. Active solar heating involves a solar panel of some type, containing a fluid, and a system of transfer of energy to and from a heat store (pipes, ducts, pumps).

There are three interrelated elements of solar heating:

• collection;
• heat storage;
• heat distribution.

Collecting solar energy

A solar collector is anything that turns the sun's energy into heat. The actual devices – windows, conservatories, mass walls and solar panels of various sorts – are all subject to the same basic physics. The key factors determining a device's effectiveness are orientation, glazing and insulation.

Fig. 10.12 The Climax solar water heater of 1892.
Source: The Golden Thread.

Fig. 10.13 CAT in the late 1970s: pioneering 100% solar space heating with a solar roof and interseasonal heat store. The two roofs are set at different angles to optimise summer and winter conditions.

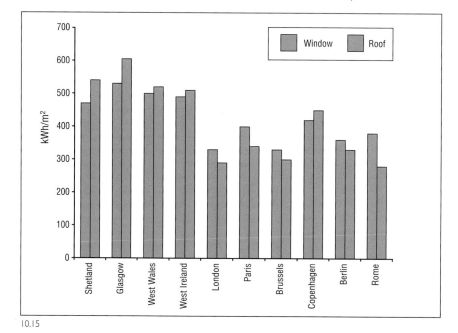

10.14

Choosing the best orientation and tilt

Orientation simply means the direction the solar collector faces in plan (south, north, etc.); tilt is the vertical angle. In the northern hemisphere, the greatest quantity of solar energy is received on a south face, assuming it is not shaded by some obstruction. The optimum orientation will depend on the job to be done: if you need a warm conservatory for a pleasant breakfast, then you will face it towards the rising sun in the east. If you want to warm the living room for evening activities, then face it west. Fortunately, precise orientation is not that critical – the solar gains from windows facing 25° off due south are only slightly lower than the maximum solar gain possible.

Figure 10.14 shows solar radiation available on a window facing different directions. You can see that the south face wins. Further, during summer, when sun angles are high, the graph takes a dive; there is less of a tendency to overheat with

10.15

Fig. 10.14 Daily solar energy falling on a window facing the four different directions, in London. South is the most useful for solar heating as it will collect the most in the winter (the heating season) and yet the high summer sun will reflect off it. Note also the 'seasonal shift' in the heating season caused by the time lag in heating up the land mass.
Source: J.K. Page Solar Energy—A UK Assessment.

Fig. 10.15 Useful solar energy collected during the heating season for some of the locations shown on the map.

Fig. 10.16 Solar energy striking a roof during the heating season (kWh/m²). In cloudy climates about three quarters of the available wintertime solar energy is in diffuse form, coming from the whole sky hemisphere. Rooflights can collect this energy better than windows (see fig. 10.15).

10.16

a southern orientation. This is because sunlight will reflect off the window glass when the angle is steep. Conversely, an east or west facing window will collect more in the summer because the sun is lower in the sky (nearer 90° to the window), and this may bring about overheating in a well-insulated house.

Optimum tilt angle will depend on your climate. Figures 10.15 and 10.16 show two interesting phenomena. You would expect northern climates to be less suitable for passive solar heating than southern, but the reverse is true. With the exception of such cold, sunny climates as the Alps and Pyrenees, passive solar design becomes a more attractive option as you go north. This is due to the fact that winter air temperatures decrease at a greater rate does solar radiation as latitude increases. Thus, in the north of Scotland, the heating season (the period when boilers are turned on) may extend throughout much of the summer, when, because of the long day length, there is almost as much solar energy available as in more southerly climes.

The second effect concerns the ratio of direct (sunshine) to diffuse (overcast) solar energy. In cloudy climates, such as Britain, most wintertime solar radiation passes through the clouds over the whole sky hemisphere. It therefore matters little in which direction a collector is facing. Rooflights see more of the sky than a window, and can be very useful in our cloudy climate, although shading devices may be necessary to protect from summer overheating.

Glazing materials

The most common form of glazing is glass – a very conductive material. Windows insulate because they separate inside air from outside air and resist heat transfer from the still air next to the glass into the glass. Glass also absorbs infrared heat radiation, warms up, and re-radiates heat both inside and outside.

There are several ways to improve thermal and solar properties of glazing.

- **Multiple sheets of glass:** each layer of glass duplicates these heat transfer processes – with each new layer, the amount of heat lost is roughly halved. Theoretically, you could add enough layers of glass for a window to have a similar insulating value to a wall, but then very little light would get through (four sheets of glass absorb 50% of the light) and the windows would be too heavy to open. The thermal resistance of the air space is proportional to distance, up to about 20mm, and then remains constant up to 60mm, after which it gets worse due to convection currents (see figure 10.30).

- **Low-E coatings:** this is a very thin layer of metal, 'sputtered' on to a glass surface, that reduces radiant heat transfer across the glazing cavity. The layer does reduce the amount of light coming through, but not appreciably. The coatings are quite soft, so they are placed on the outer surface of the inner pane – i.e. within the cavity. Pilkington 'K' glass has this low-E coating. An even more effective heat reflecting layer, made of silver and bismuth, is incorporated into Pilkington's Optitherm and the I Plus system, giving mid-pane U-values of 1.1W/m²K. There is now also a low-E plastics film that can be applied to single-glazing; this is useful for upgrading windows in historic buildings (Courtauld's Llumar low-E film).

- **Inert gas-sealed units:** gases such as argon are less conductive than air, thereby increasing the insulating value of the window with no loss in light transmission. After several years the double-glazing seals will tend to break down and the argon may seep out.

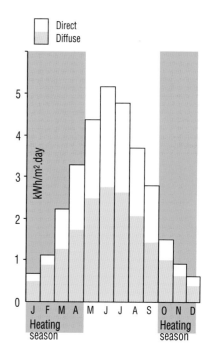

10.17

Fig. 10.17 Solar energy striking a horizontal surface during the heating season (kWh/m²). The consequence of our cloudy climate is that about three-quarters of solar radiation is diffuse during the heating season: therefore a rooflight will collect more energy than a window.

Source: European Passive Solar Handbook, CEC.

10.18

- **Very thin plastics film layer:** there are various polymers that can be made into very thin, but tough, sheets to provide a double- or triple-glazing effect without losing too much solar transmission (trade names include Tedlar and Teflon).
- **Translucent insulation:** for solar collectors where view is not important, there are waffles and foams made which allow light energy through whilst providing insulation. These are very useful as simple one-way valves for solar energy, but are very expensive at present.
- **Vacuum glazing:** still at a very promising experimental stage, this consists of two sheets of glass held apart by tiny 'invisible' glass beads. The small airspace is evacuated, which gives a very high thermal resistance – about seven times better than single-glazing.
- **Low-iron glass:** this increases the solar transmission. Iron causes the green colour you can see if you look at a sheet of glass edge on.
- **Appropriate window frame:** advanced glazing now has better thermal properties than the frame that holds it. Therefore, it makes sense not to break up the window into small panes, and to make the frame of a reasonable insulating material, such as wood.

Shutters and curtains

During the night it is very useful to be able to improve the insulation of glazing by having shutters or curtains closed. Even the most advanced glazing system will lose six times more heat than the adjacent well-insulated wall. Simple, well-fitting curtains reduce the heat loss from a window (especially if they have a silvery low-E lining). Any sort of shutter made of insulation material will improve things further, but can be awkward to use. Shutters on the outside are the best option, as they will prevent condensation forming on the glass. Outside shutters can also be used as shading to prevent overheating, and they add security. Unfortunately, British houses normally do not have shutters (unless you are going for the hacienda look), so we have not developed the habit of closing them. Roller blinds of fabric or low-E film can also be incorporated inside double-glazing.

Shading

Concerns over shading are mostly to do with whether an adjacent house, tree or hill will overshade our solar collector. While shading is most critical in terms of direct sunshine, the amount of exposure to the overcast sphere of the sky is also important. If your solar collector is a window in an existing house, there isn't much you can do about overshading, but you might be considering where to build a conservatory or where to attach a solar panel. You can use a sun chart diagram (see chapter 3, figure 3.24) to plot the whereabouts of the obstructions. This is very laborious, as you have to know the azimuth angle (the angle from due south) and the altitude angle (the angle up from horizontal) of every obstruction: you will need a compass, a spirit level, and a protractor. (There are also photographic techniques). Less laborious is a Solar Site Selector, which will enable you to make quick judgements on the suitability of a site, where to put a conservatory, the main windows, and so on. The Solar Site Selector is produced by Lewis Associates and is available from http://energyoutlet.com/products/solarsitecollector or the education website www.scolar.org.uk

Fig. 10.18 Internal folding insulated shutters: awkward to use, and you lose the window ledge.
Photo: John Willoughby.

10.19

10.20

Shading devices are used to prevent solar over heating by casting shadows at the right time of day or year. Fixed, solid shades – such as roof overhangs – are useful on the south side of a house but not on the east and west where the sun angles are lower. Fixed shades also cut out some of the view of the sky, blocking otherwise useful daylight, and fixed overhangs may cut out useful sunshine in late spring. Moveable external shutters are probably the most useful type of shading device (popular in Mediterranean countries): they can be closed when required, and they prevent solar energy getting to the glazing. Internal shutters are less effective, as the energy has to be reflected out through the glass again and much heat will enter the room. Vegetation can be used for summer shading, although the greenery is often out of phase with the solar heating requirement (tree leaves stay on too long in the autumn). The best organic solar protection device is the runner bean because its time in leaf closely matches the season of most likely solar overheating. It dies down in September/October when autumn sunshine is needed.

Heat storage

In any solar heating system, heat storage is important. Often when the sun shines you do not particularly need any heat – sometimes there is even an embarrassment of solar energy and you have to open windows or pull down shades – yet, later on, this heat would be useful. So heat storage has two purposes:

- storing surplus energy until a later time; and
- avoiding overheating.

The effectiveness of heat storage is governed by three factors:

- the heat storage capacity of the material;
- the volume of material available; and
- how heat gets in and out.

10.21

Fig. 10.19 Deciduous vegetation shades this deep verandah at a hotel in California.

Fig. 10.20 & 10.21 On single-storey houses, large roof overhangs are the simplest way of providing shading during the summer, yet allowing winter sun penetration.
10.20: Barcelona Pavilion, Mies van der Rohe.
10.21: Architect: Micheal Goulden.

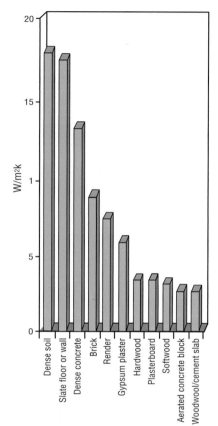

10.22a

10.22b

10.22c

Rammed earth (pisé) is the best thermal mass material.

Fig. 10.22a Heat storage admittance of selected building materials over a 24 hour period. As you would expect, the dense materials – soil, concrete, stone – are best. But suprisingly there is little difference between a whole range of materials, from timber to aerated concrete block.

Fig. 10.22b Rammed earth walls in CAT's environmental information centre.

Fig. 10.22c The graph shows the temperature variation over a 24 hour period in CAT's Environmental Information Centre – the high thermal capacity of the earth walls maintains a stable internal air temperature.

Heat storage capacity

The amount of heat that normal building materials can store depends on their density, their insulating value and their thermal capacity. By multiplying all these qualities together and putting time into the equation, we can come up with a quality called admittance. Figure 10.22a shows some common materials and their admittance over a one-day cycle. The higher the number, the better the material will be at storing heat. It will also be better at storing 'coolth' to prevent overheating in hot weather.

In a passive solar house, the thickness of thermal mass available for heat storage depends on the time taken to charge and discharge the store – the store being the walls, floor and ceiling. This usually works on a daily basis: the sun heating up the store

10.23

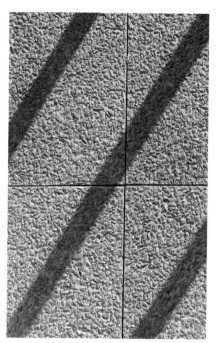

10.24

during the day for discharge at night. For most building materials, the range of useful thickness is from 50mm for lightweight materials such as aerated blocks, plasterboard, and timber, to 150mm for denser materials such as rammed earth, stone and concrete. Any greater thickness will not help in storing day-to-day solar gains, so from a heat storage point of view, there is little point in a brick wall being any thicker than 100mm (one brick).

Heat distribution

Energy contained in the heat store must now be distributed to where it is needed. In an active system this is achieved by moving the fluid through pipes and ducts to either the hot tap (if it is a domestic hot water system) or to a central heating system. With passive solar heating, the heat is transferred from the warm surfaces by heat radiation and by air convection currents. If the whole floor has been warmed by the sun, then heat given to a room will be very even and comfortable. Convection to other parts of the house will be through open doors (the taller the better) or even large high-level vents between rooms. Houses that have a warm air central heating system, or whole house ventilation, will achieve a better distribution of solar energy.

Passive and active solar heating

There are a bewildering number of possible solar heating options, but they are all just different arrangements of these elements:
- glazing: the outer, protective layer which creates the greenhouse effect;
- absorber: the element of the construction that turns sunlight into heat;
- heat store: thermal mass to store solar energy for later use;
- emitter: the part that gives out the heat to the house;
- insulation: to retain heat, either within the house or to isolate the heat store.

Fig. 10.23 Recycled rubber floor tiles, well placed to absorb solar energy in an environmental education centre, Sesseljuhus, Solheimar, Iceland.

Fig. 10.24 Concrete is one of the best thermal mass materials. Up to 150mm (6") thickness will be useful for storing daily solar gains.

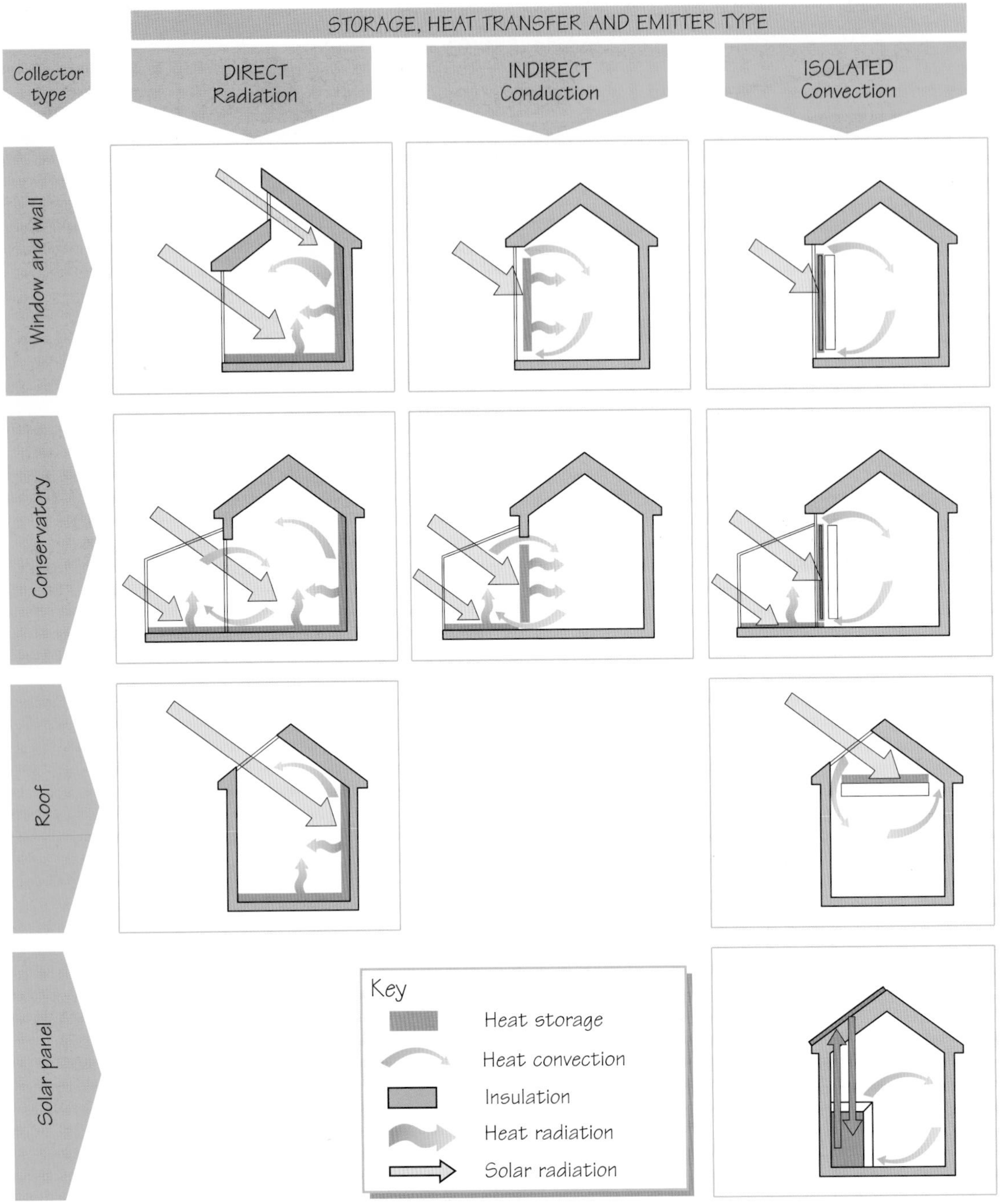

STORAGE, HEAT TRANSFER AND EMITTER TYPE

| Collector type | DIRECT Radiation | INDIRECT Conduction | ISOLATED Convection |

Window and wall

Conservatory

Roof

Solar panel

Key

Heat storage
Heat convection
Insulation
Heat radiation
Solar radiation

10.25

Fig. 10.25 Solar heating types. These diagrams recur
alongside the relevant passages in the following section.

Figure 10.25 shows a classification of solar heating by building elements (wall, conservatory, roof and collector) and different arrangements of glazing, absorber, storage, emitter and insulation. The distinction between passive and active solar heating is a little blurred. Passive solar heating means that elements of the building construction are themselves solar collectors; whereas active systems use discrete collectors and stores, with pumps and fans. However, many simple passive designs use a fan to help distribute warm air, and active collectors are often integrated into the roof or wall – it's just a matter of degree.

Passive solar heating has its limits. In a modestly insulated house, the best techniques will provide around 25-30% of the heating. Yet in a superinsulated house the heating season will be limited to maybe only three or four winter months, the very time when there is hardly any useful solar energy around. Active systems with longer term heat storage will be more appropriate for superinsulated houses.

The difference between the various solar heating designs is mainly to do with heat storage.

- **Direct gain passive solar heating:** the primary heat storage is within the living space and heat is given out (emitted) in an uncontrolled way.
- **Indirect systems:** the heat store acts as a moderator between the solar collector and living space.
- **Isolated systems:** the collector is separated from its heat store and energy must be transferred between the two systems, and subsequently to the emitters.

WINDOWS AND WALLS

Direct gain

Direct gain is the simplest form of passive solar heating. Solar energy enters the house through glazing (a window, rooflight, or conservatory) and hits a wall or floor that combines the functions of absorber, heat store and emitter. The heat is retained by the general house insulation. Much research has been done to find the optimum window size, orientation, thermal mass, house planning, etc. The basic requirements are large, south-facing windows, an exposed thermal mass and a rapid response central heating system.

In winter, south-facing windows admit the low angle rays of the sun, but in summer the high angle of the sun causes it to be partly excluded. Roof overhangs can provide additional summer shading. The optimum window to wall ratio depends largely on the thermal performance of the glazing and its cost. For normal double-glazing, about 50% of a southern façade can usefully be window. This will be about 25% of the house floor area, or 30% of floor area for low-E or triple- south-facing glazing.* There are houses that have nearly 100% south wall glazing of a very high-performance standard (quadruple-glazed, two low-E coatings and inert gas), but this costs more than an insulated wall.

10.26

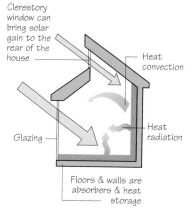

10.27

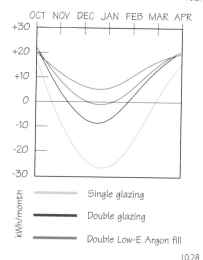

10.28

Fig. 10.26 Direct gain passive solar. This quadruple-glazed house uses 'inter-pane' blinds for shading its 100% glazed south façade.
Architects: Feilden, Clegg & Bradley.

Fig. 10.27 Direct gain – passive solar.

Fig. 10.28 Energy balance for one square metre of glazing facing south that has curtains closed at night, for different types of glazing.

*If you have lots more then overheating may become a problem, lots less and you won't be getting the benefits of passive solar.

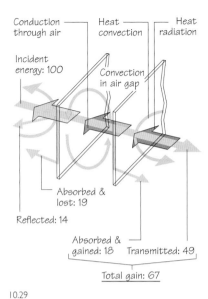

Conduction through air — Heat convection — Heat radiation

Incident energy: 100

Convection in air gap

Absorbed & lost: 19

Reflected: 14

Absorbed & gained: 18   Transmitted: 49

Total gain: 67

10.29

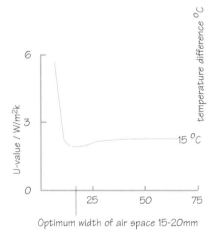

6

3

0

U-value / W/m²k

25   50   75

temperature difference °C

15 °C

Optimum width of air space 15-20mm

10.30

A double-glazed window will admit about the same amount of solar energy during the winter as it lets out as heat. If such a window has heavy curtains or shutters that are closed at night, then it will provide a net heat gain to the house. It is important to avoid overshading during the winter from buildings and trees. It is also important to avoid being overlooked – as the glazing needs to be unobstructed by curtains during the daytime. Venetian blinds are useful for scattering the sun's incoming rays, thereby distributing the energy over a wider surface; they also provide summertime shading, and reflect heat back within the house at night.

When designing a new house, ensure that as many of the windows as possible are placed on the south elevation – although east is useful for morning rooms and west for an evening room. Windows on a north elevation should be as small as is possible for the daylight requirement. The internal plan should reflect all this: place areas such as stores, utility rooms, and the garage on the north side, and the main living rooms on the south. Highly glazed houses can suffer from privacy problems – the instinctive reaction being to put up white net curtains, which reflect much of the incoming solar energy back out again (although low-E glass will help trap some). A courtyard layout, or other private back garden where the south windows are not overlooked, is the best solution.

Exposed thermal mass in the floor and walls

Many modern highly-glazed building particularly schools and offices, have large amounts of south-facing glazin, but do not have the thermal storage necessary to use solar gain and prevent overheating. Although all buildings have some thermal mass – even if it is just half an inch of plasterboard and timber floors – considerable amounts are needed to soak up solar gains from large south-facing windows. A thick concrete floor with a dark-coloured clay tiled surface would make an ideal heat store; but most people prefer carpets, which very effectively isolate the mass and prevent it doing any useful work. Dense concrete or brick partitions and inner external wall skins are the most common form of direct gain heat store.

Fig. 10.29 Energy flows through a double-glazed window. If the airspace is too large, convection will take place; if too narrow, conduction will dominate.

Fig. 10.30 Heat loss through a double-glazed window with variation in airspace gap. The optimum is 15-20mm.
Source: Hastings and Crenshaw.

Fig. 10.31 Typical direct gain passive solar houses. As they face on to the road, the windows are overlooked, so they have been screened with net curtains…

Fig. 10.32 …whereas living room windows facing private gardens take full advantage of solar gain. About one third of the 89 houses on this estate have net curtains permanently drawn, reflecting much of the solar energy. Despite this, the average solar contribution to the houses is 33%.

Architect: Bournville Village Trust Architectural Services.

10.31

10.32

Rapid response central heating system

This is common to all passive solar options. The heating system must be well-controlled and able to respond quickly to changes in temperature brought about by solar gain. For example, a solid fuel boiler or woodstove cannot be turned off at a moment's notice when the sun comes out on a winter's day. Similarly, the principal thermostat control should be in the main (solar heated) living room. However, some parts of the house may still be cold, which suggests the need to have more than one heating zone.

Advantages

- In a new house, direct passive solar heating is simple and cheap.
- Large areas of glass also provide good daylighting.

Problems

- Large energy savings require large areas of expensive advanced glazing and a lot of thermal mass.
- Privacy may be difficult to achieve.
- Furnishings may fade behind large windows.
- A responsive and well controlled back up heating system is required.

10.35

10.36

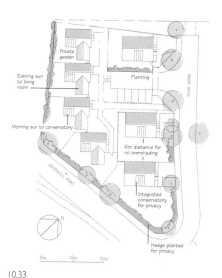

10.33

10.34

Fig. 10.33 Passive solar houses laid out for privacy to south-facing windows and minimal overshading.

Fig. 10.34 It is important that highly-glazed passive solar rooms are not overlooked. Courtyard, or L-shaped houses give the best privacy. Houses in Coalville, Leicestershire designed by CAT.

Fig. 10.35 Clerestory window bringing solar gain and daylight back into a deep building. Photo/Architect: Architype.

Fig. 10.36 Adding thermal mass to a 'lightweight' timber frame house. The infill to the timber partition wall is one brick thick; the maximum thickness worthwhile.

BUILDING A LOW-ENERGY HOUSE (7)

<u>Passive solar</u>
<u>Direct gain</u>

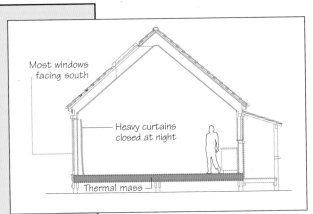

House	No. 7
SAP	100
Description:	As previous house, but with the following passive solar measures suitable for new house:
	Most windows facing south (same area)
	Thermally massive
	Solid, tiled floor and dense wall finishes and masonry partitions
	Heavy curtains or insulating blinds drawn at night

Element	U-Value	Description
Walls insulation	0.20	Cavity masonry or timber frame with 150mm
Roof	0.13	Tiled pitched roof with 300mm insulation
Floor	0.20	Insulated solid or suspended
Glazing	2.20	Double low-E in timber frames, draughtstripped

Window/floor	22%	Proportion of window to floor area
Ventilation	0.55 ac/hr	
Heat loss	0.57W/m³ of internal space	

Heating sources	per year (kWh)
Casual gains	2508
Solar gains	1890
Heating system	1855
Water heating	3900

Boiler efficiency   85%

Use of gas	Cost (£/p.a.)	Savings (£/p.a.)
Space heating	£31	£379
Water heating	£60	£25

CO_2 emissions	1.08 tonnes per year
CO_2 savings on House 1	4.47 tonnes per year

Note: Passive solar gains are not very useful in a superinsulated house if there is little thermal storage. Night-time insulation for windows is a way of improving their overall U-value without losing any solar gain.

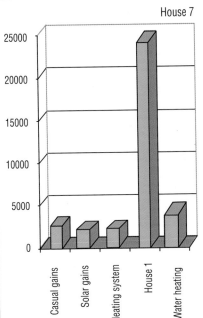

House 7

Heating supply, energy conservation and passive solar measures to House 7 in kWh/p.a.

10.37

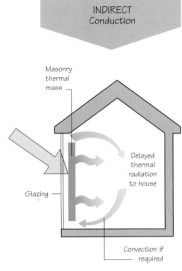

10.38

Indirect gain

Mass walls

Rather than the whole south face of the house being window, some of it can be window with a masonry wall behind. This is often called a Trombe Wall after its French designer, Felix Trombe.

Masonry wall behind glazing

In theory, the black-painted masonry (earth, brick, block, stone or mass concrete) wall heats up during the day behind the glazing. The heat is conducted through the wall to the living spaces behind. There will be a time lag between the collection of solar energy and its admission to the house: about three hours per 100mm in concrete. The wall acts as absorber, heat store and emitter. The warm air from the space between the wall and the glazing can be ducted into the house.

In practice, this system works very well in climates where bright, sunny winter days are followed by cold nights, such as Alpine climates. However, in normal UK wintertime conditions – overcast, but not very cold – the poorly insulated wall will lose as much heat as it collects. One beneficial aspect of solar mass walls is that they can be used to upgrade an existing south facing masonry wall, but it may well be more appropriate to increase the amount of glazing and direct solar gain. Overheating in summer can be prevented by shading and venting the top of the airspace to the outside. The wall can then act as a solar chimney, drawing cool air through the house.

10.39

Fig. 10.37 This house in the Pyrenees mountains, designed by Michel and Trombe, is 70% solar heated by the mass wall collector. The climate is ideal for passive solar, being sunny during the winter day and very cold at night. The black painted brick wall behind the glazing is designed to store up to a day's-worth of solar energy, which conducts through the wall to heat the space behind in the evening.
Photo: CEC Design: Trombe/Michel.

Fig. 10.38 Indirect gain – mass walls.

Fig. 10.39 The same design, built in the Wirral, Cheshire, benefits very little from its Trombe wall (7% of heating requirement, the window in the middle contributes more – 9%). A poorly insulated mass wall will lose almost as much heat as it gains during our cloudy, mild, but long, winters. Photo: John Willoughby.

10.40

10.44

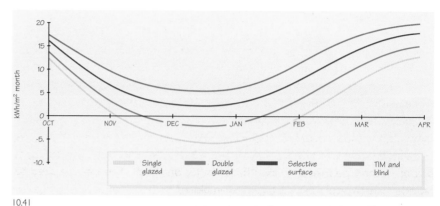

10.41

10.42

10.43

Fig. 10.40 Part of an all-glazed façade in Berlin, with (on the left) translucent insulation material fitted in front of a concrete wall.

Fig. 10.41 Energy balance through a square metre of mass wall collector with different glazing options.

Fig. 10.42 Water wall. As water has a higher specific heat than masonry, it makes a much better heat storage medium. Water will absorb in the infrared end of the solar spectrum whilst allowing much of the visible light energy through. These are acrylic tubes filled with water.

Fig. 10.43 Experimental solar air collector wall at CAT. The collector continues up into the roof, which collects as much energy as the whole wall (the wall is overshaded by a hill, and the roof 'sees' more of the cloudy Welsh skies). There are domestic hot water solar panels at the base of the wall.

Fig. 10.44 Solar house built by the Fraunhofer Institute for Solar Energy Systems, Freiburg, Germany. (The TIM insulated wall produces a heat surplus on all but 15 days in a year).

Improved construction

To improve indirect gain, we need to reduce the heat loss from a mass wall – simply making the wall itself more insulating will prevent heat being conducted through it. Past solutions have been to improve the glazing, install an insulated shutter, or to apply a low-E (selective) coating to the wall surface. The most promising solution, although pricey at present, is to add a layer of Translucent Insulation Material (TIM) between the outer glass and the wall surface. The wall will then have a much better insulation value (typically U=1.0-0.4W/m²K), but during the day solar energy is trapped against the wall. The construction will also have to incorporate some shading to prevent summertime overheating and to improve night-time insulation.

Isolated collector

Solar air heaters

In order to allow solar-warmed air to circulate around the house, mass solar walls often have holes punched through their top and bottom. The solar air heater uses this collection device alone: the dividing wall is insulated as normal, so there is not much conduction heat gain (or loss).

Lightweight collector

The collector consists of glazing, which covers an absorber panel of black painted metal. Solar-warmed air passes up the back of the absorber and circulates to the house, where it gives out heat, cools, and then returns to the collector. To work well in mid-winter, the air heater should be double-glazed and have a selective surface absorber.

HEAT STORAGE

Warm air simply circulates by natural convection (thermosiphon) in living spaces, warming room surfaces, and returns to the collector. Heat transfer to the storage (walls, floor, and ceiling) is not very efficient, but it is simple. Solar air collectors need a one-way valve – usually a flap of polythene fixed inside the ductwork – to prevent the warm inside air passing through the collector at night and cooling the house down (reverse thermosiphon). To improve overall performance, the air can be ducted down the inside of a hollow wall, or into an insulated heat store, usually a box of washed pebbles or rocks. The collector and rock store can be sized to provide several days' heating for a well-insulated house. However, the design of such a system is pretty difficult to get right. Many don't work, or use excessive fan power to get over heat distribution problems. Some way of venting hot air in the summer is necessary, as the collectors can get very hot, melting plastics parts and charring timber.

Figure 10.43 shows an experimental air heater with isolated heat store at CAT. The collector was built on to an existing blank, south-facing stone wall. Solar-heated air can either pass direct into the house or down in front of the existing insulated stone wall and then through ducts into the house. In practice, recovering the stored heat is only intermittently successful due to the particular construction of the stone wall. In theory, warm air can be extracted from the heat store wall and passed into the house at night or during cold days. Such a collector should be able to meet 30-40% of the heating demand on a good site.

Advantages

- Can be used to upgrade an existing wall.
- A simple natural convection panel can provide useful heating at modest cost.
- Gives solar gains without problems of large windows (privacy, fading furnishings).

Problems

- Careful design is needed to avoid excessive heat loss or overheating.
- Summer shading or ventilating is necessary.
- Simple systems require flaps to prevent reverse thermosiphon at night.
- Advanced systems with separate heat stores are difficult to design and are expensive (considering the output).
- Not very visually attractive.

CONSERVATORIES

Conservatories are the most popular form of solar heating, primarily because a pleasant, useful space is created that can also save energy. Conservatories can be attached to most houses with little difficulty. It is important that the conservatory can be separated from the heated house – if there is no division the conservatory will be a large heat loss.

The UK Building Regulations now recognise this problem – in the recent past, many houses have had their heating systems extended into the new conservatory. The requirement now is for a complete thermal separation between the house and the conservatory. If a heating system is installed in the conservatory, it must be

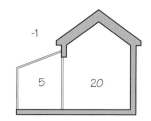

10.46

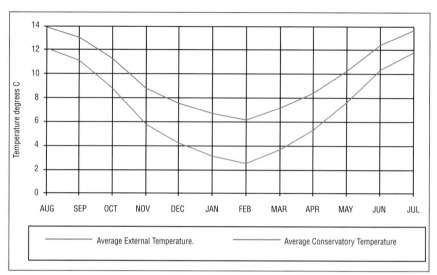

10.45

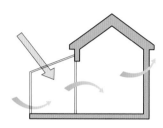

10.47

10.48

Fig. 10.45 The seasonal shift. The average February temperature inside this attached conservatory is around that experienced outside in April. The walls of the house are subject to a warmer climate than they would be otherwise and therefore lose less heat. Ventilation air drawn from the conservatory is preheated similarly.

Fig. 10.46 Buffer effect.
(The numbers represent temperatures in °C).

Fig. 10.47 Solar ventilation preheat.

Fig. 10.48 Lobby to external doors.

Facing page: Fig. 10.49 Conservatory in Devon with blinds and creepers for summertime shading. Architect/Builder: Roderick James.

Fig. 10.50 Dark stone floors are the best for collecting and storing solar heat. Architect/Builder: Jonathan Hines.

controlled independently of the main house system. It is perhaps better to integrate the conservatory into the house design and to insulate it to the same high standards as the rest of the house – this passive solar element is called a 'sunspace'.

There are four ways in which the conservatory works as an energy saver.

- **The buffer effect:** a conservatory will be the first line of defence against the weather – a solar 'crumple zone'. Walls and windows covered by the conservatory are subject to a far milder climate than their uncovered neighbours. The glass skin traps escaping heat, raising the temperature in the conservatory a little; thus, because the temperature difference between the house and its exterior is less extreme, heat escapes at a slower rate from the house (the greater the temperature difference, the quicker the heat loss). In effect, a conservatory (or porch or garage) is just a layer of insulation you can sit in. Soon after sunrise, the solar energy entering the conservatory is greater than the heat escaping, and it heats up. This heat rise enhances the buffer effect. Once the conservatory temperature is the same as the house temperature, there is no heat loss. Figure 10.45 shows average temperatures in a typical conservatory at night (when there are no solar gains). Providing the house is being heated (assumed temperature of 20°C), the conservatory will experience a seasonal shift. It will be approximately one month warmer than outside.

- **Solar ventilation preheat:** fresh air entering the house via the conservatory will be warmed on its way. This is a valuable energy saver as much of the heat loss in a well-insulated house is due to ventilation. Some of this air will circulate back to the conservatory for reheating. Solar ventilation preheat has been found to be a better option (providing you are building a conservatory anyway) than many whole house heat-recovery ventilation (HRV) systems – it gives similar energy savings, is cheaper to run and uses less electricity for fans. An HRV system benefits from taking its fresh air from the conservatory.

- **Lobby to external doors:** a conservatory reduces the ventilation heat loss caused by draughts from external doors and acts as an airlock when the doors are used.

10.49

10.50

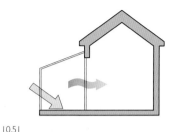

10.51

Conservatory

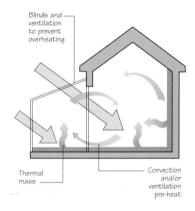

10.52

10.53

• **Heat conduction to the house:** conduction takes place whenever the conservatory is warmer than the house. The sun warms conservatory wall surfaces. Some of this heat warms the air in the conservatory, while some migrates through the wall to the house. As outdoor air temperatures cool, the wall radiates heat into both the house and the conservatory, extending its usefulness as a living space into the evening.

Making the most of a conservatory

• **Direct Gain:** solar energy passes through the glazing to strike the floor and solid walls of the conservatory. Thermal mass moderates air temperatures, storing heat for later use. Good ventilation, with low and high level openings and shading for the roof, is vital to prevent overheating in the summer. Windows facing into a conservatory can be larger than normal: the buffering effect means that they are better insulated. These windows also need to be larger as the conservatory rafters and extra layers of glazing cut out daylight. In a new house, an integrated conservatory courtyard is a beneficial way of bringing solar energy and daylight deep into the house.

• **Buffering:** a conservatory with a small surface area relative to the surface it covers has a considerable buffering effect. Walls and windows opening into the conservatory can be less well insulated than those opening directly on to the outside. Indeed one glazed street in Norway was paid for out of savings made by cheaper external walls facing into it. The better the glazing (double- low-E, etc.), the more useful the conservatory is as additional living accommodation. The trouble is, we like them so much that they end up being decorated as living rooms (carpets, curtains), and portable heaters find their way in, which rather defeats the energy saving object. Many elaborate conservatories are more expensive per square metre than the rest of the house.

Fig. 10.51 Heat conduction to the house.

Fig. 10.52 & 10.53 A single-glazed conservatory on a lightweight timber frame house can provide solar ventilation preheating, but the buffering effect is reduced as there is little thermal mass in the conservatory to soak up solar gains. It overheats quickly for the same reason. A floor finish of concrete paving slabs and tiles helps. There is little conduction to the house, as the separating wall is insulated. In summer, a two storey conservatory is more comfortable than a single storey one, since the hot air rises above head height and is dispersed via roof windows. During the heating season, first floor windows can be opened to encourage warm air circulation. Architect: Architype.

10.54

10.55

10.56

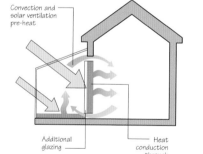

Convection and
solar ventilation
pre-heat

Additional
glazing

Heat
conduction
through
separating
wall

10.57

- **Orientation:** the direction a conservatory faces is not so critical as it is for other direct gain options, such as windows. The positioning of a conservatory depends on the layout of the house and which rooms it can best serve. A south-east aspect is ideal: the conservatory greets the early morning sun and therefore its benefits can be felt throughout the day. This also makes a wonderful place to have breakfast. Overheating of a south-east conservatory will be less of a problem as the house will shade it from the westerly sun at a time when the outside air temperature is at its warmest; and the high south summer sun will not be striking the roof at such a square angle.
- **Conservatory with mass wall:** adding a conservatory to an existing masonry-walled house creates a solar mass wall which works on the same principal as the Trombe Wall, but with the same defects. Further, the airspace between the glazing and the mass wall is now living space, with plants and people to consider. Interestingly, the Trombe Walls at a housing scheme in the Wirral, where the gap between glazing and wall was 600mm, were found to be more useful for growing tomatoes than for supplying heat to the house.
- **Conservatory with air heater:** mounted on the rear conservatory wall, a lightweight solar air heater with glazing and black or selective surface absorber can be connected, by ducts, either directly to the house, or to its own heat store. The air heater will have insulation material on its back face to prevent unwanted heat loss to the separating wall of the house. This wall will now be effectively insulated. As with the solar air heater, warm air simply circulates by

Fig. 10.54 Glazed street at the Swansea Foyer project, which provides home and training for the young unemployed homeless. The street provides a buffer zone and useful sheltered space for casual interaction.
Architect: PCKO Architects.

Fig. 10.55 Conservatory as entrance. This triple-glazed conservatory at the 'Centre of the Earth' in Birmingham acts as an entrance lobby and circulation space between the various function rooms. Using a conservatory in this way doesn't work very well in houses, but here, where the occupants are dressed in outdoor clothes, it is fine. Note the ceramic tiles for solar collection and storage.
Architect: David Lea.

Fig. 10.56 Glazed street. Linking three buildings at this Family Centre, the conservatory saves energy and provides a low-cost circulation space where active infants can play safely in all weathers.
Architect: Benedicte Foo.

Fig. 10.57 Indirect conduction – conservatory.

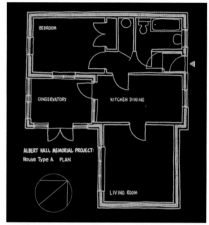

10.58

10.60

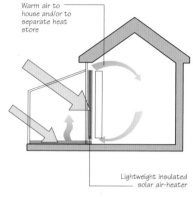

10.61a

Warm air to house and/or to separate heat store

Lightweight insulated solar air-heater

10.59

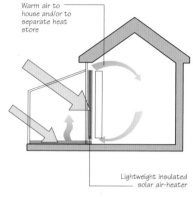

10.61b

natural convection (thermosiphon) around the living spaces, warms the room surfaces, and returns to the collector or into an insulated heat store (a rock bed).

Advantages
- Provides extra, delightful living space.
- Buffering effect and solar gains reduce heat loss from house.

Problems
- Can get in the way of views from the house.
- Can get uncomfortably hot.
- If fitted with heaters, it does not save energy.

Fig. 10.58 Plan showing a conservatory built into the corner of an L-shaped house, which will heat up quickly from the morning sun and get some shading from the west. Coalville, Leicestershire.

Fig. 10.59 Same house as the plan (figure 10.58) with the mid-morning sun shining straight into the conservatory. The living room windows on the right face the afternoon sun to heat the room for the evening.

Fig. 10.60 Solar gains absorbed by the dense block and brick construction help to minimise overheating and to extend the usefulness of the conservatory into the evening. However, it will take longer to heat up and become comfortable in the morning. The photograph is taken early afternoon—the west wall is already starting to shade the conservatory. Note the high-level window for ventilation, with automatic opener.

Fig. 10.61a Isolated convection – conservatory.
Fig. 10.61b View of high-level solar collector and insulating shutters. The living rooms all face the conservatory and have French doors with shutters. Some of the solar collectors are simple water heaters – a black painted tank of water within the 'hot box'.

BUILDING A LOW-ENERGY HOUSE (8)

Passive solar
Attached conservatory and solar water heating

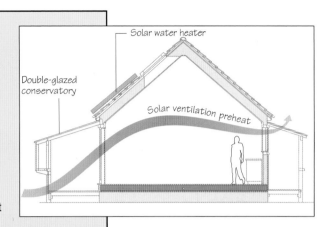

House	No. 8	
SAP	100	
Description	As House 6, but with the following passive solar measures suitable for a new house:	
	Most windows facing south (same area)	
	Thermally massive	
	Heavy curtains or insulating blinds drawn at night	
	Double-glazed 20m² conservatory on south face	
	Ventilation to house preheated through conservatory	
	4m² solar collector	

Element	U-Value	Description
Walls	0.20	Cavity masonry or timber frame with 150mm insulation
Roof	0.13	Tiled pitched roof with 300mm insulation
Floor	0.20	Insulated solid or suspended
Glazing	2.20	Double low-E in timber frames, draughtstripped
Window/floor	22%	Proportion of window to floor area
Ventilation	0.55	ac/hr through conservatory
Heat loss	0.40W/m³	of internal space

Heating sources	per year (kWh)
Casual gains	1650
Direct solar	805
Conservatory	900
Heating system	1020
Water heating	2200
Boiler efficiency	85%

Use of gas	Cost (£/p.a.)	Savings (£/p.a.)
Space heating	17	393
Water heating	34	51

CO_2 emissions	0.60 tonnes per year
CO_2 savings on House 1	4.95 tonnes per year

Note: The conservatory acts as extra insulation and preheats ventilation air, whilst still allowing solar gains through the windows it covers.

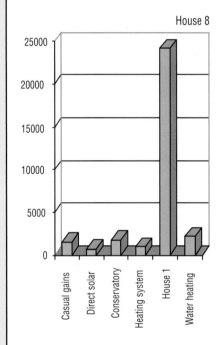

House 8

Heating supply, energy conservation and passive solar
measures to House 8 in kWh/p.a.

10.62a

10.62b

10.62c

Fig. 10.62a Tradional 'gallerias' in northern Spain have
evolved from balconies. Windows fitted on the front
edge of each balcony create a sheltered winter
sunspace. The floor above each one reduces
summer overheating.

Fig. 10.62b A modern version of 'gallerias'. The extra
layer of glazing reduces street noise and can open up
to become a balcony. No.1 Deansgate, Manchester.
Architects: Ian Simpson.

Fig. 10.62c A double height sunspace fitted with
triple-glazed low-E windows and doors forms part of
the living room. Bells Court, Shropshire.

10.63

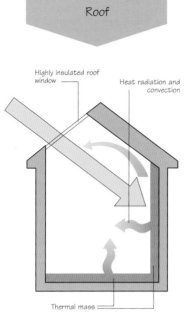

Roof

Highly insulated roof window

Heat radiation and convection

Thermal mass

10.64

SUNSPACES

The heating – and overheating – problems associated with conservatories can be avoided by building a sunspace. South facing low-energy glazing will bring energy benefits to the house throughout the year (see figure 10.28). As the cost of such glazing has reduced considerably in the last few years, it has become possible to include a large passive solar space into a house that has all the delightful benefits of a conservatory without the energy penalties. A sunspace will have an insulated roof and floor, built to the same high standard as the rest of the house – but the solid roof will ameliorate the summertime overheating suffered in glass-roofed conservatories. If the sunspace is double height, not only will it be a wonderful, light, convivial space but the entire house will also benefit from solar gains.

Roofs

Direct gain

A roof sees much more of the sky dome than a window, partly because of its angle and partly because it is less likely to be overshaded. This is very useful in densely populated areas where windows may not be exposed to direct sunlight at all. A rooflight or sunpipe is also useful for getting daylight into deep buildings and stairwells, and bringing delight to dull areas.

Orientation is not as critical as for windows, and there should be no problems of privacy. The tilt of a roof is obviously not ideal for collecting winter sunshine (around 75° is best, and most roofs are around 35°) but, due to the cloudiness of our climate in the winter, the tilt is not that critical. Ideally, direct sunshine should fall on thermally massive surfaces such as masonry walls and solid floors. Unfortunately, this is rarely the case in 'room-in-the-roof' attic conversions, which are prone to overheating. A south-facing glazed roof will collect a huge amount of solar energy in the summer, so good ventilation and shading are vital.

Fig. 10.63 Daylight and passive solar heat from roof glazing above a stairwell.
Fig. 10.64 Direct radiation – roof.

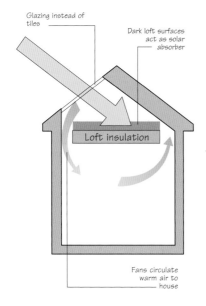

Glazing instead of tiles

Dark loft surfaces act as solar absorber

Loft insulation

Fans circulate warm air to house

10.65

The passive solar roof at CAT, which was built over an office, was constructed from glazing consisting of eight layers of plastic film, giving an insulating value four times greater than single glazing. Its energy balance (solar in versus heat out) was very good – with a net heat gain even on dull cold days of approx 60W/m². The room underneath was very well daylit, and there were shutters which reflected light back into the room and prevented glare and overheating in the summer.

Loft space air heater

An ordinary loft will get quite warm on a sunny day. If the tiles are replaced by glazing, and the inside of the loft is a dark colour (acting as a solar absorber) it will get very, very warm. The loft air can be pulled down into the house when it is warmer than the house air. This will require a fan and a thermostat controller, which may be powered by a convenient photovoltaic panel – the PV array producing electricity at the very time it is needed to power the fans. The air will warm the surfaces of masonry walls, which will act as a heat store. When the house is unoccupied during winter, the system can be allowed to overheat on sunny days in order to try and get as much energy stored up in the house mass as possible. When the house is occupied, there will have to be an upper temperature limit. As the loft air will always be warmer than outside air, a trickle fan can be left on permanently in winter to provide ventilation preheating. The ceiling between the loft and the rest of the house needs to be insulated as normal – both to keep the house warm in cold conditions, and cool when the collector is over hot – but the insulation must be covered up (by flooring) to prevent insulation particles drifting into the house.

During the summer, the loft space collector will get very hot, so temperatures must be controlled by shading devices and ventilation. This hot air can be passed through a heat exchanger to provide solar water heating.

Starting with a simple idea, you can see that – to cover every eventuality – the loft space collector can become quite complex and still suffer from the basic problem shared with other passive systems: in well-insulated houses, using the walls and floors as heat storage is not very effective.

Fig. 10.65 Isolated convection – roof.

BUILDING A LOW-ENERGY HOUSE (9)

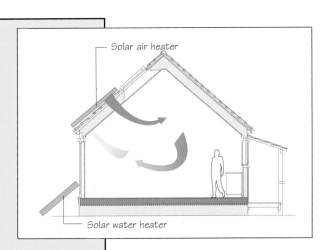

Solar air heater

Solar water heater

Passive solar

Solar air heater and solar water heating on a superinsulated house

House: No. 9
SAP   100
Description: As House 6, but with the following passive
                solar measures suitable for new house:
                Most windows facing south (same area)
                Thermally massive
                Heavy curtains or insulating blinds drawn at
                night
                20m² solar air heater or loft space collector
                Solar water heater and extra hot water tank insulation

Element	U-Value	Description
Walls	0.20	Cavity masonry or timber frame with 150mm insulation
Roof	0.13	Tiled pitched roof with 300mm insulation
Floor	0.20	Insulated solid or suspended
Glazing	2.20	Double low-E in timber frames, draughtstripped

Window/floor	22%	Proportion of window to floor area
Ventilation	0.55ac/hr	
Heat loss	0.46W/m³ of internal space	

Heating sources	per year (kWh)
Casual gains	1275
Direct solar	865
Solar heater	1740
Heating system	1165
Water heating	2200

Boiler efficiency	85%

Use of gas	Cost (£/p.a.)	Savings (£/p.a.)
Space heating	19	391
Water heating	34	51

CO₂ emissions	0.63 tonnes per year
CO₂ savings on House 1	4.92 tonnes per year

Note: The air heater has no discrete heat storage, but uses the thermal mass in the house – its performance could be improved by an insulated rock store. Solar water heating can be by heat exchanger in the air heater system.

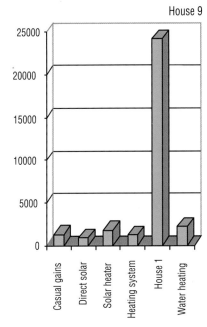

House 9

Heating supply, energy conservation and passive solar measures to House 9 in kWh/p.a.

10.66

10.67

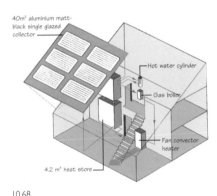

40m² aluminium matt-black single glazed collector

Hot water cylinder

Gas boiler

Fan convector heater

4.2 m³ heat store

10.68

ACTIVE SOLAR SPACE HEATING

Quite apart from whether they save energy, many passive solar options (large windows facing south, conservatories, roof windows) are worth installing simply because they improve the quality of the living spaces. Indeed, most passive solar options struggle to make any significant contribution towards heating a superinsulated house. (The exceptions are those that buffer the external skin or preheat ventilation air.) To further reduce fossil fuel use, or to do without it altogether, requires an active solar system made up of separate, thermally isolated elements. An active solar system comprises a collector (glazing covering an insulated absorber), a heat transfer system to an insulated heat store, and a supply system to give out heat to the house when required.

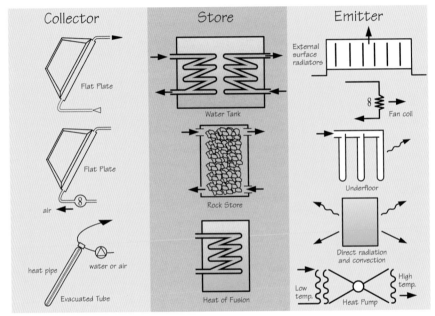

10.69

Individual house systems

Thirty years ago, many active solar systems were designed, built, and tested in Britain, Northern Europe and North America. The solar contribution of these schemes ranged from 30-100% of the heating demand, but they all suffered from being hopelessly uneconomic. In many industrialised countries, the price of fossil fuel is so low that until fuel shortages, pollution-control or grant aids dictate otherwise, active solar space heating will remain in the province of society's innovators.

District heating systems

Whilst active solar space heating for individual houses may be difficult to justify, larger village-scale systems have been successful. In Scandinavia there have been several schemes that employ huge arrays of solar collectors – sometimes distributed on the house roofs – combined with a district heating main and a large underground heat store. The heat stores are large enough to store up summertime heat for the winter – interseasonal heat storage. Where there is a heat demand all year round, such as is the case at CAT for dish washing, in the restaurant (which is used most in

Fig. 10.66 Isolated convection – roof.

Fig. 10.67 Solar space heating system in a house in Milton Keynes. Many systems like this were installed at the end of the 1970s, which provided up to 50% of the annual heating supply. Photo: CEC.

Fig. 10.68 Schematic of the solar space heating in the Milton Keynes house. The 40m² collectors heat a 4.2m³ water heat store. Hot water is fed to the fan convector unit after passing through a boiler to bring it up to temperature if necessary. It supplies 45% of the demand. The collectors also supply heat to the domestic hot water cylinder.

Fig. 10.69 Types of collector, heat store and emitter.

10.70

10.71

10.72

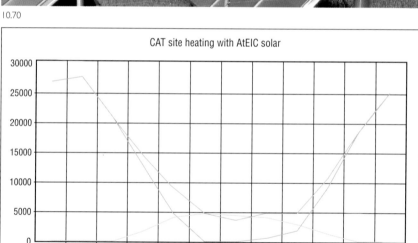

10.74

10.73

the summer), the heat storage can be drastically reduced – thereby reducing the capital costs considerably. The Autonomous Environmental Information Centre (AtEIC) is a zero-CO_2 building by virtue of the heat energy from its large solar array replacing gas that was previously used for summertime hot water in the Restaurant. A heat main connects all the buildings on the CAT site, with a biofuel boiler providing heat during winter when the output from the solar array is inadequate.

Types of active solar system

Figure 10.69 shows some variations on the basic theme of collector, heat store and supply system (emitter), with the two common heat transfer media of water and air. While there is considerable scope for variations in the design configuration, it is sensible to stick to one medium rather than mixing, say, an air collector with a water heat store. Complex schemes do not perform any better than their simpler counterparts. Slight inefficiencies can often be compensated for by a slightly larger collector area or store. In Britain, almost all solar systems have used water as the heat

Fig. 10.70 A 10,000 square metre solar thermal array, powering a district heating system together with a biomass boiler, in Kungalv, Sweden.

Fig. 10.71 This building – called the Autonomous Environmental Information Centre (AtEIC) – is mostly heated by its 120m² high-performance solar water heating array.

Fig. 10.72 The CAT solar/biofuel district heating system. Surplus solar heat can be sent down the 'heat main' to other buildings on the site.

Fig. 10.73 When there is not enough solar heat available, a biofuel (wood chip) boiler, also connected to the 'heat main', can heat the buildings. Overall, the solar roof on AtEIC saves more fuel for CAT than the building consumes – therefore it is a 'zero-CO_2' building.

Fig. 10.74 Graph showing the contribution made to the total CAT heating demand by the surplus solar heat generated by AtEIC.

transfer medium, mainly because we have lots of plumbers around and not many ventilation installers. Water is much more thermally dense than air, and a water heat store will contain about three times the energy of the same-sized air/brick store. During the summer, the huge surplus of solar heat can be used to heat domestic hot water.

Water-based systems

Advantages

- High energy density results in compact systems and stores.
- System permits ease of control and regulation with scant use of electricity.
- Technology and systems are familiar.

Problems

- System must be protected from frost and internal corrosion.
- Response to short bursts of winter sunshine is slower than air systems.
- Leaks can be damaging.

Air-based systems

Advantages

- Efficient response to short bursts of winter sunshine.
- Leaks not damaging.
- Rock heat stores stratify well.
- Warm air from panel passes directly into house.

Problems

- Low-energy density results in larger heat stores (about 1:3 compared with water).
- High electricity required to power the fan.
- Generates noise.
- Awkward, bulky and expensive to move energy around and divert the flow.

An evaluation of all the above pros and cons suggests that an air system might be appropriate for short-term heating (storing enough heat for a day or two), while a water system seems best where the intention is to store up enough energy for a week, a month, or the whole winter.

Solar collectors

A solar space heating collector needs to be well insulated to work effectively in wintertime conditions. The recommended types are detailed below.

- **Evacuated tube:** this has a selective surface absorber and a 'heatpipe' or water pipe surrounded by a glass tube from which the air has been evacuated. The tube is mounted in an array with a water manifold at the top to take away the heat.
- **High performance flat plate:** water passes through a selective surface absorber. Double-glazing or better. The back and sides are insulated.

Flat plate collectors are best integrated into the roof rather than mounted on it. Indeed, with this sort of system the whole roof is usually the solar collector. Evacuated tubes are mounted in arrays clear of the roof surface.

10.75

10.76

Heat stores...

The heat store will be sized according to the daily and seasonal heating load and the available solar energy. Climates that enjoy bright winter sunshine will only require heat stores large enough to carry the daily solar gains through to the night. A gloomy winter climate may necessitate storage over several days or weeks. Even then, the midwinter months will not produce enough solar energy to heat the house. To maximise the contribution of solar space heating, the store must be large enough to carry some summer sunshine into the winter. This is called interseasonal storage.

Fig. 10.75 An integrated, high-performance solar array at CAT with selective surface absorber underneath double-layer polycarbonate glazing.

Fig. 10.76 Evacuated tube solar collector. Thermomax.

10.77

Heat stores must be well insulated to prevent unwanted heat loss into the house. The more long-term the heat store, the thicker its insulation must be. The no longer extant interseasonal heat store at CAT had an insulated lid 600mm thick.

… with air systems

The design needs to ensure an even distribution of warm air across the heat store. Rock heat stores stratify well: the top layer of rocks will be hottest, as conduction between the rocks is poor and there will be little convection movement. Hot air from the collector is passed into the top of a bed of washed, fist-sized rocks (usually sandstone or limestone). The air passes down through the rocks and is extracted from the bottom to return to the collector. Air for domestic heating is extracted by passing room air in at the bottom (coolest), which gradually gets hotter as it moves up through the store.

… with water systems

These can be anything from a larger version of the familiar domestic hot water cylinder; to a swimming pool sized interseasonal store, as at CAT; to a vast rock cavern 50m across serving 55 houses, as at Lyckebo in Sweden. Water is the best medium for storing solar energy: it is cheap, has a high energy density, and can be moved around easily. The only drawback (apart from the mess caused if it leaks) is that it does not stratify well. Although hot water rises within a heat store and will collect at the top, the introduction of new water disrupts the heat stratification. This may result in a large quantity of lukewarm water instead of a small amount of water hot enough for use. Solar collectors will work at their most efficient level when supplied with cold water and when the heat supply system (emitter) requires the hottest water. Heat stores can be split up to store energy at different temperatures or can have various baffles and floating inlet tubes fitted to reduce mixing.

Heat supply systems

To be efficient, a solar heating system must be run at the lowest temperature possible. During the winter, a collector cannot supply water hot enough to operate a normal central heating system. The heat supply system has to be designed to deliver energy to the house at low temperatures by using a larger area of cooler radiator. Conventional central heating systems operate at high (70°C) temperatures, so that the radiators can be compact and not take up a lot of wall space, but a radiator covering a large area will emit the same amount of heat at a cooler temperature.

Emitters (devices that give out heat)

- **Extended surface radiators:** these are similar to conventional steel radiators but much larger.
- **Underfloor heating:** if the whole floor is an emitter, the solar system can operate at very low temperatures (30°C or so). Very good radiant comfort conditions lead to lower air temperatures and hence less heat loss from the house. If the underfloor heating is set in a concrete floor, the extra thermal mass is useful.
- **Fan coil and convection from solar air heaters:** for warm air heating to work with a solar system at low temperatures, the air has to be introduced carefully and slowly to avoid draughts.

Fig. 10.77 Large solar collector feeding an inter seasonal heat store – one that stores up the summer surplus heat until the winter – in this system at CAT built in 1976.

10.78

—Shows a **Climax Solar-Water Heater**
supported by a bracket on the wall.
A.—Is the cock to use when the hot water is
wanted. This passes cold water into the heater,
displacing the hot water and forcing it through a
pipe to the bath tub.
B.—Is the drain cock which is used to prevent
freezing.
C.—The air opening which prevents vacuum
in the heater and siphonic action.

10.79

- **Heat pump:** if a solar system is to be added to a conventional central heating system, then its temperature can be raised using a heat pump. This works in a similar way to a domestic refrigerator: an electric compressor turns a large quantity of low temperature heat into a small quantity of high temperature heat. The solar system can still run at low temperatures.

DOMESTIC SOLAR WATER HEATING

The habit of regular bathing in hot water, prevalent in Roman times, was re-acquired during the 19th century following Pasteur's discovery of germs and the importance of hygiene. To save their customers the chore of heating water on a stove, inventors in America combined the ancient idea of the hot box (a pot of water in a glass-topped box) with the new technology of plumbing – and the solar water heater was invented. Thousands of solar water heaters were installed in the US right up until World War II, when a copper shortage and the discovery of cheap oil killed off the industry. Solar technology was re-discovered during the 1970s oil crisis, though it has only really become a popular option in sunny countries with few fossil fuel resources (e.g. Greece, Japan, Israel, Australia).

Even in cloudy Britain, the potential for energy savings is huge. It has been estimated that about half of our 22 million dwellings could usefully have a solar water heating system fitted (at present there are around 42,000). Such a measure would reduce total CO_2 emissions by about 1%. The average house will need about 3000kWh of energy per year for domestic water heating and it is estimated that solar thermal panels can provide 40-50% of that demand.

The area of installed solar water heating has risen from 7596m² per year in 1995, to 11,850m² per year in 2000. Unfortunately, the installation costs have risen, too, and are currently around £2,500 to £4,000, although this could be less for DIY systems, or for new build where the panels are integrated into the roof. However, domestic solar water heating still offers a reasonable financial payback of between seven and fifteen years, depending on the cost of fuel that is being replaced. This equates to a rate of return on your investment of 14% to 6.5%.

Fig. 10.78 The heat store (figure 10.77) was connected to an underfloor heating system. In its best year the system supplied 80% of the heating for the 170m² building, and computer simulations of the system have since shown that 100% heating would have been achieved easily, had a sealed, modern selective surface solar collector been installed.

Fig. 10.79 The Climax solar water heater.
Source: The Golden Thread.

Under the Clear Skies scheme, the Government is currently subsidising solar water heating along with other renewable technologies. It has also reduced the VAT rate on professional installations of solar thermal systems to 5%.

Using second-hand steel radiators as absorbers, a DIY system costs very little. Although efficiency of such systems is low in cold weather, this can be offset by having a large number of panels that provide ample hot water during the summer.

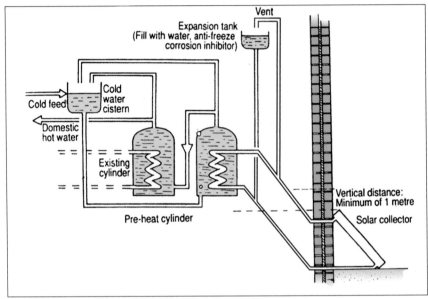

10.80

A SOLAR WATER HEATING SYSTEM

A solar water heating system consists of a **collector** and **hot water storage.**

A **collector** is made up of the absorber – the black metal bit that turns the sun's radiation into heat – a glass cover to trap the heat and insulation to prevent heat escaping from the back of the absorber. Collectors are either 'flat plate', which may be double-glazed or have a selective surface absorber, or 'evacuated tube' type, where the insulation is in the form of a vacuum.

The **hot water storage** will either be inside the house, as part of the general plumbing, or integrated into the absorber.

Separate panel and hot water storage

The solar array can be mounted as a free-standing box on the ground; on a flat or pitched roof; or integrated into the roof finish. If mounted at low level, the system can be a thermosiphon system; if at high level, it will have to be a pumped system.

Fig. 10.80 Thermosiphon (gravity) system.

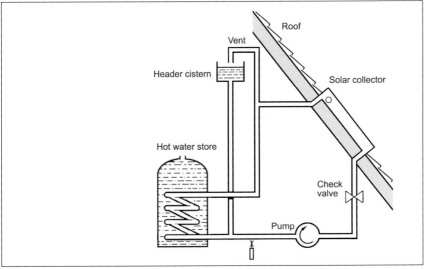

10.81

Thermosiphon system
- The panels must be lower then the hot water cylinder by at least one metre.
- The absorber must be of a 'flooded plate' or 'headers and risers' type.
- Pipework must be large diameter (22mm or 28mm) and it must be near to, and always slope up to, the cylinder.
- No pump or electronic controller is necessary.
- The response to bursts of sunshine is slower than that of a pumped system.
- Panels at low level are easier to maintain, but may get broken and are easily overshaded.

Pumped system
- Panels can be mounted anywhere.
- Any sort of absorber can be used.
- Pipework can be small diameter.
- The pump and thermostatic controller require maintenance and electricity.
- Response to small bursts of sunshine is efficient.
- Panels at high level are safely out of the way and have good solar access, but may be more difficult to maintain.

Both systems can be either direct or indirect. In a direct system, the solar panels are connected directly to the hot water cylinder – the same water that comes out of the hot tap runs through the collector. In northern latitudes, such a system requires some form of frost protection. This might consist of draining down the system before the first frosts, or having a frost-resistant collector with plastic pipework. In an indirect system, there is a separate hot water system for the solar collector, which runs through its own coil in the hot water cylinder. The water has an anti-freeze solution added to protect it from frosts. An indirect system is not as efficient as a direct one, but improved heat exchangers are reducing the difference. 'Drain-back' systems are becoming increasingly popular – the water is drained out of the system when the temperature falls below a certain point – and most of these are indirect systems.

Fig. 10.81 Pumped system.

10.82

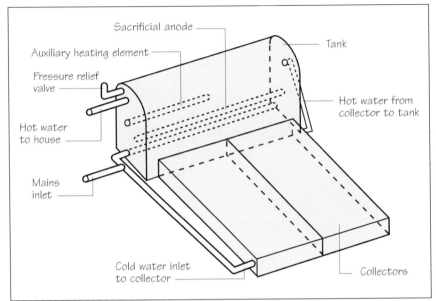

10.84

10.83

Fig. 10.82 Evacuated tube integrated collector/storage on the roof of the public toilets roof at CAT. Hot water storage is contained within each evacuated glass tube. Low installation costs (cold feed in, hot supply out) should overcome to some extent the higher capital cost. Manufacturer: Hitachi.

Fig. 10.83 Flat plate collector.

Fig. 10.84 Diagram of a close-coupled solar water heating system.

Integrated collector/storage

This type of 'close-coupled' system, where the collector and heat store are combined, offers a much-simplified installation, which reduces the overall cost significantly. Plumbing connections are reduced to a cold feed and hot water take-off; these can be inserted into most existing hot water systems. The drawback of an integrated collector/storage system is the difficulty in protecting it against freezing.

In brief

- An integrated collector/storage system can be mounted anywhere.
- It permits simple integration into existing plumbing.
- Installation costs are low.
- The unit is a heavy weight to put on an existing roof.
- Only viable in climates with frost-free winters.

Efficiency of solar collectors

When comparing solar collectors, the first question is one of efficiency. Like most worthwhile questions, there isn't a simple answer. A solar collector is not like a light bulb, the efficiency (converting electricity into light) of which is constant; a collector is subject to the following variables:

- available solar energy;
- external air temperature; and
- water temperature.

There are four design factors for the collector itself.

- The amount of solar energy that passes through the glazing.
- The efficiency of the absorber surface.
- The speed of heat transference from the absorber into the water.
- The insulation level of the collector.

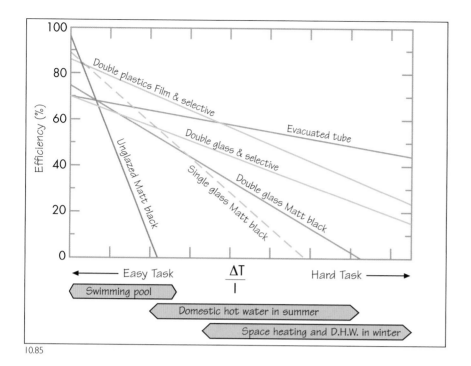

10.85

Put all these factors together, and the result is a straight-line graph that describes collector performance over a range of conditions. Once we know the sort of job we are expecting the collector to do, a suitable one can be selected. For example, a swimming pool collector that only operates when it is warm and sunny, and only has to raise the pool temperature a few degrees, can be a simple, unglazed, uninsulated device. Ask this collector to heat up water for a shower on a dull, cold winter's day and nothing will happen – the solar energy being absorbed will be lost too quickly. For this job, an advanced, well-insulated collector is required.

There are five basic types of solar collector.

• Matt black, unglazed, uninsulated. Used for swimming pool heating.

• Matt black, single-glazed in insulated box. Basic solar collector, often DIY, using central heating radiators or 'clip fins'.

• Matt black, double-glazed in insulated box. This model gives better performance in colder weather.

• Selective surface, glazed, in insulated box. This collector gives higher performance under inclement conditions. A selective surface absorbs energy well in the light spectrum (it appears blackish), but emits less in the heat radiation spectrum (it is shiny). Similar in principle to low-E glazing, it greatly improves performance.

• Evacuated tubes. Single-glazed with a selective surface absorber, these collectors will perform best of all, per square meter of collector surface, under really difficult circumstances (cold, dull day).

So, it is a matter of choosing the right collector for the job. If, for example, your house is heated by an Aga or woodstove that provides ample hot water all winter, your main concern is with summertime performance. In this case the simpler, cheaper collectors would be the right choice. If, however, you are looking for savings all year round, or for solar space heating, it would be sensible to go for the more efficient and expensive collector types.

Fig. 10.85 Performance of various solar collector types. The efficiency of each collector will vary with the difficulty of the task. To the left of the graph the work is easy; it is a sunny warm day and you just want to heat up some swimming pool water a few degrees above ambient air temperature – any old panel will do that, even running water through a black hose. The next job is more difficult: heating water from 10°-60°C during the summer, for domestic hot water. A simple matt-black single-glazed collector will do much of the job, but will struggle when it is cloudy or when the water is already quite hot. Better results will come from improvements such as double-glazing or a selective surface absorber. To do a demanding job of work, such as heating up domestic water, or space heating in mid-winter, the most sophisticated collector is needed – multiple glazing with selective surface or evacuated tube type.

10.86

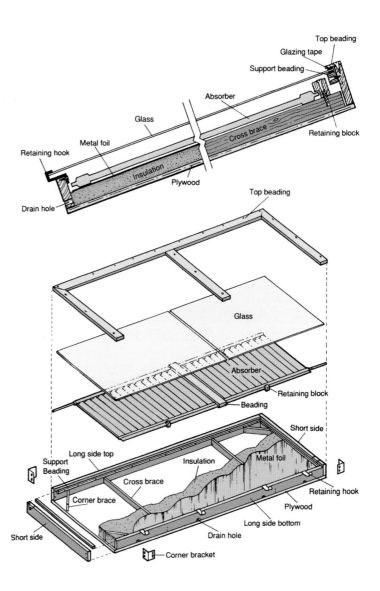

10.87

Sizing, orientation and performance

If you are designing your own water heating system in the UK, you should refer to the British Standard (BS 5918), which gives all sorts of useful information and procedures for estimating performance. Like many energy saving measures, there is an optimum size of system: a 10% saving is quite easy, a 100% saving would require a huge system in our climate. Somewhere in between lies the optimum. So, for an average house you will need:

- 5m² of single-glazed matt black flat plate collector; or
- 4m² of selective-surface absorber flat plate collector; or
- 3m² of selective-surface evacuated tube collector.

The best orientation at the UK latitude is slightly west of due south, and the optimum tilt is around 32°. With our cloudy climate the orientation and tilt are not very critical – a collector set anywhere from SE to SW with a tilt of 10°-60° will perform at 90% of the optimum efficiency, and the decrease can be offset by a greater panel area.

Fig. 10.86 DIY solar collectors sited on a south-facing bank below the house. The (thermosiphon) pipework is buried under the garden. These panels have been reliably producing hot water for about 20 years, for a negligible capital outlay – so solar heating can pay for itself. Architects/builders: Brian and Maureen Richardson.

Fig. 10.87 DIY solar water heating, using central heating radiator.

The output in hot water will be around 1200-1800 kWh per year (about 40-60% of total hot water energy use). You will probably not need backup heating from early May until the end of September. The value of this will be from £30-£100, depending on the type of fuel being saved. It is a very satisfying energy saving measure to have. Back from a sunny day on the beach, you can bathe in the glory of a solar heated bath. You can alter your lifestyle slightly to use hot water when you know it has been solar-heated (around 5pm), and solar-heated water feels so much cleaner than that heated from fossil fuel.

Greater savings can be wrung out of a solar system by using hot water at the lowest temperature possible. For example, a typical shower temperature is around 40°C, and if your solar panels never had to get hotter than this they would work at much higher efficiencies, and thus collect more solar energy. Unfortunately, since the onset of Legionnaires Disease, all hot water must be stored at a minimum of 55°C, so it is no longer possible to recommend this.

RENEWABLE ELECTRICITY SUPPLY

On the plus side, electricity from renewable sources (hydro, wind, photovoltaic cells, wave, biomass) is clean, apart from the fossil fuel used to build the installations (which is paid back very quickly). Despite being blessed with a huge renewables resource (particularly wind and wave), Britain is lagging behind comparable countries in developing renewable electricity generation. However, following on from the Energy White Paper (February 2003), the Government has a target of 20% renewable generation by 2020. Given that the previous target of 10% by 2010 is now unlikely to be met, the aims of the White Paper require substantial commitment and investment.

As awareness of the damaging effects of conventional power generation has grown, many have dreamt of having an electricity supply that does not involve the use of polluting fossil fuels or nuclear power. But for most of us, having no windswept hill or handy mountain stream to tap, this has remained a dream. Even if we generally support the idea of wind turbines and solar panels, there doesn't seem to be a lot we can do about it, except to invest any spare cash in renewable energy companies. However, three recent developments bring hope of change to this frustrating situation.

Green electricity

In 1998, the Regional Electricity Companies (MEB, SWEB, MANWEB, etc.) lost their monopoly on supply and were replaced by Public Electricity Supply Companies. As a result of privatisation, you can now buy renewably generated electricity from any supply company, via the National Grid. This is really quite exciting, as the demand for renewable electricity will probably outstrip the supply, even if the cost is slightly above the cost for non-renewable electricity. It will help to ensure the economic success of such sustainable sources as wind farms, and to encourage the building of more renewable generators.

10.88

There are at least ten suppliers of what is claimed to be 'green' electricity, but they all offer different packages – there are two basic types of package:

- **Energy based tariffs:** this is the one that actually offers you renewable energy in return for your money. The suppliers guarantee that a proportion of the energy you buy will be matched by the equivalent amount of renewable energy supplied to the grid. With Good Energy (formerly Unit-E) that proportion is 100%.
- **Fund-based tariffs:** a proportion of the money you pay is paid into a fund, administered by an independent body, which supports new renewable capacity, green causes or other related initiatives.
- **Combination tariffs:** are a mix of the above two.

(See Friends of the Earth Green Energy League Table[1])

Whatever the relative merits of the different schemes, it is always a positive step to switch to a green electricity supplier and the process is quick and easy. It can be done over the phone, or via a website – www.uswitch.com

According to the Government's Renewable Energy Advisory Group, the accessible potential is about three times our current electricity use. The difficulty is in matching the unpredictable nature of renewables against our fluctuating demand for electricity (although there is a general match between increased demand in winter and higher wintertime winds.) The Grid could cope with up to about 20% of its supply coming from renewables, but higher percentages would require a much more flexible system. Research into developing this flexibility is being carried out and the benefits of diverse sources of generation, geographical separation and demand-side management are being explored.

Community renewable schemes

Baywind in Cumbria launched the first community renewable scheme when local people bought shares in Harlock Hill wind farm in 1997. Since then it has sold £2million worth of shares and has 1,300 members. It was so successful, both financially and environmentally, that Baywind has since launched subsequent schemes, and other communities have formed their own, including one in the Dulas valley around CAT. A Renewable Energy Investment Club has been set up to establish communication between developers and investors. Community benefits include financial support for energy saving measures, available to all local residents.

Fig. 10.88 Community owned wind turbine: a Vestas V17 75kW machine in the Dulas valley.

10.89

Your own supply: photovoltaics

Photovoltaic (PV) technology is the direct conversion of solar energy into electricity in a solid-state silicon cell. It has been around for a long time and is familiar to us in the form of solar-powered calculators and watches. The high price of PV generation has limited its use to providing power to remote telecommunication installations, where a conventional electricity supply would be even more costly. They can be more commercially viable when used on a relatively large scale, integrated into the cladding or roofs of industrial or office buildings. The unit price is falling slowly and the efficiency increasing, to the point where more and more buildings get a proportion of their electricity from PVs. However, there is a long way to go before PVs make economic sense or even significant CO_2 savings, compared with other renewable technologies.

A typical domestic installation

Electricity requirement assuming essential uses only	1500 kWh/year
PV installed capacity assuming 10% efficiency & 1000 kWh/m² average solar radiation/year	1.5kWpeak
Cost of a roof-integrated system, including inverter	£10,000
Cost per kWh, assuming 15 year life and 10% discount rate	75p

The cost of a unit of PV electricity in this case will be 10 times that of one bought off the Grid. Thanks to the Government's desire to support this industry, grants are currently available for up to 50% of the cost of PV installation.

Fig. 10.89 12.5kWp integrated photovoltaic roof at CAT.

10.90

10.91

The independent electricity supply: off the grid

If you are in a remote location and facing a cost of several thousands of pounds for a Grid connection, an independent renewable electricity system begins to look much more attractive. There are two renewable options, apart from PVs:

- **Hydro:** if you have a reliable stream that 'falls' a reasonable height, then installing a micro-hydro system is likely to be financially attractive. A large, slow-running river at the bottom of your garden will not be very useful; the engineering works necessary to dam the water to provide a few feet of 'head' will be prohibitively expensive.
- **Wind/PV:** a typical isolated house system might have a small PV array, a small wind turbine and a battery store. Such a system will cost a few thousand pounds and will provide for modest, essential electricity needs. A stand-by diesel generator is usually installed to cope with occasional large electrical demands.

References

[1] *The Good Energy Guide* published by the Ethical Marketing Group. Purchase copies direct from www.thegoodshoppingguide.co.uk.

Fig. 10.90 A tiny independent renewable energy system. A wind turbine and PV array (mounted on a trailer so that it can be faced to the sun) provide for the modest power requirements of these yurts.

Fig. 10.91 There are now several systems for PV 'tiles' that are more easily integrated into the roof finish and may be more visually acceptable, but without sufficient ventilation these are less efficient than conventional PV panels. (Solar Century).

Water conservation and quality

We used to take water for granted. But now, both its quality and quantity are under threat.

WATER CONSERVATION

As 75% of the European population lives in cities and their suburbs, and so cannot collect all their own supply, water has to be collected from rivers or pumped from underground aquifers, stored in reservoirs, filtered, treated and pumped to each house, often in fairly ancient, leaky water mains. As a resource, water is being used at an unsustainable rate – underground aquifers are being emptied faster than they are replenished. Due to higher standards of hygiene and cleanliness, domestic water use has doubled from 75 litres/person/day in 1960 to 150 litres/person/day now.

There is a significant charge for all this, which has risen steeply in the last decade. Water meters are an effective way of reducing individual profligate use. It is certainly possible for a low-energy house to have a higher water bill than the heating, hot water, cooking and electrical bills put together.

It is important to conserve water, not only from the financial point of view, but also from the viewpoint of energy savings (treatment and pumping consume energy). Treating water and sewage for an average family creates 78kg of CO_2 emissions per year.

On average we use water in the home in the following proportions:

Flushing the toilet	33%
Washing machines	21%
Baths and showers	17%
Kitchen sink	16%
Wash basin	9%
Dishwashers	1%
Hosepipes	3%

There are a number of ways to reduce our overall water consumption, and to use water more efficiently.

Water leaks

Having processed water at great cost and then expended energy to pump it around, the water companies promptly lose a third from leaky old mains. There is not much you can do about that, and new pipelines are being laid. However, a further 5-10% is estimated to be lost within the house, through dripping taps and cistern valves.

Water meters

Although we hate having to have one fitted, water meters concentrate the mind wonderfully and allow you to check how you are succeeding on the water saving front. Water consumption does drop considerably once a meter is installed – usually by around 30%. The new water companies are 'voluntarily' installing pre-paid water meters in some low-income households, ostensibly as a way of helping consumers plan their spending. In practice, it is a form of self-disconnection, enabling the suppliers to avoid their public health responsibility. Water poverty is now almost as common as fuel poverty, and the dangers to the general public are far greater, as it could lead to outbreaks of those diseases we thought were extinct in the developed world.

11.1

Fig. 11.1 Water shortages should not be a problem in our rainy climate but the resource is very variable across the UK.

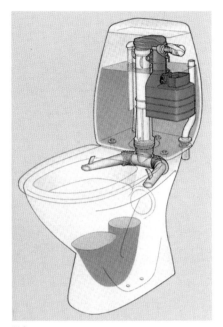

11.2

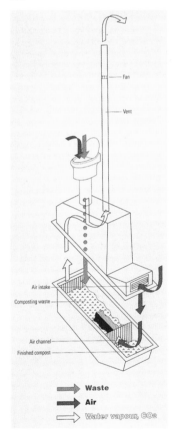

11.4

11.3a

Fig. 11.3b

Fig. 11.2 The Ifo Aqua ultra-low flush toilet.
Source: Ifo Products (UK) Ltd.

Fig. 11.3a & 11.3b A public toilet at CAT with access to the twin composting vaults outside (Andy Warren).

Fig. 11.4 The workings of a Clivus Multrum composting toilet.

Toilets

New toilet cisterns are required to be no more than six litres, but most existing ones are nine litres. Most European toilets use a 'valve flush', which is usually more water efficient than the British siphon flush. The Water Regulations, which came into force in 2001, now allow valve flush mechanisms to be fitted in the UK to mains water installations. However, the Regulations also stipulate that all WCs must be approved by the Water Regulations Advisory Scheme (WRAS), or as an interim measure tested and certified by the manufacturer to the standards of the Water Regulations.

A four litre siphon flush toilet, approved by WRAS, is now available in the UK, but at the moment only in concealed cistern versions at the moment[1]. As most siphon toilets will flush perfectly well with less than nine litres of water, a water-filled plastic bottle in the cistern will make significant inroads into what is probably your largest water use. Most siphons have a dual flush device fitted, consisting of a little plastic plug fitted to the plastics siphon unit. Remove the plug and you will be able to use a small flush for urine. 'Ecoflush' cistern handles are available, which are less liable to double flushing. Other ways to save on flushing water are (politesse allowing): the age-old 'have a pee in the garden' technique, pee cans, and not flushing the loo after every pee.

Compost toilets

There are also dry compost toilets of DIY or manufactured designs, which avoid water use altogether. Compost toilets are the very best way to deal with human waste: not only do they use no (expensively processed) water, but they also produce a useful fertiliser. Sewage, in fact, should be seen as a resource rather than a waste product. It will break down harmlessly into plant nutrients over a period of about one year. The pathogens in human waste are killed during this process, but it is still a good idea not to use it directly on edible crops. There are now designs of compost toilets for every domestic situation. The most reliable is probably the twin vault system[2].

One make, the Clivus Multrum, has been installed on various sensitive or remote sites by the National Trust and the Caravan Club, as well as in the 'autonomous house' built by architects Robert and Brenda Vale.

Showers and taps

A bath uses about 110 litres of water, a shower 30-40 litres. As they are so quick and convenient, we tend to take more showers than baths, which evens out the score somewhat. A power shower can use as much water as a bath. Further water reductions can be achieved by installing low-flow showerheads which aerate the spray more effectively, so you get just as wet with less water. Or you can turn it off whilst you work up a lather, or just be under it for less time. Spray taps work more efficiently for hand washing and thus use less water and energy.

'Dead legs'

When designing a new house, or renovating an old one, keep the length of hot pipe between the cylinder and the most frequently used taps (usually the kitchen sink and wash basin) as short as possible, and install insulation round the pipes. Waiting for the hot water to come through a long pipe run wastes a considerable amount of water, and the heat left in the 'dead leg' gets wasted. In addition, if your hot pipe is not well insulated, it will heat up the cold water pipe next to it, and you will waste water waiting for cold water to come through.

Washing dishes and clothes

For dishes, it is debateable whether machine- or hand-washing is more water efficient. Most dishwashers use less than 20 litres on a full load. A standard washing up bowl holds 7 litres and a standard sink, around 15 litres. So the way in which you wash up will be crucial – if you rinse the dishes in another sink full of water, you will be using more water than a dishwasher. According to the Environment Agency, the major environmental impacts of dishwashers are related to detergents rather than water or energy use. Beware of economy or half-load settings, which typically reduce water and energy use by only 10-25%.

Most clothes washing machines now use less than 50 litres per full load. There are machines that allow you to adjust the water usage, and some that re-use rinse water. Small amounts of washing are better done by hand.

Using grey water

'Grey water' is contaminated household waste water from a sink, a bath or shower. Although you may think it would be good to use this water for flushing toilets, it is more practical to use grey water for the garden. Use eco-soaps and cleaning products to avoid sodium salts, which are present in conventional soaps and detergents, from damaging the soil. Look for 'phosphate free' or 'low sodium' on the package. If you have taken all the necessary measures to reduce/recycle water, you should not have much grey water to dispose of. Grey water must not be stored, as the organic matter in it will start to rot.

Water quality

Given that most of our water supply comes from rain running off the surface of the land, on its journey to our taps it picks up whatever pollution is around in the air, on the land and discharged into the rivers. Agricultural land makes up about 70% of our total land area, so pollution from biocides and fertilisers may be a major source of contaminants. Add to this industrial effluent, municipal landfill, leaks from sewage works and toxic wastes, together with airborne pollutants absorbed by the rainwater, and it is not surprising that water has to be treated to make it safe. Although water quality has improved considerably in recent years (in 2001, of 2.82 million tests, only 0.1% failed to meet European standards), the resulting water is considered by many to be pretty well undrinkable – hence the popularity of bottled spring water and kitchen water filters.

Water filters

- **Activated carbon:** carbon granules will trap organic chemicals and chlorine. Under-the-sink versions are best, with a particle filter to prevent the carbon filter getting blocked up too quickly. Removing chlorine potentially allows bacteria in. Filtered water should be stored in the fridge and drunk within the day. Filters should be changed at the recommended intervals.
- **Distillation:** a well-designed distilling filter will produce the cleanest water, but such a device is expensive and the water is a little bland. Add minerals to taste. This is not recommended, as the process is very energy-intensive and the resulting water can be bad for your health in the long term.
- **Ultra violet treatment:** private water supplies often need treating for micro-organisms. An under-sink UV unit, connected to the drinking water tap, does this effectively.

Collecting rainwater

While water conservation measures should be the first step, rainwater may be collected for various uses, such as garden watering. Rainwater collected for toilet flushing needs no treatment. The rainwater store should be covered to prevent the ingress of sunlight and animals. There are now several manufacturers offering packaged rainwater collection, storage and pump units. At present these are quite expensive (approximately £1,500 including installation), but may still have a reasonable payback if you are on a water meter. Pollution and debris can be filtered out.

It is quite simple to collect enough rainwater to keep your garden happy, but what if you want to supply all of your domestic water needs? For those interested in collecting rainwater for their own use, and trying to be autonomous (having no mains connection), how much collection area would be needed? With no water conservation measures, a household of four will use maybe 240m³ per year. With an average rainfall of 800mm/m² and adequate storage for rainless periods, you would require a collecting area of 300m², or about three times the size of an average house roof, and 30 cubic metres of storage. However, using draconian conservation measures, this consumption could be reduced by three-quarters, which makes home collection a possibility.

Preference

- Water meters.
- Low flush toilets.
- Low flow showers.
- Spray taps.
- Rainwater collection for garden.
- Compost toilets (require a certain level of management).
- Rainwater harvesting for house.

Your own well

For rural and suburban areas, there is no reason why you cannot have your own well or borehole. You will be required to connect to the mains as well, if it is available, and your private supply will have to be tested for contamination. You can extract a certain amount (up to 20,000 litres a day) from your own land without a licence. You may be required to demonstrate that the rate of extraction is sustainable and not damaging to local ecosystems. The Water Authority can object to any extraction they consider will affect the water table – but this is unlikely from a single household's consumption.

Sewage treatment

Sewage is unwanted water-borne wastes: mostly water with solid matter (faeces, paper) and various solutions of urine, fats, soaps, household detergents and other chemicals. The vast majority of our houses are connected to the mains, and our effluent is dealt with by the local sewage treatment works. For those not connected, there are various ways of treating sewage on your own land, all with ecological pros and cons.

11.5

Compost toilets

Once again, the message is to conserve first. Water-borne sewage takes two very useful substances (fresh water and human manure) and mixes them together to create a problematic substance, which then takes time and energy to separate and dispose of safely. A saner approach mimics the natural processes that deal with millions of tonnes of wild and farm animal manure a day[2]. Compost toilets can range from the rural simplicity of the CAT Twin Vault to the hygienic charm of the Clivus Multrum, and with care they will all do the job of breaking down human wastes into a material much like soil.

The 'autonomous house' in Southwell, built and lived in by architects Brenda and Robert Vale, houses a Clivus Multrum in the cellar, which has proved simple and trouble-free in operation. Indeed, it was the Clivus tank which helped to determine the house design (size of bays, etc.) and which reduced the water consumption to a level that made rainwater harvesting from the roof possible.

11.6

There are several drawbacks:
- bulky, difficult to fit into a compact house design;
- social inhibitions; and
- waste grey water still has to be treated.

Primary sewage treatment

This is the process of removing most of the solids and partially reducing the Biochemical Oxygen Demand (BOD) of the effluent. BOD reflects the amount of organic material in the sewage, measured by the oxygen required by micro-organisms to break it down over a given period.

- **Septic tank:** the most common rural solution to treatment, the septic tank only half-treats the effluent, which must be further treated in a soakaway or reed bed. The effluent is anaerobic and smelly.
- **Aquatrons:** use surface tension to separate the solid faeces and toilet paper from the liquid that carries it. The solids then drop into a composting chamber, with the liquids diverted for further treatment. This means you have the potential

Fig. 11.5 Twin-vault compost toilet at CAT.

Fig. 11.6 The end product, sweet smelling soil.

11.7

11.8

for nutrient recovery from the solids (like in a compost toilet) whilst still having a conventional looking flush toilet.

Secondary sewage treatment

- **Mechanical plant:** there are many packaged mechanical secondary treatment systems available, that use a variety of rotating discs, filters and aerating devices. They all work fairly well and can be installed out of sight, but they use electricity and require regular maintenance.
- **Vertical flow reed bed:** a bed of gravel planted with aquatic species (often common reed) whose roots fix oxygen to keep the process aerobic. The effluent spreads over the whole surface and percolates down through the active biological layers of the bed[3].

Tertiary treatment

Final polishing can be by horizontal reed bed, leachfield (land drains), pond, or willow plantation.

References

[1] Available from Green Building Store, www.greenbuildingstore.co.uk

[2] Harper & Halestrap, *Lifting the Lid*, CAT Publications, 1999

[3] Grant, Moodie & Weedon, *Sewage Solutions*, CAT Publications, 2nd edition, 2000

Fig. 11.17 Reed bed sewage treatment at CAT. Primary treatment is by a bark ring strainer, secondary by vertical flow reed bed, and tertiary by horizontal flow reed bed, with final polishing by a willow plantation. Design: Camphill Water.

Fig. 11.8 The Aquatron at CAT diverts solids from water-borne sewage into the composting chambers below.

Finance, legislation and assessments

FINANCE, LEGISLATION AND COSTS

When building a new house or remodelling an existing one, you will have to find your way around the worlds of building finance and law. You may also want, or may be required, to prove the worth of your actions by undergoing an environmental assessment.

Costs

Most of this section applies only to the UK. The cost of the work you have in mind can only really be assessed once all the plans are complete. Even then it is not very easy to estimate accurately and decisions you make about the type and quality of materials and fittings will affect the end price considerably. But for a modest new house, superinsulated with ecologically benign materials, the build costs are going to be in the range of £1,000-£1,500 per square metre of internal floor area. The cost of land, fees, service connections and so on, would have to be added to this figure.

Of course, if your design includes a hand-built oak frame (£20,000-£25,000) or solar water heating system (£2,000-£3,000) or other special features, you can spend much more. But there is no reason why an ecological house should be significantly more expensive than a conventional one. It is mostly a matter of careful selection of materials and sensible design. On the other hand, you may decide to invest more in a product that is exceptionally durable, or brings predictable future savings.

Self-management is one way to reduce costs and keep control of the project. If you do all the building yourself, the costs will be even lower. Building is still (fortunately, in many ways) a craft industry, so labour costs are high. Many of the crafts themselves are not too difficult to master, particularly if the house is designed for self-build using simple techniques such as those employed in the Segal Method.

Sources of finance

There are two sources of finance, presuming you do not have enough of your own cash: commercial lenders or the Housing Corporation.

- **Commercial lenders:** these consist of building societies and banks (nowadays indistinguishable from each other). If building your own house you should try the Ecology Building Society (www.ecology.co.uk), whose aims will be closest to your own. They encourage self-build, unconventional techniques of construction, and sustainable lifestyles – and they invest their profits ethically.

- **The Housing Corporation:** the Governmental organisation that funds and regulates Housing Associations (now known as Registered Social Landlords) – the main providers of 'social' or 'affordable' housing. Through their Approved Development Programme, the Housing Corporation have around £1bn to invest every year. They also operate an Innovation and Good Practice Programme, which can provide 'seedcorn' grants to projects promoting sustainability measures of long-term benefit to residents. A self-build group can register as a self-build housing co-operative and apply for funding through a Housing Association. Grants are not available for individuals.

LEGISLATION

Planning permission

Planning Permission is required for any development, which in planning parlance means either building work (including landscaping) or change of use. Planning regulations are the means by which Local Authorities control what is built, where, and how buildings and land are used.

Before work starts, an application must be made to the local Planning Authority and permission granted. The Authority will be concerned primarily with whether your site is in an area scheduled for development, and secondarily with what the building will look like. There are many circumstances where planning permission is not required, but you should make sure by obtaining the small useful leaflet 'Planning: A Guide for Householders' published by the Department of the Environment, Transport and the Regions (DETR), or visit your local planning office and have a chat. Planning officers are, on the whole, helpful and would prefer to discuss a scheme and influence design in the formative stages, rather than to have to reject something later on.

If your property has already had planning permission, you should check that you still have rights under the General Development Order for 'Permitted Development'. This is most important for householders, as it allows you to add to your holding quite considerably without having to go through the planning process. It allows such things as conservatories, porches, garages and separate structures (for studio, granny house, etc.). A separate structure may be quite a substantial, proper little house – so long as the building meets the following criteria:

- the use is 'for the benefit of the occupants of the house' (i.e. not a separate household);
- no part of the structure projects forward of the existing house;
- it is not higher than three metres for a flat roof, or four metres for a pitched roof;
- not more than half the garden is covered by buildings; and
- it lies more than five metres from your existing house and no closer than two metres to a boundary.

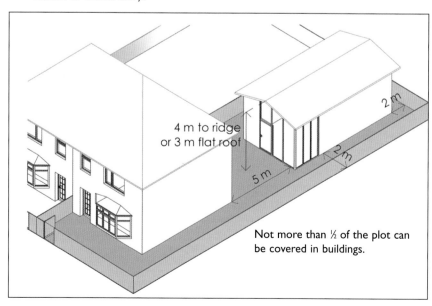

4 m to ridge or 3 m flat roof

2 m

2 m

5 m

Not more than ½ of the plot can be covered in buildings.

Fig. 12.1 The criteria for 'permitted development' for a home.

12.1

Outline planning permission

Outline planning permission establishes the principle of development on a particular site – you do not even have to own it, providing the owner is informed. No designs are required – outline planning permission is used to decide on contentious matters, such as whether a house can be built at all in a particular location. Permission will be granted subject to reserved matters – e.g. the materials to be used and what it looks like.

Full planning permission

It is usually cheaper and quicker to go for full permission (rather than outline and reserved matters), providing you are confident that the principle is acceptable. You will need a reasonably detailed set of drawings showing layouts, elevations, materials, and the location. Most Local Authorities have simplified forms for householders. For any type of application there is a fee.

The actual decision is usually taken by the Planning Committee made up of local councillors, advised by the Planning Officers. The Planning Officers have delegated powers to decide on applications where no objections have been registered and on minor matters. A reply has to be given within eight weeks of your application, although the local authority can ask for an extension of time. If your application has not been dealt with in time, or is refused, you can appeal to the Secretary of State within three months.

It is possible for Local Authorities to grant planning permission for developments that fall outside the requirements of the Local Plan when there is a perceived local need. Planning permission can be granted using a Section 106 Agreement, which may restrict the development for local housing only, or, as is the case in the Hockerton Project, it is considered to be a 'sustainable development'.

The planning process, which is a relatively new phenomenon, has its good and bad sides. On the one hand, it does not seem to have prevented massive, inappropriate development in our city centres or countryside. Zoning has created monocultures of industry, offices and housing, while the cities we admire are much more diverse and lively. The planning process tends to resist innovation in design, only allowing a narrow range of styles and lifestyles, and has, until recently, ignored environmental matters, such as pollution and unfettered car-use. On the other hand, it is difficult to imagine what would result from a complete free-for-all, whilst the imperative behind development is still one of commercial greed and insensitivity. Either way, spare a thought for the planning officer, always assumed to be in the wrong.

Changes to the planning system

Following a Green Paper in 2001, the Government has promised legislation to reform the planning system in England. Part of the background for this is the current failure to meet targets for new-build homes – 2001/2002 saw the lowest number of new houses built for more than 50 years. The changes are intended to facilitate development (e.g. Area Plans are replaced by 'Local Development Frameworks') and to make the planning system more efficient and transparent.

There will be enforcement of time targets for planning decisions – at present only 20% of applications are decided within 8 weeks and only 40% within 13 weeks. Full and outline permissions will only be valid for three instead of five years, and the time allowed to register an appeal will be reduced from six to three months.

Element	Required 2002 standards
Roof	0.20 – 0.16 W/m²k
Walls	0.35 W/m²k
Floors	0.25 W/m²k
Windows/Doors	2.2 – 2.0 W/m²k
Air tightness	10 ach at 50pa*
Boiler efficiency	75% – 85%

* for non domestic buildings greater than 1000m²

12.2

The legislation will allow the Government to enforce certain densities in areas such as the South East, where demand for new housing and availability of building land are not compatible at current housing densities.

BUILDING REGULATIONS

Significant building works also require approval under the current Building Regulations. Small buildings and conservatories under 30m² are exempt. Again, check with your Local Authority Building Control office. The Regulations refer to a series of technical 'Approved Documents', which interpret the general laws and are basically all very sensible and sound. The Approved Documents illustrate constructions that will comply with British (or European) Standards setting out the science of construction.

The principle is that of providing safe constructions in terms of the following:
- structural stability – part A
- protection from fire – part B
- materials, workmanship, site preparation and moisture exclusion – Part C
- cavity insulation – Part D
- sound Insulation – part E
- ventilation – part F
- bathrooms and hot water storage – part G
- drainage and waste disposal – part H
- heat producing appliances – part J
- stairways, ramps and guards – part K
- conservation of fuel and power – part L
- means of access and use – part M
- glazing materials and protection – part N

Building Control officers are well versed in building science and will happily discuss technical queries, either at the drawing board stage or on site. They do not, however, take kindly to contractors concealing bad constructions.

There are two main types of Building Control approval.
- **A building notice:** this is the simplest form of approval, suitable for simple, well-understood constructions. The officers require three days' notice of intent to start work, and all matters are dealt with on site.
- **Full plans:** these are required for most constructions and involve submitting all drawings, specifications and details for approval at least one month before your anticipated start date. Queries will come back from the officers, usually asking for more information on a particular area or pointing out some

Fig. 12.2 Required U-values to demonstrate compliance with the Building Regulations Part L, 2002, using the elemental method.

contravention of the Regulations. When approval is gained, you will be sent a series of cards which must be sent off at the appropriate time in the work programme so that the construction can be inspected. On completion, a certificate will be issued.

Changes to the Building Regulations

In April 2002, certain aspects of the Building Regulations were revised, including Part L relating to the 'conservation of fuel and power' in buildings. As a result, the required minimum insulation standards were improved and increased boiler efficiencies were specified.

Also, for the first time, the Building Regulations were extended to apply to 'material alterations' and/or change of use in existing buildings. The intention is to achieve the same standards of thermal performance as for new build. In particular, this will have a major impact on the type of replacement glazing and boilers that are fitted.

When these changes were introduced, warning was also given that further improvements to thermal performance standards were in the pipeline for 2005/6. These are likely to include:

- 25% reduction of buildings-related carbon emissions on 2002 levels;
- encouragement for 'low carbon' solutions e.g. solar water heating;
- airtightness standards to be progressively improved, aiming at a figure of 3 ach at 50Pa, by 2010;
- condensing boilers as standard; and
- in line with European legislation, performance targets to be set for existing buildings

THE NEW EUROPEAN DIRECTIVE

This Directive, the Energy Efficiency of Buildings Directive, became UK law in January 2003 and must now be implemented within the next three years. It will apply immediately to all new buildings and existing buildings over 1000m^2 or undergoing major renovations. The objectives are: to improve energy performance through cost-effective measures; and to bring about a convergence of building standards to meet the highest (e.g. those in Sweden). The Directive centres round the idea of Energy Performance criteria, measuring primary (not net) energy use.

Key elements envisaged as crucial to the process are:

- minimum standards of energy performance applied to new buildings and existing buildings over 1000 square metres;
- energy certification of buildings as defined above and compulsory display of energy certificates in public buildings; and
- regular inspection of boilers and air conditioning units.

Energy certificates will describe the actual or predicted energy performance of the building and are issued on construction, sale or rent. They will last a maximum of 10 years, include benchmarks and advice on cost effective improvements and be displayed on all public buildings over 1000m^2.

The Home Information Pack

This is the mechanism whereby the European Directive will be implemented for owner occupied housing. A Housing Information Pack or seller's pack will have to be prepared for any house offered for sale and will include a Home Condition Report. As well as standard conveyancing material, such as copies of searches and planning consents, this will include an energy efficiency assessment of the house, based on a SAP rating. This information will allow prospective purchasers to compare homes in terms of energy performance and may encourage vendors to improve this aspect of the house before selling.

ENVIRONMENTAL ASSESSMENT

Energy rating schemes

The Standard Assessment Procedure (SAP) and the Carbon Index (CI)

The Standard Assessment Procedure for the energy rating of dwellings was developed to ensure that houses are designed to a reasonable level of energy conservation. It is based on the calculated annual energy cost for space and water heating – it assumes a standard occupancy based on floor area, a standard heating pattern and a standard climate, so that houses can be compared anywhere in the country. The SAP rating allows for floor area, so that large houses are not penalised (indeed large houses will generally have a better SAP rating as they have a better volume to surface area ratio). The rating goes from 1 to 120, the higher the better, and must now be displayed on all new buildings.

The Carbon Index was introduced along with the new Part L in 2002, and is one of the ways in which builders and developers can demonstrate compliance. On a scale of 1-10 (currently a score of 8/10 is required), it is based on calculations of annual CO_2 emissions associated with space and water heating. Like the later versions of SAP, it is based on the carbon intensity of fuels, rather than primary energy use, and as such is a better indicator of pollution levels associated with energy consumption. It is also adjusted for floor area and so is independent of house size.

The method for calculating the Carbon Index, which is an extension of the latest version of SAP (2001), is printed as Appendix G in Approved Document L1 of the Building Regulations, 2000, available from the Stationery Office, www.thestationeryoffice.com

National Home Energy Rating (NHER)

The formulae used in the SAP calculations are based on a work called 'The Building Research Establishment's Domestic Energy Model' (BREDEM), which has also been developed into another rating schemes which is considerably more accurate and sensitive: the National Home Energy Rating (NHER). With a rating scale of 1 to 10, this energy rating scheme can only be undertaken by a trained and registered assessor – thus it is slightly more expensive to do than a SAP – but can yield more meaningful results tuned to the individual householder's desires and financial constraints. The best approach is to employ an NHER assessor for the basic service (from house plans). They will issue you with a SAP Rating for Building Regulations purposes and an estimate of your annual heating bills. If you wish to pursue things further and calculate the effectiveness of various energy conservation measures (extra insulation, conservatory, etc.), this can be done easily, using the more sophisticated NHER software programmes.

BREEAM and Eco-Homes

Currently, the only whole house environmental assessment (as opposed to energy-only, or materials-only) is the Building Research Establishment Environmental Assessment Method (BREEAM). This covers a range of environmental issues within one assessment and there are versions of BREEAM for offices, industrial and retail buildings, and bespoke versions. The version for domestic buildings is called 'Eco-Homes' and covers new, converted or renovated, houses and apartments.

Designs and/or completed buildings are assessed in the following areas:

- energy use;
- water use;
- materials specified;
- transport issues;
- pollution associated with all the above;
- ecology and land use;
- health and well-being.

Scores are awarded within each category then passed through a 'filter' of environmental weightings (based on consultations with a wide range of interest groups), to achieve a final score. These are expressed as four possible grades: Pass; Good; Very Good; Excellent[1]. As well as evaluating finished buildings, it can also be used as a tool to enhance environmental design and specification.

Increasingly, as legislators and policy makers seek to discriminate in favour of low-impact housing and establish a benchmark for sustainable construction, there will be a need to define and assess which buildings are indeed 'eco'. Currently, the BREEAM model is the only credible environmental assessment scheme in the UK To the extent that it is not perfect, it needs to be continually reviewed and refined.

References

[1]: 'EcoHomes: the environmental rating for homes', Construction Research Communications Ltd, London, 2000.

Case studies

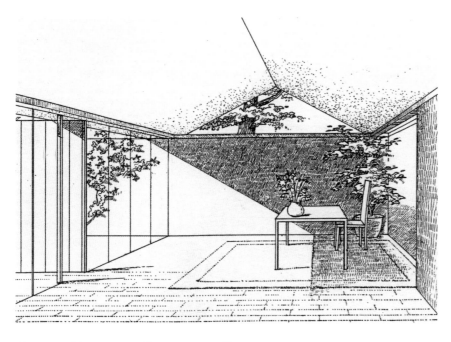

BRIDGE POTTERY, CHERITON, GOWER

In 1999 the architect David Lea was commissioned by the potter Micki Schloessingk to design a new kiln, and a small gallery in which to show finished work. The site lies on the northern bank of the wooded valley of Burry Pill. The budget was modest.

'These are the bare facts of programme and site familiar to all architects. But from these, architect and client have fashioned a work that rises far above the ordinary'. Touchstone, Spring 2002

The building consists of two pavilions, linked by a flat glass 'Reglit' gutter. It sits on a platform of 150mm square oak piles, driven into the bank, and oak beams. The structure is of Welsh Larch, the posts tied together with stainless steel rods to prevent the roof 'spreading'. The same material provides the floor finish, external cladding and roof surface. Most of the south gallery wall is glazed, with a sliding panel, as is the gable that frames views of the upper branches of trees.

Client:	Micki Schloessingk
Architect:	David Lea Architects
Cost:	£30,000

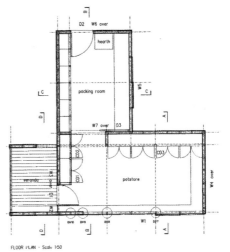

BELLS COURT, BISHOP'S CASTLE, SHROPSHIRE

The Living Village Trust commissioned the design of five ecological houses, to be built behind the Six Bells public house – which itself had been bought by the Trust as a community resource.

The houses – constructed by a benign developer, Ecostruct – were designed to the highest 'green' standards. They have post and beam timber frames of home-grown Douglas Fir and high levels of thermal insulation, using Warmcel recycled cellulose. The external joinery is triple-glazed with low-E coatings and argon fill in softwood frames. High performance condensing gas boilers with solar water heating and advanced controls complete the low-energy package. Natural finishes, such as recycled brickwork, lime renders and limewash, home-grown oak floors and organic paints are used throughout.

The design layout reflects the dense street pattern of Bishop's Castle, with 'shuts' – pedestrian alleyways running along the contours – leading to houses. All houses are south-facing with small, private courtyard gardens, and are accessed off a shared covered way and courtyard. Car parking is on a lower level. Each house has a highly glazed two-storey 'sunspace' that makes a spectacular studio room, or just a pleasant place to be on a cold sunny day.

Bells Court was the protoype for a larger development by The Living Village Trust of 40 houses at The Wintles, Bishop's Castle.

Location:	Bishop's Castle, Shropshire
Client:	Living Village Trust / Ecostruct
Architect:	Pat Borer
Frames:	Carpenter Oak and Woodland
Construction:	2002
Cost:	£500,000
Area:	450m^2
Floors:	Timber 225mm joists, counterbattens and oak flooring. U=0.14W/m^{2}K Or Limecrete slab with oak flooring on 150mm perlite insulation. U=0.19 W/m^{2}K
Frame:	Douglas Fir post and beam frame exposed internally, on recycled brick piers and plinth wall.
Walls:	Spaced stud timber frame with 200mm Warmcel insulation, VCL, services zone and plasterboard. Externally, lime-washed hydraulic lime render on wood wool slabs. U= 0.18 W/m^{2}K
Tower:	Dense concrete cavity blockwork with lime-washed hydraulic lime render, 200mm cavity filled with perlite. U= 0.21 W/m^{2}K
Windows:	Triple-glazed, low-E, argon filled, Swedish redwood. U= 1.5 W/m^{2}K
Roof:	10"x6" new Welsh slates on spaced rafters, with 300mm Warmcel insulation, VCL, services zone and plasterboard. U= 0.12 W/m^{2}K

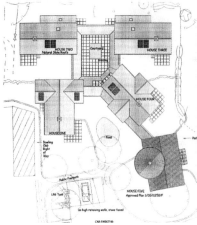

ANGELL ESTATE, SOUTH LONDON

Faced with refurbishing a block on a large estate in south London, Lambeth Council were persuaded by the tenants to adopt an eco-friendly approach. The Angell Estate had been built in the early 1970s when central heating was becoming standard but before the oil crisis. There was no insulation in the fabric, the flats were cold and draughty and condensation problems were exacerbated by the use of mobile paraffin heaters.

The first step was to install insulation in walls, roofs and ceilings, new timber frame windows with double-glazed, low-E units, and insulated render on exposed concrete floor slabs. Full height metal-framed windows were replaced with timber panelling and 'breathing' construction. In consultation with the residents, the architects removed individual external 'dog leg' stairs between first and second storeys, which were seen as a major safety and security problem. Condensing boilers and passive stack ventilation systems have helped to increase comfort and reduce bills.

Subsequent monitoring found that temperatures in the renovated flats were on average 1°C higher than in the original flats, but the heating energy consumption had been reduced by about 50%. Over the three month monitoring period, CO_2 emissions were reduced by an estimated 500kg per flat. Damp, draughts and cold floors were no longer cited as problems.

Now tenants from Angell Estate, supported by Community Self Build London, are planning to self-build 11 eco-friendly homes as the beginnings of a mutually supportive sustainable community.

Architects: Anne Thorne Architects
Monitoring: Bohn & Viljoen Architectst

CASTELL Y GWYNT

'The name of this house beautifully evokes its exposed and elevated site, with spectacular panoramic views across the Severn Valley and far into the high Welsh mountains to the north.

'The present house replaced a derelict farm, adopting the same orientation and simple vernacular forms. Recent additions have aimed to develop the relationship of the house to the wonderful landscape, soften the severity of its exposure, and reduce the environmental impact.

'The living area has been extended and linked to a pavilion, the Ark, which steps and turns the principal axis of the house downhill, around a large existing tree, and out towards the mountains, culminating in a fully glazed gable wall. The longer side wall on the south west, also fully glazed, opens via big sliding doors onto a sheltered south west facing verandah, under the extended overhang of the new roof and the large sycamore tree. On the north east side the timber wall becomes more opaque and highly insulated, like the roof and floor, and, at mid point, divides for a semi circular unplastered brick inglenook with wood burning stove, adding thermal mass and an anchor point to the oak framed structure, and a comforting focus for the room at night. A glazed corner to the east admits morning sun. Smaller vertical slots in the extended sitting room frame views to the pond and the monument on the adjoining peak to the east. More sheltered outdoor areas and more domesticated views across the cultivated garden have been created with a new oak framed shelter that wraps around the south end of the house.

'At the eastern end of the sitting room extension another brick structure houses the plant for the new ground source heat pump, which replaces the original oil boiler as the primary heat source for the under floor heating and hot water systems.

'Extensive tree planting has sheltered the house and improved the microclimate for growing fruit and vegetables.

'The construction uses green oak framing timbers with pegged carpentry joints, oak cladding, reclaimed Welsh roof slates, limestone paving, cellulose fibre insulation, low emissivity and argon filled double-glazing'.

Michael Goulden, architect.

BedZED

BedZED, the Beddington Zero Energy Development, is an environmentally friendly, energy efficient mix of housing and workspace for the Peabody Trust in Beddington, Sutton. On a 'brownfield' wasteland site, the development provides 82 dwellings in a mixture of flats, maisonettes and town houses, for sale or rent. There is approximately 2500m² of workspace/office and community accommodation, including a health centre, nursery, organic café/shop and sports clubhouse.

BedZED only uses energy from renewable sources generated on site. It is the first large-scale 'carbon neutral' community. BedZED shows how housing can be built without degrading the environment and that an eco-friendly lifestyle can be easy, affordable and attractive – something that people will want to do.

Where possible, building materials were selected from renewable or recycled sources and more than 50% were from within a 35 mile radius of the site. Every aspect of construction was considered in terms of its environmental impact.

'The BedZED urban system reconciles high-density three-storey city blocks with high residential and workspace amenity. Workspace is placed in the shade zones of south facing housing terraces, with skygardens created on the workspace roofs, enabling all flats to have outdoor garden areas with good access to sunlight, at the same time as providing well day lit workspace without problematic summer overheating. The combination of super insulation, a wind driven ventilation system incorporating heat recovery, and passive solar gain stored within each flat – by thermally massive floors and walls – reduces the need for both electricity and heat to the point where a 135kW wood fuelled combined heat and power (CHP) plant can meet the energy requirements of a community of around 240 residents and 200 workers.

'The community treats all its black and grey water on site, and collects rainwater to minimise mains water consumption. To avoid over-sizing the CHP unit, a 109kW peak photovoltaic installation provides enough solar electricity to power 40 electric cars, some pool, some taxi, some privately owned. The community has the capability to lead a carbon neutral lifestyle – with all energy for buildings and local transport being supplied by renewable energy sources'. Bill Dunster, architect.

Client: The Peabody Trust
Architect: Bill Dunster Architects
Environmental Consultant: BioRegional Development Group
Cost: £1,450/m²

Cobtun House

The name: Cobtun – 'cob' for the walling and 'tun', from the Anglo-Saxon for a walled dwelling enclosure.

Design: The site, falling gently down to the Severn, lies within the Worcester Local Plan Green Network and the Riverside Conservation area. The client's stated brief is: 'Humour, mystery and fantasy.
Ecological, sustainable, independent.
Contextual, agricultural, invisible'.

The house is approached along a quiet unmade road. An encircling earth wall, which appears to crumble or decay at its southern end, encloses the site. The wall construction, known as cob, uses site soil and locally sourced clay, with straw acting as the binding ingredient. Following the wall round, an entrance leads through the massive wall to the front door and circular top-lit hall. The wall continues past the entrance, the house abutting its south face in horizontally boarded oak and glass.

Unheated buffer storage and service functions line the north wall internally. Living and bedroom spaces, separated by a secret sliding screen, open out in two wings to the west and the south. Accommodation is planned on one wheelchair-accessible level.

Materials: Low environmental impact building materials are specified throughout. These include paints and varnishes, sustainably sourced timber, recycled newsprint insulation, PVC-free wiring, etc. Render, screeds and mortar use sieved site sand, avoiding imported material; doors use linen canvas with leather handles.

Earth for cob walling: earth excavated on site was predominately fine sand with layers of gravel and clay. Study by the Centre for Earthen Architecture, University of Plymouth School of Architecture recommended adding an additional 25% of imported spoil from another of the contractor's nearby sites. This soil was high in silt and clay fines, to give an ideal mix of compressive strength, minimal shrinkage, crack control and erosion resistance. As the majority of earth is from the site itself, and as there are virtually no transportation or manufacturing costs, the 'embodied energy' of the material is almost zero. Cob is here the preferred earth material as the curved form is easier to achieve than using facetted shuttering for rammed earth. The U-value of a cob wall is better than that of rammed earth, as there are more air voids. Cladding is untreated locally grown oak. High insulation levels are achieved with recycled cellulose insulation.

Servicing: Energy conservation measures include solar panels to provide much of the hot water supply, south facing insulated glazing, seasonally shaded by vines, and rainwater harvesting for washing machines, WC cisterns, and gardening. Medium thermal mass in floors, chimney, cob walling and concrete worktops allows the environmental advantages of timber construction elsewhere. Low-energy lighting and energy efficient appliances are installed, with a high efficiency underfloor heating system and gas-fired condensing boiler with intelligent controls.

Heating performance

U -values:

Floors 0.21W/m²K

Roof 0.17 W/m²K

Walls 0.19 W/m²K

SAP rating 100

Total solar gains 3084W

Useful solar gains 2905W

Total space and water heating 5.06 CO₂ tonnes/yr

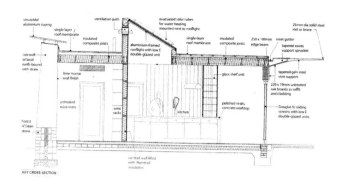

Client:	Nicholas Worsley
Architect	Associated Architects
Main contractor	GF Hill (Malvern) Ltd
Completion	September 2001
Building cost total	£1,038/m²

Gross internal floor area is 246m² total, made up from 219m² house plus 27m² outbuildings. Note external works includes cob wall where this does not form part of the building.

External works (not included above)	£293/m²
Cob walling	£16/m² (1.5% of total)

Information from John Christopher, www.associated-architects.co.uk

Photographs by Martine Hamilton Knight, www.builtvision.co.uk

The cob wall curves around the garden and then forms the outer wall of the 'buffer spaces' – utility room, wine store, garage, etc. – that do not need high levels of thermal insulation.

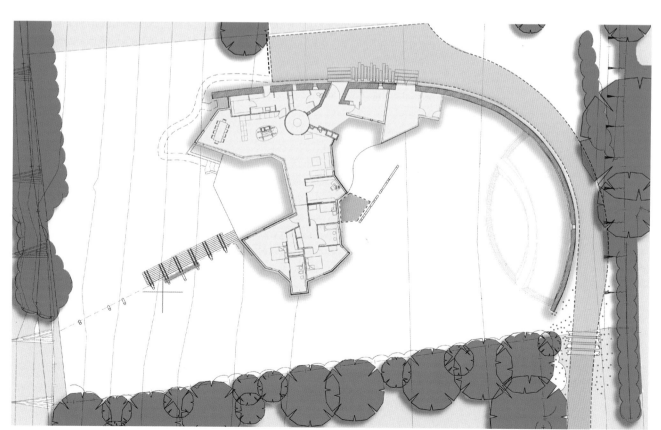

COLORADO COURT AFFORDABLE HOUSING

Built in 2002 in Santa Monica, California, this 44-unit, five-storey block is the first affordable housing project in the USA to be 100% energy neutral. It is claimed to be an excellent model of sustainable development in an urban environment, is built using a model for private/public partnership that benefits the whole community and promotes diversity through strategically placed affordable housing.

The building is sited for climate-responsive, passive solar design with no air conditioning. Over 90% of glazing is on the north and south facades, to minimise summer overheating. All the electrical demands are met on site through a combination of photovoltaic panels (producing around 21,000 kWh/year) and a gas-fired CHP unit. The National Grid serves as a buffer, smoothing out any mismatch between energy generation and demand. Waste heat from the CHP micro-turbine supplies domestic hot water and meets the small space heating demand. Appliances are highly efficient – specially selected refrigerators use only 1kWh/day.

Materials were chosen specifically to be recycled, locally sourced and beneficial to indoor air quality. All carpets were made from 100% recycled material and natural linoleum is used in all units. Cabinets were made from formaldehyde-free MDF. Low- and no-VOC paints, sealants and adhesives were used throughout the building and natural stucco pigments were used. Building insulation is made from recycled newsprint and certified oriented strand board (OSB) was used instead of plywood. Composite structural members such as laminated i-beams were used instead of dimensioned timber. The concrete has a high fly-ash content. Over 75% of construction waste was recycled.

All units have low-flow toilets and shower controls.100% of the storm water runoff from the entire city block is collected on-site in an underground chamber system and allowed to percolate naturally back into the aquifer.

EVA-LANXMEER PROJECT, CULEMBORG, NETHERLANDS

This pilot project comprises 200 houses/flats together with an environmental information centre, city farm and permaculture gardens, built alongside a protection zone around an area set aside for the extraction of drinking water. Planning permission was granted only on condition that development was based on the sound ecological principles of integrated water resources management (IWRM), based on local water storage and reuse. Rainwater from roofs is collected in ponds and old riverbeds, and from streets in wide infiltration trenches which allow it to filter slowly and recharge the groundwater. Domestic sewage is treated with reedbeds and in future a 'living machine' will be installed to treat waste from a congress centre and hotel.

In the process of extracting groundwater, it was discovered that its temperature was over 12°C, and it could be used to provide heating for the homes, via a heat pump and district heating system. Thus the drinking water company became an energy production company as well! All the (predominantly brick and block) houses are well insulated and have solar hot water and solar electric systems fitted. Heat delivery is through a low temperature water-based system integrated into the walls.

Built to a medium density (25 dwellings per hectare) all the housing blocks are surrounded by private and communal gardens. Streets are mostly pedestrianised and the site is right next to a railway station with regular local and inter-city services. From the beginning, project development was an interactive process involving the municipality, the drinking water company, and future residents. The area is divided into small scale 'neighbourhoods' and great emphasis is placed on education and information to guide consumer behaviour, e.g. in the disposal of wastes so as not to prejudice the functioning of the ecological treatment systems.

Architect: Joachin Eble Architectuur
Construction: begun 1999, ongoing
Number of dwellings: 200
Email: gem.culemborg@culemborg.nl
Website: www.eva-lanxmeer.nl

Burry Port

Integrated Care Scheme for the Elderly at Plas Y Mor, Burry Port, South Wales.

The Burry Port Integrated Care Scheme is a new development of 38 one and two bedroom flats for people over the age of 55. Situated close to the harbour, train station and local shops, the accommodation has been specially designed with older people in mind. It is designed to cater for the needs of both the fit and frail elderly, with accommodation providing the flexibility appropriate to the varying care requirements of individual tenants. Part of the building includes a day centre for older people from the local community, a kitchen delivering hot meals, hairdressing, chiropody and guest bedrooms. It was developed as a partnership project between Gwalia Housing Group, Carmarthenshire County Council and the Welsh Assembly Government. All three partners provided a share of the funding. Gwalia provided the project management and development expertise.

Procured through a partnering contract, the construction is 200mm deep timber frames filled with recycled cellulose insulation and clad with FSC certified Red Luro hardwood. A main feature is the glazed street, from which warm air can be extracted and ducted into communal areas by thermostatically controlled fans. Rooflights and sunpipes above a central corridor allow daylight penetration and passive gains. A district heating system has been installed fuelled by a central biomass boiler, which is part of an integrated central heating and domestic hot water system. 30m² of solar thermal panels pre-heats water for this integrated system, and there is provision to add PVs at a later date. Sensor controlled low-energy lighting is installed throughout. Total energy costs for a two bedroom flat are in the region of £5.75 per week. This includes heating, domestic hot water, cooking and all electricity.

This scheme has won the Welsh Housing Design Award, 2004, and was praised by the judges for its clear design principles and commitment to sustainability.

Design and construction team:

Contractor:	Tycroes Group
Architects:	PCKO
Quantity Surveyors:	Shaun Condron Partnership
M&E Engineers:	Hicks Titley Partnership
Structural Engineers	Ateb Consult

Development statistics:

Total development cost:	£3,700,000
Construction contract, including fees:	£3,100,000
Total gross floor area:	3,730m^2
Construction cost per m^2:	£751.00/m^2
Completion date:	28th November 2003

Gross cost of key environmental technologies:

Bio-mass boiler and district heating:	£100,000
Solar panels:	£30,000
Heat recovery:	£11,000
Environmental controls, etc. to M&E Specification:	£30,000

Matzdorf House in Islington

Built on a tiny (12x15m) 'brownfield' site in London, this house includes within its design many features associated with 'green' architecture.

Large glazed sliding doors open out on to a densely planted, inward looking garden, whilst a long, curved roof light and panels of glass blocks bring light and sunshine into the house – without overlooking neighbours' gardens. The structure is a timber frame, which sits on deep piles so that existing mature trees can be retained. The curved, planted roof wraps over the double height rooms, and as the tops of the internal partitions are glass, there is a surprising sense of space and long views for such a small house. The external shell is timber construction, with a good thermal performance – using recycled cellulose insulation.

Embodied energy has been considered and minimised by using recycled materials (e.g. the insulation), local materials (e.g. home-grown timber) and renewable materials wherever possible (e.g. timber windows and cladding). Materials have also been selected to avoid potential health hazards; formaldehyde-free building boards, for example; using durable timber species to avoid toxic timber treatments; natural organic paints and stains to reduce manufacturing pollution and to provide harmless finishes.

Client: David Matzdorf
Architects: Jon Broome and Tim Crosskey of Architype Ltd

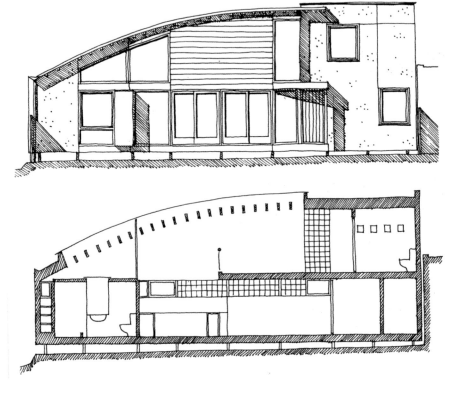

Solar Renovation Project, Gardsten, Sweden

This eco-renovation project, funded by the EC, is based on nine medium-rise apartment blocks (three- to six-storeys), built in the 1960s but which by the late 1990s had become very rundown, associated with a high rate of crime and drug use, and with an occupancy rate of only 65%.

Up to mid-2003, 225 apartments have been renovated and 750m² of solar thermal heating panels installed, mainly as a pre-heat for domestic hot water with storage tanks located in the basement. Existing open balconies have been single-glazed, to preheat the supply air into the flats and new ventilation systems with heat recovery installed. Insulation levels and glazing systems have been upgraded. A district heating system fuelled mainly by municipal waste incineration feeds a radiator based heat delivery system.

These works have reduced energy use (for space heating and ventilation) by 40% from 270 to 160 kWh/m²/yr. Energy for domestic hot water has been reduced by 30% and electricity consumption decreased by 25-30%, to 50kWh/m²/year, including communal spaces. Water consumption, too, has fallen by 50%. There is individual metering for electricity and water heating, while, in the case of space heating, tenants are charged according to the indoor temperature, rather than energy use. The standard setting is 21°C, and tenants with lower set temperatures (<18°C) pay less, while those with higher set temperatures (>23°C) pay more.

Communal facilities include a greenhouse, laundry, and large-scale composter which, together with recycling, has replaced the conventional waste management system. Courtyards are well landscaped. There has been a high degree of tenant participation during the renovation works, and a subsequent feeling of 'ownership' of the estate. The crime rate has dropped and the area is now seen as a desirable place to live. Renovation costs are approx 600Euro/m², which is 25-30% of the equivalent new-build cost.

An experimental system installed in one block, consisting of a large exposed gable wall with external insulation and a vented space between the insulation and the wall, into which solar heated air is introduced at low level from a solar air collector on the roof, has led to 30% drop in heating demand.

HOUSE IN FURNACE, CEREDIGION

This house has a cross-shaped plan, centred on a two-storey, cruck framed 'sunspace' – which, like a medieval hall, is the main social and circulation space. The plan steps in and out, so that all major rooms get some east and west views and sunlight – with the help of corner windows. The north side, facing a busy road, is faced in a protective natural stone wall (from the derelict cottage that stood here and other local demolitions) that continues either side to form a walled garden. The south side is open and highly glazed.

Every design decision was informed by the client's desire to use the best environmental practice. It has an engineered green oak frame – which allows for a high degree of flexibility in the layout and the possibility of large glazed openings; it is built of materials with the highest 'green', healthy credentials; it is superinsulated, and most of its energy comes from renewable sources. The natural finishes, the high daylight and sunlight levels and thick insulation combine to provide a relaxed, comfortable and ever-changing internal environment.

Constructed:	2000-2001
Contract:	Self-build with contract management by CAT, Machynlleth
Architect:	Pat Borer
Oak frame:	Carpenter Oak
M&E:	Rob Gwillim, CAT
Solar heating installation:	Chris Laughton, Solar Design Company
Sewage adviser:	Nick Grant, Elemental Solutions
Heat pump:	John Cantor

Foundations:	Hydraulic lime concrete with brick plinth walls.
Ground floor:	Limecrete slab with underfloor heating pipes, on 150mm cork slab insulation. Finished with home-grown ash boarding or 25mm slate slabs. U=0.19 W/m2K
Walls:	Lightweight spaced stud infill, with 200mm sheep's wool insulation, services zone and plasterboard. External Keim mineral paint on hydraulic lime render on Heraklith woodwool slabs. North wall faced in 450mm random rubble with lime mortar. U=0.15 W/m2K
Roof:	Natural second hand slate on spaced rafter cut roof, with 300mm Warmcel insulation. U=0.12 W/m2K
External joinery:	Laminated Welsh oak with ash inner face, low-E argon filled glazing.
Internal joinery:	Welsh ash doors, stairs and skirtings. Auro organic wood and wall finishes.
Heating:	Initially, a 12kW wood pellet boiler was fitted, but this gave a few problems and perhaps is not the best match for a very low-energy house. Recently it has been replaced by an 8kW ground source heat pump. There is a 4 square metre solar domestic water heating array, integrated with the roof finish. 'Intelligent' optimised controls increase the efficiency of fuel use.
Electricity:	A 2kW photovoltaic array is integrated into the garage roof. This is grid-linked and provides around 1600kWh per year.

Top: The 150m long, 2m deep trench being dug in the garden for the 600m of ground source heat pump (GSHP) pipes.

Bottom: The single phase heat pump. Although expensive to install, GSHP's, if well-designed and installed, will provide heat at the lowest cost and with the lowest CO_2 emissions.

HOUSES FROM HEMP, HAVERHILL, SUFFOLK

The two 'hemp houses' at Haverhill in Suffolk, are the first to be constructed in Britain using this ecological and highly sustainable building material.

'The project has been undertaken by the Suffolk Housing Society, of Bury St Edmunds, with support from the Housing Corporation and St Edmundsbury Borough Council.

'It was prompted by the enthusiasm for using hemp as a principal building material by local architect Ralph Carpenter, of Modece Architects in Bury St Edmunds, who had seen the method being used in France where the hemp processing system was developed.

'Suffolk Housing Society and St Edmundsbury engaged the support of the Housing Corporation to fund the Building Research Establishment to carry out extensive research into the project. The purpose of this was to demonstrate that hemp and lime construction is a viable low energy alternative to the more conventional forms of construction based on brick and concrete blocks.'[1]

The materials for the wall construction of the two houses – which were compared to two brick/block houses that were identical in every other way – were:

• 'Isochanvre' – a French product made of hemp waste (shiv) that has been 'petrified' by treating with an alkali and an acid to form a protective salt;

• hydraulic, hydrated lime;

• sand; and

• locally sourced timber.

The construction process is to erect a conventional timber 'stud' frame and to lightly pack the damp hemp/lime mixture into shuttering fixed either side, but spaced apart from, the timber frame. The hemp/lime wall is 200mm (8") thick, and after being rendered outside with lime/sand, provides a complete, insulated and weatherproof construction – from just the one material. The internal face was left un-plastered, which gives a 'warm' and hygroscopic finish. The same material was also used to fill the internal partitions – to improve sound insulation, and to bring thermal mass into the otherwise fairly 'lightweight' house. The solid ground floors used a thick screed of hemp/lime/sand.

The research project[2] looked at differences in construction time and cost, thermal performance and sound performance, between the two types of construction. Strength and durability were also studied.

On the whole the BRE report is very encouraging. Although the costs of construction were a bit higher than the conventional houses, this was felt to be mainly due to the method being unfamiliar. The construction proceeded much faster as the scheme progressed, and many improvements could be made in the shuttering and mixing processes. The construction is reported to be very durable, resistant to fire and vermin, and the timber frame is well protected by the hemp/lime material.

The thermal performance was much better than the theoretical U-values would suggest, and comfort levels were better than for the brick/block houses. It is, at present, unclear why the hemp houses performed so well thermally. Possible explanations (apart from the depressing thought that conventional British houses are so badly constructed that anything else appears good) are that the all-enveloping nature of the construction would be expected to be quite airtight, and that the higher comfort levels experienced would encourage energy saving.

Client: Suffolk Housing Society & St Edmundsbury Borough Council
Architect: Modece Architects
Cost: £54,000 – £526/m² (brick/block control houses £478/m²)
Hemp: Chenovette Habitat
Contractor: DCH Construction Ltd

[1] 'Homes from Hemp: Summary Research Findings', Suffolk Housing Society

[2] 'Final Report on the Construction of the HempHouses at Haverhill, Suffolk' BRE
    Client report number 209-717 Rev1, © Building Research Establishment Ltd, 2002

WOODLANE HOUSE, TRURO

This house, by architect and owner Chris Hendra, replaced a derelict chalet on the site in rural Cornwall. As a 'Replacement Dwelling' under Planning Policy it was expected to be '...traditional in character and appearance..'.. But instead of pandering to the pastiche, Chris used the rather more interesting form of the traditional corrugated iron hay barn for his eco-house.

Within the shelter of the recycled steel frame and metal roof is a house with the following low-energy systems:

- Passive solar gain via the conservatory and south facing openings – small openings to the north and other elevations.
- Timber clad externally insulated single leaf block and brick wall construction and generally high levels of insulation throughout.
- Ground source heat pump: a 50m deep vertical borehole with heat pump, compressor and heat exchanger to a hot water tank, for space heating and domestic hot water.
- Mechanical heat recovery ventilation (MHRV) system.

Solar energy enters the house, and, with any internal ambient gains from lighting, cooking, etc. is both absorbed into, and stored within, the thermal mass of the externally insulated walling. Warm air rises in a normal stack effect within the central double height volume of the dining room.

The ground source heating system slowly extracts stored solar energy from below ground surface (there is an even temperature all year round from 2m down), and aggregates it via the heat pump and compressor into a water tank, maintaining 48°C within the tank. Under computer control, heat is delivered to underfloor heating in the ground floor only at around 30°C, and to the domestic hot water. Space heating is not required to the first floor. The capital cost of the heating system is around 2.5 times that of a conventional system, but the running costs (on Green

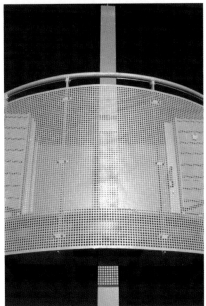

Tariff electricity) are working out at about 40% of the equivalent conventional house. Payback is expected within 5 years.

As well as ventilating the house and recovering around 80% of the heat from the outgoing air the MHRV system serves to distribute heat around the house. An effective energy conservation measure, the system also contributes to a pleasant indoor environment by removing dust, smells and allergens, whilst also helping with the radon issue.

Client:	Mr & Mrs C Hendra
Architect:	Chris Hendra, Dip. Arch. RIBA CAD Architects Ltd, Penryn
Contractor:	Davey Bros, Redruth
Floor area:	220m²
Cost:	£1,000/m² over a 10 month build

Springfield Co-housing, Stroud

Co-housing is basically a form of co-operative housing in which individual households form a company that acts as a developer to secure land, develop the site and construct their individual houses. Initiated in Denmark and now also common in the US, Springfield Co-housing in Stroud is the UK's first new build co-housing scheme. The Stroud scheme was initiated by David Michael who developed the financial and legal structure for the project, initially risked his own money to secure the purchase of a piece of land, and has acted throughout as the managing director of the Co-housing Company, steering this pioneering project through to completion.

The demand for co-housing proved to be huge, with 30% of the plots pre-sold before the completion of the land purchase and 100% before the planning application was submitted, without any formal advertising.

The scheme is designed around a number of well established co-housing principles.

Participatory process: the group as a whole worked with Architype to design the site layout and then individually to design their own houses, and were fully involved in every decision during the development process, including the selection of contractors.

Private and common facilities: each household has their own private house with all normal facilities, but in addition there is a shared 'common house' which is best described as an extension to each household's living space. It contains a communal kitchen and dining room, lounge and workshop spaces. Shared meals are served every evening, cooked by members on a rota basis.

Neighbourhood design: the site layout is designed to enhance the sense of community. Cars are kept to the periphery and the whole site is pedestrian and child friendly. The majority of the houses are arranged along a pedestrian street. All garden space is shared although there are areas of privacy. The common house is located at the heart of the site and provides disabled access from the parking area, two-storeys down, to the pedestrian street. The land is a steeply sloping difficult-to-develop site within a few minutes' walk of Stroud Town Centre.

Resident management: the scheme is managed by the residents and all decisions are democratically reached, based on consensus where possible. Individual houses are owned leasehold, with the company (itself owned by the householders) owning the freehold.

Sustainability: co-housing seeks to go beyond environmental sustainability and create a truly sustainable community. A car share scheme and bulk organic food buying is being established.

The scheme is designed to be ecologically sustainable – the houses are timber frame using breathing construction, with good levels of insulation, clad in UK grown Douglas Fir and render. The houses have excellent daylighting and face south for passive solar gain. Internally the upper floors are open to the roof slope creating light airy rooms with opportunities for high level platforms. The 20 houses have grid connected photovoltaic roof tiles making it the largest array on a private housing scheme in the UK. An innovative sustainable urban drainage scheme (SUDS) collects all the rainwater and directs it through a series of rills, swales and ponds to ensure that the water runoff from the site is maintained at greenfield levels. In very heavy rainfall a 'village green' takes the overflow, becoming a temporary pond.

The scheme comprises 20 houses of various sizes, 8 flats, 7 studio units and the shared common house. Within a limited number of house types, each household has designed a completely unique individual house tailored to their needs.

Client:	The Co-housing Company
Architect:	Architype Ltd (and Pat Borer)
Contractor:	Hodson Building Company Ltd
Timber frame:	Adaptable Development Company Ltd
Value:	£4.5million

HOCKERTON HOUSING PROJECT

This is a ground-breaking project in many ways: a successful community self-build group which won planning permission for earth sheltered houses (without heating systems) and a wind turbine on a greenfield site and, having built their homes, went on to set up an educational and consultancy business on eco-building products and services.

The houses are based on a modular system, with modules – or 'bays' – six metres deep by three metres wide. Each one of the five houses has six bays. Bay sizes, window/door openings and frames were standardised to simplify construction and reduce costs. The rear walls have two skins of dense concrete blocks with reinforced concrete poured into the cavity, 300mm of expanded polystyrene on the outside and 400mm of earth. The roof is concrete beam-and-block, exposed internally. The high thermal mass results in very stable temperatures throughout the year. South facing conservatories have double-glazed low-E units, and the glazing between conservatories and living space is triple low-E. Hence the conservatories are treated as buffer zones rather than heated spaces.

There is no central heating, but some of the houses have woodstoves for use during the coldest months. It is judged that superinsulation and incidental gains are more effective at reducing heating demand than passive solar measures. The measured energy consumption is 75% lower than that for comparable conventional housing. Domestic hot water is heated by an air-to-water heat pump taking air from the top of the conservatories. Mechanical ventilation systems with heat recovery run in large clay pipes hung from the ceilings.

Grid connected renewable energy systems include a 6kW Proven wind turbine and an array of photovoltaic panels rated at 6.5kW. A reed bed system treats septic tank runoff. Rainwater is collected and pumped to storage tanks for potable and non-potable uses, the former treated with string, carbon and UV filters; the latter with a sand filter.

Residents are expected to give 300 hours per year to collective maintenance, food growing and other income generating or cost avoiding activities. One fossil fuel car per household only is allowed and there is one shared electric car.

Architects:	Robert and Brenda Vale
Construction:	1996-1998
Building costs:	£450/m², including labour.

'Houses without Heating', Lindas, Sweden

This development comprises 20 terraced houses, modestly sized at around 120 square metres each, in rows oriented north/south. Built without externally fuelled heating systems, the heating requirements, calculated at 4100kWh/year, are mostly met by solar and casual gains from occupancy, lighting and appliances, and by heat recovery on the whole-house mechanical ventilation systems, which have an efficiency of 85%. This system has an optional heating coil on the incoming air, but it is little used according to the architect. The external design temperature was taken as -16°C, but in recent bad weather the houses stayed warm at temperatures of -21°C.

This extraordinary performance comes from extremely well insulated, airtight construction and a compact built form. A relatively deep floor plan of 11 metres front to back gives minimal external wall surface. There is 500mm of insulation in the roofs and 420mm in the external walls. Triple-glazed, low-E, Krypton filled units give a U-value of 0.8W/sqmK. Airtightness was measured at 0.4ach at 50Pa, which is the equivalent of a hole the size of a human palm in the whole building envelope. First floor balconies and projecting eaves shelter large south facing windows, and rooflights provide daylight and summer ventilation.

Five square metres of solar water heating panels are fitted to each house, which provides 50% of the domestic hot water requirement. The houses are connected to the Grid (which in Sweden is supplied mostly by hydro and nuclear) but electrical energy use is low at approx 40kWh/m²/yr.

Architect: Hans Eek

Costs: c.200,000 Euro/house

(Extra 'eco' costs, c.4-5,000 Euro, equal to cost of a conventional heating system.)

SPARROW HOUSE

This design responds to the constraints of its infill site in a 1920s housing estate in Lewes, East Sussex, by creating a sense of openness and space within a confined suburban plot. It is a modern, solar powered house constructed of local environmentally friendly materials – a courtyard house that opens up to the south bringing the garden into the house and vice versa.

Keeping the house quite narrow (at 6m) meant that Sparrow House keeps a polite distance from its neighbours, and has a reasonably sized garden down one side – but it is long at 17m. Hence the need for the south-facing courtyard with folding doors creating the main source of natural light and the 'hub' of the house.

Planning constraints meant that the house had to be low in profile, but the site is made the most of by allowing for a studio mezzanine to the front of the site, with a sloped roof creating a double-height space above the dining room. The front living accommodation is linked to the rear by a long galley-type kitchen overlooking the courtyard.

The architects, BBM, have built their practice on sustainable solutions, Sparrow House responds to this.

- The timber frame, decking and cladding is all of locally-grown sweet chestnut, as is the shelving within the house. This tree is extensively grown locally: there are at least 160 square kilometres of fast-growing sweet chestnut coppice in Kent and Sussex.

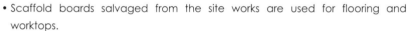

- Scaffold boards salvaged from the site works are used for flooring and worktops.
- English sheep's wool is used for insulation.
- Home-grown softwood is used for the timber studwork framing.
- Building papers and vapour checks are made from recycled paper and plastic.
- The ground floor has an underfloor heating slab fuelled by a flat plate solar array.
- Timber pulp insulation is used under the floor slab.

From the RIBA Ibstock Downland Prize 2004 jury's report: 'This is an ingenious project on a very difficult site, surrounded by 1930s houses. Given this starting point, every detail of the building has been very well thought through. In particular, the architect has tackled the challenges of privacy and use of space in a cohesive way'.

Client:	Duncan and Katie Baker-Brown
Completion Date:	Spring 2004
Gross Floor Area:	95m^2
Cost:	£130,000
Architect:	BBM Sustainable Design Ltd www.bbm-architects.co.uk
Stuctural Engineer:	BEP Consultant Engineer
Main Contractor:	Chalmers & Co. Ltd
Main Suppliers:	Inwood Developments/Construction Resources/Second Nature

Bo01, Malmo, Sweden

This development of the Western harbour in Malmo was begun with a Building 'Expo' in 2001. Eighteen different architects participated in the scheme, although there was one overall 'planner'. The aim was to achieve a dense, urban feel, with narrow passageways between buildings leading into open squares and prompting a sense of curiosity and discovery.

Part of the brief was to achieve an overall energy use of less than 105 kWh/m²/year. However, some blocks have fallen short of this target, especially those on the seafront which have large areas of glazing. The scheme includes a 2.4MW wind turbine, which makes it overall self-sufficient in electricity although it is grid connected. The district heating system is fuelled partly by solar water heating (20%) and the rest by underground water (at 18°C) or sea water (at 5°C), passed through a heat pump. Water features integrated into the landscaping filter rainwater and road run-off.

Building systems range from timber frame to brick and concrete. High levels of insulation and triple-glazing are standard. Although the area round the blocks are pedestrianised, developers insisted on including underground car parks, to make the units more saleable.

There has been some local criticism of this development, based on the lack of 'affordable' housing and the high sale value of the units. One block (designed by Ralph Erskine) remains empty, allegedly because of the high prices. In future, a more 'mixed' development, including small retail outlets, would probably be more successful.

PENWHILWR, ST DOGMAELS, CEREDIGION

Artist and healer Rachel Whitehead has been developing the design for this house for several years, with the help of like-minded professionals and with the approval of the local planning authority. She has been involved with every aspect of the construction, and has also relied on local builders, friends and volunteers.

The 2/3-storey house rests on strip foundations and the walls are mainly full height load-bearing straw bale, with some timber frame (local larch and oak) and stone wall to first floor level. The ground floor is part solid limecrete, part suspended timber and the roof is finished with cedar shingles. The unique curved shape of the building expresses the kind of internal spaces that Rachel wanted to create, and is achieved relatively easily with straw bale construction.

The straw bales are finished with lime render externally and clay plaster internally. The timber is mainly larch and oak with maximum use made of recycled floorboards, doors and windows.

The site is not connected to mains electricity or water. A borehole will be sunk in adjoining land, and a wind turbine and PV panels will be installed. A Proven WT600 wind turbine (600 watts) already has planning permission. An underfloor heating system will be fed by a central 'Osier' ceramic woodstove, supplied by the Ceramic Stove Co. Unusually, there is no vapour control or sarking felt in the pitched roof construction, but there will be a 50mm gap left above the insulation, to allow the elements to 'breathe'.

Along with an outdoor dry composting toilet, a low flush Ifo Cera toilet will be fitted inside, supplied by the Green Building Store.

Designers: Rachel Whitehead / Barbara Jones / Lindsay Halton
Space: 72m²
Cost: £60,000
Time: Ongoing, begun April 2003

QUARRY HOUSE – A 'GREEN' ARCHITECT'S OWN EXTENSION

'Quarry House is typical Herefordshire stone cottage. It features internal oak frame partitions, intermediate floors and roof structure that have been dated to the mid 1600s. The cottage has been continuously adapted and modified during its life. In the early 1900s it was transformed from a single to a two-storey cottage when the whole roof structure was lifted up. In the 1950s an extraordinary extension was added to the south side, extending the house out by 2.5 metres and upwards by three storeys. In the 1980s a poorly built single storey extension was added to the west, which included a front door obscured from visitors, a very small hall and cramped dining area. When we purchased the house in 1996 it had a classic cottage atmosphere, with thick stone walls and small windows, cosy but rather dark. It had an open aspect to the south, but no windows to the west.

'The extension is designed to do more than simply make the house larger. We have sought to transform our living environment by creating a light and airy modern extension that contrasts and complements the existing 'cottage atmosphere'. Specifically the extension brings sunlight into the heart of the house through glazed roof slots, Veluxes, tall spaces open to the roof, and large glazed walls. The new front door, now clearly visible to visitors, opens into a double height space, which is overlooked by a gallery housing a small office. A glazed slot and high level windows link the hall with the new conservatory. The walls of the conservatory slide to open up and link the inside space with the outside space'.

Client:	Hilary, Jonathan, Matthew and Emily Hines
Design:	Jonathan Hines & Howard Meadowcroft of Architype
Builder:	Mike Whitfield
Structural design:	Pat Borer
Cost:	(New extension) £70,000
The structure:	A modern interpretation of traditional timber frame construction, using Welsh Douglas Fir and traditional pegged joints. Oiled with Holzweg UV oil.
Wall:	'Breathing construction' of plasterboard, Proclima airtight barrier, panel line board, 200mm studs with Warmcell, Panelvent, Proclima breather membrane, ventilation slot and Douglas Fir cladding or lime render on Herakilith board.
Windows and doors:	Triple-glazed, with argon and low-E with warm edge spacers with U-value of 1.1, from the Swedish Window Company. Direct glazing into the frame is double-glazed i-plus with warm edge spacers. The front door is 100m thick, purpose designed and locally made in Herefordshire oak, with an insulated core.
Central roof finish:	Reclaimed second hand clay tiles.
Lower roofs:	Sedum roofs over an EPDM pond liner membrane.
Internal floor finishes:	FSC certified English ash finished with Auro floor varnish and Welsh Pennant Sandstone tiles from Swansea, finished with OS Polyx Oil.
Window-sills and shelves:	Herefordshire ash.
Internal doors:	Herefordshire oak.
Internal walls:	Finished with Keim Ecosil or Auro Emulsion.
Heating and hot water:	Rayburn linked to a thermal store tank, supplemented by a Solartwin solar thermal panel. The conservatory is vented passively via a high level window that opens at floor level into the office gallery, which has two large Velux windows.

'The existing house was also extensively renovated – with all windows replaced with triple-glazed units, ground floors taken up and insulated, the roof battened out and insulated and walls replastered with lime plaster. Original timber walls were uncovered and restored. The 1950s extension was reclad with Douglas Fir to link with the new extension and improve the previously rather ugly elevation.

'Landscaping around the extension uses Welsh Pennant Sandstone flooring, rocks dug out of the ground during the excavations for retaining walls and Herefordshire oak for decking'.

Text by Jonathan Hines

The authors

Following seventeen years working for the Centre for Alternative Technology, first as a builder and then project manager, consultant and lecturer, Cindy Harris is now the Design Review Officer for Design Commission for Wales. Whilst working at CAT she was involved with all new constructions, including the self-build house, the eco-cabins, the top station of the water powered cliff railway and, most recently, the award winning Autonomous Environmental Information Centre (AtEIC). Trained as a carpenter, she is a strong advocate of timber frame building.

Pat Borer is an architect with his own practice in mid Wales. He has worked with the Centre for Alternative Technology for thirty years. During this time he has been influential in the evolution of the ecological self-build approach to design apparent in the Centre's buildings. His current projects include low-energy housing schemes and CAT's Wales Institute for Sustainable Education.

Cindy and Pat wrote the first edition of *The Whole House Book* in 1998 and have also collaborated on CAT's *Out of the Woods: Ecological Designs for Timber Frame Housing*. They are both guest lecturers on CAT's highly regarded and popular MSc Architecture: Advanced Environmental and Energy Studies.

Abbreviations & measurements

°C: degrees Celsius

ac/hr: airchanges per hour

AECB: Association for Environment Conscious Building

BBA: British Board of Agrément

BFS: blast furnace slag

BIF: bitumen impregnated fibreboard

BOD: biochemical oxygen demand

BRE: Building Research Establishment

BREDEM: Building Research Establishment's Domestic Energy Model

BREEAM: Building Research Establishment Environmental Assessment Method

CAF: compressed agricultural fibre

CAT: Centre for Alternative Technology

CCA: chrome, copper, and arsenic

CFC: chlorofluorocarbon

Clo: the insulating value of clothing

CO_2: carbon dioxide

dB: decibels

DPC: damp-proof course

EMF: electromagnetic fields

EPDM: ethylene propylene diene monomer

FICGB: Forest Industry Committee of Great Britain

FIDOR: Trade Association for the Fibreboard Industry

FoE: Friends of the Earth

FSC: Forest Stewardship Council

GJ: gigajoules (1GJ=278kWh)

ha: hectare (1ha=2.47 acres)

HAG: Housing Association Grant

HCFC: hydrochlorofluorocarbon

HFC: hydrofluorocarbon

Hz: hertz

K: degrees Kelvin

k-value: measure of thermal conductivity

kg: kilogram (1kg=2.2 pounds)

km: kilometre (1km=0.62 miles)

kWh: kilowatt hours

LCA: life cycle analysis

LD50: lethal dose required to kill 50% of a given population

LETS: Local Exchange Trading Scheme

low-E: low emissivity

LVL: laminated veneer lumber

m: metres (1m=1.09 yards)

MDF: medium density fibreboard

MDI: methyl bisphenyl di-isocyanate

Mets: the metabolic rate in watts per m² of an individual's body surface area

mm: millimetres (1mm=0.04 inches)

mT: microtesla

NEF: New Economics Foundation

NFFO: Non-Fossil Fuel Obligation

NFHA: National Federation of Housing Associations

NHBC: Natural House Building Council

NHER: National Home Energy Rating

NIF: Neighbourhood Initiatives Foundation

OPC: ordinary Portland cement

OSB: oriented strand board

Pa: pascal

PBF: Portland blastfurnace cement

PCB: polychlorinated biphenyl

PCP: pentachlorophenol

PET: polyethylene terephthalate

PFA: pulverised fuel ash

PSL: parallel strand lumber

PV: photovoltaic

PVC: polyvinyl chloride

PVC-u: unplasticized polyvinyl chloride

RSJ: rolled steel joint

R-value: thermal resistance of a construction

SAP: standard assessment procedure

SBS: styrene-butadiene-styrene

SLF: secondary liquid fuels

TBTO: tributyl tin oxide

TIM: translucent insulation material

Index

CAT Publications

Other CAT publications and CAT services

Printed below is a selection of CAT publications. To view details of all 80 titles visit www.cat.org.uk/catpubs or phone 01654 705980 for a publications list. Visit www.cat.org.uk to find out about CAT's 80 professional and leisure courses (including our MSc Architecture: Advanced Environmental and Energy Studies), mail order catalogue (featuring hundreds of green products and books), visitor centre and consultancy and membership services.

Building

Out of the Woods: Ecological designs for timber frame housing
Pat Borer and Cindy Harris
The Energy Saving House
Thierry Salomon and Stéphane Bedel
Rebuilding Community in Kosovo
Maurice Mitchell
The Lemonade Stand: Exploring the unfamiliar by building large-scale models
Maurice Mitchell

Renewable energy

Solar Water Heating: A DIY guide
Paul Trimby
Tapping the Sun: A guide to solar water heating
Chris Laughton
Windpower Workshop: Building your own wind turbine
Hugh Piggott
It's a Breeze: A guide to choosing windpower
Hugh Piggott
Going with the Flow: Small scale water power
Billy Langley and Dan Curtis
Power Plants: Biofuels made simple
Brian Horne

Ecological sewage treatment and water systems

The Water Book: Find it, move it, store it, clean it, use it
Judith Thornton
Lifting the Lid: An ecological approach to toilet systems
Peter Harper and Louise Halestrap
Sewage Solutions: Answering the call of nature
Nick Grant, Mark Moodie and Chris Weedon

Organic gardening
The Little Book of Garden Heroes
Allan Shepherd
The Little Book of Slugs
Allan Shepherd and Suzanne Galant
How to Make Soil and Save Earth
Allan Shepherd
Creative Sustainable Gardening
Diana Anthony

General
52 Weeks to Change Your World
Allan Shepherd and Caroline Oakley

NOTES

NOTES

NOTES

NOTES

NOTES

NOTES

NOTES

NOTES

NOTES

NOTES